CURRICULUM DEVELOPMENT FOR THE GIFTED

C. June Maker
University of Arizona at Tucson

8700 Shoal Creek Boulevard
Austin, Texas 78758
512/451-3246

Library of Congress Cataloging in Publication Data

Maker, C. June
Curriculum development for the gifted.

Bibliography: p. 365
Includes index.
1. Gifted children—Education. 2. Curriculum planning. I. Title.
LC3993.M29   371.95'3   81-14985

ISBN 0-89079-130-9
(formerly ISBN: 0-89443-347-4)   AACR2

8700 Shoal Creek Boulevard
Austin, Texas 78758

10 9 8 7 6 5 4 3 2   90 91 92

To my Mother and Father
Arnold David Shartzer
Bernice Smith Shartzer
with love

Table of Contents

Preface

PURPOSE OF THE BOOK

The purpose of this book is to provide teachers and prospective teachers of the gifted with a comprehensive handbook of theoretical and practical approaches to teaching these special children. My philosophy is that there is no one right way to teach gifted children, so a book on the topic of curriculum development needs to present a variety of approaches that can be combined or integrated into a unique plan that fits each situation.

In developing such curricula, consideration must be given to:

a. the philosophy of the teacher, the school, and the community regarding the purpose of education for the gifted;
b. the underlying assumptions of the theoretical and practical approaches as well as how these assumptions mesh with the philosophies of everyone concerned;
c. child characteristics;
d. parental concerns;
e. the teaching style, strengths, and preferences of the educator; and
f. the physical setting of the school.

It is highly unlikely that any model or way of teaching the gifted now in existence can fit these requirements for every possible situation. Therefore, the purpose of this book is to present information, resources, and examples that will enable each teacher and school to develop its unique program. The best program may be a "pure" approach advocated by Renzulli, Parnes, Taba, or any of the other teaching-learning models used in programs for the gifted. However, the best program may be an integrated entity based on the complementary aspects of these various approaches.

The book is for practitioners: teachers, curriculum development specialists, program coordinators. A major intent is to show how to put theory into practice. To this end, the text provides a framework of general principles and theory, gives examples of the practical application of each principle, describes processes for developing curricula for the gifted that will incorporate each principle, gives sample curricula, then analyzes the examples to show how they are developed from the general principles. All curricular plans have been developed and field tested by teachers of the gifted.

Since the primary focus of the book is on curriculum development, it does not cover aspects of program development that are an integral part of the overall school operation such as identification procedures, overall program evaluation, or research on characteristics of gifted and creative children. These topics are discussed only as they relate to the curriculum and its development or evaluation.

Perhaps this author's definition of curriculum is important: it is simply any kind of interaction between someone (or something) whose intent is to help someone learn and the learner. Thus, a curriculum includes both direct (i.e., through teaching activities) and indirect (i.e., through materials, mentors, instructional aids) teacher involvement in a child's learning. The teacher may arrange learning activities or may provide them.

ORGANIZATION OF THE BOOK

The book is separated into three major sections for easy reference:

   I. an introduction to general principles of curriculum development for the gifted;
  II. procedures and suggestions for developing one's own program; and
 III. examples of four different integrated approaches.

Section I presents general principles for making the curriculum for gifted students qualitatively different from the basic program for all children and assuring that it is appropriate to the characteristics and needs of the gifted. These general principles involve modification or extensions of the basic curriculum in all areas: content, process, products, and learning environments.

Section II provides methods for educators to develop their own program after the general principles and available teaching-learning models have been examined. Chapter 5 discusses general influences on curriculum development. Next is a step-by-step plan for curriculum development, emphasizing the process involved, along with procedures for inclusion of key individuals from the school and community. Work sheets to be used in the process are provided and explained. Chapter 7 covers the adaptation of a curriculum based on the characteristics and needs of certain special populations of the gifted (e.g., culturally different, low income, highly gifted, handicapped, highly creative/low IQ, high performing/low IQ). The final chapter in this section concerns the development of individualized programs based on the unique characteristics and needs of each child. Methods for developing talent/ability profiles and Individualized Education Programs (IEPs) are presented, along with a specific example of how these methods are used.

Section III consists of a description of four programs that have combined two or more of the recommended teaching-learning models in the development of a curriculum. These include (1) a world cultures curriculum for a program in a middle school in which children spend the majority of the day in a special classroom, (2) an elementary resource room program, (3) an early childhood program for potentially gifted, culturally different children, and (4) a high school seminar class. In each case, the curriculum (including philosophy, objectives, lesson plans, IEPs, student evaluation, resources) is described, then analyzed to show the essential elements, how they were developed from teaching-learning models, and how they incorporate the general principles described in Section I.

It is hoped that the book will be practical and useful for educators of the gifted. If it stimulates you, the reader, to use one of the models or to develop your own unique program, it will have fulfilled its purpose. Perhaps together we can develop school programs that will keep us from wasting our nation's most precious natural resource—the strengths and talents of our children.

In this context, however, let us remember the words of "The Prophet" as he cautions us against assuming we own our children:

Your children are not your children.
They are the sons and daughters of Life's longing for
*   itself.*
They come through you but not from you,
And though they are with you yet they belong not to
*   you.*
You may give them your love but not your thoughts,
For they have their own thoughts.
You may house their bodies but not their souls,
For their souls dwell in the house of tomorrow,
*   which you cannot visit, not even in your dreams.*
You may strive to be like them, but seek not to make
*   them like you.*
For life goes not backward nor tarries with yesterday.

(Kahlil Gibran, 1972, p. 17)

Acknowledgments

The writing of my first major book has been an exciting and rewarding process. It has been exciting and rewarding because of the assistance of friends, colleagues, and students. I can mention only a few of the most significant.

Several colleagues in education for the gifted have contributed to my thinking on the subjects in this book through courses, discussions, or arguments: Dr. Carolyn Callahan, Dr. Jim Gallagher, Dr. Faye Shaffer, Dr. Joe Renzulli, and Dr. Virgil Ward.

I would like to thank the many students who have taken "Teaching the Gifted Person" before and during the writing of this book. They provided the inspiration for its content and an audience for its field testing. The book was written to provide future students with a real textbook instead of a collection of articles or unpublished manuscript pages.

To some of these students, a special thank-you is appropriate. Many have tried my ideas and have shared their results with me: Patricia Kerr, Pat Carpenter, Peggy Robinson, Donna O'Dell, Anaida Pascuale-Sosa, Sue Harrell, Vivian Edge, Jane Limburg, and Wayne Gordon. Others have developed written curricula that are exemplary and have allowed me to include them: Patti Williams, Suzanne Keisel-Stagnone, Evelyn Morris, and Jan Bodnar.

Without my doctoral students, I could not survive. They have assisted with my teaching, planned conferences, held or attended meetings, and helped when asked. Most importantly, they have challenged my thinking: Diane Montgomery, Jan Bodnar, Dick Howell, and Ray Veseth. To a very special doctoral student, Jocelyn James, I would like to add an extra thanks for being "the first" and for her assistance in all phases of the early childhood project described in Chapter 11.

Without the continued support of my colleagues in the Department of Special Education at the University of New Mexico, this book could not have been written so quickly. I especially acknowledge the encouragement of Drs. Deborah and J.O. Smith, who appreciate professionalism and productivity in their colleagues, and the support of my department chairperson, Dr. Gary Adamson. More than a supervisor, Gary is a friend who appreciates my abilities and forgives my mistakes.

For her help in the preparation of this manuscript, I express my appreciation to Arietta Maria. A very special thanks goes to my secretary, Connie Baca, for her typing of parts of the manuscript, her organization of many of the tables, her screening of telephone calls and requests, and, most of all, for her loyalty. Anne Udall, research assistant and friend, deserves special recognition for her dedication to the project, as evidenced by careful checking of references, proofreading, typing, abstracting, and generally managing the production of the manuscript.

A very special thanks is expressed to my editor, Curt Whitesel, who provided the vehicle, inspiration, advice, continued support, and "push" that enabled the expression of these ideas in print. His confidence in me as a young author and patience with my mistakes is unequalled in my professional career.

Finally, to my most loyal supporter, most vocal advocate, and best friend, Steve Curtis, I give my most special thanks for making this book possible.

C.J.M.
December 1981

General Principles of Curriculum Development for the Gifted

Introduction to Section I: Qualitative Differences

The most basic principle underlying curriculum development for the gifted is that the experiences for these children must be qualitatively different from the basic program provided for all children. To enable educators to justify providing special services to this already "advantaged" group of students, good answers are absolutely essential for questions such as "What's so different about this program?" and "So why are you pulling these children out of my class? You're not doing anything I don't do." Admittedly, the concept of qualitative differences is tough to define. Even the experts disagree on its meaning. One thing they do agree on, however, is what it is not: more work. Indeed, one of the most frequent reasons for parents' removal of gifted children from special programs is their all-too-prevalent complaint, "Now my child has twice the amount of homework, extra reports in addition to basic assignments, and two pages of math problems instead of one . . . and is getting lower grades."

Qualitatively different also implies that the program be designed to enhance or take into account what is special about these children. If they are considered different enough (in needs, learning styles, cognitive styles, motivational characteristics) to need a special program, then the curriculum must be built around the characteristics that make the program necessary. Sounds like common sense, doesn't it? Nevertheless, developing, providing, and justifying a qualitatively different curriculum based on the unique characteristics of gifted children is not easy. Perhaps most of the difficulty lies in disagreement over the purpose(s) of such special programs or in the differing values of today's multicultural society. Certainly, the lack of research comparing the effectiveness of different approaches is a major contributing factor.

Regardless of the difficulties in defining something as value-laden and ambiguous as qualitatively different, or the underlying causes for the trouble, several attempts have been made. The U.S. Office of Education's Office of the Gifted and Talented provided the following definition:

3

"Differentiated education or services" means that process of instruction which is capable of being integrated into the school program and is adaptable to varying levels of individual learning response in the education of the gifted and talented and includes but is not limited to:

(1) A differentiated curriculum embodying a high level of cognitive and affective concepts and processes beyond those normally provided in the regular curriculum of the local educational agency;
(2) Instructional strategies which accommodate the unique learning styles of the gifted and talented; and
(3) Flexible administrative arrangements for instruction both in and out of school, such as special classes, seminars, resource rooms, independent study, student internships, mentorships, research field trips, library media research centers and other appropriate arrangements. (USOE, 1976, pp. 18665-18666)

Virgil Ward (1961), unique in the field of education for the gifted because of his development of a comprehensive logical theory, defines "differential education for the gifted" by presenting a series of formal propositions and corollaries that take into account both the superior characteristics of these individuals and the probable societal roles they will assume because of their superior intellect. His propositions and corollaries relating to the design of curricula are:

I. That the educational program for intellectually superior individuals should be derived from a balanced consideration of facts, opinions based on experience, and deductions from educational philosophy as these relate to the capacities of the individuals and to the probable social roles which they will fill. (p. 81)
II. That a program of education for the intellectually superior should be relatively unique. (p. 86)
III. That the curriculum should consist of economically chosen experiences designed to promote the civic, social, and personal adequacy of the intellectually superior individual. (p. 102)
IV. That in the education of the gifted individual there should be considerable emphasis upon intellectual activity. (p. 126)
V. That the educative experience of the intellectually superior should be consciously designed as generative of further development, extensively and intensively, along similar and related avenues. (p. 141)
VI. That the education of the gifted child and youth should emphasize enduring methods and sources of learning, as opposed to a terminal emphasis upon present states of knowledge. (p. 156)

VII. That the instruction of intellectually superior individuals should emphasize the central function of meaning in the acquisition of fact and principle, and the varieties of reflections of meaning in the developed communicative devices of man. (p. 161)

VIII. That the instruction of the intellectually superior should include content pertaining to the foundations of civilization. (p. 170)

IX. That scientific methods should be applied in the conception and in the execution of the education for personal, social, and character adjustments of the intellectually superior individual. (p. 195)

X. That instruction in the theoretical bases of ideal moral behavior and of personal and social adjustments should be an integral part of the education of intellectually gifted individuals. (p. 201)

Renzulli's (1977) ideas about qualitative differences are contained in his definition of "enrichment" as experiences that (1) are above and beyond the regular curriculum; (2) take into account the students' specific content interests; (3) take into account the students' preferred styles of learning; and (4) allow students the opportunity to pursue topic areas (where they have superior potential for performance) to unlimited levels of inquiry. His description of Type III enrichment, the only one considered uniquely appropriate for the gifted, provides a clearer picture of what he perceives as qualitative differences in experiences for gifted students. The goals of Type III enrichment are:

1. To assist youngsters in becoming actual investigators of real problems or topics by using appropriate methods of inquiry.

2. To provide students with opportunities for taking an active part in formulating problems to be investigated and the methods by which the problems will be attacked.

3. To allow students to use information as *raw data* rather than reporting about conclusions reached by other persons.

4. To provide opportunities for students' inquiry activity to be directed toward some tangible product.

5. To provide students with an opportunity to apply thinking and feeling processes to real situations rather than structured exercises. (Renzulli, Note 1, p. 9)

According to Kaplan (1974), "differentiation" of curricular activities for the gifted and talented relies on the elaboration of (1) procedures for presenting learning opportunities, (2) nature of the input, and (3) expectancies for learning outcomes. She provides the following guidelines for differentiating learning within the regular curriculum:

Procedures for Presenting Learning Opportunities

Exposure: Students are exposed to experiences, materials, and information which is outside the bounds of the regular curriculum, does not match age/grade expectancies, and introduces something new or unusual.

Extension: Students are afforded opportunities to elaborate on the regular curriculum through additional allocation of working time, materials and experiences, and/or further self-initiated or related study.

Development: Students are provided with instruction which focuses on thorough or new explanation of a concept or a skill which is part of a general learning activity within the regular curriculum. (p. 123)

In relation to differentiating learning as a separate curriculum, she provides suggestions for the type of input and the expectancies. She describes the input appropriate for gifted as (a) accelerated or advanced, (b) more complex, (c) beyond the regular curriculum, (d) selected by the students according to their interests, and (e) concerned with the more abstract concepts in each content area. The level and type of resources used or available to these individuals is different from those available for all students.

The expectations for gifted learners are different from those for all children in: (a) setting aside longer time periods for learning; (b) creating new information, ideas, or products; (c) providing more depth of thought or investigation; (d) transferring and applying knowledge to new areas; (d) showing personal growth or sophistication in affective areas; (e) developing new generalizations; (f) developing higher levels of thinking; and (g) designing and implementing their own study.

Gallagher (1975), in describing how to modify the regular curriculum to make it more appropriate for meeting the needs of gifted children, suggests that there are three aspects that can be changed: the content of the material to be taught (i.e., stressing more complex and more abstract concepts), the method of presentation of material to the students (going beyond the mere absorption of knowledge to the development of a learning style that will be useful in later studies and in later life), and the nature of the learning environment (moving the child to a different setting or changing the nature of the existing instructional setting).

As can be seen from inspection of the various definitions, there are several common elements in that they: (1) build upon the characteristics unique to gifted students, (2) include concepts at higher levels of abstraction or greater complexity, (3) emphasize the development of thinking skills at a higher level than acquisition and memory, and (4) provide any administrative or other arrangements necessary to enable all pupils to utilize their full potential. Other ideas included in some, but not all, of the descriptions above involve considering not only the present characteristics but also the probable societal roles of gifted individuals, expecting different kinds of products or outcomes, and basing instruction on a principle of economy making possible a depth and breadth of learning within a reasonable period of their lives.

What follows now is this author's attempt to develop a comprehensive, organized approach to the development of a qualitatively different curriculum based on the present and most likely future characteristics of gifted children.[1] Table 1 summarizes the curricular modifications presented in this section and shows graphically how they relate to the identified or potential characteristics of gifted children. This chart lists the behavioral characteristics of gifted students in four areas: learning, motivation, creativity, and leadership. This particular listing has been chosen because of its comprehensiveness, its method of development, and its frequency of use in programs for the gifted. The characteristics listed are contained in the four most commonly used of the *Scales for Rating the Behavioral Characteristics of Superior Students* (SRBCSS) (Renzulli, Smith, White, Callahan, & Hartman, 1976). Curricular changes appropriate for the gifted in the areas of content, process, product, and learning environment are listed across the top. When a curricular change is suggested by or built upon a particular child characteristic, an x is placed in the appropriate row and column.

In addition to providing a summary of the ideas presented in this section, the chart is an easy reference for those who need to justify or explain how their program is based upon the characteristics of their gifted students. It also can serve as a guide for making decisions about curricular modifications for special populations or for individual children based on their characteristics. These uses of the chart are explained in more detail in Chapters 6, 7, and 8.

In this section, the basic principles summarized in Table 1 are described in more depth. After each explanation, a justification based on the relationship between the curricular change and the characteristics of gifted children is presented. The four chapters also contain specific examples of how these general principles can be implemented.

NOTE

1. For discussions of characteristics of gifted children, the reader is referred to the following publications: Gallagher (1966); Getzels & Jackson (1962); Stanley, George, & Solano (1977); Stanley, Keating, & Fox (1974); Terman (1925); Terman & Oden (1947, 1959).

Table 1 Summary of Characteristics of Gifted Children and Their Implications for Curriculum Modifications

Child Characteristics and Probable Social Roles	Content							Process/Method								Product				Learning Environment					
	Abstractness	Complexity	Variety	Organization	Economy	Study of People	Methods	Higher Level Thought	Open-Endedness	Discovery	Proof/Reasoning	Freedom of Choice	Group Interaction	Pacing	Variety	Real Problems	Real Audiences	Evaluation	Transformation	Student Centered	Encourages Independence	Openness	Accepting	Complex	High Mobility
Learning																									
Has unusually advanced vocabulary for age or grade level; uses terms in a meaningful way; has verbal behavior characterized by "richness" of expression, elaboration, and fluency. (National Education Association, 1960; Terman & Oden, 1947; Witty, 1955)	X	X	X					X			X								X	X				X	X
Possesses a large storehouse of information about a variety of topics (beyond the usual interests of youngsters his age). (Terman, 1925; Ward, 1961; Witty, 1958)		X	X	X				X						X		X	X		X	X	X			X	X
Has quick mastery and recall of factual information. (Goodhart & Schmidt, 1940; National Education Association, 1960; Terman & Oden, 1947)	X	X	X					X						X					X	X					X

Table 1 continued

	Content							Process/Method								Product				Learning Environment					
Child Characteristics and Probable Social Roles	Abstractness	Complexity	Variety	Organization	Economy	Study of People	Methods	Higher Level Thought	Open-Endedness	Discovery	Proof/Reasoning	Freedom of Choice	Group Interaction	Pacing	Variety	Real Problems	Real Audiences	Evaluation	Transformation	Student Centered	Encourages Independence	Openness	Accepting	Complex	High Mobility
Has rapid insight into cause-effect relationships, tries to discover the how and why of things; asks many provocative questions (as distinct from informational or factual questions); wants to know what makes things (or people) "tick." (Carroll, 1940; Goodhart & Schmidt, 1940; Witty, 1958)	×	×	×	×	×	×		×	×	×	×			×		×	×			×	×	×	×	×	×
Has a ready grasp of underlying principles and can quickly make valid generalizations about events, people, or things; looks for similarities and differences in events, people, and things. (Bristow, 1951; Carroll, 1940; Ward, 1961)	×	×			×	×		×	×	×	×					×	×		×	×	×	×	×	×	×
Is a keen and alert observer; usually "sees more" or "gets more" out of a story, film, etc., than others. (Carroll, 1940; National Education Association, 1960; Witty, 1958)	×	×	×	×	×			×	×	×												×		×	

Table 1 continued

Child Characteristics and Probable Social Roles	Content							Process/Method								Product				Learning Environment					
	Abstractness	Complexity	Variety	Organization	Economy	Study of People	Methods	Higher Level Thought	Open-Endedness	Discovery	Proof/Reasoning	Freedom of Choice	Group Interaction	Pacing	Variety	Real Problems	Real Audiences	Evaluation	Transformation	Student Centered	Encourages Independence	Openness	Accepting	Complex	High Mobility
Reads a great deal on his own; usually prefers adult level books; does not avoid difficult material; may show a preference for biography, autobiography, encyclopedias, and atlases. (Hollingworth, 1942; Terman & Oden, 1947; Witty, 1958)	X	X	X	X		X		X				X							X		X			X	X
Tries to understand complicated material by separating it into its respective parts; reasons things out for himself; sees logical and common sense answers. (Freehill, 1961; Strang, 1958; Ward, 1962)	X	X		X				X	X	X	X									X	X	X	X	X	
Motivation																									
Becomes absorbed and truly involved in certain topics or problems; is persistent in seeking task completion. (It is sometimes difficult to get him to move on to another topic.) (Brandwein, 1955; Freehill, 1961; Strang, 1958)			X									X				X				X	X	X		X	
Is easily bored with routine tasks. (Terman & Oden, 1947; Ward, 1961, 1962)	X		X		X			X		X		X		X	X						X	X		X	

Table 1 continued

Child Characteristics and Probable Social Roles	Content							Process/Method								Product				Learning Environment					
	Abstractness	Complexity	Variety	Organization	Economy	Study of People	Methods	Higher Level Thought	Open-Endedness	Discovery	Proof/Reasoning	Freedom of Choice	Group Interaction	Pacing	Variety	Real Problems	Real Audiences	Evaluation	Transformation	Student Centered	Encourages Independence	Openness	Accepting	Complex	High Mobility
Needs little external motivation to follow through in work that initially excites him. (Carroll, 1940; Villars, 1957; Ward, 1961)			×					×	×			×				×	×	×		×	×	×		×	
Strives toward perfection; is self-critical; is not easily satisfied with his own speed or products. (Carroll, 1940; Freehill, 1961; Strang, 1958)						×	×		×									×			×	×	×		
Prefers to work independently; requires little direction from teachers (Gowan & Demos, 1964; Makovic, 1953; Torrance, 1965)			×				×		×	×								×		×	×	×			×
Is interested in many "adult" problems such as religion, politics, sex, race—more than usual for age level. (Chaffee, 1963; Ward, 1961; Witty, 1955)	×	×	×									×				×	×		×	×	×	×		×	×
Often is self-assertive (sometimes even aggressive); stubborn in his beliefs. (Buhler & Guirl, 1963; Gowan & Demos, 1964; Ward, 1961)								×	×	×	×	×						×		×	×				

Table 1 continued

Child Characteristics and Probable Social Roles	Content							Process/Method								Product				Learning Environment					
	Abstractness	Complexity	Variety	Organization	Economy	Study of People	Methods	Higher Level Thought	Open-Endedness	Discovery	Proof/Reasoning	Freedom of Choice	Group Interaction	Pacing	Variety	Real Problems	Real Audiences	Evaluation	Transformation	Student Centered	Encourages Independence	Openness	Accepting	Complex	High Mobility
Likes to organize and bring structure to things, people, and situations. (Buhler & Guirl, 1963; Gowan & Demos, 1964; Ward, 1961)	X			X			X	X		X	X		X							X	X	X		X	X
Is quite concerned with right and wrong, good and bad; often evaluates and passes judgment on events, people, and things. (Buhler & Guirl, 1963; Carroll, 1940; Getzels & Jackson, 1962)						X		X			X		X					X		X		X	X		
Creativity																									
Displays a great deal of curiosity about many things; is constantly asking questions about anything and everything. (Goodhart & Schmidt, 1940; National Education Association, 1960; Torrance, 1962)			X									X		X		X				X	X	X	X	X	X
Generates a large number of ideas of solutions to problems and questions; often offers unusual ("way out"), unique, clever responses. (Carroll, 1940; Hollingworth, 1942; National Education Association, 1960)								X	X									X	X			X	X		X

Table 1 continued

Child Characteristics and Probable Social Roles	Content							Process/Method								Product				Learning Environment					
	Abstractness	Complexity	Variety	Organization	Economy	Study of People	Methods	Higher Level Thought	Open-Endedness	Discovery	Proof/Reasoning	Freedom of Choice	Group Interaction	Pacing	Variety	Real Problems	Real Audiences	Evaluation	Transformation	Student Centered	Encourages Independence	Openness	Accepting	Complex	High Mobility
Is uninhibited in expressions of opinion; is sometimes radical and spirited in disagreement; is tenacious. (Getzels & Jackson, 1962; Gowan & Demos, 1964; Torrance, 1965)									x		x							x	x	x	x	x	x		
Is a high risk taker; is adventurous and speculative. (Getzels & Jackson, 1962; Torrance, 1965; Villars, 1957)			x						x			x				x	x		x	x	x	x	x	x	
Displays a good deal of intellectual playfulness; fantasizes, imagines ("I wonder what would happen if . . .") manipulates ideas (i.e., changes, elaborates upon them); is often concerned with adapting, improving, and modifying institutions, objects, and systems. (Getzels & Jackson, 1962; Gowan & Demos, 1964; Rogers, 1959)								x	x	x									x	x	x	x	x	x	
Displays a keen sense of humor and sees humor in situations that may not appear to be humorous to others. (Getzels & Jackson, 1962; Gowan & Demos, 1964; Torrance, 1962)																						x	x		

Table 1 continued

Child Characteristics and Probable Social Roles	Content							Process/Method								Product				Learning Environment					
	Abstractness	Complexity	Variety	Organization	Economy	Study of People	Methods	Higher Level Thought	Open-Endedness	Discovery	Proof/Reasoning	Freedom of Choice	Group Interaction	Pacing	Variety	Real Problems	Real Audiences	Evaluation	Transformation	Student Centered	Encourages Independence	Openness	Accepting	Complex	High Mobility
Is unusually aware of his impulses and more open to the irrational in himself (freer expression of feminine interest for boys, greater than usual amount of independence for girls); shows emotional sensitivity. (Gowan & Demos, 1964; Rothney & Koopman, 1958; Torrance, 1962)						×						×	×		×			×			×	×	×		
Is sensitive to beauty; attends to aesthetic characteristics of things. (Villars, 1957; Wilson, 1965; Witty, 1958)			×						×													×	×	×	
Is nonconforming; accepts disorder; is not interested in details; is individualistic; does not fear being different. (Buhler & Guirl, 1963; Carroll, 1940; Getzels & Jackson, 1962)							×										×	×				×	×	×	
Criticizes constructively; is unwilling to accept authoritarian pronouncements without critical examination. (Martinson, 1963; Torrance, 1962; Ward, 1962)							×	×			×							×		×	×	×	×		

Table 1 continued

Child Characteristics and Probable Social Roles	Learning Environment						Product				Process/Method								Content						
	High Mobility	Complex	Accepting	Openness	Encourages Independence	Student Centered	Transformation	Evaluation	Real Audiences	Real Problems	Variety	Pacing	Group Interaction	Freedom of Choice	Proof/Reasoning	Discovery	Open-Endedness	Higher Level Thought	Methods	Study of People	Economy	Organization	Variety	Complexity	Abstractness
Leadership																									
Carries responsibility well; can be counted on to do what has been promised and usually does it well. (Baldwin, 1932; Bellingrath, 1930; Burks, 1938)	x				x	x		x						x					x						
Is self-confident with children his own age as well as adults; seems comfortable when asked to show his work to the class. (Bellingrath, 1930; Cowley, 1931; Drake, 1944)	x	x			x	x			x				x												
Seems to be well liked by classmates. (Bellingrath, 1930; Garrison, 1935; Zeleny, 1939)					x								x												
Is cooperative with teacher and classmates; tends to avoid bickering, and is generally easy to get along with. (Dunkerly, 1940; Fauquier & Gilchrist, 1942; Newcomb, 1943)					x	x							x												

Table 1 continued

Child Characteristics and Probable Social Roles	Content							Process/Method								Product				Learning Environment					
	Abstractness	Complexity	Variety	Organization	Economy	Study of People	Methods	Higher Level Thought	Open-Endedness	Discovery	Proof/Reasoning	Freedom of Choice	Group Interaction	Pacing	Variety	Real Problems	Real Audiences	Evaluation	Transformation	Student Centered	Encourages Independence	Openness	Accepting	Complex	High Mobility
Can express self well; has good verbal facility and is usually understood. (Burks, 1938; Simpson, 1938; Terman, 1904)													X				X			X	X		X		
Adapts readily to new situations; is flexible in thought and action and does not seem disturbed when the normal routine is changed. (Caldwell & Wellman, 1926; Eichler, 1934; Flemming, 1935)													X	X						X	X	X			X
Seems to enjoy being around other people; is sociable and prefers not to be alone. (Bonney, 1943; Goodenough, 1930)													X								X				
Tends to dominate others when they are around; generally directs the activity in which he is involved. (Bowden, 1926; Hunter & Jordan, 1939; Richardson & Hanawalt, 1943)							X					X	X		X			X		X	X				

Table 1 continued

Child Characteristics and Probable Social Roles	Abstractness	Complexity	Variety	Organization	Economy	Study of People	Methods	Higher Level Thought	Open-Endedness	Discovery	Proof/Reasoning	Freedom of Choice	Group Interaction	Pacing	Variety	Real Problems	Real Audiences	Evaluation	Transformation	Student Centered	Encourages Independence	Openness	Accepting	Complex	High Mobility
	Content							Process/Method								Product				Learning Environment					
Participates in most social activities connected with the school; can be counted on to be there if anyone is. (Courtenay, 1938; Link, 1944; Zeleny, 1939)													X								X				X
Excels in athletic activities; is well coordinated and enjoys all sorts of athletic games. (Flemming, 1935; Partridge, 1935; Spaulding, 1934)																									X
Probable Roles																									
Scholar	X	X	X	X	X	X		X		X	X	X			X	X	X	X	X	X	X	X	X	X	X
Leader				X	X	X	X	X			X		X			X	X	X	X	X	X			X	X
Creator			X			X		X	X			X							X	X	X	X	X	X	X

Chapter 1

Content Modifications

The content of a curriculum is what is taught—the ideas, concepts, or facts presented to the student. This content can assume a variety of forms (Guilford, 1967). It can be *figural* (e.g., concrete items such as apples, cups, and balls; or figures such as circles, squares, and amorphous shapes), *symbolic* (letters, numbers, mathematical symbols, and other materials that are representative of something), *semantic* (words or ideas with an abstract meaning), and *behavioral* (information pertaining to the actions, perceptions, intentions, and emotions of people). To make the subject matter more appropriate for gifted students, educators can teach content that is more complex, more abstract, more varied (e.g., areas not usually included in schools), and organized differently. Teachers also can follow the principle of economy of experiences. Content should include the study of creative/productive people, and the methodology of areas of study as well as the concepts from these areas.

ABSTRACTNESS

Objects, shapes, and noises are concrete. They can be seen, touched, or heard. Very few people would disagree over their existence or their properties. Concepts such as love, hate, and altruism are abstract. Although most would agree that they exist, few individuals agree on their meaning or how they are manifested. Within every subject taught or every traditional content area, the information can be ordered on a rough continuum from concrete to abstract, based on how far removed it is from objective reality. For example, in mathematics, the concept of addition is near the concrete end, the algebraic concept of addition with unknowns is more abstract, and the idea of infinity is near the most abstract end of the continuum.

Gallagher and his associates (Gallagher, Shaffer, Phillips, Addy, Rainer, & Nelson, 1966), in an attempt to classify content according to its abstractness, use a system with three levels: data, concepts, and generalizations. They present the following definitions and examples:

Data Level

These are topics where the focus of discussion is on specifics where a particular event, object, action or condition is considered. The emphasis is on things and people rather than abstract ideas. The student should be able to touch, see, hear, etc., the entities that are the focus of this type of topic.

Examples:

A description of one of Winston Churchill's brushes with Laborites in the House of Commons.

A story of how I trapped a skunk.

A teacher demonstrates how to interpret the colors on the classroom globe.

An argument over whether George Washington had false teeth or not.

A student explains how he developed the material for his report on Angola.

A descriptive report on the class play.

A discussion of the use of a tool or method in specific regard to a particular instance (as in an experiment or exercise in class). (pp. 21-22)

Concept Level

This type of topic focuses on ideas and classes of objects, events, processes, etc. It often deals with class inclusion or exclusion. Topic focus is thus on an abstraction, even though specifics may be used in the topic for illustration.

Examples:

Discussions which deal with the definition of virus, sales tax, social group, mammal, etc.

Explanations of the operation of a social group.

Discussions as to whether sales taxes are equitable.

Who belongs in the mammalian category.

How gasoline ignites. (p. 22)

Generalization Level

The differentiation between the *Concept* and *Generalization* is difficult since the line to be drawn across many actual levels of abstraction is an arbitrary one. The following criteria are used to determine the presence of *Generalization*.

1. Two or more concepts are involved. The topic focus thus represents a complete sentence or a statement in a logical sense.
   Examples:
   Great men made history.
   Frustration breeds aggression.
   Water seeks its own level.
   The presence of *Data* in the topic focus (i.e., Thomas Jefferson was a great President) automatically eliminates this topic from consideration as *Generalization*.
2. These concepts are interrelated either as a set of component parts in a system (i.e., the transportation system, the number system, the balance of trade, etc.) or as part of a larger generalization.
3. The topic focus in a *Generalization* is on a large idea having broad applicability. Another way of expressing this point is that the concepts making up the *Generalization* do not themselves have concrete referents. (i.e., War is Hell; As pressure increases, the volume of a gas decreases; Great novels deal with deep human emotions, etc.)

Each of these three criteria are necessary but not sufficient conditions for *Generalization*. All three must be present.

Generalization—Special Issues

a. An emphasis on a piece of a system without focusing on the system itself would not be *Generalization*.

Concept	Generalization
The nature of the Presidency.	The balance of powers within the federal system.
A description of an electron.	The nuclear system— electron, proton, neutron, etc.

b. A *Generalization* representing as it does high level mental functioning cannot be sustained for very long. A topic should be classified as *Generalization* if that high level is clearly reached, however briefly during the topic, and that *Generalization* can be considered as the topic focus.
   Example:
   In a discussion of seaports on the Atlantic Ocean someone remarks how important it is to be on a body of water since all

major metropolitan areas are on or close to navigable water. (This *Generalization* would be the topic focus since what has preceded could clearly be subsumed under it even though it is a small part of the total topic.)

c. *Generalization* may be noted as appearing as an upward conceptual step in the discussion. One may move from the weather patterns of a specific region to weather systems in general, or from photosynthesis to energy transfer or from multiplication problems to a discussion of the changing of number bases.

d. If through *explicit* statement, an implication is drawn from a *Generalization,* it will be categorized on the *Generalization* level despite the lower conceptual focus involved. (i.e., If man is evil, then we need a larger police force in our town.)

Examples:

Concept	Generalization
A discussion judging whether we are doing a good job in choosing a President.	If we accept the idea that Great Men Make History, what does this imply for our choice of a President?
Possible changes in future farming practices.	Population growth will continue to reduce the number of persons engaged in farming. (pp. 23-26)

Within each of these levels, of course, are additional levels of abstraction. For example, descriptions of concrete objects are considered data as are definitions of the three branches of government. Since the concrete objects are closer to a child's experience and more tangible, descriptions of them are more concrete. The levels of abstraction within the generalization category are most important for purposes here. A generalization can be stated or presented in differing degrees of abstraction even when the same underlying principle is involved. Womack (1966) gives the following example of four levels of statement of the same general idea:

1. All families divide the work among the family members so they can meet their basic needs.
2. A division of labor takes advantage of the best skills of each member of the family or any working group.
3. A division of labor produces specialized workers, thereby leading to an increase in the production and quality of goods.

4. A division of labor leads to increased productivity and a rising standard of living. (p. 8)

As can be seen by inspecting these statements carefully, their level of abstraction is determined mainly by how far they are removed from a student's concrete experience. Most children are part of a family that divides chores among its members; division of labor in a nation, leading to an increase in the standard of living, is much further from their experience.

Womack (1966) also classifies generalizations into four types, depending on their inclusiveness and generality: subgeneralizations, normative, methodological, and substantive. Substantive generalizations are the most abstract while the three other types have more limited applicability.

Subgeneralizations are those that have limited rather than universal application. The degree of application usually is identified by an introductory phrase as in this example: "In fascist countries, the people are the servants of the state rather than served by the state" (p. 4).

Normative generalizations express a value judgment and thus have only limited application, as in this example: "Democracy has survived only because of the role played by political parties" (p. 5). These generalizations also lack the objectivity of those that are more abstract.

Methodological generalizations are principles or rules that describe a skill or technique for a field of study. An example is: "Area geographical relations can be seen most readily by the use of map symbols and scales" (p. 5).

A substantive generalization, the most abstract of the types, is "A broad inclusive statement in complete grammatical sentence form which serves as a principle or rule. . ." (p. 1).

Some of the characteristics of these generalizations are the following: (1) they are derived from factual descriptive information but are not facts themselves; (2) they not only come from factual, descriptive information but also are substantiated or proved by facts; (3) they have universal application and admit no major exceptions; (4) they contain no specific references to any particular people, places, or times; and (5) they have a thesis or, in other words, they make a point about the subject of the sentence. The Gallagher et al. (1966) system and the Womack (1966) definitions provide a useful way of looking at the abstractness of content.

A word of caution is in order, however. Specific facts and concrete/descriptive information are necessary components of the curriculum. They provide the raw material or food for thought in the development of ideas. The point of this discussion is that the content *focus* should be on abstract concepts and generalizations rather than on the facts and descriptions. Gifted students need much less emphasis and much less time spent on concrete information in the development of their abstract concepts.

Characteristics of the Gifted

The major characteristics of gifted children upon which this curricular modification is built generally are in the area of their learning characteristics. First, as noted in Table 1, they "possess a large storehouse of information about a variety of topics," have "quick mastery and recall of factual information," and read a great deal on their own, especially adult level books; thus, they do not need content emphasis on the acquisition of factual data. In fact, they need an emphasis on abstract ideas as a way to integrate and make sense out of conflicting, disparate bits of knowledge.

Other characteristics contributing to the success of and need for this approach are "rapid insight into cause-effect relationships," a "ready grasp of underlying principles," and a desire to "reason things out," "look for similarities and differences," and "find out what makes things tick." These attributes indicate that gifted children need this curricular emphasis not only to enable them to make sense out of their storehouse of information, but also to enjoy it. In relation to their expected roles in society, it seems clear that emphasis on the enduring abstract ideas in the various disciplines is necessary for children who are likely to become scholars and researchers in some academic discipline. These abstract ideas and general principles are much less likely to become obsolete before they are used.

COMPLEXITY

The second content modification, closely related to abstractness, is complexity. Although it is difficult to conceive of a complex idea that is not also abstract, it seems possible that some abstract ideas are quite simple. In the Gallagher et al. (1966) system, for example, generalizations by definition are more complex than concepts since they involve two or more concepts as well as the relationships between them. It is most useful to think of levels of complexity within the three identified levels of abstraction, particularly at the generalization stage. A more complex generalization (a) involves more concepts, (b) contains more complex and/or abstract concepts, (c) involves more relationships between concepts, (d) involves more complex relationships, (e) cuts across more disciplines or fields of study, or (f) integrates knowledge or concepts from fields or areas of study that are more diverse than does a less complex one. Any one of these characteristics indicates a higher degree of complexity.

Consider, for example, the following two generalizations (Womack, 1966):

(1) Natural resources are insignificant if unused by man, and if used, their manner of use reflects man's wants as well as his level of technology. (p. 2)

    (2) In a capitalist country, the regulator of supply and demand is the
        marketplace. (p. 4)

    Each involves at least four concepts—the first, natural resources, insignificant, wants, and level of technology; the second, capitalist country, regulator, supply and demand, and marketplace. However, the relationships among concepts in the first generalization are more complex than in the second; in the latter, they are very similar. A second difference between the two statements is the number of disciplines or fields of thought involved. The first takes ideas from the natural sciences (i.e., natural resources), psychology (humankind's wants), and the physical sciences (level of technology), while the second involves mainly those from economics (regulator, supply and demand, marketplace) and relates them to the social science concept of capitalism. The economic concepts and the relationships among them can be considered definitions of capitalism. The two generalizations cited would seem to involve a similar, if not the same, level of abstraction.

    Taba (1962) offers a classification of content into four levels combining the characteristics of abstractness and complexity. The first, or lowest, level of abstractness is specific facts or descriptive ideas. The second is basic ideas or principles, including scientific laws, mathematical principles, or what Bruner calls the structure of the discipline. Concepts such as democracy, social change, and bases (in mathematics) are at the next level of abstractness and complexity. The fourth level, thought systems, is most important for present purposes. According to Taba, the academic disciplines represent thought systems "composed of propositions and concepts which direct the flow of inquiry and thought" (p. 178). A system of interrelated principles, concepts, and definitions directs the questions asked, the kinds of answers sought, and the methods by which the questions are answered. By learning the "structure" or "thought system" of a discipline such as mathematics (i.e., consisting of the separate subjects of arithmetic, algebra, and geometry), Taba says the individual can effectively acquire "mathematical thinking." To relate this idea to Womack's (1966) classification of generalizations, a thought system could be defined as a set of interlocking substantive, normative, methodological, and subgeneralizations that form the basic structure of an academic discipline or field of inquiry. This system is much more complex, but not necessarily more abstract, than any of the individual generalizations that are a part of it.

Characteristics of the Gifted

    As with the content modification of abstractness, the learning characteristics of the gifted are the traits most suggestive of a need for complexity in subject matter. These children's high level of vocabulary development, vast store of information, quick mastery and recall, and extensive reading of adult level material, as well as their desire to identify and understand underlying principles (including thought systems) necessitates the teaching of complex ideas. Not only do these complex ideas provide a structure for using and remembering a vast store of information, they also are a source of challenge for the children. The more complex the generalizations or systems of thought, the greater the challenge to the gifted who enjoy figuring out how things work and how things are similar or different. The teaching of complex content also provides a setting where gifted students can attempt to organize and bring structure to things.

For children who are likely to become scholars and researchers in academic fields, the study of complex ideas and systems of thought seems essential. Its importance lies both in the scholar's need to understand a discipline or area of study thoroughly (including its basic thought systems) and in the individual's need to have a working understanding of several disciplines in order to make an informed decision about the area of most interest. Most people do not begin to understand the thought system in their respective fields until in graduate school.

VARIETY

A third type of content modification for gifted children is that of variety. This idea is one that is easily understood and commonly included in programs for the gifted. In fact, in some programs, variety appears to be synonymous with the word enrichment. Children in gifted programs are taught oceanography, geology, herpetology, and other exotic topics while other children are learning basic biology or general science. Part of the motivation for this practice, it seems, comes from the need for teachers of the gifted to avoid encroaching upon the territory of regular classroom teachers. By avoiding the traditional subject areas, one can avoid the wrath of next year's teacher who hears a gifted student say, "But I learned that last year in the gifted program."

In addition to simply considering whether a subject area is taught, the concept of variety also suggests considering the systematic sampling of different types of content. Perhaps the idea is best expressed by Ward (1961) in a corollary to his sixth proposition, "That in the education of the gifted child and youth the scope of the content should extend into the general nature of all the chief branches of knowledge" (p. 144).

Using scholarly references, such as Phenix's (1964) *Realms of Meaning* or Adler's (1952) *The Great Ideas: A Syntopicon of Great Books of the Western World,* a curriculum can be developed that samples a broad range of ideas or systems of thought. The teaching of varied content not only meets some of the intellectual needs of gifted children but also facilitates the teaching and understanding of complex systems of thought. A wide range of disciplines contributes varied concepts and generalizations as the raw material in the development of a thought system.

Characteristics of the Gifted

The learning characteristics of wide vocabulary, broad range of information, quick mastery and recall, and extensive reading suggest that variety of content is an important modification to use and extend a child's store of knowledge. However, the gifted pupil's motivational attributes may be more important determinants. These students tend to become (as in Table 1) "absorbed and truly involved," needing "little external motivation to follow through in work that initially proves exciting;" they are "easily bored with routine tasks," "prefer to work independently," and are "interested in many adult topics." By providing a wide range of content, there is a greater chance that the teacher will find areas of intrinsic interest to turn on gifted students. Their creativity characteristics of curiosity and willingness to take risks suggest that they enjoy involvement in very different content areas. Their sensitivity to the aesthetics as well as their possible future involvement in areas such as the arts indicate that this should be one of the varied content areas in the curriculum. If these children become scholars, knowledge of a wide range of academic disciplines can contribute to their thinking in a chosen field as well as assist them in their initial choice of a study area.

ORGANIZATION AND ECONOMY

Although different, the two related modifications of organization and economy are discussed together since it is almost impossible to achieve economy without the kind of content organization suggested here. Ward (1961) was perhaps the first to suggest the principle of economy in his third proposition: individuals select learning experiences with the greatest potential for transfer or generalization. He defines economy in terms of abstractness of ideas. Abstractness certainly is a consideration. However, Taba (1962) provides more guidance in her discussion of what to teach within each of her four levels of abstraction. To understand and implement her ideas, the concept of organization must be added. Rather than arranging the content according to chronology (e.g., time periods of history), functional similarities (tools, equipment), categorical groups in an existing classification (chemical elements, classes of animals or plants), or descriptive similarities (geographical environments, types of government), Taba and others (c.f., Bruner, 1960; Henry, 1958; Womack, 1966) suggest that it be organized around the basic concepts or abstract generalizations that "represent the most necessary understandings about a subject or field" (Taba, 1966, p. 177).

By organizing the content taught (including both data and concepts) around central ideas, educators can provide a setting where the specific facts are chosen carefully to illustrate abstract ideas. The information gathered must be related to and interpreted in the context of the ideas they serve. Content can be sampled so that sharp contrasts and comparisons are available as examples and nonexamples of the ideas. Furthermore, the method of presentation of the material can reveal the method of thinking for that discipline. For example, it is possible to learn the essential ways of being a historian not by covering all of history but by studying some historic phenomenon in sufficient depth to "discover the essential ways of thinking, of discovering appropriate causalities, of handling generalizations, and of establishing conclusions" (p. 180). Taba gives the following example from history:

> It should be possible, for example, to study a few crucial social phenomena, such as wars, by asking all the questions a historian might ask: what are the factors that create wars; how are wars affected by conditions, such as the tools of warfare and the political institutions that surround them; what is the history of causation of wars, and so on. (p. 180)

Womack (1966) suggests that the basic principles or abstract generalizations in an academic area can serve as a guide for (a) selecting content at each grade level, (b) organizing learning activities for each unit of study, and (c) serving as a major articulating strand for the entire K-12 curriculum. He provides a step-by-step procedure for using generalizations to select content.

1. Compile an authoritative list of generalizations.
2. Choose from the list those generalizations which most likely can be discovered from the prescribed content of the course.
3. Arrange the chosen generalizations in a priority order of those which must be learned to those which may or may not be necessary for the particular course.
4. Decide which of the *must* generalizations the students can discover from a particular unit of study. The teacher now has a list of generalizations that students can discover unit by unit.
5. Decide which unit has generalizations that absolutely must be learned and which has generalizations that could be omitted if necessary.
6. Arrange the units with the *absolutely must* generalizations in a sequence based on one of the usual criteria, such as chronology, expanding environments, or a topical approach. (pp. 19,20)

Both his and Taba's suggested way of using generalizations to articulate the K-12 curriculum depend on the concept of a spiral curriculum, where an idea is introduced again and again and expanded each time it is revisited. The degree of abstraction is increased as children become more capable of handling abstract ideas, more familiar with the ideas, and have a wider range of experience to bring to the classroom.

To provide guidelines for using the selected generalizations to choose and/or organize learning experiences at each grade level, the generalization is restated in the form or level of abstraction children are believed capable of understanding at that level. For example, the idea of supply and demand can be restated for five grade levels.

Grade 3

Some workers make more money than others because their services are needed more.

Grade 5

Both the supply of workers and the demand for workers operate to determine the wages paid for particular kinds of workers.

Grade 7

The more income one has, the greater his claim on the goods available, and thus the higher his standard of living.

Grade 9

The standard of living a person has is a major criteria for determining the social class to which he belongs.

Grade 12

The supply and demand of particular categories of workers leads to wage and standard of living differentials, and thereby stratification of social classes. (Womack, 1966, p. 9)

To make use of Taba's ideas regarding thought systems as the highest level of complexity and to illustrate, through these methods, the type of thinking prevalent in a certain field, Womack's classification of types of generalizations is helpful. Ideas to be taught can be arranged with the substantive generalizations as the overarching content. Subgeneralizations, normative generalizations, and methodological generalizations related to the more abstract idea can serve as a further guide for selecting and organizing the content. Extending this example provides a framework similar to that in Exhibit 1-1, which gives the generalizations, concepts that must be taught or understood before the generalization can be understood, the data (e.g., specific facts, information) to be used in developing the concepts and

Exhibit 1-1 Use of Generalizations to Help Select and Organize Content and Learning Activities

Substantive Generalization: The supply and demand of particular categories of workers leads to wage and standard of living differentials and thereby stratification of social classes.

Related Generalizations	Concepts	Sample Data	Sample Teaching Activities
In a capitalist country the regulator of supply and demand is the marketplace (subgeneralization)	Capitalism Regulator Supply and demand Marketplace	• A study of the Industrial Revolution • A study of a major trade center such as New York City with particular emphasis on its economic development	• Students read both primary and secondary source materials describing the Industrial Revolution and the economic development of New York City • Students play a simulation game such as *Trade*[1]
Few events have single causes or single effects (methodological generalization)	Cause Effect Event	• An analysis of different people's perceptions of the causes and effects of the Industrial Revolution • An analysis of the different theories of the causes and effects of the economic development of New York City	• Class discussion of the possible causes and effects of the Industrial Revolution and the economic development of New York City • Brainstorming (without judgment) all the possible causes and effects; each student then selects and justifies what the pupil perceives as the most important causes and effects; comparisons are made of the students' differing conclusions

| Throughout history, man's incentive to advance has been the desire to attain material wealth rather than to serve the causes of humanity (normative generalization) | Incentives
Desires
Values
Humanitarianism | • An examination of the possible values or motivations of different people involved in or opposed to the Industrial Revolution
• An examination of the differences in values or motivations of people engaged in various occupations in New York City and a contrasting area such as a farm community in upstate New York | • Students are instructed to examine the list of causes and effects generated through brainstorming to see how many involve values and desires; they then examine and classify these values as to whether they relate to humanitarianism or a desire for material wealth
• Students discuss their participation in the simulation games and the underlying motives for their behavior |

1. A complete catalog of simulation games, including "Trade," is available from INTERACT, P.O. Box 262, Lakeside, Calif. 92040.

generalizations, and some sample teaching activities that can promote the development of an underlying thought system. By using a procedure similar to this social studies example, content and learning experiences can be chosen economically while important abstract and complex ideas necessary for understanding a particular discipline still are being developed.

Characteristics of the Gifted

Learning characteristics of gifted children that contribute to the need for economy include (a) rapid insight into cause-effect relationships, (b) a ready grasp of underlying principles, and (c) an ability to see more or get more out of a story or film than others. These attributes imply that gifted children need fewer learning experiences and less data to enable them to understand abstract complex ideas. Because they are easily bored with routine yet potentially will become leaders in their fields, the principle of economy is an increasingly important content modification.

Organization of content according to abstract generalizations is built on the fact that gifted children have a vast store of information that needs to be related to higher level ideas, they have rapid insight into causes and effects, they read a lot on their own, they get more out of their experiences, they try to understand complicated material by breaking it down, and they like to organize and bring structure to a situation. If learning experiences are arranged in the way described in this section, children have an ideal setting to exercise and be challenged to grow in these characteristics. The future social roles of leadership and scholarship also suggest that content organization according to these important ideas is necessary.

THE STUDY OF PEOPLE

To build upon the interests of gifted children and to help them become more effective adults, teachers should guide them in the study of individuals (including themselves) and how they interact with each other as well as how they function in a career. This study should include an examination of the following aspects of people's lives: (a) their personal or internal characteristics, such as their motivations, their family backgrounds, and their personality types; (b) their career characteristics, including the creative processes they use, their leadership styles, the type of products they have developed; and (c) their social characteristics, or the ways they interact with others and others with them.

In all of these three factors, the study of people should concentrate on the actual processes or skills used, the development of the individual, and the interaction among all three aspects. For example, in studying an individual's personal characteristics, it is important to examine the person at a point in time as well as to examine how those traits developed—how parents, teachers, siblings, or peers contributed to their motivation; how the social or political setting of the community or nation influenced their personality and/or motivation. A study of the career traits of an individual should include the development of the person's creative or leadership style (e.g., characteristic style of painting or sculpture and ways of handling people), including how teachers or events may have provided an influence, and how personal and social aspects of their lives interacted with external ones in their development.

There should be a definite focus on problems unique to gifted or creative individuals and how they have resolved these situations. Some issues worthy of study are lack of social recognition of the value of creative products, defining success in a personal vs. a social sense, resolving conflicts between self-expectations for success and the expectations of others, coping with the perception of being different or abnormal, and many others that can be identified by the students through their own personal experiences or through their relationship to the lives of others.

In a study of individuals, numerous methods can be used, ranging from in-depth examination of one person's life through biographies, autobiographies, and personal case studies, or through comparison of several different individuals in one field of study or in different fields. When studying one individual, for example, students can examine all of the products of that person, noticing their similarities as well as the changes in products as the subject matures or changes focus. Students can note periods in which products are similar as well as the events or personal factors that might have caused a move from one period to another. Students can study in depth one individual in a certain field who lived in the past and one who is living now and compare their lives, noting the anomalies that might be the result of differing external conditions as well as the similarities that relate to human nature and the creative process. Other methods can include comparisons of individuals in different types of careers from different cultural or ethnic groups, different sexes, or those with handicaps vs. those without handicaps. The study of individuals certainly should include direct contact with one or more gifted, talented, or creative persons.

Characteristics of the Gifted

With regard to the learning characteristics of gifted students, the study of people should build upon their natural interest in how people tick, their ready grasp of underlying principles regarding events, people, and things, and their desire to look for similarities and differences in events and people. Gifted children often show definite interest in reading biographies and autobiographies of famous people. Most of the motivational characteristics suggest a need to study creative/productive people and leaders in the sense that by analyzing the motivations of others and relating them to their own lives, these students may be better able to understand and cope with their own motivational characteristics.

Other motivational characteristics specifically contributing to the need for this modification are the tendency to be self-critical (or strive toward perfection) and the tendency to evaluate or judge people. The study of others gives a more human perspective to this latter tendency. Creativity characteristics of the gifted also suggest the study of creative individuals since this could help students understand and deal more effectively with their own originality. In addition, the students' self-awareness and emotional sensitivity suggest the value of examining their own characteristics and how they are different from or similar to those of creative/ productive adults. Gifted students' future participation in a career is enhanced by consistent study and observation of others and how they could be more effective.

METHODS OF INQUIRY

A final content modification, discussed briefly, is the inclusion of both the study of substantive information and the methods of inquiry in a discipline. This idea was discussed in the two previous sections in relation to Taba's concept of thought systems, so it does not need further in-depth explanation. Suffice it to say that this curricular modification is necessary if a setting is to be provided where pupils can understand the complexities of an area of study. It also is necessary because of gifted children's characteristics such as independence (i.e., their ability to structure their own inquiry appropriately), their adult level interests (they enjoy studying phenomena the way an adult does and are interested in ways of thinking about ideas), their desire to organize and structure things, their tendency toward constructive criticism, and their leadership abilities in assuming responsibility and directing the activities in which they are involved. These last attributes as well as gifted children's probable future roles as scholars and leaders suggest that they need and can profit from an analysis of the methods used by scholars and leaders in the various disciplines.

SUMMARY

This chapter has described modifications of the basic curriculum's content. These changes in ''what to teach'' are designed to enhance and extend the present characteristics distinguishing the gifted from other children. They also are designed to develop the skills required by the future roles gifted students probably will assume. Most of these content changes build upon the learning and motivational characteristics of gifted students, but some emerge from their creative traits. Perhaps not all of these modifications are necessary for all gifted students but a comprehensive, well-established program should include most, if not all, of them.

Chapter 2

Process Modifications

Process or methodology is the *way* educators teach and involves the way material is presented to children, the questions asked of them, and the mental or physical activities expected from them. Although the way practitioners teach cannot be separated completely from what is taught, especially if the content modifications suggested here are implemented, a discussion of process provides another set of curricular modifications that need to be made.

Of all the curricular modifications suggested for programs for gifted students, process has received the most emphasis in the past. To make the process more appropriate for gifted children, the teacher can modify the level or type of thought processes (i.e., mental activities) emphasized, the pacing of instruction, and the overall approach (deductive vs. inductive). Other associated changes include using a variety of methods and encouraging or even requiring students to express both the products of their reasoning processes (i.e., their answers) and the logic or reasoning process they followed to arrive at the answers. Each of these modifications is explained in the sections that follow, using the same format as in Chapter 1.

HIGHER LEVELS OF THINKING

One of the most frequently discussed modifications is a change of emphasis from the so-called lower levels of thinking such as memory or recall to the so-called higher levels such as analysis, synthesis, and evaluation. This change essentially involves an increasing emphasis on use rather than acquisition of knowledge and on progressively more difficult mental activities. Teacher questions usually provide the vehicle for implementation of this change. Classic studies of classroom interaction (e.g., Gallagher, Aschner, & Jenné, 1967; Taba, 1966) have shown clearly that, when it comes to mental activity, teachers get what they ask for. If they ask a low-level question, they get a low-level answer, and if they ask a question calling for a high-level analysis, that is what they get. Teaching activities also can provide the setting for emphasis on higher levels of thinking, but instructor questions are the major vehicle.

Numerous classification systems exist for analyzing levels of thought and guiding teacher questions. The most common is the *Taxonomy of Educational Objectives* proposed by Bloom and his colleagues (Bloom, 1956) that describes six levels of thinking in a hierarchical taxonomy in which each higher level includes and depends on all those below it. This taxonomy classifies thought processes into knowledge or recall, comprehension, application, analysis, synthesis, and evaluation. In a related project dealing with affective behaviors, the same group of educators (Krathwohl, Bloom, & Masia, 1964) developed a taxonomy consisting of the categories of receiving, responding, valuing, organizing, and characterizing by a value complex. Other classifications emphasizing strategies for use rather than acquisition of information are the following:

a. Bruner's (1960) three aspects of a learning episode (e.g., acquisition, transformation, evaluation);

b. Parnes's (1966) Creative Problem Solving Process, which has five steps emphasizing use of information in the process of solving problems (fact finding, problem finding, idea finding, solution finding, acceptance finding);

c. Kohlberg's (1966) six levels of moral reasoning (obedience and punishment orientation, instrumental relativist orientation, interpersonal concordance orientation, "law and order" orientation, social contract/legalistic orientation, universal ethical principle orientation);

d. Taba's (1964) four types of thinking skill clusters, also including sequences of skills within each cluster (concept development, interpretation of data, application of generalizations, resolution of conflict);

e. Taylor's (Stevenson, Seghini, Timothy, Brown, Lloyd, Zimmerman, Maxfield, & Buchanan, 1971) six talent areas (academic, creative, decision making, planning, forecasting, communication) that include levels and types of thinking skills;

f. Williams's (1970) thinking processes (fluency, flexibility, originality, elaboration) and feeling processes (curiosity, risk taking, complexity, imagination); and

g. Guilford's (1967) five operations (cognition, memory, divergent production, convergent production, evaluation).

Another useful concept in the context of higher levels of thinking is that of critical thinking as opposed to an uncritical analysis (i.e., acceptance without examination) of information. Ennis (1964) provides a practical listing of aspects of critical thinking derived from his study of the literature in education, philosophy, and psychology. If students are taught these skills, there is a greater likelihood that they will become critical thinkers:

1. Judging whether a statement follows from the premises,
2. Judging whether something is an assumption,
3. Judging whether an observation statement is reliable,
4. Judging whether a simple generalization is warranted,
5. Judging whether a hypothesis is warranted,
6. Judging whether a theory is warranted,
7. Judging whether an argument depends on an ambiguity,
8. Judging whether a statement is overvague or overspecific, and
9. Judging whether an alleged authority is reliable. (Ennis, 1964, pp. 600-610)

Within each of these skill areas, Ennis presents a series of criteria to be applied to information in making judgments of its validity. For example, a hypothesis is warranted (skill 5) to the extent that:

5.1 It explains a bulk and variety of reliable data. If a datum is explained, it can be deduced or loosely derived (in the fashion of the application of principles) from the hypothesis together with established facts or generalizations.
5.2 It is itself explained by a satisfactory system of knowledge.
5.3 It is not inconsistent with any evidence.
5.4 Its competitors are inconsistent with the evidence. This principle is the basis of controlled experiments.
5.5 It is testable. It must be, or have been, possible to make predictions from it. (Ennis, 1964, p. 605)

Criteria such as these can be used for the related purposes of teaching students the component skills involved in critical thinking, evaluating their progress, and planning learning activities that will develop these component skills systematically.

Characteristics of the Gifted

Child traits contributing to the need for emphasis on higher levels of thinking include all their learning characteristics and most of their motivational ones. The gifted do not need much practice in acquiring knowledge. This fact can be seen in the storehouse of information they possess in a variety of areas. They also are proficient in the use of information at higher levels. However, there certainly is room for improvement and challenge in these high levels as evidenced by their less than perfect performance on tests of critical or higher level thinking (Ennis &

Millman, 1971; Ross & Ross, 1976; Taba, 1964, 1966; Watson & Glaser, 1964). Motivational attributes such as the tendency to become bored with routine tasks as well as tendencies toward making personal judgments rather than accepting the opinions of others suggest that gifted children need to be challenged and given practice in making informed, logical, and appropriate uses of information rather than simply acquiring it. Their creative characteristics (generating a number of ideas, manipulating ideas) as well as their probable future roles as scholars, leaders, and creators, indicate a need for emphasizing a high level of mental activity.

OPEN-ENDEDNESS

A second process modification often discussed in the literature is that of encouraging "open" rather than "closed" thinking. A popular way of describing this difference is through the definition of convergent and divergent thinking. Convergent thinking involves an individual's attempt to reach the "right" or best conclusion or come up with the right or best answer; divergent thinking is the attempt to generate a variety of possibilities or many answers. In this context, convergent thinking often is seen as a lower level of thought or as a process to be avoided. Such a perception is unwarranted and could be harmful. Decisions are, and must be, made every day. Everyone constantly is required to make judgments about the adequacy, appropriateness, or usefulness of something. Making decisions necessarily involves converging on the best solution or the best answer. Gifted students need practice in making decisions and judging them as well as in generating a variety of possibilities. The point is that one type of thinking— covergent or divergent—should not replace the other in a curriculum for gifted children.

The concept of open-endedness is different from and more important than the convergent-divergent dichotomy stressed in the popular literature. Open-endedness implies a different teacher attitude reflected in (a) questioning techniques as well as the content of questions, (b) the design of learning experiences, and (c) evaluation of student responses to questions. In asking questions, teachers often have in mind what they want to hear, and go through a probing or fishing process with children until they hear it. The questions may even be those calling for divergent thinking as in situations where the teacher asks a question such as, "What are some other ways we can evaluate this solution?" and continues to ask the question until someone comes up with the one answer the instructor thinks is most important.

Questions can be phrased in an open fashion but asked in such a way that students know there is only one acceptable answer. Needless to say, this closed attitude on the part of the teacher stimulates the mental activity of figuring out what the teacher wants rather than high-level divergent or even convergent thinking. As most educators know from experience, many gifted children have become experts at this mental activity.

The content or phrasing of questions is easier to modify than are attitudes and may be just as important. An open-ended question is one that satisfies two basic requirements: it cannot be answered by ''yes'' or ''no,'' and there is no predetermined or expected right answer. Some examples of closed questions changed to open are the following:

Closed: Do you think that excessive TV watching has an effect on family interaction?

Open: What, if any, effect do you feel TV watching has had on family interaction?

Closed: What did Thomas Jefferson say about democracy?

Open: What do you think were some of Thomas Jefferson's most significant ideas about democracy?

Although open questions usually require higher levels of thinking than do closed ones, even recall questions can be made open-ended:

Closed: Would you like to add any other information?

Open: What information would you like to add?

Closed: What did Jim do in the film when his dog was shot?

Open: What are some things you noticed about the behavior of the characters in the story?

Open questions have the added advantages of (a) permitting and encouraging many rather than only one student response; (b) developing student-to-student rather than teacher-student, teacher-student interaction patterns; (c) eliciting complete responses rather than parts of answers; and (d) encouraging the pupils to question themselves, their classmates, and the teacher.

A related aspect of open-endedness involves the selection and design of learning experiences or teacher questions that encourage further thought or exploration of a topic rather than an ending. Womack (1966) calls this type a ''provocative'' or ''leading'' question and describes it as one that focuses student attention on a specific part of the content, is concise and to the point, and is particularly of the ''how'' or ''why'' variety. Williams (1972) also includes a teaching strategy called ''provocative questions.'' He describes this as ''inquiry to bring forth meaning; inquiry to incite knowledge exploration; summons to discovering new knowledge'' (p. 95). These questions generally are of three basic types:

1. What do you think would happen if _____?
2. What effect do you think _____ would have on _____?
3. How would _____ have been different if _____?

They also can be questions calling for a quantity of ideas or requiring the student to assume a viewpoint other than the usual or conventional one. Some examples of provocative questions are:

- What do you think would happen if all of the trees in the country were suddenly destroyed?
- What effects would a population decrease have on our governmental system?
- How would the story have been different if the children lived in New Mexico instead of West Virginia?
- How do you think a cave man would react to a television set?
- How would the developers of our Constitution react to our present interpretations of interstate commerce regulations?

Ward (1961), in discussing his principle dealing with this idea, suggests that a curriculum that is "generative of further development" (p. 141) is one in which (a) the scope of content extends into the general nature of all the chief branches of knowledge, (b) concepts are only introduced and initially explored (i.e., only the essential nature and structure of a curricular segment should be presented, leaving more thorough examination to the child's own initiative), (c) content is organized so that the concepts are of a generic nature, and (d) the theoretical bases for facts, opinions, and principles are always given to the student.

Taken together, Ward's, Womack's, and Williams's ideas can be used as guides for developing experiences that encourage exploration. As can be seen by comparing these ideas with the content modifications suggested earlier, if the material taught is complex, abstract, varied, chosen economically, and organized appropriately, further thought is likely to be generated, assuming that Ward and Womack are right in their analysis. However, one of Ward's ideas needs further examination. He states that theoretical bases should be *given* to the students. "Given" seems an unfortunate choice of word. Based on the characteristics of gifted children and what is known about the phenomenon of curiosity, a teacher who always provides the theoretical bases for information would seem to eliminate pupils' joy of discovery. A more appropriate suggestion, in this writer's opinion, is that the educator always should elicit, discuss, or analyze the underlying theory— implying that a teacher needs to arrange experiences and ask questions that will necessitate the student's analyzing theoretical ideas but not necessarily in a didactic manner. The use of an inductive or discovery approach, in fact, is one of the process modifications suggested in this chapter as important for gifted children.

Characteristics of the Gifted

To provide a justification for the process modification of open-endedness, the teacher should consider the learning characteristics of rapid insight, quick grasp of underlying principles, and awareness of more aspects of situations. If educators provide an atmosphere where children are encouraged to do their own thinking regardless of what the teacher might have in mind, and a setting where all students are encouraged to offer ideas and to interact, gifted pupils can contribute to each other's thinking while developing their own. Their motivational tendencies toward becoming involved in topics of intrinsic interest also are facilitated. Perhaps the most important justification comes from their creativity characteristics. There does seem to be a relationship (though not a one-to-one correspondence) between intelligence and creativity (c.f., Dellas & Gaier, 1970; Gallagher, 1966; Guilford, 1967). Those who are more intelligent are more likely to be creative and possess characteristics such as fluency and originality, lack of inhibition, willingness to take risks, playfulness and imagination, awareness and sensitivity. These strengths can be fostered and allowed to flourish only in open-ended learning situations. Future roles involving these attributes further justify the concept of open-endedness.

THE IMPORTANCE OF DISCOVERY

Inductive thinking is a mental process in which an individual sees a number of items, events, or phenomena that are presented separately and reasons that they fall into a particular pattern. This pattern may be based on some criterion such as size, shape, quantity, order, or distance. Once the pattern has been discovered, the individual can make a prediction about new items based on knowledge of previous phenomena and how they fit together. Deductive reasoning is the process of predicting future events or patterns, while inductive reasoning is the discovery of the rule or principle underlying the perceived pattern. For example, in a problem involving numbers in a series (e.g., 2, 6, 14, 26, 42), inductive reasoning is involved in figuring out the pattern (e.g., the numbers are separated by multiples of 4 as in $2 + (1 \times 4) = 6; 6 + (2 \times 4) = 14; 14 + (3 \times 4) = 26$), while deductive reasoning is involved in predicting the next number in the series (e.g., $42 + (5 \times 4) = 62$). The use of formal logic also is an example of deductive thinking.

When practitioners utilize an approach in their teaching that guides children through an inductive approach, they are said to be using guided discovery. In its most extreme form (often found in law school classrooms), the process is called "hiding the ball." In a discovery approach, students are encouraged to form hypotheses and make informed guesses. Suchman (1965) calls the process "in-scientific events presented to them. In the first stage, episode analysis, the child attempts to verify the facts of the situation. In the second stage, determination of relevance, the pupil isolates the relevant or necessary conditions that will cause the event. With a big jump further in the third stage, induction of relational constructs, (i.e., discovering the generalization or underlying principle) the child realizes what has happened and why.

Suchman has collected a series of what he calls "discrepant" events that illustrate important scientific concepts. These events are presented to students through film loops. The pupils attempt to formulate theories explaining the events by asking questions of the teacher and reading on their own. The teacher's role is to answer students' questions with "yes" or "no" and to assist them in identifying resources. An important aspect of the process, however, is that the teacher never replies to an hypothesis question with yes or no. If this were done, and the answer were yes, the student (along with the whole group) would achieve closure and the inquiry process would end. Suchman believes that motivation is seriously hampered by closure. Another reason for avoiding these answers, it seems, is that it promotes the attitude that the teacher is the final authority rather than the students through their own competent methods of inquiry. The Suchman program was used successfully as a model in gifted programs in Illinois.

Womack (1966) gives a sequential order for one way of using a discovery approach when teaching generalizations:

1. Decide what generalization or generalizations should be discovered from the content or unit of study.
2. Organize the learning activities of the unit so that all "strands" or important parts of the generalization are exposed to the students.
3. Have students write summaries of the content.
4. Have students trace sequences or identify patterns of events and omit specific references to particular people, places, or times.
5. Ask the students to combine the patterns or sequences identified and make one complete sentence expressing this synthesis. In this process, students are clearly attempting to develop a generalization.
6. Ask the students to provide proof that their statement fits the requirements of a generalization. To do so, they must give examples of its applicability to situations, periods, places, and people other than those initially studied. (p. 13).

In following this process, it should be noted that there is a definite concentration on generalizations that should be discovered from the content. Teachers must be careful to avoid preprogramming the answers and allowing only certain kinds of generalizations. In other words, students must be allowed and even encouraged to discover generalizations other than those identified by the teacher. They also should be encouraged to examine generalizations developed by others to determine whether they are accurate. This examination certainly would need to include the ones developed by the teacher.

Gallagher (1975), on the other hand, cautions against having children verbalize their discovery. Instead, he recommends encouraging them to demonstrate their understanding through applying ideas or solving problems. He bases his cautious stance on two factors: too-early verbalization of the principle will "short-circuit" the other students' discoveries, and too-early verbalization often is poorly stated, leading to concentration on the form and organization of the statement itself rather than on its meaning. On the other hand, Taba's (1966) research does not suggest that educators be overly concerned about avoiding the attempt to verbalize a general idea resulting from discovery. In fact, she suggests, as a result of her many years of research on the *Hilda Taba Teaching Strategies Program,* that it is important to have children reach their own conclusions and generalizations about a topic. Students always must provide an explanation of their logic in reaching this conclusion. They are encouraged to interact with each other as well.

Over a period of years, Taba developed four teaching strategies, two of which are guided discovery techniques. The second, called Interpretation of Data, has the following general procedures, with student behavioral objectives guided by "Focusing Questions" asked by the teacher:

Step 1

Behavioral Objective:

    a. Enumerates data relevant to the focus of the discussion

Thinking Objectives:

    a. Recalls data from prior knowledge or intake experience
    b. Differentiates relevant from irrelevant data

Focusing Question:

    a. What did you read? See? What do you recall about _____?

Step 2

Behavioral Objectives:

    a. States inferences about causes and/or effects
    b. States evidence or reasoning to support inferences

Thinking Objectives:

    a. Infers causes and/or effects of events or phenomena (items of data)
    b. Identifies evidence or reasoning to support inferences

Focusing Questions:

    a. What are some causes for (*data*)?
       What have been some effects of (*data*)?
    b. Why do you think (*inference*) is a *cause* (*effect*) of (*data*)?

Step 3

Behavioral Objectives:

    a. States inferences about prior causes and/or effects
    b. States evidence or reasoning to support inferences

Thinking Objectives:

    a. Infers causes and/or effects of previously inferred and supported causes or effects
    b. Identifies evidence or reasoning to support inferences

Focusing Questions:

    a. What are some causes of (*cause*)?
       What are some of the effects of (*effect*)?
    b. Why do you think *(inference)* is a *cause (effect)* of *(cause/effect)?*

Step 4

Behavioral Objectives:

    a. States conclusions based on cause/effect inferences
    b. States evidence or reasoning to support conclusions

Thinking Objectives:

    a. Synthesizes inferences to form conclusions
    b. Identifies evidence or reasoning to support conclusions

Focusing Questions:

   a. What could you conclude about _____?
   b. From what we've discussed, what would lead you to conclude
       that?

Step 5

Behavioral Objectives:

   a. States generalizations based on conclusions
   b. States evidence or reasoning to support generalizations

Thinking Objectives:

   a. Generalizes about all of the inferences and to other like situations
   b. Identifies evidence or reasoning to support generalizations

Focusing Questions:

   a. What could you say generally about the causes/effects of
      _____?
   b. What from our discussion would lead you to make that statement?
      (Institute for Staff Development, 1971b, p. 8)

At Step 5, the generalization step, as with all the others, the teacher asks questions to get children to clarify, extend, and elaborate on their statements as well as to cite evidence or reasoning in support of their ideas.

Perhaps a way to resolve the opposing positions of Gallagher vs. Taba and Womack is to consider the idea of "too early" in Gallagher's statement along with Taba's overall philosophy of teacher encouragement tempered with acceptance of all student responses. In Taba's teaching strategies, a focusing question calling for a general statement is asked of the entire group of students; although no one is required to answer. More importantly, even though attempting through questions to get students to think on as abstract a level as possible, the teacher accepts responses at any level of sophistication. The instructor does not criticize any student's ideas and does not allow other pupils to be critical. They may challenge or ask questions to clarify meanings. If not ready to attempt verbalizing an idea, the pupil is not required to do so. Through methods such as this, the teacher can ascertain the approximate level of sophistication of the children's thinking on a certain topic. If they are not encouraged to verbalize until they are absolutely certain, their level of sophistication may be unknown or uncertain.

Kagan (1965) presents four major arguments favoring a discovery approach based on psychological and educational principles:

1. Studies of both animals and young children indicate that the more active involvement required of the organism the greater the likelihood of learning. . . . A major advantage of the discovery strategy is that it creates arousal and as a result maximal attention.
2. Because the discovery approach requires extra intellectual effort, the value of the task is increased. . . . It is reasonable to assume that activities become valuable to the degree to which effort is expended in their mastery.
3. The inferential or discovery approach is likely to increase the child's expectancy that he is able to solve different problems autonomously. . . .
4. The discovery approach gives the child more latitude and freedom and removes him from the submissive posture ordinarily maintained between teacher and child. (p. 216)

In discussing the merits of a discovery approach, Gallagher gives arguments both for and against this method of teaching. On the pro side, in addition to the above arguments, is the enthusiasm and excitement generated in children; on the con side, is, first of all, the lack of empirical research demonstrating its value. Although not conclusive on the subject of discovery vs. didactic formal presentation, however, Taba's (1966) research on the effectiveness of her teaching strategies shows the inductive approach valuable both in increasing academic achievement and in enhancing abstract reasoning skills. She finds that children tend to be very tentative at first in their generalizations, then become "overgeneralizers," and finally begin to make valid generalizations.

A second argument against a discovery approach involves the costs of time and teacher preparation. Perhaps the time element is the greatest cost. Guiding a student, through selection of examples, to discover a rule or principle may take four or five times as long as it would for the teacher to state a principle and give four or five examples to illustrate the point. The time element certainly is an important consideration for most children. However, it is this author's opinion that given the learning and motivational characteristics of gifted children, combined with carefully and economically chosen examples (they can even be selected to illustrate several concepts or generalizations in the course of study of a content area), the extra time spent in using a discovery approach with gifted children is well worth the expense.

One final point needs to be made. It is not suggested that teachers emphasize inductive reasoning to the exclusion of deduction, nor that they always use a discovery approach. In fact, the argument is for a balance between inductive and deductive reasoning, and for the use of a guided discovery approach whenever possible and appropriate. A discovery approach is both necessary and appropriate when developing complex, highly abstract ideas in gifted children and attempting simultaneously to develop higher levels of thinking. If they are simply given the ideas, they will neither fully understand them nor have an opportunity to develop their own inductive reasoning processes.

Characteristics of the Gifted

The learning characteristics of rapid insight, quick grasp of underlying principles, breaking down things for better understanding, and seeing more or getting more out of a situation suggest that the time cost of using a discovery approach is minimal. In addition, motivational characteristics of becoming bored with routine, enjoyment of bringing structure to things, independence, and stubbornness, when considered with Kagan's (1965) comments about the value of discovery methods, suggest that gifted students enjoy and become involved in learning through such an approach. Their probable future roles as researchers and scholars further justifies such an approach since valid inductive thinking is an absolute necessity in facilitating productive research, synthesis of the results of previous research, and formulating scientific theories.

CITATIONS OF PROOF AND EVIDENCE OF REASONING

An integral aspect of a discovery approach and an important element in the development of higher levels of thinking is the requirement that students express not only their conclusions but also the logic or reasoning process they use in arriving at those conclusions. To emphasize its importance, however, this method is discussed separately. Each time students offer an answer (i.e., a conclusion or inference) or make statements arrived at through a thinking process at a level higher than recall or low-level comprehension, they should be asked to explain or cite evidence to support their statements. Most teachers ask only for reasoning or evidence when they disagree or think the children are wrong and wish to call attention to the incorrect answer or faulty reasoning process. For this reason, "why" questions often are perceived as a threat when they are extremely important for gifted students.

Explaining the logical analysis or reasoning process behind an answer is important for gifted children for two related reasons. First, children can benefit from hearing how someone else analyzed a problem, in a way that may have been different from their own process. They also have an opportunity to evaluate the process as well as the products of others' thinking. Theoretical justification for the learning of reasoning from other children can be found in the research and writing of Piaget (Piaget & Inhelder, 1969) and Kohlberg (1970). Children can understand and profit from expressions of reasoning by students one or two stages above their own but cannot from adults' reasoning if it is several stages higher because it is too sophisticated. This is one way to help students refine their higher level thinking skills in all subject areas and in a variety of contexts. For the teacher, expressions of reasoning provide an opportunity for assessing the student's level of development.

As an example of the application of this idea, consider some of the open-ended questions presented earlier as illustrations of that principle:

> Question calling for an inference: What, if any, effects do you feel television watching has had on family interaction?
> Student's answer: It has caused a lowering of the level of interaction.
>
> Question calling for clarification: What do you mean by "lowering the level?"
> Question calling for elaboration: What is an example of "lowering the level of interaction?"
> Sample question calling for support: How did you arrive at the conclusion that television watching lowers the level of family interaction? or What are your reasons for thinking that television watching lowers the level of family interaction? or What was your thinking in reaching that conclusion?

See also the "b" focusing questions in the Taba discovery process example earlier in this chapter.

Characteristics of the Gifted

Justification for this method is similar to that for teaching higher levels of thinking and using a discovery approach. Another, and perhaps more important, source of support is the vocabulary development of gifted children and their tendency to cover up a lack of knowledge by using big words and high-level concepts they do not really understand. Teachers often are fooled by their tricks and assume pupils are more sophisticated than they are. Needless to say, the students' intellectual development is not facilitated by being allowed to get away with this intellectual bluffing. As potential scholars and leaders, they need to be able to explain clearly the processes for arriving at conclusions and generalizations resulting from their work.

FREEDOM OF CHOICE

Allowing gifted students the flexibility to choose topics to study, methods to use in the process, and the environments in which to pursue them is an important method for facilitating success with other systems as well as a way to build upon the learning and motivational characteristics of these children. Common practices such as independent study, self-directed learning, learning centers, contracts, and projects all are methods that allow a certain degree of freedom of choice. Many programs for gifted children are run completely on an independent study basis, and are successful. Regular classroom teachers often use this method as a way to extend the learning of gifted children and allow them to pursue topics of their own choosing in more depth than can be incorporated into the basic curriculum.

Crucial aspects in the implementation of these methods are (a) the degree and kind of freedom allowed, and (b) the student's ability to handle or profit from the freedom given. Each of the procedures above (e.g., independent study, learning centers, contracts) can be designed to permit differing degrees or kinds of freedom. An independent study program, for example, can be placed on a continuum from the one extreme of complete freedom to study any topic for any length of time anywhere, with any person, develop any product, have it evaluated by anyone or no one, and even to not study at all, to the opposite extreme of a defined choice between only two topics, a well-defined short period of time, in a classroom, and a specified product (i.e., a report) that is evaluated on predetermined criteria by the teacher. In the 1960s, the extreme of complete freedom was common in programs for the gifted, and continues to be used in some systems.

Treffinger (1975) provides a useful way to look at the degree and kind of freedom that can be allowed. He presents a basic model of instruction that includes (1) identification of goals and objectives, (2) assessment of entering behavior, (3) identification and implementation of instructional procedures, and (4) assessment of performance. These four areas suggest types of freedom that can be given. Within each of these areas, degrees of freedom can be provided. For example, within the area of identifying goals and objectives, four levels of freedom (i.e., self-direction) can be provided:

Teacher-directed: Teacher prescribes for class or for pupils
Self-directed, 1st step: Teacher provides choices or options for pupils
Self-directed, 2nd step: Teacher involves pupil in creating options
Self-directed, 3rd step: Learner controls choices, teacher provides
    resources and materials (p. 52)

Della-Dora and Blanchard (1979) also describe different levels of choice, dividing the process into four areas: (1) deciding what is to be learned, (2) selecting the method and materials, (3) communicating with others about the subject, and (4) evaluating achievement of goals. They describe typical practices ranging from school-directed to self-directed with a midpoint to give an example of the nature of changes that might be involved in moving from school-directed to self-directed learning.

Deciding What Is to Be Learned

School-Directed: At this level, the school and teacher make decisions about the required content. They define all goals and even decide upon optional courses and activities.

Midpoint: In the transition between school- and student-directed learning, pupils have a part in creating or suggesting elective courses or selecting from learning options in required courses. They are allowed to select what they learn for a part of each day or for a part of the year.

Self-Directed: Students are active participants in the process of selecting subject matter, working cooperatively with their teachers and the school. Teachers help students in establishing criteria for selecting content, which may include long-range goals, current interests and needs, usefulness in preparation for college, and contribution to overall development.

Selecting Methods and Materials for Learning

School-Directed: Materials are chosen by the teacher or a committee of teachers responsible for textbook adoption. The selection of films, other media, field trips, speakers, and instructional aids also are the complete responsibility of the teacher.

Midpoint: The transition between school and student direction consists mainly of the creation of options for methods, materials, and media. Students choose from these options subject to the approval of the teacher.

Self-Directed: At this level, the teacher and students cooperatively examine what learning resources are available in the school and community. They look at each of the resources creatively to determine new ways of using them. As in the self-directed level of deciding what to learn, teachers concentrate on assisting students in determining criteria for selecting the methods and materials to be used or the combinations of resources that will best meet student needs. Some possible criteria for selection include the potential value of the methods or resources for meeting the student's long-term goals, how the method fits with the pupil's preferred style of learning, and the potential for expanding the individual's experience with a variety of materials. Once the selection is made, the instructor's role is that of teaching students how to use materials, assisting in the location of materials, and serving as a general guide to learning.

Communicating with Others about What Is Being Learned

School-Directed: At this level the teacher usually specifies what type of product the students are expected to develop. These could be oral or written reports, completed pages of workbooks or work sheets, laboratory notebooks or manuals, answers to oral or written questions, debates, slide presentations, displays, etc.

Midpoint: Involvement in a transition suggests, again, that both teachers and students provide options. Final selections are made with the approval of the teachers. Students can propose new and different reporting options but the final approval of their selection rests with the teacher.

Self-Directed: The procedure here again is the development of criteria for making decisions about the appropriate reporting procedures. When establishing these rules or criteria, emphasis is placed upon learning new ways of communicating, appropriateness for the audience, appropriateness of the subject matter, improving skills in previously used methods of reporting, and use of a variety of methods within a group or classroom. Students also are encouraged to expand their methods of communication to include visual and performing arts and the use of media (tape recording, photography, filming, slides, multimedia presentations). The teacher's responsibility is either to teach the methods to be used or to assist the students in finding ways to learn new methods.

Evaluating Achievement of Goals

School-Directed: Teachers (or other school personnel) decide when to assess student progress, what to measure, and how to make this evaluation. In recent years, emphasis has been on establishing schoolwide, consistent behavioral objectives or competencies, then evaluating the student's progress toward reaching each of these. These evaluations usually are done on a continuing basis, with major assessments at the end of each school year. Often, the evaluation includes only an assessment of recall or memorization. Methods usually include pretests and posttests, demonstrations, and analysis of products.

Midpoint: The student creates alternative times or methods of assessment although the teacher usually still decides what is to be measured. Students also may be encouraged to provide their own evaluation of activities they have chosen and may be allowed to complete their own recordkeeping.

Self-Directed: Students and teachers decide cooperatively how, what, and when to evaluate. Outcomes to be appraised include knowledge, skills, feelings, interests, and behaviors that relate to the original goals. Students and teachers both suggest what outcomes to assess and reach agreement about the most important ones. The teacher's role includes assisting the student in developing criteria for selecting means of evaluation, helping in the development of assessment procedures, and locating or helping the student find appropriate instruments.

Comparison of Della-Dora's and Blanchard's (1979) descriptions of the self-directed level with the levels provided by Treffinger (1975) reveals that the latter's system actually suggests a level higher than that of the others. For instance, in the highest level of Della-Dora's and Blanchard's system, the teacher continues to impose some restrictions on the students or at least to invoke the practitioner's own values in the development of criteria for selecting options. In Treffinger's system, students are encouraged to go beyond this level and to be completely responsible for their own learning. They are allowed to seek help from the teacher if they feel a need for assistance but the teacher does not supply this if it is not requested.

Underlying the need for degrees and types of freedom are student characteristics. Gifted students need to be allowed to progress to a high level of self-direction. However, educators must make careful decisions about how much freedom to allow even gifted children. Even though they do possess many of the attributes necessary for success with a self-directed approach, just because they are gifted does not imply complete freedom without preparation. Children who have been told what to learn, how to learn it, where, and when beginning with their first day of school should not be expected to know how to structure their own learning experiences completely.

A checklist for assessing a student's learning characteristics can be a guide to making decisions about the level of self-direction to encourage. Based on the checklist, the educator can match up student characteristics, teacher roles, and learning activities. Student competencies or skills needed at each of three levels are listed in the areas of identification of objectives, assessment of entering behavior, implementation of instruction, and evaluation of performance. For example, the skills or competencies required for effective participation at level 3 of self-direction in Treffinger's (1975) model are that the student:

1. can determine criteria for evaluation of progress with only teacher advice when needed
2. can closely match self-evaluation with the assessment made by others
3. can pinpoint general and specific areas of strength and weakness in own products
4. can determine criteria that would be used by various audiences in evaluating a product.

Characteristics of the Gifted

Gifted children's motivational attributes provide the most valuable impetus for this process modification. They tend to be independent, become absorbed and involved in topics or problems, need little external motivation if excited initially, and like to organize and structure things. All these characteristics suggest that these special students enjoy and profit from methods allowing them as much freedom as possible. Other characteristics such as their outside reading, their awareness of themselves, curiosity, willingness to take risks, acceptance of responsibility, and desire to take charge contribute to the need and potential for success of this educational method.

Future roles involving leadership and scholarliness indicate this method's value in giving practice in important skills. Indeed, evaluations of student attitudes toward independent study programs indicate that the programs have (a) a positive influence on motivation and career (e.g., increased excitement about learning, helping decide on careers and majors in college), (b) a positive effect on study habits and thinking processes (organizing and focusing thoughts, developing study habits, increasing critical thinking), and (c) an atmosphere that is highly challenging.

GROUP INTERACTION ACTIVITIES AND SIMULATIONS

During the height of the human potential movement of the 1960s, group process or group interaction activities were very popular. They were used in all phases of business, industry, and education as tools for enhancing a working group's effectiveness as well as for unlocking the potential of each individual by developing the ability to relate to others more effectively. In most of these activities, essential elements were (a) a contrived, structured, or simulated group interaction situation, (b) honest feedback from other participants regarding one's behavior, and (c) honest self-analysis or critique by each participant. Often, simulated social situations or other games were included as the group interaction setting during which observations were made. A facilitator trained in the skills needed to establish an atmosphere of trust, foster the willingness to self-disclose, encourage honesty, and develop a group support system structured the group's activities. In their extreme form, these were labeled sensitivity groups.

In that extreme form, such groups would not be appropriate in a classroom. However, structured group interaction activities can provide a setting in which gifted students can learn valuable social and leadership skills. In such situations they learn by interacting and how to do so more effectively. The essential elements of such activities are (a) a simulated situation (e.g., a simulation game, a role-playing situation, a structured discussion) in which the individuals follow a set of rules and must interact with at least a small group of pupils; (b) self-analysis through verbal critiques, viewing of videotapes, or listening to audiotapes; and (c) critique of performance by others in the group. These critiques are much more effective if the students actually must watch or listen to themselves on a tape, since gifted pupils often are unwilling to accept others' criticism.

One method that is very useful in a wide variety of situations is called the fishbowl technique. Students are seated in two circles, inner and outer. The inner circle is given a structured activity, discussion, or simulation. Members of the outer group serve as observers, unable to participate or to interfere with the inner circle in any way. In some cases, the observers are given specific behaviors to look for or are assigned to watch particular individuals. When the structured activity ends, the inner circle discusses the activity and critiques itself. The outer circle of observers then adds its comments. Next, the two groups change places and the process is repeated. Following are descriptions of activities that can be carried out by the inner circle, along with specific observations that can be made by the outer circle.

Lost on the Moon: A Decision-Making Exercise (Stanford & Stanford, 1969).

In this activity, participants are told they have made a crash landing on the moon 200 miles from the rendezvous point with the mother ship. Survival depends upon reaching that module. Participants are given a list of 15 items and told to rank order them according to their importance. Each individual ranks them separately, and the group then discusses them and reaches a consensus on the rank order. When this is completed, members compare their individual and group rankings to those made by scientists of the National Aeronautics and Space Administration (NASA). Questions for analyzing the process include the following:

Was the group or an individual more accurate? What member or members influenced the group the most? How was this done? How did the group reach agreement? How did you interact with the group? (e.g., What was your role?) How could you have interacted more effectively?

Observers are given the task of watching for roles played by different members of the group, such as a leader, a harmonizer, a summarizer, a dominator, or a follower. Observers also can be assigned to concentrate on a particular individual and take notes or complete a checklist on certain behaviors such as interpersonal communication skills (verbal and nonverbal expression, listening, responding) or group role (leader, summarizer, harmonizer).

The Echo Game (Stanford & Stanford, 1969).

This game is most effective if used in the fishbowl setting. First, the inner circle members are given a topic of interest to discuss. After the discussion is well under way, the teacher interrupts and rules that before anyone speaks, the person must repeat what was said by the previous speaker to the latter's satisfaction. Observers note which participants give accurate accounts of what previous speakers have said, how many trials must be made by each person, and whether the participants actually are listening to each other.

The Murder Mystery (Stanford & Stanford, 1969).

Each of the participants is given one or more clues to a murder mystery. They must solve it by compiling their clues but must share them orally. They may not give all clues to someone to sort out. Observers watch for group roles, cooperation of members, and other aspects of interaction. They also note the problem-solving approach of the group as a whole.

Role-Playing Activity (Bushman & Jones, 1977).

The purpose of this activity is to teach students the variety of roles members of a group can assume. Each member is given a specific role—either positive or negative. While the group is discussing a topic, the individual must assume the assigned role. Members can be assigned randomly to a certain role but the teacher also can choose those that are opposite the student's usual role so that person can experience a different way of participating. Observers can be told the roles so they can judge how effective an individual is, or they can try to guess each person's role by their participation. Possible group roles are the following (Gage & Berliner, 1979):

a. unifying roles, or those concerned mainly with climate and harmony in the group (e.g., encouraging, harmonizing, compromising, gatekeeping, energizing);
b. task roles, or those concerned with accomplishing the job (initiating, information seeking, information giving, opinion giving, orienting, coordinating); and
c. antigroup roles, or those concerned with meeting the needs of an individual at the expense of the group (aggressing, blocking, attention seeking, dominating, noncooperating).

In addition to these types of structured games and activities, any simulation game[1] that teaches content or process can serve much the same purpose. The same elements of a structured activity, self-analysis, and critique from others should be included. Long-term games or committee work can serve similar ends and can provide a setting where students can assess, change, and reevaluate their own behavior. Such situations should be structured so that self-analysis and group critique are a frequent and continuing part of the process.

Characteristics of the Gifted

Group process activities and simulation games generally build upon and develop the leadership characteristics of gifted students. In these structured settings, the pupils can practice their skills in cooperating, influencing, and motivating others. At the same time, in many of the games, they also can exercise their problem-solving skills, develop higher levels of thinking, and exercise their abilities in predicting consequences of their own actions. Because of the high degree of participation and the rapid pace of most games, gifted students retain their interest in them. According to Cline (1979), there is some indication that simulation games may be more effective with gifted than with other students. Addison (1979) discusses the value of simulation games in developing leadership skills that may be lacking in gifted girls.

PACING AND VARIETY

The last two process modifications—pacing and variety—need less explanation, although they are no less important. In many ways, their function is facilitative in relation to the other recommended content and process modifications. Pacing refers to how slowly or rapidly information is presented in the learning situation; variety is the range and number of types of procedures used. Both are necessary to maintain student interest and avoid boredom. To provide variety, teachers can use discussions, learning centers, logic games, simulation games, lectures, films, role playing, committee work, and numerous other techniques. Appropriate pacing, however, is more difficult to achieve and takes some experimentation.

Gifted children do not need as much time as others to assimilate information or commit it to memory. In the *Study of Mathematically Precocious Youth* (SMPY) program at The Johns Hopkins University, for example, four and a half years of precalculus mathematics was taught successfully in 120 hours of instruction (George, 1976). Normally, this amount of material would have been covered in approximately 600 hours over four to five years. The classes initially were held for two hours each Saturday morning for 13 months. With these talented students, the material could be mastered in approximately one-fifth the usual time. The concept subsequently has been adopted in numerous school systems throughout the country.[2]

It is important to note at this point, however, that pacing refers to the introduction of new material, not to the time allowed for children to think. Teachers often seem to feel compelled to fill the silence with words or questions; after asking a question calling for a high level of thinking, if someone has not answered within a couple of seconds they either answer it themselves or pose it in another way. As a child, I often complained to my mother that teachers always asked tough questions and then kept talking so I couldn't think. Indeed, this childhood observation has been supported by research. Taba (1964, 1966) cites research showing that the average amount of time teachers wait for answers to their questions is two seconds.

Two of the most distinguishing characteristics of gifted children are how quickly they learn and how easily they are bored if not challenged. In attempting to show that even slow learners are capable of abstract thought, Taba (1964, 1966) introduces the concept of pacing assimilation and accommodation activities. The Piagetian concept of assimilation is incorporating information as it is or adapting it so that it fits into an individual's existing cognitive structures; accommodation is changing the structures so that new information that previously would not fit will now do so. Although this is a very simple description of two complex concepts, the essence is there. Slow learners and average children need many assimilation activities with concrete materials before they begin to accommodate and progress toward a more abstract level of thinking. Gifted children need far fewer of these assimilation activities to enable accommodation to occur.

Quickening the rate of instruction in individual classrooms as well as condensing year-long courses into a semester or less are important elements of appropriate pacing for meeting the needs of gifted children and facilitating the other recommended content and process modifications.

SUMMARY

In the past, programs for the gifted have been described almost solely in terms of the processes being used. Although process is only one dimension of the curriculum needing modification, these changes must not be deemphasized. They continue to be an essential aspect of a curriculum for these students. Several necessary process changes have been described in this chapter, along with examples of methods for implementing them.

NOTES

1. For readers interested in simulation games and group process activities, the following resources are helpful: Carlson & Misshauk (1972); the entire issue of *Gifted Child Quarterly,* Summer 1979; Heitzman (1974); Youngers & Aceti (1969); and Zuckerman & Horn (1973).

2. For discussions and reviews of the research on acceleration and fast pacing of instruction, the reader is referred to the following publications: Keating (1976); Stanley, Keating, & Fox (1974); and Whitlock (1978).

Chapter 3

Product Modifications

A third area of the curriculum that can be modified for gifted students is the nature of the products expected from these individuals. Although products cannot be separated entirely from content or input and the process used to develop it, the product—the end result of the process—is what usually is evaluated to determine the validity or effectiveness of the program. Products can be of many types, both tangible and intangible, and can assume an almost infinite number of forms. Ideas, research reports, dances, musical compositions, displays, constructions, slide-tape presentations, books, and dramatic productions all are products.

Each of these products involves the use of a certain type of information or content, is directed toward a particular audience, and is evaluated or judged by someone. A research report, for example, could involve the student's reading an encyclopedia article on a teacher-determined topic (or perhaps two different encyclopedias) and paraphrasing the content. Or it could be a report of original research, with the topic area and research methods chosen by the student, in which raw data related to some phenomenon are studied and the information interpreted in terms of a particular theoretical position. The report could be intended solely for the teacher's reading or it could be directed toward a professional audience through publication in a scholarly or scientific journal. A research report submitted only to a teacher usually is read and evaluated only by that individual while a report submitted to a journal is read and evaluated by the publication's manuscript reviewers (i.e., editor and field reviewers) and, if printed, by the subscribers.

In the two examples above, the basic difference is that one is a "student-type" product, the other a "professional-type" (Renzulli, 1977). Student-type products tend to be contrived and somewhat artificial, often resulting from a teacher's need to have a tangible product that can be evaluated. Professional-type products have a real purpose in the life of the individual and result from the individual's desire to investigate or develop something. Professionals usually have a particular audience in mind as they develop their products. These audiences may be as specific as teen-agers in a suburban midwestern town as an intended audience for a play or movie. They may be the Republican senators in the Arizona State Legislature as an audience for a bill to control government spending. The intent of the product is to please, convince, impress, or otherwise have some impact on the audience.

In modifying the curricular area of what is expected from students, the basic guideline should be that the products approximate to the extent possible those developed by professionals—that they address a real problem or concern, be directed toward a real audience with an identified purpose, be a transformation or synthesis rather than a mere summary of information, and be evaluated by someone other than the teacher. Two of these aspects—a real problem and a real audience—are discussed together since they are almost impossible to separate. Evaluation and transformation then are discussed separately.

REAL PROBLEMS AND REAL AUDIENCES

If the content and process modifications just discussed are implemented, it is impossible to assess the student's progress appropriately if educators expect (or will accept, for that matter) only a student-type, contrived product. When students are learning abstract, complex ideas or thought systems, the very learning requires active investigation in the way that a scholar or inquirer (a professional) approaches problems. As Taba (1962) suggests, it should be possible to study a few crucial phenomena "in sufficient depth to discover the essential ways of thinking, of discovering appropriate causalities, of handling generalizations, and of establishing conclusions" (p. 180).

A student who is learning these ways of handling generalizations and establishing conclusions, and who also is using higher level mental activities or critical thinking powers, cannot conclude the process with a report taken from an encyclopedia. Indeed, to carry the process to its logical conclusion, the student's product would have to be evaluated by scholars in the field (or at least by the teacher's using a process as closely resembling this assessment as possible). In this way, the student learns not only how professionals go about developing products but also how they judge the value of what results.

Few experts address the problem of how to modify the curriculum area of the expected products so as to better meet the needs of gifted students. Only Renzulli (1977), Guilford (1967), and Torrance (1979) address the question directly. Others (c.f., Parnes, Taba, Treffinger, Gallagher, Ward) do so indirectly through discussions of problem finding or problem solving.

Focusing on Real Problems

In assisting students to focus on real problems, one of the first things teachers can do is to ask the kind of provocative or leading questions suggested by Womack

(1966) (Chapter 2). Students then are presented with a model of the kind of questions or problems investigated by professionals.

In one resource seminar program for gifted students at a middle school (Lethem & Osborn, Note 2), two important aspects of the program are seminar discussions and student investigations into topics of their own interest. In the seminars, teachers present provocative questions for the pupils to discuss. Students may select these questions, others inspired by the discussions, or entirely different ones to guide their research. Some of the questions chosen for the 1980-1981 school year are the following:

1. Urban planning in Albuquerque: What are some ideas that would help make Albuquerque a more viable place to live?
2. What is relevant and irrelevant about today's education system?
3. How responsible should we be for our fellow man?
4. How were the early witch trials justified? Unjustified?
5. What have been important contributions to society from minority groups?
6. What are some of the effects of television on our lives?
7. How does the media, or advertising, discriminate against women?
8. What is meditation? Why do people meditate?
9. What are some of the problems of the elderly?
10. What would be a workable alternative transportation system to the automobile in Albuquerque?
11. How does art in the form of paintings, literature, movies, and plays reflect and often shape the culture and customs of a specific time and place?
12. Divorce: What happens to the children?
13. Migrant workers: How could the problems they face be lessened or solved?
14. What happens after W. W. III????
15. What are the effects on people of our computer society?
16. If good looks, money, and popularity do not always bring happiness to a person, what do you think does bring happiness?
17. The Depression: What should the government do to help people when there are hard times?
18. What should be done about the problem of illegal aliens in this country?
19. A nation affects and is affected by other nations with which it interacts: How could this concern us? (Lethem & Osborn, Note 2, p. 1-4)

A second aspect of the program that provides models of provocative questions is a resource box or idea file of all the questions and topics that have been investigated since the program began. Each child develops a 5″ × 8″ note card with the topic, question, and a short description of the investigation carried out so far. These are filed in the resource file for future students' use. Anyone who does not have a topic can choose one from the resource file or can use the file to stimulate new ideas.

In discussing teacher questions appropriate for discussions using the *Hilda Taba Teaching Strategies Program*, Durkin (1971) gives two criteria for evaluating questions: open-endedness and focus. Open-endedness was discussed in Chapter 2, so those ideas are not repeated. However, focus needs some explanation. Focus pertains to how narrow or broad a question can be. For example, the question, "What would you like to investigate?" is unlimited in its range while, "What do you want to know about states of matter?" is somewhat narrower but still very broad. A focused question is, "What would you like to know about the effect of different temperatures on water?" It often is necessary to use increasingly more focused questions with students to help them identify areas of interest. The teacher also can provide a model by always asking students questions that are focused.

One example from the author's own experience may help to clarify this point. In a classroom I was supervising, a student teacher was leading a discussion about solar heaters and how they worked. The children had spent a week or more designing and carrying out tests of their own solar heaters. The teacher's major purpose was to get the pupils to talk about the differences in heater design and how this affected the amount of heat collected.

The teacher's opening question was, "What did you notice about the experiments you did last week?" Students started talking about how a dog had knocked over one of the heaters and how students in other classes were envious. The next attempt at getting them back on track was, "What happened in the experiments you conducted this week?" The answers were more to the point but included such statements as, "We had trouble keeping records because there was so much to do in class." The next question became, "What did you notice about the different heaters you made and the temperature changes inside and outside the heaters?" I breathed a sigh of relief until I heard their answers. For these young children, this was too focused for a beginning question. They had no idea how to answer. A bit frustrated by now, I could not resist intervening to help the student teacher, who by now was also becoming very frustrated. I brought in two of the children's data charts (from two different solar heaters) and suggested that the teacher first ask, "What do you notice about the temperature changes inside and outside Tommy's heater?" then, "What do you notice about the changes inside and outside Free-land's heater?" After that, the instructor could ask, "What do you think caused _____?" about each factor they noticed that related to differences in design. It worked. After discussing each of these separately, the children finally could answer the question, "What do you think are the major effects of differences in design on the working of a solar heater?'' Interestingly enough, this is also an example of successful guided discovery.

Renzulli (Note 1) presents a series of questions from the problem-focusing section of an exercise dealing with the methodology of historical investigation:

(1) The first set of questions is geographical. They center around the interrogative: "Where?" What area of the world do I wish to investigate? The Far East? Brazil? My country? My city? My neighborhood?

(2) The second set of questions is biographical. They center around the interrogative: "Who?" What persons am I interested in? The Chinese? The Greeks? My ancestors? My neighbors? A famous individual?

(3) The third set of questions is chronological. They center around the interrogative: "When?" What period of the past do I wish to study? From the beginning till now? The fifth century B.C.? The Middle Ages? The 1780's? Last year?

(4) The fourth set of questions is functional or occupational. They center around the interrogative: "What?" What spheres of human interest concern me most? What kinds of human activity? Economics? Literature? Athletics? Sex? Politics? (pp. 2, 3)

Other works dealing with the methodology of investigation in a defined area provide problem-focusing questions specific to that area. Parnes (Note 3) suggests that educators look at "fuzzy situations" or "the mess" and develop a chart similar to Figure 3-1 showing the information known as well as needed about the situation. He also suggests trying several restatements of the problem in an attempt to formulate it in a creative, solvable way.

Using a process similar to the one that Parnes produced, Koberg and Bagnall (1976) designed a series of steps and specific techniques useful in problem solving. The aspects of their process of most interest in this discussion are related to the analysis and definition of a problem.[1] These two aspects are described next, along with methods for assisting in the process.

Analysis

The basic processes in analyzing a problem involve getting to know more about the situation and clarifying what is known already. Analysis includes taking the problem apart, sorting its aspects into categories, gathering facts and opinions, comparing this situation with others, researching the issue and developing questions about it, and dissecting it. Several different types of methods can be used to analyze problems (Koberg & Bagnall, 1976):

Figure 3-1 Fact Finding Chart

Aspects of Situation	Known Facts	Needs to Be Known

1. *The Basic Question Method* is asking oneself questions about the problem such as: Who could help in solving it? What has been tried already? What is the total scope of the problem?
2. *The Pack Rat Method* consists of the students gathering items that have come to their attention as having some relationship to the problem. After a collection of these items has been made, they stretch their imagination and relate each collected item to the problem in some way.
3. *Synectics/Forced Relationships Method* is forcing oneself to develop relationships between items or ideas that seem to be unrelated. Answers can help in gaining a deeper understanding of the problem.
4. *The Back-to-the-Sun Method* consists of tracing a problem or one of its aspects back to its source, which may even be the sun. The teacher can make a game of this process by having the student attempt to identify as many steps in the process as possible.
5. *Attribute Listing* consists of making lists of the attributes of different aspects of the problem. For example, the list could involve physical attributes such as color, texture, or weight; psychological attributes; and social attributes such as group membership, values, or responsibilities. Such an analysis exposes the specific aspects of all parts of the problem.
6. *The "Record All You Know" About It Method* simply involves writing everything the individual knows about the problem. It is important for the teacher to adopt an open attitude, however, because it is easy to assume the student knows nothing or very little. Such an attitude can inhibit the process.
7. *The "What Have Others Done?" Method* consists of critically examining the methods others have used as well as their results.

8. *Analysis Models* involve examining a problem by building a model of it. Models can be three-dimensional as well as schematic. They can include charts, prototypes, or Performance Evaluation and Review Technique (PERT) charts.

9. *The Morphological* method is a way to organize attributes or components of a problem so they can be interrelated. It consists of (a) listing the attributes or variables, (b) classifying them, and (c) determining the relationships by systematically matching an attribute from one list with all others on each of the other lists. A model expressing the relationship then can be developed. Educators and psychologists often use three-dimensional morphological models such as cubes (e.g., Guilford's *Structure of Intellect Model)* or rectangular solids (e.g., Frank Williams's model).

10. *The Matrix* model is similar to the morphological one but is two-dimensional. One category of attributes or aspects of the problem is listed across the top of a grid and a second category down the side. The intersection of the attributes on the grid (or plot) is used to generate ideas about how the attributes are related. Matrix methods are suggested in Chapters 6 and 8 as ways to analyze the needs of children and to generate evaluation procedures or questions.

11. *The Search for Patterns* method consists of looking for subproblems or problems within the problem.

12. *The Expert Consultant* method can consist of actually calling in an expert to provide advice or of consulting this person through one's mind. Ask, "I wonder what _____ would have to say about this problem?" (Koberg & Bagnall, 1976, p. 55).

13. *Expanding Objectives* is an analysis method consisting of continually examining and expanding or clarifying objectives in the problem situation.

14. *The Idea-Dump* method may be one of the most useful processes, since it simply requires the individual to get the ideas out of the way (to dump them out of the mind). Gifted students, as well as others, often begin generating ideas long before a problem is even defined. These ideas can inhibit thinking in many ways by short-circuiting the process. In this strategy, ideas are listed now and analyzed later to determine their usefulness after the problem is defined.

15. The *Sensitivity Game* examines each aspect of the problem using all the senses.

16. The *Squeeze and Stretch* method is one in which the problem-finder first stretches out the problem to discover its parts by asking a series of questions beginning with "What." Next, the problem is squeezed by asking a chain of questions beginning with "Why." For example, a series of stretching questions might be (a) What is this problem all about? (People's motivations.) (b) What are people's motivations? (What makes them want to do

something?) (c) What are some examples? Squeezing questions would be (a) Why am I studying this problem? (It is important.) (b) Why is it important? (A solution would make me famous.) (c) Why do I want to be famous?

Any one or any combination of these methods provides specific ways to examine any type of problem students or teachers encounter. Pupils can be taught to use all of these means of analysis and encouraged to develop a variety of strategies for use when needed.

Definition

After the problem has been analyzed, it needs to be defined. This provides a focus for later idea generation and serves as the statement of essential elements or the essence of the problem. A definition can be a verbal analogy, the individual's concept or attitude about the problem, or the underlying meaning of the issue. Several methods can be used to develop problem definitions (Koberg & Bagnall, 1976):

1. *The "Whys" Guy* method extends the stretch and squeeze procedure for analysis. By continuing through a series of "Why" questions, the distilled purpose begins to appear. A chain of at least ten questions should be asked.
2. *Essence-Finding* through the matrix method consists of extending this method of analysis. Using the matrix already developed, the problem solver chooses the crucial intersections of attributes and concentrates only on these.
3. The *Happiness Is* method is a takeoff on the techniques used by Charles Schulz in developing his *Peanuts* cartoons and books (e.g., Happiness is . . . , Love is . . . .). To use this strategy, the problem solver simply develops as many definitions as possible for the problems. Others can be asked to assist in making this list.
4. *King-of-the-Mountain,* as a method for defining a problem, consists of matching each element or aspect of the problem with each other element to determine which is more important. After these comparisons are made, a hierarchy or rank order can be developed, with those having the greatest number of "wins" as the essential elements.
5. *Key-Word Distillery* is a method in which a long description (or list) of aspects of the problem is developed. The key words from the description then are selected and put together into one statement. This also can be an extension of many of the analysis methods. For example, the key words could be selected from a list of attributes, a list of "All You Know About It," a list of what others have done, or from what the expert consultant has said.
6. *Problems Within Problems* is an extension of the search-for-patterns method of analysis. After subproblems have been identified, the crucial one is

pinpointed. This subproblem is attacked first because its solution often can provide the solution for the whole situation.

7. *Talk It Out* is a method consisting simply of the teacher's and/or the student's discussing their analysis of the problem with someone. Several persons can be involved in such discussions.

8. *Essence-Finding by Consensus* suggests that several persons be involved in identifying the most important aspects of the situation. This method is most useful if a large number of individuals ultimately will be affected by the solution.

Students can be taught these methods for problem definition and should be encouraged to develop a repertoire of strategies to use when needed.

Directing Problems toward Real Audiences

To help students develop products that have a purpose for some audience, Renzulli (Note 1) states that the key question is, "What do [ecologists, photographers, teachers, choreographers, short story writers, etc.] do with their creative products?" (p. 6) and gives two examples:

1. *Ecology*

Key Question: What does the ecologist do with the results of his/her research?

Answer: He or she attempts to use the information to influence (a) the general public and/or (b) policy-making bodies regarding ways in which we can preserve our environment and make better use of our natural resources.

2. *Creative Writers, Puppeteers*

Key Question: What do creative writers and puppeteers do with their stories, scripts, and puppet shows?

Answer: Attempt to bring enjoyment into people's lives by evoking emotions (happiness, understanding of a social problem, humor, etc.) or make them better informed about a particular issue or topic. (p. 6)

He also provides a form (Exhibit 3-1) useful for both teachers and students in analyzing areas of study and potential audiences.

Exhibit 3-1 Analysis of Areas of Study and Potential Audiences for Products

Type of Professional Activity		How Is It Communicated?	Who Are Some Potential Audience(s)?
1.	Ecology (study of pollution in a local stream)	a. Audio-visual Presentation (graphs, tables, photographs, and verbal report)	- Rotary Club - City Council - Local Environmental Protection Agency (EPA)
		b. Written Report	- Readers of local news-paper - Readers of EPA news-paper - Members of City Council or State Legislature
		c. Radio or Television Report (local, state, or within-school closed circuit	- Listeners - Viewers
		d. Display	- Shopping mall - Town Hall - Bank lobby
2.	Creative Writers, Puppeteers (working together on an adventure story/ presentation for young children)	a. Live Puppet Show	- Children in primary classrooms - Children in day care center - Children in state home for the handicapped - Children in pediatric wing of hospital - People in senior citizens' center - Parent Teacher Association
Note: By adding this dimension, additional areas of interest and talent expression (i.e., Cinematography, TV Production) can be combined with the work of creative writers and puppeteers.		b. Video-tape (To be used with 1. individual groups, 2. closed circuit TV, 3. educational TV, 4. local TV station)	- Any or all of the above - Various groups of viewers in general

Source: Reprinted from *Inservice Training Worksheets for the Enrichment Triad Model: Summary Sheet 1;* pp. 6-7, by Joseph S. Renzulli by permission of the author.

Parnes (Note 3) also provides valuable suggestions in the acceptance-finding step of his problem-solving process. He suggests use of a work sheet divided into three columns (Exhibit 3-2) to list (a) ways of implementing an idea, (b) who, when, where it would be done, and (c) how, why (e.g., how would one gain acceptance of the idea). Deferring final judgment, the individual lists as many possibilities as the person can think of, then goes back and chooses the best.

Two other sources (Atwood, 1974; Stevenson, Seghini, Timothy, Brown, Lloyd, Zimmerman, Maxfield, & Buchanan, 1971) provide helpful guidelines for addressing products to real audiences in their discussions of the concept of communication. Atwood offers a useful listing of communication skills for students involved in independent study:

I. Communication
   A. The communication process
      1. Recognize the four basic elements of communication
         a. Identify the communicator
         b. Identify the audience
         c. Identify the media being used
         d. Identify what is being communicated
      2. Understand the function and value of communication
         a. Recognize communication as a means of contacting or influencing other people
         b. Recognize communication as a way to share ideas and thoughts
         c. Recognize communication as a way to preserve events, ideas and thoughts
   B. The communicator and his audience
      1. Understand the relationship between the communicator and his audience
         a. Recognize what the communicator contributes to communication
         b. Recognize what the audience contributes to communication
      2. Understand the role of the communicator
         a. Decide what to communicate.
         b. Choose media appropriate to the audience
         c. Use the selected media effectively
      3. Understand the various purposes of the communicator
         a. Warn or give orders
         b. Inform
         c. Explain or educate
         d. Persuade

Exhibit 3-2 Work Sheet for Using Creative Problem Solving in Gaining
Acceptance for an Idea

First idea (or combination of ideas) to be developed (selected from previous worksheet)

WRITE IDEA HERE:

Column A	Column B	Column C
Ways of implementing, carrying out, accomplishing, gaining acceptance for, ensuring effectiveness of, improving, etc. -- the above idea (deferred judgment)	Who, when &/or Where?	How &/or why? (How to gain acceptance and enthusiasm of others for idea)

Now go back and circle the best ones in Col. A (Judgment); then for each circled one, list further thoughts re: the who, when, where, how, and why, as indicated in Cols. B & C. Search for several alternatives in Cols. B & C for each item circled in Col. A. Then circle the best alternative(s) in each case.

Source: Reprinted from *Creative Potential and the Educational Experience* (Occasional Paper No. 2) by S.J. Parnes by permission of the Creative Education Foundation, © 1967.

e. Evoke emotions

f. Entertain

4. Understand how the communicator affects the communication

a. Recognize the impact of personal experience

b. Recognize the impact of personal beliefs and emotions

c. Recognize the impact of faulty thinking

C. Media

1. Recognize the kinds of media available and how they can be used

a. Identify and use examples of demonstrative media

b. Identify and use examples of representational media

c. Identify and use examples of symbolic media

2. Use a variety of media to achieve specific purposes

a. Use media within one's own capabilities

b. Use media appropriate to a specific purpose

c. Use media appropriate to a specific audience (Atwood, 1974, pp. 9-10)

The Stevenson et al. (1971) description of communication talent includes three developmental facets—expressional fluency, association fluency, and word fluency. Expressional fluency includes skills related to providing a concise explanation of thoughts and ideas, including both verbal and nonverbal modes. Association fluency pertains to the ability to understand how things are related. In other words, communicators who have associational fluency can perceive how their ideas are related to the experiences or ideas of their audience. They will be able to capitalize on these associations when communicating with the audience. Word fluency, the third facet, consists of the use of a variety of words to add to the conciseness or clarity of the ideas being communicated. Descriptive words or phrases are used to add color, beauty, or depth to the communication.

Atwood (1974) also provides exercises and guidelines for use in developing students' skills in communication. First, students need to understand the variety of purposes available for communication. They also should realize how their own experiences affect their communication. Finally, they must understand some basic information about forms or levels of media and how these can be used to reach a variety of audiences more effectively. To teach students these skills, some possible techniques are the following (Atwood, 1974):

1. Display examples of some of the most familiar kinds of communication. Have students identify the communicator, how and why she is communicating, the audience, and how the communication is being accomplished.

2. From the display, have students think of ways each communication can be changed.
3. Teach children the three levels of media, *demonstrative* (i.e., literal forms such as displays, exhibits, demonstrations, collections), *representational* (i.e., forms that represent the communication, such as photographs, drawings, sculptures, models), and *symbolic* (i.e., abstract forms such as oral discussions, speeches, monologues, written reports, tables, graphs). Have them express a particular idea in all three forms so they can learn the differences. Provide experiences in developing all three types, and in classifying other communications according to the type.

Koberg and Bagnall (1976) provide a very useful checklist to assist students in developing products that are directed toward real audiences:

COMMUNICATION involves translating a meaning which is in your mind into a medium and through the environment to the mind of an intended receiver. The meaning is affected by your background and is formed by your ability as well as by the background and ability of the receiver.

IMPORTANT DETERMINANTS OF SUCCESSFUL COMMUNICATION SEEM TO BE:

YOU, THE SENDER (knowledge and attitudes)
YOUR ABILITY TO SHAPE AND SEND MESSAGES OF YOUR MEANING (skill)
THE QUALITY OF THE MESSAGE (substance and relevance)
THE SELECTED MEDIUM
THE ENVIRONMENT (external elements which facilitate or block the message)
THE RECEIVER'S ABILITY TO RECEIVE
THE RECEIVER'S BACKGROUND AND ATTITUDES

SENDER AND RECEIVER BACKGROUND

Age, personal relationship to each other, expectation based on experiences
Attitude and potential ramifications or consequences
Beneficial outcome; motives, values, needs
Recent experience; uplifts, traumas, sickness, diversions, fatigue, anxiety, etc.
Habits, customs, rituals, taboos, prejudices, biases, assumptions

Education, travel experience, breadth of outlook
Influential aspects; idols, models, aspirations
Areas where influence can be affected
National, religious, racial heritage
Social attitudes, politics
Insecurities and strengths
Specific knowledge of message area
Concurrent focus of attention

SENDER AND RECEIVER ABILITIES (Skills)

Experience, breadth or scope of practice
Preferences related to training
Physical handicaps
Mental blocks
Vocabulary
Awareness; ability to relate to other interests
Propensity to distraction (attention span)

QUALITY OF THE MESSAGE

Content; completeness
Relevance to receiver familiarity
Facilitates recognition
    clarity
    simplicity
    strength of stimulus
    orderly

CHARACTERISTICS OF THE MEDIUM

Potential for sensory stimulation
Appropriateness to message content
Appropriateness to sender's skills, knowledge and attitudes
Within receiver's limits of acceptance
Energy required
Symbolic characteristics
Speed
Noise (distraction) characteristics

THE ENVIRONMENT

Harmony with message and sender-receiver relationship
Noise (distractions)

movement
sound interference
temperature discomfort
threat to physical or mental security
Pressure to perform (Koberg & Bagnall, 1976, pp. 119-120)

In addition to its usefulness in assisting students in analyzing their own skills, the audience, and the situation so they will be more effective communicators, the checklist can provide criteria for evaluation of student products (by the pupil, teacher, peers, or audiences).

Characteristics of the Gifted

In justifying the emphasis on products that address real problems and are directed toward real audiences, Renzulli (1977) cites a study by the American College Testing Program showing that adult accomplishments are unrelated to test scores, high school grades, and college grades, but are related to comparable high school nonacademic or extracurricular accomplishments. In analyzing what might explain these relationships, he gives three important advantages of the nonacademic activities: children have the freedom to choose their own activities, there seldom is a grading system, and they have a tangible product at the end—a performance, a basketball game, or a school newspaper.

The current learning characteristics (e.g., their rapid insight and grasp of underlying principles), motivational characteristics (becoming absorbed and involved in topics of interest, needing little external motivation if interested, their adult interests, self-criticism, tendency to judge), creativity characteristics (curiosity, willingness to take risks), and leadership characteristics also can be considered as indicative of a need for the product modifications suggested in this section. As the probable future scholars, leaders, and creators in society, gifted children need continued experience in the development of professional-type rather than student-type products.

APPROPRIATE EVALUATION

Each product developed by a gifted student should receive an appropriate evaluation, including assessment by the teacher using preestablished criteria, self-evaluation by the pupil, and evaluation by the real audience or a simulation of one. If students are developing products that are directed toward real audiences, a single assessment by the teacher will not provide a comprehensive, appropriate evaluation. Judgment of the product in a way that professionals would evaluate it is not discussed by Renzulli. However, Parnes (1977) and Guilford (1967) offer some suggestions as outlined in subsequent pages.

Evaluation by a 'Real' Audience

It may be helpful, in an attempt to generate ideas for evaluation, to look back at Renzulli's chart (Exhibit 3-1) and add a fourth column—How Is the Product Judged? For example, consider the first area: The professional activity is ecology, the study of pollution in a local stream; the type of product is an audiovisual presentation; and some potential audiences are the Rotary Club, the City Council, and the local Environmental Protection Agency.

Different audiences may tend to evaluate the product in different ways. For example, the Rotary Club may be more interested in the photographs and the investigator's report of the status of the stream and what a citizen (or their organization) could do about the problem. The City Council may be more interested in the possible causes for the current state of affairs and whether new regulations (or stricter enforcement of old regulations) would be the most effective way to handle the problem. Since most City Councils are made up of very busy people, they no doubt will be impressed with clarity and brevity. However, the EPA, because of its familiarity with such problems, may be more interested in the technical aspects of the report, such as graphs, tables, etc., as well as the appropriateness of data collection activities. All audiences will judge the product's overall effectiveness in presenting the results of the study clearly and efficiently.

What this example says for teachers, then, is that whenever possible, they should give students the opportunity to present their products to real audiences. If this is not possible, a simulated role-playing situation should be arranged. In all cases, however, students should be encouraged to look at the product from several viewpoints and think carefully about the criteria that different audiences may use in judging it. These criteria can be used as a guide for the teacher, the pupil, and other classmates to evaluate the product. If students are presenting products to real audiences, however, it must be remembered that they are not yet professionals even though they may be acting like real inquirers. They should be encouraged to refine the product, present it to a simulated audience first, and look at it critically themselves.

Self-Evaluation

Practicing professionals in every field need to be able to examine their own products, especially as an aspect of the refinement process. They must be able to recognize the positive as well as negative aspects of a product so that needed changes can be made without total revisions or complete dismay. According to Guilford (1972), since gifted and creative individuals are independent and often pay no attention to others' criticisms of their products or performance, they should be taught the value of self-evaluation. They also should be taught methods for assessing their own performance. Several of the models recommended for use in gifted programs contain guidelines for developing the thinking process of evaluation or related abilities. For instance, Bloom's (1956) highest level of thinking is evaluation; one of Guilford's (1967) operations is evaluation; Parnes (1977) describes a process of solution finding in which all ideas are evaluated; and Stevenson et al. (1971), based on Taylor's (1968) model, describe the talent of decision making as including evaluation of alternatives in that process. The exact processes in different models are not reviewed here as they are described in the Introduction to Section II; however, they are invaluable as guides for teaching students to evaluate their own products.

The essential elements of evaluation seem to be (a) developing criteria for judgments (i.e., what aspects of the product will be examined as indicators of quality), (b) developing methods for making the assessment (checklists, tape analysis, tests, rating scales), (c) deciding when and by whom the assessment should be made, and (d) applying the criteria as consistently as possible by using the selected methods.

Methods of evaluation can be arranged along a continuum of "objectiveness" or of "intuitive" assessment made without specific criteria in mind to guide the process. At the other extreme is the most specific judgment possible, in which the criteria are explicit and their application always consistent. At this extreme, there can be no disagreement about the judgments made. Students need to be taught each step of the process, as well as a wide range of procedures, including both objective and subjective methods. They also should be provided with experiences in making different types of evaluations, including, for instance, assessment of written products as well as of performances, both physical and verbal.

When teaching students to evaluate their performance, it is helpful to follow a process similar to the one the author has developed for educating teachers in how to assess their own performance. This procedure also has been successful in teaching graduate assistants to evaluate the performance of teachers-in-training in my classes. In one of the programs described in Section III (Chapter 12), the teacher has taught her students in much the same way.

First, present the student with a listing of the criteria and a form to be used in making the assessment. Discuss the criteria, what they mean and why they are important, and provide concrete examples of how each criterion is manifested (how it can be observed). Allow the pupil to ask questions. Request the individual to generate examples of each criterion. It also is helpful to provide a list of concrete examples along with the descriptions of criteria.

After the form and process are understood clearly, the student and teacher both apply the criteria to the product or performance. This is done concurrently but individually. For example, if a teacher's performance on audiotape or videotape is the subject of analysis, both evaluators listen to or watch the tape at the same time. They sit so that checkmarks cannot be seen. After a few judgments have been made (usually checkmarks after a certain behavior is observed), the tape is stopped and the two evaluations are compared. If they do not match or if there is some confusion about the criteria or process, the tape is replayed at the point of confusion. This process is continued, with discussions as needed, until both are satisfied that the process has been learned.

After the initial learning period, the teacher randomly selects a tape evaluated by the student and analyzes it without checking the student's assessment (this is done often at first). If there are differences, they are resolved through discussion. This checking process continues but is done less frequently as the procedures are learned.

A next level of self-evaluation involves the development of criteria for assessment and development of methods of evaluation. To teach this level, it is important to examine a variety of evaluation instruments and criteria, analyzing each in terms of its appropriateness for particular situations or products. An essential element is continuous, detailed feedback to the student about that pupil's evaluation process and about the product or results of the individual's evaluation.

After students have evaluated their own products using the same forms or the same criteria as others, they should attempt to match the assessments of others, then compare the two perceptions. Grading, if grades must be assigned, can reflect both the quality as perceived by others and the closeness of the match between self-evaluation and assessment by others.

Characteristics of the Gifted

Justification for the ideas presented in this section comes from a wide variety of characteristics of gifted children. In the area of motivation, the trait of striving toward perfection and being highly self-critical suggests that gifted students find it necessary to evaluate their own performance. They need to be taught alternative methods for this analysis. Their independence, internal motivation, individualism, and tendency to criticize also indicate that they want to make their own judgments about quality. Skill in assessment of their own progress also can contribute to a greater degree of independence or self-direction.

A concern for making evaluations as well as a high degree of stubbornness in their own beliefs suggest that students may not accept or appreciate a teacher's sole assessment of a product. Since creative students can generate a large number of creative ideas and solutions, they need to develop appropriate ways to evaluate them. Leadership qualities such as responsibility and a tendency to dominate or direct activities also justify the use of peer and audience assessment and self-evaluation. All the probable future roles indicate that evaluation of gifted students' products must be as realistic and comprehensive as possible.

TRANSFORMATION VS. SUMMARIES

A final modification is that educators expect students to develop products that are more than mere summaries of the thoughts and ideas of others. In the example presented earlier, for instance, the student who wrote a research paper by paraphrasing the information in one or two encyclopedias was giving a summary rather than a true synthesis or transformation of the information (i.e., content). The student who reported on original research, however, had to transform the information through collection, analysis, synthesis, and interpretation. For example, doctoral dissertations, even though at a higher level, and even though they contain discussions that are transformations, often contain reviews of the literature and research that are mere summaries of the thoughts and conclusions of previous investigators.

Guilford (1967) provides a helpful way to look at differences in products. He classifies products into six different types:

1. *Units,* the lowest level, are individual items of information—a picture, a letter, a word.
2. *Classes* are recognized sets of information grouped by common properties.
3. *Relations* are recognized connections between two items of information.
4. *Systems* are organized or structured collections of information, consisting of interrelated and interconnecting parts.
5. *Transformations* are changes of known information—changes in meaning, significance, use, interpretation, mood, or sensory qualities.
6. *Implications* are "expectancies, anticipations, and predictions" (p. 104).

Products that are considered units, classes, relations, and systems in Guilford's system involve only a summary of existing information.

Guilford (1975) recommends that, for gifted and creative children, programs concentrate on the product area of transformation and implications. Part of the justification for this emphasis stems from the fact that creative, productive adults rank these abilities highest in importance for their work. The product abilities, in fact, are ranked higher than the divergent thinking abilities.

Related to the concept of transformation is Renzulli's (Note 1) emphasis on the use of raw data in the development of products by, for example, artists and scientists. Raw data include an artist's impressions, sensations, and perceptions as well as the scientist's "quantifiable pieces of evidence that can be tabulated and counted" (p. 9). The artists may collect data through observation and self-awareness while scientists resort to surveys, questionnaires, and tests or rating scales. In short, looking up information just for the purpose of reporting material gathered, summarized, and interpreted by others is not what investigators and scholars do. They may use others' conclusions or data as additional support for their own position or to suggest other avenues to pursue. However, as Renzulli states so succinctly, "chewed and digested is not raw!" (p. 9).

Evaluating and Developing Transformations

The concept of transformation or synthesis presented here includes the ideas of Guilford (1967, 1975), Bloom (1956), Renzulli (1977), and Torrance (1979). However, they are combined with the author's own perceptions to form a new definition of transformation. The concept of transformation contains the following elements: (a) viewing from a different perspective, (b) reinterpreting, (c) elaborating, (d) extending or going beyond, and (e) combining. When viewing a gifted student's product to determine the degree to which the individual has transformed the raw data, some or all of these elements should guide the examination. These same elements can be used as guides for teaching students ways to develop products that are real transformations instead of mere summaries.

Viewing from a Different Perspective

Torrance (1979) emphasizes the value of seeing things in different visual perspectives or looking at them from different points of view as an important aspect of the creative process. By viewing life in new ways, creative writers communicate their own perspective through plays, poetry, and novels, while creative artists communicate an unusual visual perspective through a sculpture, painting, or drawing. Often, perception of the idea of viewpoint is limited to visual perspectives such as drawing objects from underneath (the bottom of a foot or the underside of a bird), drawing objects from an unusual angle or distance (an animal shown from the rear or objects lying down that usually are seen upright), and objects shown in depth perspective such as the bottom of a bottle seen from the top or one end of a tunnel seen from the other end.

However, the element of unusual perspective should include other ways to view both ideas and objects. In addition to visual perspective, this can include philosophical (e.g., viewing an idea from a completely different philosophical orientation), historical (viewing a current event from the perspective of a historical character or future time period), theoretical (looking at an individual's behavior from the perspective of both a behaviorist and a psychoanalyst), logical (viewing a conclusion derived through principles of formal logic from a humanistic viewpoint), or emotional (viewing an event through the eyes of one who is coolly detached or one who is emotionally involved, one who is angry or one who is satisfied). A viewpoint also can be changed by viewing an event or idea from the perspective of an individual in a different scientific or social discipline. Viewpoint can include evidence of an individual's own personal perspective.

Reinterpreting

The element of reinterpretation is very similar to Guilford's (1967) concept of transformations. His concept includes adapting objects to new uses; shifts in meaning, symbols, figures, or behaviors; or substitutions of figures, symbols, meanings, or behaviors. Reinterpreting also includes redefining a problem, clarifying an idea by translating or narrowing its meaning, illustrating ideas, paraphrasing, and simplifying ideas or images. Torrance (1979) discusses a useful concept that is a part of reinterpreting: "highlighting the essence." He describes this element of creativity as involving, simultaneously, the processes of "synthesis, discarding erroneous or irrelevant information, abandoning unpromising facts or solutions, refining ideas, establishing priorities, and letting a single problem or idea become dominant" (p. 52). Reinterpretation also can be viewed as finding a new kernel or core of an idea—a different focus.

Elaborating

A familiar aspect of transformation is the addition of new details or explanations that will enhance the meaning of an idea or the enjoyment of a visual image. Elaborating can add to the richness or color (Torrance, 1979) of a visual image, enhance the humor of an image or a joke. It can assist the recipient in that person's own fantasy by producing a new auditory, olfactory, tactile, kinesthetic, or taste sensation or image. In other words, elaboration is the addition of details to enhance the product's uniqueness and its sensory, emotional, or ideological appeal to the audience.

Extending or 'Going Beyond'

Going "beyond the information given" (Bruner, 1973) is referred to as predicting, extrapolating, or generalizing. It includes both the extension of present trends (Guilford, 1967) and the development of new trends that may not be consistent with the given information but rather are a transformation of the given data. Extrapolating or going beyond in a way that is consistent with the given information is discussed by Guilford (1967) as an implication (in the formal logic sense). This includes extending a series of numbers or letters by adding to them, making conclusions, or making new deductions by use of formal logical principles. Extending or going beyond should include the development of new relationships or ways to connect old data with new conclusions. It also includes the application of generalizations to new situations (Taba, 1964).

Combining Simultaneously

Perhaps the essence of the concept of transformation is the element of simultaneous combination of ideas, objects, or images. In the familiar example of reviews of literature or children's "research" reports, teachers often find a sequential listing of ideas or conclusions rather than a combining of these ideas into one presentation or one conclusion. When examining the original research reports of gifted youngsters, for example, the author often is struck by their inability (or perhaps unwillingness) to develop abstract categories or groupings for organizing their papers. An educator can read a 25-page paper with millions of facts and ideas without a single subtitle or subheading. Out of seven excellently written papers from middle school gifted children that the author examined (the best of one great teacher's products), not a single paper included a subheading. The vocabulary, writing style, ideas, and conclusions were faultless but often there was no simultaneous combination of the ideas. The ideas were connected laterally or sequentially but not put together into one big organized idea.

Simultaneous synthesis also includes the development of conclusions, formation of generalizations, developing abstract categories, and labeling the categories developed. Sigel (1971) suggests that in evaluating children's development of categories or classes, the teacher should be concerned with the characteristic style of categorization and with the development of flexibility in these styles. As children grow older, they make less use of unsophisticated groupings (i.e., using more than one different reason for a grouping) and of those based on their own experiences with objects. Groupings based on subjective or concrete experiences can include the relational-contextual (i.e., locational—linked because items are found together in the student's experience, temporal—grouped because of some relationship in time, functional—grouped because the items are operated or used together) and the descriptive. Descriptive groupings are those based on appearance, texture, or material. Older youngsters and adults tend to rely more on categorical or inferential groupings, which are abstract categories that refer to a class of items. These classifications are made on the basis of abstracted qualities of the whole group.

Individuals tend to develop characteristic styles of categorization. They should be assisted in the increased use of abstract categories as well as the development of flexibility in their styles of categorizations. Hilda Taba's concept development teaching strategy can be used as a tool for assessing the ability to group, label, and regroup in a sophisticated manner as well as for developing this ability.

To examine children's generalizations—another aspect of combining—Mc-Naughton (1971) provides the following criteria for evaluating sentence generalizations:

1. *Abstractness, Conciseness* or *Inclusiveness* of the words used. The most effective are those which have the greatest amount and depth of the story's meaning invested in them. Less effective are those which are so abstract that their meaning is vague, and those which are relatively concrete. The least effective are those which are used the same way as in the text.

2. *Qualification* or *Subordination* in the form of either a relevant explanation or qualification of a main clause, or a complementary relationship between two clauses.
3. *Tentativeness* in the form of an explicit recognition of the conditional nature of a generalization or an inference within it.
4. *Comparison* in the form of an evaluation of relationships within the data or between parts of the story and data outside of it. The latter kind of comparison could also be described as an *inference*. (pp. 143-144)

The ability to develop products that are transformations rather than summaries of existing information should be a direct result of the growth of higher levels of thinking, the use of a discovery approach, and open-endedness of questions and methods. However, if the products students develop are not real transformations, exercises to enhance the elements just described can be helpful. In addition, the reader is referred to Torrance (1979), Guilford (1967), de Bono (1970, 1976), and Gordon (1961) for other ideas.

Most of the learning and creativity characteristics of gifted children, as well as their future roles in society (Table 1) as creators, scholars, leaders, and others who would be involved as "reconstructionists rather than participators" (Ward, 1961) suggest that these students should be expected to transform existing information rather than simply report or accept it as it is. Gifted students possess the ability to grasp underlying principles and make valid generalizations, and they have an advanced vocabulary with a great storehouse of information on a wide variety of topics. They need to synthesize this information and transform it by filtering it through their own conceptual structure. This also builds upon their creativity, originality, and concern with adapting, improving, and modifying.

SUMMARY

The product modifications suggested in this chapter build upon the process changes described in Chapter 2. If the changes are implemented, students can be expected to develop more sophisticated and more creative products than other children since these grow naturally out of the use of particular processes. It is the thesis of this chapter that the products developed by gifted students should approximate, to the extent possible, those of creative, productive professionals. This means that their products should address a real problem or concern, be directed toward a real audience whenever possible, have an identified purpose, be evaluated appropriately, and represent a transformation or synthesis of existing information rather than only a summary.

NOTES

1. Their complete process includes the following steps: the birth of a problem, acceptance of the problem, analysis of the problem, ideation, idea selection, implementation, and evaluation.
2. The reference citations for all tests listed in the text are presented in the Appendix.

Chapter 4

Learning Environment
Modifications

Changes in the learning environment to enhance its effectiveness for gifted students primarily serve a facilitative function. They enable the teachers' more successful implementation of the content, process, and product changes recommended in Chapters 1 through 3. These modifications also facilitate the success of the changes by increasing students' motivation to learn, interest in pursuing topics, and freedom to learn in a way that is comfortable and happy. Many of these elements are important to a degree in programs for all children. For this reason, the elements of classroom/school environments are conceptualized as continuums with opposite extremes. The most appropriate environment is at some place on each continuum. Generally, this place is in the same direction for all classrooms but is closer to one of the extremes in programs for the gifted.

Before examining the modifications to be made in learning environments, it is necessary to recognize the range of learning preferences of gifted children. There are many elements of the learning environment, particularly the physical one, that gifted students perceive as having differing degrees of importance. For example, some prefer some sound in the environment, others want complete quiet. Some prefer more privacy than others. These preferences, however, may change over time. Since preferences vary in the gifted population, no general statements about their importance can be made except that the environment must accommodate a range of choices. For these reasons, all modifications discussed in this chapter are perceived as important because they are preferred by gifted students as a group or are necessary environmental changes for implementing other curricular modifications.

Learning environments for gifted children must (a) be student-centered rather than teacher-centered, (b) encourage independence rather than dependence, (c) be open rather than closed, (d) be accepting instead of judging, (e) be complex rather than simple, and (f) permit and encourage high mobility instead of low mobility. Most of these are aspects of the psychological environment but the complexity-simplicity dimension includes the physical as well. The high mobility-low mobility dimension is entirely physical. These six continuums are discussed in the sections that follow.

STUDENT-CENTERED VS. TEACHER-CENTERED

A classroom and program for gifted children must be focused on students rather than the teacher. In a teacher-centered classroom, the focus is on the ideas and methods of the educator, who is the final authority should disagreements arise or decisions need to be made. Other elements that signal a focus on the instructor are (a) a high proportion of class time spent on the teacher's lecturing or informing, (b) pressure or perceived pressure on students to produce teacher-selected answers for a grade, and (c) a pattern of interaction in discussion situations that has the practitioner as the central figure.

On the other hand, the major focus in a student-centered classroom is on pupils' ideas and interests. The teacher's major goals are to find out what interests the students, determine what they know, and arrange learning experiences that will help them find out what they want to know. Other elements characterizing a student-centered classroom are (a) a high proportion of class time spent on discussion in which the pupils do most of the talking, (b) an absence of pressure to produce teacher-selected ideas for grades, and (c) a general pattern of discussion interaction that includes mainly student-to-student rather than student-to-teacher talk.

Teacher Talk

As noted, perhaps the most revealing factor indicating a classroom focus on the teacher is the percentage of class time consumed by teacher talk, either through lectures, informing, asking questions, or responding to student answers. The more teacher talk, the more passive the role students can and must take. According to Steele, House, Lapan, and Kerins (1970), teacher talk occurring 75 percent or more of the time generally indicates an authoritarian instructor and passive or bored students, while teacher talk 40 percent or less of the time usually signals a student-centered classroom with involvement and excitement on the part of the pupils. Although active student participation certainly is possible in a classroom where the teacher talks a great deal, it is most difficult to maintain student interest, stimulate reflective thinking, and increase individuals' productivity.

In their study comparing average classes, those for the gifted supported by state funds, and demonstration gifted classes, Steele et al. (1970) found that the teacher talked 75 to 90 percent of the time in 55 percent of the average classes, in 43 percent of regular gifted classes, and in only 6 percent of demonstration classes.

On the other hand, the teacher talked only 10 to 25 percent of the time in only 3 percent of average classes, 14 percent of regular gifted classes, and 21 percent of demonstration gifted classes. It should be noted that demonstration classes were considered the best possible examples of good educational practice for the gifted because they were selected to model these practices for others in the state.

Most of the process modifications described in Chapter 2 are best facilitated by an atmosphere where students talk more than the teacher. Open-endedness, discovery, freedom of choice, and group interaction cannot be incorporated to a significant degree in a classroom dominated by teacher talk. The teacher cannot provide appropriate pacing without attending to the students' ability to assimilate the material; this would be unknown if the classroom allows for little feedback from pupils. Finally, variety in methods requires that teacher lecture or informing be only one of several used in the classroom. This of necessity will lower the amount of time available for teacher talk.

Teacher Authority

One of the toughest aspects to change when moving from teacher-directedness to student-directedness is to convince children that the instructor is not or should not be the final authority in answering questions. Gifted students often become frustrated when the teacher will not tell them whether an answer or hypothesis is "right" or "wrong." When implementing the Suchman (1965) Inquiry Development Program, for example, teachers of the gifted found this was one of the most frustrating aspects of the approach for the students. Even though the children found several authoritative sources (science books, encyclopedia articles, journal articles) that supported their hypotheses, they still wanted the teacher to affirm that they were correct. Teaching the children to have confidence in their own ability to judge the validity and appropriateness of references is a slow process. Perhaps the difficulty results from pupils' early experiences when they are taught to accept an adult's word as the final authority and that it is wrong to doubt or question that voice.

Regardless of the difficulty in implementing such a change, movement away from teacher authority, especially in the realm of ideas, is an important step toward developing a student-centered classroom. With such an approach, gifted children build confidence in their own ability to formulate ideas and check their validity. An approach that teaches students to judge ideas using appropriate methods such as logical coherence, support through research, comprehensiveness of examples, generalizability, replicability, and other acceptable scientific procedures also will achieve other important objectives besides changing the focus of authority. Methods for judging ideas can be taught that (a) are generalizable to other situations, (b) allow the teacher to challenge student conclusions to make certain the appropriate support is present, and (c) improve the pupils' ability to challenge each other's ideas without focusing on or hurting the person. In other words, such an approach removes the focus for judgment from the realm of people and into the realm of ideas and logic.

Changes in content, process, and product all are facilitated by a focus away from teachers as the final authority. To enable children to deal effectively with abstract, complex ideas, the teacher must encourage and even require that students seek out their own sources, provide their own examples, and trust their own judgment. An emphasis on higher levels of thinking certainly demands that students evaluate their own ideas. Open-endedness, discovery approaches, freedom of choice, and group interaction activities are more successful if the teacher is not considered the only or final authority. Implementing all the product changes, especially appropriate evaluation, necessitates a focus on several authorities, including the audience, peers, self, and the teacher.

Patterns of Interaction

In a student-centered classroom where the focus is on pupils' ideas, interests, and needs, the interaction pattern will reflect greater student involvement and less teacher direction. This pattern is most noticeable in a discussion situation. One way to represent the two extremes of interaction (Figure 4-1) is to show graphically how the lines of communication can be arranged. In Figure 4-1A, the obvious focus in the discussion is the teacher, who is the center of attention and through whom all comments to the other students are directed. No comments go directly from one student to another. By contrast, in Figure 4-1B, the teacher is not the central figure and intervenes only when necessary to redirect the discussion, refocus it, or seek clarification or extension of student ideas. Many comments are directed to other students without being sifted by the teacher.

Another way to represent patterns of interaction is to show how they can be recorded by an observer. A method developed by Taba (1964) for analyzing success in discussions is presented in Figure 4-2. When using this system, the observer notes teacher behaviors in the top row and student behaviors in the bottom row. In a simple analysis, only three codes are used: "A" when someone asks a question, "T" when someone tells, and "SS" when students respond to student ideas. The observer can be an outsider watching classroom interaction, the teacher watching a videotape or listening to an audiotape, or a student. In the first example (Figure 4-2B), the interaction pattern is teacher-centered. The teacher asks a question, one student responds, the teacher comments on the answer, asks another question, and another student replies. The pattern continues.

A more student-centered interaction pattern is presented in the second example (Figure 4-2C). The teacher opens the discussion with a question, a student responds by asking for clarification, the teacher clarifies and restates the question, then several students respond. Later, the teacher intervenes with a question that

Figure 4-1 Student-Centered and Teacher-Centered Interaction Patterns

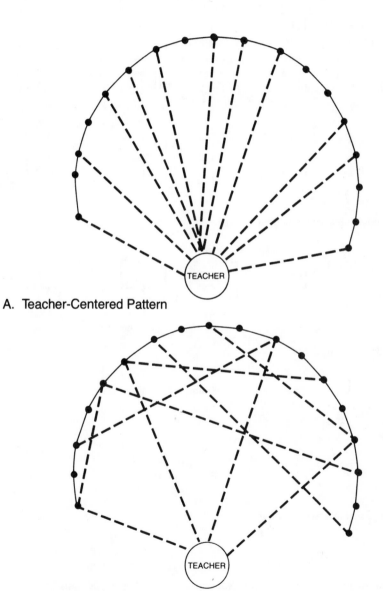

A. Teacher-Centered Pattern

B. Student-Centered Pattern

Figure 4-2 Coding of Classroom Interaction Patterns

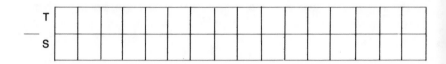

A. Coding System: T = Teacher Behavior, S = Student Behavior, A = Asks, T = Tells, SS
       = Student Reaction to Student Idea

T	A	T	A	T	A	T	A	T	A	T	A	T	A	T	A	T
S	T		T		T		T		T		T		T		T	

B. Teacher-Centered Interaction Pattern

T	A	T	A						A							A
S	A			T	T	T	T	T	T	T	T	SS	SS	SS	SS	SS	T

C. Student-Centered Interaction Pattern

Example B	Example C
TA = 8	TA = 4
TT = 8	TT = 1
ST = 8	ST = 8
SS = 0	SS = 6
Teacher = 16	Teacher = 5
Student = 8	Student = 14

D. Analysis of Interaction Patterns

Source: Reprinted from *Hilda Taba Teaching Strategies Program* by Hilda Taba by permission of Institute for Curriculum and Instruction, ©1971.

calls attention to differences in student ideas. This results in a long series of student reactions to each other's ideas. To compare the interaction patterns numerically (See Figure 4-2D), the numbers are calculated for each behavior for teacher and students. A ratio of student behavior to teacher behavior is then calculated. In these examples, the difference is very apparent, with a ratio of teacher-to-student behavior of 2 to 1 in the teacher-centered example and a ratio of 5 to 14 (almost 1 to 3) in the student-centered example.

To achieve a more student-centered interaction pattern, the teacher can take several basic actions. The first and perhaps most important is to ask open-ended questions. However, this is not enough. The teacher must permit and encourage a variety of responses to each question by (1) asking questions that call for variety (e.g., What other ways would you suggest for solving the problem?); (2) avoiding making a response to every student answer (avoid "good," "right," and even noncommittal responses such as "OK"); and (3) waiting for other students to answer. When a comment on student answers is avoided, the focus is diverted from teacher approval or disapproval and students gradually will stop expecting this. Because of the teacher's waiting, other students are encouraged (and given time) to offer their answers. A third teacher tactic that can be highly successful is to ask specific questions that force students to respond to the ideas expressed by their classmates. Some examples of teacher questions are the following:

Jane, it seems to me that what you are saying about economic freedom is very similar to Susan's earlier comment about political freedom. How do you see your ideas as similar or different?

Ronnie, what do you think about the opposite point of view presented earlier by Jimmy?

The teacher also can acquire the habit of self-analysis using a procedure such as the coding system in Figure 4-2. Taping and self-analysis seem to be the most effective ways of changing teacher behavior (Maker, 1975).

Characteristics of the Gifted

Development of a student-centered classroom and program builds upon the motivational, learning, and creativity characteristics of gifted pupils. It allows these traits to be exhibited as well as providing the setting where other curricular objectives can be implemented. By listening to students, the teacher can assess their level of knowledge and understanding on many issues as well as gather clues about what might interest them. Students' motivation is increased because of their greater involvement in learning.

Student-centered classrooms have been shown to provide effective climates for achieving many of the goals of gifted programs, while teacher-centered classrooms are more effective in teaching specific facts (Chickering, 1969). In his review of research on curricula and teaching methods, Chickering found significant differences in ability to apply concepts, in motivation, and in group membership skills when teacher-dominated classes were compared with those emphasizing a greater degree of student participation. In 10 out of 11 studies, these differences favored the student-centered classrooms. He concludes that the goals will determine the choice of focus: ''The more highly one values outcomes going beyond acquisition of knowledge, the more likely that student-centered methods will be preferred'' (p. 1140).

INDEPENDENCE VS. DEPENDENCE

In Chapter 2, much is said about the importance of developing independence, focusing mainly on more structured methods for encouraging independence, particularly freedom of choice. The explanation here focuses more on the classroom climate variables necessary to achieve student independence. Most of these variables are subtle, unstructured strategies reflected in teacher attitude and behavior.

It is impossible to separate completely the elements of a climate that encourage independence from one that is student centered. Certainly a student-centered classroom is a necessary prior or attendant condition for the encouragement of independence. However, there are other essential elements that go beyond those described earlier.

The basic definition of the dimension is the degree of tolerance for and encouragement of student initiative. This tolerance and encouragement is reflected in many aspects of the classroom, including academic factors such as student choice of what to learn, how to learn, and how to evaluate that learning, as well as in nonacademic elements such as classroom management, social interaction in class or school, the establishment of requirements such as deadlines for completing assignments, and the planning of class activities. Since academic aspects have been discussed, the focus here is on nonacademic elements and on having students solve (and of course prevent) their own problems rather than having them solved for them.

For example, when two students are arguing, fighting, or having other difficulties in getting along, an adult tends to intervene and suggest or even implement a solution. When there is a problem with classroom management such as a group discussion in which everyone is talking at once and everyone is interrupting everyone else, most teachers will intervene, stop the activity, and/or impose some punishment on the offenders. However, in both of these cases, if the teacher's goal is to develop independence rather than dependence, intervention tactics must be different.

Some sort of stop-action definitely is needed in these situations, but the next step should be eliciting rather than imposing a solution. In the right setting, students can propose at least as many solutions to their own problems as can a teacher (and usually more). Solutions generated by gifted students usually are more effective since these individuals are more committed to making their own ideas work.

Creative problem solving in a group setting with a positive atmosphere is an excellent means of developing ways to solve social or classroom management problems. Issues can be proposed before they arise and students can develop possible solutions; real, immediate problems can be presented after they occur. The author once observed a classroom of 17 gifted students who were reporting their analysis of artifacts they had collected. Two teams had analyzed each other's artifacts and developed their hypotheses about the other culture. All were eager to present their ideas, so the team leaders were unable to control their groups. The teacher almost panicked because it was impossible to reduce the noise level—to even a mild roar. After attempting to control the group, the teacher stopped the action, said there seemed to be a problem, and asked if the students agreed. They all did. The teacher then asked what they saw as subproblems or contributing factors. In a brainstorming situation, they listed several issues, then a variety of solutions to each. Student volunteers then were given the task of developing a plan of action. The original activity was deferred until the following day so the plan could be implemented. The next day, the students managed their own discussion and imposed strict penalties on their own group members who broke rules. The teacher reported a return to sanity and said future management problems definitely would be handed over to the class.

Another way of handling classroom management is to establish student "government" through a system the pupils design in which they develop their own laws or rules as well as methods of enforcement. The system can include elected officers, appointed committees, or any other methods the group chooses. Functions of these committees or officers can be expanded to include not only management and solution of problems but also activity planning. If students are responsible for the planning and coordinating of class activities such as field trips, parties, and guest speaker schedules, two positive results can occur: (1) the children can learn valuable skills in planning and (2) the teacher can be freed from much of the handling of details. Obviously, much teacher time is needed when students are first learning how to plan activities, but as these skills are developed, pupils can take over a great deal of the responsibility.

Even due dates for assignments and late penalties can be the students' responsibility. They should be able to establish their own reasonable time limits and assume the responsibility for meeting them. Either the teacher or some group of students can enforce the rules or impose the penalties.

One last teacher behavior needs to be stressed. When developing a classroom where independence in thought and action is the objective, teachers must be prepared to answer questions about their own actions without becoming irritable or defensive. This means being prepared to explain their reasons for actions or for certain school rules. Teachers also must avoid authoritarian pronouncements or answering "why" questions with "because *I* said so."

Characteristics of the Gifted

Because of the motivational and leadership characteristics of gifted students, emphasis on independence in nonacademic pursuits is particularly important as a way to build upon their strengths. It also is impossible to develop independence and self-direction in academic areas if the teacher is unwilling to tolerate or encourage independence in areas other than academics. In the study of classroom climate reported earlier (Steele et al., 1970), independence characterized the atmosphere in classes for the gifted but not in average classes. Although only 28 percent of the average classes permitted and encouraged student initiative, 71 percent of regular gifted and 79 percent of demonstration gifted classes emphasized independence. Closely related to this was the degree of student enthusiasm. In 65 percent of gifted classes and 70 percent of demonstration gifted classes, students perceived that there was enthusiasm, excitement, and involvement in learning. By contrast, in 51 percent of the average classes, students saw a lack of enthusiasm and in none of the classes did they discern its presence. Most in average classes perceived the climate as neutral in this dimension.

It is interesting to note that even though children in 28 percent of the average classrooms believed that student initiative was encouraged, none perceived that pupils were enthusiastic and excited about learning. There is no basis in this study for assuming that the reason for a lack of enthusiasm in the 28 percent of classes that encourage independence is that students do not desire or cannot handle independence when it is encouraged, but one could infer this as a possible explanation.

However, there is some indication from research on student instructional preferences that the gifted do prefer a greater degree of independence. For example, Dunn and Price (1980) report that gifted students show a desire for less structure in their learning environment than do their nongifted peers. Further, they indicate they are less teacher-motivated than the nongifted. Using a different instrument, Stewart (1979) finds that gifted students rank independent study higher than do their average peers, and research with the *California Psychological Inventory* (CPI) shows the gifted to prefer "achievement via independence" over "achievement via conformity" while their average peers opt for achievement via conformity (Gallagher, 1966; Gough, 1957). Connolly (1976) reports that independent study is included in the top three instructional modes in gifted students' rankings of methods according to both their learning importance and their enjoyment. From these results using different instruments, it does seem valid to conclude that gifted students prefer a greater degree of independence than do their average peers.

OPEN VS. CLOSED

A second dimension of classroom atmosphere discussed in Chapter 2 (on process modifications) is open vs. closed. This dimension, although closely related to the teacher's development of open-endedness in methods and learning activities, also goes beyond the academic realm into nonacademic areas. Elements of open-endedness already discussed are encouragement of and tolerance for many ideas, many solutions to problems, many answers to questions, and learning experiences that provoke further study. The basic definition of the environment dimension of open vs. closed is the extent to which restrictions affect the environment. Jones (1977) provides this definition in his description of the physical environment. Although the dimension does include physical aspects, Lethem and Osborn (Note 4) expand the concept to include openness in the psychological environment as well.

With regard to aspects of the physical environment (Lethem & Osborn, Note 4), an open situation permits new people, new materials, and new things to enter. The environment is not static but rather changes when necessary or desirable. As to the psychological aspects of the environment, an open climate permits new ideas, exploratory discussions, and the freedom to change directions or procedures to meet different situations. In other words, when confronted with unexpected or unpredicted factors, the planned situation can be changed. Not only are different student ideas encouraged or permitted, so, too, is different behavior. Not all students are expected to conform to the same standards of classroom behavior nor to meet the same instructional requirements.

The dimension of open vs. closed is closely related to independence vs. dependence in that openness is necessary in order to achieve an atmosphere in which students can become independent. It also is related to the dimension of student-centered vs. teacher-centered because openness to student ideas and interests is necessary if the practitioner is to focus on them. Open vs. closed, as a dimension of classroom climate, is different from the two other dimensions, however, in its focus on divergence. Rather than simply accepting differences in students, the teacher of the gifted should be encouraging these pupils to be different and to avoid conformity. This focus on divergence also should extend to the teacher. Students need to recognize a different teacher style and to avoid placing unnecessary or unrealistic restrictions on that individual.

An open rather than closed environment can facilitate the success of both product and process modifications that are important in gifted programs. In particular, if students are expected to develop original products that are investigations of real problems, are directed toward real audiences, and represent transformations rather than summaries of existing data, restrictions in the environment must be minimized. Students should face minimum restraint on topics to be studied, methods to be used, and products to be developed. With regard to the process modifications, an open environment is necessary to the success of all changes listed. To provide variety in methods, for example, the educator must be able to try out a variety of teaching styles and must accommodate a number of learning styles. This means that as many restrictions as possible must be eliminated and new people, new materials, and new ideas must be welcomed. To allow freedom of choice and encourage higher levels of thinking, the teacher also must encourage as much divergence as possible.

Characteristics of the Gifted

Emphasis on divergence mainly facilitates the learning and creativity characteristics of gifted students. Creative students are very much in need of a climate that encourages and permits divergence. They tend to offer clever or way-out answers to questions and to scorn social conformity. A very special teacher is needed because it is difficult and sometimes impossible to see the connection between a student's answer and the question asked. Pupils' skills can leave much to be desired, and the children are stubborn and tenacious in their beliefs. Patience and a high tolerance for diversity are much-needed traits for teachers who wish to be successful with creative children.

In their study of classroom climate, Steele et al. (1970) report that divergence is a characteristic of most average classes (69 percent) and almost all gifted classrooms (96 percent of regular and 97 percent of demonstration). In 0 percent of average, 71 percent of regular gifted, and 82 percent of demonstration gifted classrooms, however, students perceive much emphasis on divergence. Regarding the element of openness to new people and new ideas, in Connolly's (1976) study, students ranked guest speakers as their second most enjoyable instructional mode.

ACCEPTING VS. JUDGING

As with other dimensions of classroom climate, the judging-accepting dimension cannot be separated entirely from the open vs. closed element. Openness implies acceptance, closed indicates nonacceptance. Perhaps the best distinction, however, should be in the definition of acceptance as the absence of judgment. In other words, the judging-accepting dimension is more concerned with avoidance of value judgments than with the absence of restrictions and encouragement of divergence. It seems obvious that encouragement of divergence implies avoidance of value judgments, but the emphasis is somewhat different.

Three elements are important in describing the accepting-judging dimension of classroom climate: attempting to understand, timing, and evaluation rather than judgment. Although related, these elements reflect a somewhat different emphasis and are important in different contexts.

Attempting to Understand

Adults often jump to conclusions about an idea or a method before getting all the facts or listening to a different point of view. This tendency to make a judgment takes the focus away from an attempt to really understand another point of view, and perhaps occurs with greater frequency when adults are dealing with children than with other grown-ups. Adults tend to believe that because of their wider range of experience and greater depth of knowledge, their perspective is better or more valid than the child's. Perhaps because of their stubbornness and their confidence in their own ideas, gifted students are highly unlikely to listen to their teachers' perspective if they do not believe the educators have made an honest attempt to understand their point of view.

The element of attempting to understand is very much related to Jung's (1923) concept of the continuum of judging vs. perceiving as a dimension of every individual's personality. This dimension also is included in the *Myers-Briggs Type Indicator* (MBTI) (Myers & Briggs, 1962), a personality assessment instrument based on Jung's theory. Characteristics indicating a "judging" personality are

Settled	Planned
Decided	Completed
Fixed	Decisive
Plan ahead	Wrap it up
Run one's life	Urgency
Closure	Deadline!
Decision-making	Get show on the road
	(Keirsey & Bates, 1978,
	pp. 25, 26)

while the characteristics indicating a "perceiving" personality are

Pending	Emergent
Gather more data	Tentative
Flexible	Something will turn up
Adapt as you go	There's plenty of time
Let life happen	What deadline?
Open options	Let's wait and see
Open ended	(Keirsey & Bates, 1978,
	pp. 25, 26)

A perceiving person prefers to keep things open and fluid while a judging one feels a sense of urgency until a decision has been made, then feels comfortable afterward. The perceiving person, on the other hand, may resist making a decision because of a need to collect more data first. Thus, the perceiving person may feel uneasy rather than comfortable after a decision is made.

In a teaching situation, judging types should be careful in their interactions with children because of their tendency to live by defined standards and beliefs that are not changed easily (Lawrence, 1979) and because of their desire to be "right." These tendencies contribute to judgment of student ideas on the basis of the teacher's own standards and values rather than on an attempt to understand another point of view and avoid passing judgment on it.

Students need to feel that the teacher is making a genuine attempt to understand their feelings, their values, and their beliefs. To convince them that this attempt is genuine, teachers must listen actively to what their students are saying. Teacher responses to student ideas often are no more than cursory acknowledgments of the fact that the pupils have said something. Active listening or attending behavior is, first of all, nonverbal. The teacher by physical actions displays an interest in the student's ideas—that they have worth and significance. Nonverbal behavior includes such factors as:

facial expressions: smiling
eye contact: looking at the speaker
spatial distance: moving toward, or near the speaker
body positioning: leaning forward, inclining the head, tone of voice, rate of
            speech, timing
head movements: nodding, inclining the head, gestures

These are not the only types of behavior that show interest nonverbally but do indicate generally the kinds of actions people unconsciously take when they are interested and listening.

After attending to the student's ideas, the teacher who has listened actively will indicate acceptance, implying that the ideas are worthwhile, significant, relevant, pertinent, or sincere. It does not suggest either agreement or disagreement. To accept an idea is to grant it importance and to recognize its worth for examining, elaborating, perhaps clarifying, and ultimately challenging. Expressions of acceptance are particularly susceptible to becoming rote, distracting mannerisms. A teacher therefore must consciously vary the ways of accepting student responses. There is an almost infinite number of ways this can be accomplished. For example, here are some expressions:

Yes, I can understand that.
That seems reasonable enough to me.

I see what you mean.
I think I see the idea you're getting at.
You are developing some interesting ideas here.
That certainly makes a lot of sense.
That's an interesting difference you just pointed out.
This might work.
I hadn't thought about that before.

Expressions that are subject to becoming mannerisms when used too often are the following:

Yes, I see, OK, Good, Fine.

Having displayed acceptance and encouragement, the teacher then can request that the student explain, elaborate, and clarify ideas. Not all ideas require this so the teacher must exercise judgment about the need for additional explanation. Gifted children, who often give their ideas in abstract or ambiguous terms, need practice in providing concrete examples and in offering different explanations for them. The clarification process is accomplished by restating the ideas in some manner that is acceptable to the student and clearer to the teacher. Another way, which permits more student talk, encourages critical thinking, and sounds less condescending, involves asking questions such as those below. Two subcategories of questions/behaviors are included:

Clarification/Elaboration
Please tell us more about the idea.
What is an example of what you are talking about?
Please explain that a bit more clearly.
When you say _____ , what do you mean?
Please give us more details.

Extension
What is an example of that idea in a different area?
What do you think have been some of the results of that?
What would be some good and bad points about this?
What kinds of facts can we use to support your idea?

Often it is helpful to preface these questions with statements such as:

Let's explore this idea.
Let's discuss this.
Let's develop your ideas.

These generally should come after the teacher has displayed attending behavior and after clearly indicating acceptance of the student's ideas. "Give us some more details" tends to have a critical overtone unless prefaced by smiling or nodding and saying, "Yes, this might well work. Give us some more details." The difference may seem inconsequential but experience indicates that it is not.

It is important to remember with this as with the following two behaviors that the teacher's tone of voice and the other nonverbal clues must be appropriate or congruent with the verbal statements. The same statement made in a sarcastic tone and while glancing out a classroom window hardly builds a feeling of acceptance.

While attending, accepting, and encouraging behaviors are designed to increase the quantity of expression, the questions and statements of clarification and challenge are meant to increase the quality. The transition takes place with teacher encouragement.

Timing

The element of timing in the accepting vs. judging dimension of classroom climate simply pertains to when evaluations are made. The previous section noted that teachers go through a series of behaviors while attempting to understand a student's ideas. These include attending, accepting, clarifying, and extending. Only after clearly understanding the ideas should the teacher consider the merits of an idea or permit students to do so. At this time, the teacher can pose challenging questions or require the student to cite evidence or reasoning to support the idea. Teachers under the guise of getting students to really think often begin discussions early in a class by asking challenging and probing questions that force pupils into defensive positions. Such a technique can be effective, but only after an appropriate student-teacher rapport has been established. This rapport must include a sense of respect on the part of both teacher and students. In one sense, the previous teacher behaviors are designed to create this feeling of respect so that open, rigorous debate can take place. Examples of challenge questions are:

What is your reasoning that led you to that conclusion?
How did you reach that conclusion?
What are some facts that would support your idea?
What led you to believe that?
Why?
Why do you believe that?
What are some of your reasons for saying that?
What are your reasons for saying that?

Questions of challenge help the teacher understand ideas better and allow the student freedom to reorganize, restate, qualify, and possibly rethink the response.

Properly worded, they should not force the pupil to be defensive or antagonistic. The student may begin qualifying the generalization, indicating which parts can be supported and labeling those that are only guesses or hypotheses.

Another aspect of timing is related to the stage of problem solving. When the purpose of an activity is to generate a quantity of ideas or possible solutions to problems, evaluation of any kind is completely inappropriate. For example, during idea production in a brainstorming situation (Parnes, Note 3), the most important rule to enforce is deferred judgment. Some of the most creative, original ideas will be inhibited and thus not even considered later if the person cannot avoid the natural tendency to judge an idea as good or bad before saying or writing it. Several studies (Parnes, 1975) show that (1) individuals instructed to defer judgment during idea production tend to produce more unique and useful ideas than those allowed to judge at the same time; (2) individuals trained to use deferred judgment produce more unique and useful ideas under deferred judgment instructions than do untrained people; and (3) groups also produce more and better ideas when trained and when using this principle.

It is important to note that in the Parnes method as in other creative problem-solving processes, judgment is not eliminated—only deferred. The teacher waits until a quantity of ideas is produced, then reviews them and selects the most important or most promising. The teacher thus can look objectively at all the ideas and can develop and apply appropriate criteria for evaluation rather than imposing an initial judgment that perhaps is emotional or based on past experience and that does not involve open-minded consideration.

Evaluation Rather Than Judgment

Judgment implies rightness or wrongness and goodness or badness as global concepts. When judging an idea, individuals tend to consider it entirely good or entirely bad, entirely right or entirely wrong. Evaluation, on the other hand, implies considering both the right and wrong or good and bad aspects of an idea. Evaluation also involves constructive rather than destructive criticism. Both the manner of speaking and the timing of the critique are important in this context. For example, the teacher says: "Your description of the operation of the state penal system is accurate in that you have said _____ . However, that description could be improved if you also included _____ ." The statement considers both accurate and inaccurate aspects of the idea but the focus of the critique is on how the description can be improved rather than on how or why it is wrong or bad.

In evaluating students' products, the teacher's focus always should be on both the positive and negative and should suggest ways to improve. If only the positive is considered, students cannot grow (and may not even believe the critique) but if the positive is not emphasized, the critique will not really be constructive. Students also need to practice the same kind of evaluation of other pupils' ideas. The teacher can be both a model and a teacher in these situations. Koberg and Bagnall (1976) provide what they term a foolproof method for painless criticism that can be a guide to both teachers and students:

> The trick is to place the criticism within a context of positive reinforcements . . . just simple diplomacy. (1) Begin with two positive reinforcements: "You really are a well-seasoned traveler." "You have all of the best gear for hiking." (2) Insert your criticism: "I wish we could stay in step when we hiked." (3) Add one more positive reinforcement: "I notice that you can adapt easily to most things." (4) Finish with a ray of hope: "If we work on this together, I'm sure we'll be able to get harmony into our stride." (p.118)

Facilitation of Success

The learning environment dimension of accepting vs. judging is important for facilitating the success of content, process, and product modifications for gifted students. It is perhaps most important for process and product changes but also is necessary for the complete development of abstract, complex ideas. With regard to process changes, the development of higher levels of thinking and open-endedness are entirely dependent upon an atmosphere that emphasizes acceptance of ideas rather than judgment. A discovery process also necessitates the teacher's willingness to accept and allow the children's mistakes so they will reach their own conclusions and discover their own principles. The series of teacher behaviors from attending and accepting through clarifying and extending is a necessary prerequisite to requiring that students offer their proof or evidence of reasoning to support their ideas. These questions of challenge are nonthreatening only if they are preceded by teacher behavior indicating acceptance, understanding, and recognition of the worth of the idea.

The product modification of appropriate evaluation also requires a climate of acceptance to be successful. Emphasis on evaluation and constructive criticism rather than judgment is necessary in teaching children to assess their own products as well as to evaluate the products of other pupils. The teacher's own behavior in modeling appropriate evaluation is especially important.

Characteristics of the Gifted

Enhancing the creativity characteristics of gifted children requires that the teacher develop a classroom climate where all ideas, regardless of how far out, unique, or clever they may be, are accepted as having value. Teachers do not want to destroy the students' intellectual playfulness or their imagination and fantasy by requiring too much evaluation or too early judgment, or by not recognizing the importance of these characteristics and their manifestation. The teacher must be able and willing to recognize when children are not ready for their ideas or products to be evaluated or challenged and must provide an atmosphere where other students also accept the importance of timing in the evaluation process.

Another creativity characteristic of gifted children is their ability to criticize constructively and their unwillingness to accept authoritarian pronouncements without examining them thoroughly. This trait suggests that the teacher's efforts to develop a climate of acceptance will be more successful with creative children than with those who possess the tendency to judge events, people, and things. The tendency to evaluate needs to be refined and channeled in such a way that judgments are timed appropriately and are constructive rather than destructive.

COMPLEX VS. SIMPLE

Complexity vs. simplicity as a dimension of classroom environment is defined by Jones (1977) as the degree of complexity or simplicity present in the physical environment as well as in the kind of tasks students are asked to perform. It seems clear that gifted students should be expected to carry out complex intellectual tasks. They are given assignments that require higher levels of thinking; they are expected to consider abstract, complex ideas; and they should transform rather than summarize the ideas of others. Their interactions, both academic and social, need to be complex (Lethem and Osborn, Note 4).

As Lethem and Osborn also have noted, gifted students need a complex physical environment. This complexity includes a variety of materials, a balance of hard and soft elements, a variety of colors, asymmetric rather than symmetric arrangements, and many types of spaces or environments for learning (tables for work areas, comfortable seating for seminars and discussions, study carrels for seclusion).

Renzulli (1977) also notes that to enable gifted children to study highly complex phenomena and develop products that are transformations, they must have available specialized equipment, a variety of reference sources, and sophisticated materials. He gives a helpful list of book and nonbook references that should be made available:

TYPES OF REFERENCE BOOKS

Bibliographies	Reviews	Concordances
Encyclopedias	Reader's Guides	Data Tables
Dictionaries and	Abstracts	Digests
Glossaries	Diaries	Record Books
Annuals	Catalogues	Surveys

Handbooks	Books of Quotations, Proverbs,	Almanacs
Directories and	Maxims, and Familiar Phrases	Anthologies
Registers	Source Books	Periodicals
Indexes	Histories and Chronicles	Yearbooks
Atlases	of Particular Fields,	Manuals
	Organizations	

TYPES OF NONBOOK REFERENCE MATERIALS

Art Prints	Globes	Charts
Talking Books	Kits	Films
Video Tapes	Maps	Study Print
Microforms	Film Loops	Models
Filmstrips	Filmstrips with Sound	Pictures
Realia	Records	Flashcards
Transparencies		Slides (pp. 59, 60)

Ward (1961) suggests that while an encyclopedia may serve as a basic reference for most children, the gifted will need specialized equipment such as slide rules, calculators, typewriters, and laboratory materials. Many of these items will be expensive but it is always possible to allow access to them by developing more flexible arrangements for their use rather than by purchasing them for every class or school.

Creative individuals also show preferences for complexity in other aspects of their physical and psychological environment. MacKinnon (1962) reviews a series of studies, including his own, that show a marked preference in creative individuals for complex and asymmetrical drawings rather than simple and symmetrical ones. The subjects in one study (Barron & Welsh, 1952) refer to the complex drawings as "vital and dynamic." All creative groups in MacKinnon's studies show this preference for perceptual complexity in scales other than drawings. Generally, the more creative the individual, the stronger the preference. He concludes:

> it is clear that creative persons are especially disposed to admit complexity and even disorder into their perceptions without being made anxious by the resulting chaos. It is not so much that they like disorder per se, but that they prefer the richness of the disordered to the stark barrenness of the simple. They appear to be challenged by disordered multiplicity which arouses in them a strong need which in them is serviced by a superior capacity to achieve the most difficult and far-reaching ordering of the richness they are willing to experience. (p. 489)

Although most studies showing that creative individuals prefer complexity to simplicity have been conducted with adults, research of others (Khatena, 1978; Khatena & Fisher, 1974; Torrance, 1972, 1979) has shown that most of the perceptual and personality characteristics of creative children parallel those of adults. The youths' preferences are not quite as strong but become more marked as they grow older.

There is a strong indication that gifted students prefer complexity when their tendency to become bored with routine activities, drill, and unchallenging tasks is considered. This characteristic is clear from the research (Terman & Oden, 1947; Ward, 1962) as well as everyday teaching experience.

HIGH MOBILITY VS. LOW MOBILITY

Jones (1977) also discusses the classroom environment dimension of mobility. However, his conception focuses mainly on the physical movements of children within the classroom, including the use of large muscles vs. small muscles. Lethem and Osborn (Note 4) have expanded his concept to include movement in and out of the classroom. It is this expanded concept that provides the dimension of concern in the education of gifted children. Mobility, then, refers to the amount of movement needed by the student and allowed and encouraged by the teacher. Gifted students need an environment that is flexible enough to allow high mobility: a great deal of movement in and out of the classroom; differing grouping arrangements within and outside the classroom; access to a variety of learning/ investigating environments; and access to a variety of materials, references, and equipment (Renzulli, 1977).

Common procedures such as acceleration to the next grade level, use of open classrooms, ability grouping, and resource rooms serve (or should be designed to serve) the same facilitative purposes as the basic concept of flexibility. Administrative arrangements such as resource rooms for bright children, although helpful and possibly necessary, should not be viewed as a program. They are only means to the end and are not the end in themselves. All too often, in special education, the administrative arrangement determines the curriculum, rather than the reverse.

It is not the purpose of this book to present evidence in favor of or against any particular administrative arrangements such as special classes, partial segregation, consulting teachers, acceleration, etc. Research on the effectiveness of these approaches, including comparisons, has shown consistently that what goes on between teacher and student is more important than the type of arrangement or provision for facilitating the process.

Regardless of the basic administrative arrangement, the most important ingredient in the environment that relates to mobility is the flexibility that will allow freedom of movement in and out of the classroom as well as within it. To enable gifted students to learn methodology, develop abstract and complex concepts, be true investigators, and have freedom of choice in their activities, administrative arrangements must be flexible enough to allow them to study outside the confinement of the school. For example, they must be allowed to collect their data on the street corner, get specimens from a local river or pond, and perhaps more importantly, study with a mentor or scholar in some field who can help them develop those systems of thought in a discipline.

Within the classroom, gifted students need to be allowed the freedom to study with different subgroups of classmates as well as alone. They need the freedom to organize themselves and direct their own activities. Thus, high mobility also serves as a facilitator of success for other learning environment changes as well as the product, process, and content changes perceived as important for gifted students.

SUMMARY

The purpose of this chapter has been to describe the dimensions of a classroom and school environment that are important in a program for the gifted. The six dimensions discussed are perceived as continuums, with the most appropriate environments for the gifted being arranged near one extreme. Student-centered, facilitative of independence, open, accepting, complex, and highly mobile are adjectives that describe the learning environments appropriate for these pupils. These dimensions and elements have been chosen for three reasons: (1) they address the group preferences of gifted students, (2) they build upon and extend the characteristics of these pupils, and (3) they are necessary to facilitate the success of other curricular modifications in programs for the gifted.

NOTE

1. For reviews of the research and discussions of the merits of various administrative arrangements, the reader is referred to the following publications: Borg (1964); Gallagher (1966); Goldberg, Passow, Justman, & Hage (1965); and Plowman & Rice (1967).

Developing Your Own Program

Introduction to Section II: The Teaching-Learning Models

There are several teaching-learning models that can be used separately or combined as a curriculum development framework in a program for the gifted. The models have different strengths and weaknesses as well as differing degrees of specificity in the strategies they suggest. They also have different assumptions and philosophical bases. How is a teacher to choose which of these or which combinations of these will guide classroom efforts? How can parental values, school restraints, and student characteristics all be considered in developing a curriculum? Section II is designed to answer these questions.

The suggestions in this part are directed toward those who are concerned with the design of learning experiences for gifted children regardless of the program's administrative structure. Of course, the administrative arrangements are a consideration in the type of curriculum to develop but this section assumes the structure is present already or that it will be developed to facilitate the success of the program.

Several factors influence curriculum design. They relate to the (a) model (i.e., philosophy, objectives, strengths, and weaknesses), (b) teacher (philosophy, personality, skills, prior experiences), (c) setting (administrative structure of the gifted program, parental philosophy, the school system, the individual school, the regular curriculum), and (d) students (their common and unique characteristics). In some way, the curriculum must reflect the intersection of all these factors. Is this an impossible task? The author does not think so. However, it certainly is not an easy one. The initial process of development must be comprehensive. It must involve knowledgeable key individuals; must be developed in a systematic, inductive manner; and must include a built-in process for review and a mechanism for change.

The chapters in this section provide answers to five basic questions about the design of curricula in programs for the gifted:

1. What are the factors that must be considered in the development of a curriculum?
2. How does the educator take these factors into account in developing the curriculum?
3. How does the teacher assess the effectiveness of the design and make the necessary changes?
4. How does the educator provide for special populations of gifted children within the framework for all?
5. How does the teacher develop a program that meets the needs of each individual child?

In effect, the focus of the section is on process—the process of curriculum development. Although it does supply some of the material needed to develop a program through suggestions of factors that should be considered or resources that are available, the section seeks to provide a step-by-step procedure. The end result is not specified but if the process is followed, the curriculum should be a real intersection of the characteristics and constraints of the model, teacher, setting, and students.

Before beginning the section, however, some introductory comments regarding the author's assumptions are in order. With all the references to teaching-learning models, it may be clear that I believe it is imperative that some philosophical and theoretical framework serve as the basis for curriculum modifications for the gifted. A program made up of a collection of games and activities or a conglomeration of bits and pieces from various, often incompatible, sources, does not constitute a qualitatively different curriculum for the gifted. Although the general principles discussed in Section I provide guidelines—a framework—for curriculum development, they do not offer enough specific teaching strategies nor adequate theoretical frameworks by themselves for implementing the kind of program needed for gifted children.

Several theoretical or structural teaching-learning models exist that are in some way appropriate for teaching gifted students. Many of these approaches are in use in programs for the gifted. These approaches do make a difference in what is learned and how well it is learned. Since each model has its own particular focus and its strengths and weaknesses for certain purposes, a comprehensive curriculum will use the models in such a way that they complement each other. Probably the best curriculum will combine more than one of the models since none is comprehensive enough by itself. On the other hand, trying to use them all no doubt would result in a strange collection of bits and pieces and a schizophrenic teacher.

Individual children are a powerful part of the process. They react differently and unpredictably to each of the approaches as well as to day-to-day activities. To increase the probability of finding something that works with each pupil, a teacher needs a wide range and good variety of tricks. Mastering several of these approaches thus enhances a teacher's effectiveness.

The purpose of this section is not to provide an in-depth discussion of each of the existing models. That is left to other publications. However, to assist the reader unfamiliar with any of these models, the following section provides a brief orientation to the ten most commonly used, and most potentially useful, teaching-learning models. The approaches are chosen for several reasons. The first is a concern for their demonstrated or potential success with gifted children. Each principle described in Section I is a consideration in this selection process. Second is their widespread use in gifted programs. Third is variety and complementarity.

No one model addresses all the content, process, product, and learning environment changes suggested in Section I. No one model will be attractive to all teachers nor fit every situation. For these and related reasons, models are chosen that can be combined in a variety of ways to enhance their effectiveness and increase the chances that educators will find a particular combination that will fit their preferred styles of teaching.

TEACHING-LEARNING MODELS

Benjamin Bloom and David Krathwohl: Taxonomies of Cognitive and Affective Educational Objectives

One of the most frequently used models for the development of higher level thinking is Bloom's *Taxonomy* (Bloom, 1956).[1] Most programs for the gifted, if not based entirely on this model, at least use it in some way. Although both the cognitive and affective taxonomies were developed by essentially the same group of educators and psychologists, the cognitive one usually is referred to as Bloom's *Taxonomy* and the affective one as Krathwohl's *Taxonomy* (Krathwohl, Bloom, & Masia, 1964).

The purpose of the taxonomies is to provide a set of criteria that can be used to classify educational objectives according to the level of complexity of the thinking required. They are generic in the sense that they are applicable to any academic subject area and any level of instruction from kindergarten through adult education (including graduate school). Although their focus and levels are different, the underlying assumptions, process of development, and use are similar.

At the time of their development, it is doubtful that anyone anticipated the widespread use of the classifications to develop teaching activities. However, they provide a simple, somewhat easy-to-learn structure for developing teaching-learning activities that take students through a sequential process in the development of a concept or learning of relationships. If the major assumption of the taxonomies is valid—that each higher level includes and depends on the behaviors below—students who have been led through the process systematically should be able to think or behave more effectively at the higher levels.

The cognitive taxonomy consists of six levels: knowledge, comprehension, application, analysis, synthesis, and evaluation. The affective taxonomy consists of five levels: receiving or attending, responding, valuing, organization, and characterization by a value complex. Although the taxonomies are viewed as parts of two different domains, human behavior, especially at the higher levels, is impossible to separate into two different components.

The taxonomies of educational objectives cannot be defended as a total approach to curriculum development for gifted children. However, they can be used as one aspect of a program, particularly to show the relative emphasis on higher vs. lower thinking and feeling processes in gifted programs. The associated uses—evaluation and development of teacher-made tests, evaluation of standardized tests, and construction of more quantifiable objectives—all are appropriate even if curriculum development is not based on the taxonomies.

Jerome Bruner: The Basic Structure of a Discipline

Of all the teaching-learning models used in programs for the gifted, Bruner's (1960) is perhaps the most philosophical. In fact, his is not actually a framework but rather is a way of approaching the development of a framework. Bruner's ideas have contributed to many of the other models, as well as to the author's overall view of curricular modifications appropriate for the gifted.

One assumption has formed the basis for most of Bruner's ideas: "Intellectual activity anywhere is the same, whether at the frontier of knowledge or in a third-grade classroom." The difference is in degree, not in kind, and the best way to learn history is by behaving the way a historian would. Thus, instead of focusing only on the conclusions in a field of inquiry, educators should look also at the inquiry itself. Most of Bruner's ideas follow from this basic conviction. A person more nearly approximates an inquirer if the basic ideas of that discipline are understood and are of concern, if concepts are revisited as understanding increases, if there is a balance between intuition and analysis, and if there is a long-term commitment to intellectual activity and the pursuit of knowledge.

A theme underlying Bruner's approach is that the aim in education should be to teach the basic structure of academic disciplines in such a way that this structure can be understood by children. This basic structure consists of certain concepts (e.g., biological tropisms in science; revolution in social studies; supply and demand in economics; commutation, distribution, and association in mathematics) and the important relationships among them. Such concepts and relationships, when understood, enable the learner to understand most of the phenomena in that discipline. Understanding the basic structure means that the individual not only has learned a specific thing but also has learned a model for understanding other things like it that may be encountered. A phenomenon is recognized as a specific instance of a more general case. Carefully developed understandings should permit the student to recognize the limits of applicability of the generalizations.

Based on what is known from the available research, the basic structure approach combined with teaching methods emphasizing inquiry and discovery rather than didactic ones can be highly successful with gifted students. Although the teaching of structure and abstract concepts is difficult for the teacher, materials and comprehensive curricula are available as aids. It seems that with Bruner's approach, the advantages greatly outweigh the disadvantages.

J.P. Guilford: The Structure of Intellect (SI)

Guilford's (1959, 1967) theory of the structure of human intelligence no doubt has had a greater influence on the field of education of the gifted than has any other theory or model. Its influence has been felt in all areas of programming, including definition, philosophy, identification, and testing as well as curriculum development and teaching strategies. Indeed, the theory is even used as the sole basis of many gifted programs. Perhaps its most important influence has been in expansion of the concept or definition of giftedness. Prior to Guilford's work, the concept of giftedness was almost synonymous with IQ, but after his ideas spread into the educational community, the multifaceted or multidimensional conception of giftedness began to form the basis for programs.

In addition to its influence on the actual operation of programs for the gifted, Guilford's model has had great influence on several of the theorists and leaders in this area of special education. For example, in this section, Parnes, Taylor, and Williams all were stimulated in some manner by the ideas in Guilford's theory. Taylor's and Williams's approaches actually were developed as educational counterparts to Guilford's psychological model.

It is important at this point to distinguish between the work of Guilford and of Mary N. Meeker. Guilford, a psychologist and theorist, spent most of his professional life conducting research on human abilities, their structure and function, and means of testing them. Using factor analytic statistical techniques, he attempted to identify or isolate the basic abilities that are a part of human intelligence. After several years of testing and analyzing various measures of ability, Guilford developed a morphological model to describe what he had found through his research. He continued in his attempts to isolate abilities predicted by the model but not yet identified by psychological tests.

Meeker, an associate of Guilford's, became interested in the more practical psychological and educational implications of the model. She developed extensive testing materials, test item mapping procedures for development of *Structure of*

Intellect (SOI) ability profiles using existing data, workbooks for use with children, computer programs for analyzing ability profiles and developing prescriptions, and materials for training teachers and others to use the model. In addition, Meeker (1969) researched on the unique ability patterns of various cultural and clinical groups as well as the effectiveness of her training materials on the development of specific abilities.

The SI model (Guilford, 1959, 1967) depicts human intelligence as consisting of three "faces" or dimensions: an *operation* is performed on a particular kind of *content,* yielding a certain type of *product.* There are four types of information or content of thought—figural, semantic, symbolic, and behavioral. There are five types of thinking processes or operations—cognition, memory, convergent production, divergent production, and evaluation. When the intellect acts upon a particular type of content, the result is one of the six types of products: units, classes, relations, systems, transformations, and implications. The intersection of each of the three dimensions results in a unique ability or a component of intelligence. This means that there are potentially 120 separate human abilities (4 $\times$ 5 $\times$ 6 = 120).

Guilford's Structure of Intellect model can be used effectively to plan Individualized Education Programs (IEPs) to develop the intellectual abilities of gifted children. Research has shown that the approaches designed by Meeker can be effective in enhancing specific abilities. However, they are not recommended as a total framework for curriculum development since they were not designed for that purpose. Perhaps the most important drawback is their tendency toward fragmentation. The SI approach needs to be combined with a different model (e.g., Bruner, Taba, or Renzulli) to provide the important elements that are lacking.

Lawrence Kohlberg: Discussions of Moral Dilemmas

Kohlberg's (1966) theory of the development of moral reasoning and his approach to moral education is a response to the failure of indoctrination programs and shows his disagreement with the idea of ethical relativity as a basis for values education (Kohlberg, 1971). He rejects the idea of ethical relativity on a philosophical basis. His key idea is that although values relating to personal choice are equally appropriate, values related to basic moral questions are not. In other words, there are certain universal ethical principles. In the late twenties, a classic study of children's cheating and stealing by Hartshorne and May (1930) shocked the educational community by showing that the indoctrination approaches had been ineffective. Children who attend Sunday school, participate in Boy Scouts and Girl Scouts, and whose parents emphasize ethical behavior do not behave more ethically than children who do none of these things, their report shows.

In direct contrast to the attempts to develop ethical behavior through indoctrination is the values clarification approach, which takes the position that the school's and teacher's responsibility is not to indoctrinate children as to what values they should hold but to assist them in following a process whereby they think seriously about the values they have and those they should hold. A fundamental idea behind this approach is that of ethical relativity; there are no universal ethical principles because values and ethics are relative. As long as an individual has followed the values clarification processes of choosing, prizing (i.e., believing in the importance of a value), and acting, all values developed are equally valid.

Relative to his philosophical position, Kohlberg (1966) studied the development of moral reasoning by interviewing 50 boys over a period of time, posing moral dilemmas to them, and asking them first to tell what would be morally right for the individual to do and second to tell why this action would be right. He found that children's reasoning about moral issues proceeded through certain stages in a sequential order and became more sophisticated at each stage. Numerous individuals, including Kohlberg, his colleagues, and his students, subsequently have studied how this development can be facilitated. They have concluded that educators can encourage the development of higher levels of moral reasoning through methods emphasizing class discussion of moral dilemmas.

Kohlberg's (1966) most basic assumptions form a comprehensive theory of moral development and are based on Piaget's theories and research on the development of thinking. Essential to the understanding of Kohlberg's stage theory is the realization that his is a cognitive approach. He is studying, and suggesting that educators attempt to develop, moral reasoning rather than moral behavior. He holds that sophisticated moral reasoning usually leads to ethical behavior, so educators should concentrate on reasoning. By establishing a setting in which students are exposed to moral dilemmas and encouraged to discuss them, educators set the stage for cognitive conflict to occur and for pupils to hear reasoning at a higher stage than their own. This then leads to more rapid movement through stages than would occur if the normal course of development were followed.

The most important practical aspect of Kohlberg's approach is the discussion of moral dilemmas. These are chosen or created on the basis of several criteria: (a) a central character must decide between alternative possibilities for action, (b) at least one moral issue must be involved, and (c) society should lend support for any of several actions that the protagonists could take. Dilemmas are presented to students and a discussion follows.

Since the major advantages of the Kohlberg approach involve content modifications and its major disadvantages are in the process area, his would seem to be a valuable method to use in gifted programs when combined with one of the process models such as the Taba *Strategies*. It also could be combined effectively with a *Creative Problem Solving* approach if the teacher were to select moral or ethical problems as the focus. Although the research is inconclusive about the validity of Kohlberg's Stages 5 and 6 (the principled level) as natural developmental stages, the model does provide a valuable goal for programs for the gifted: the development of sophisticated moral reasoning.

Sidney J. Parnes: Creative Problem Solving

One approach widely used in programs for the gifted is the creative problem-solving model developed by Sidney J. Parnes, director of the Creative Problem Solving Institutes held at the State University of New York at Buffalo (SUNY) and other locations around the country. Influenced greatly by the work of Alex Osborn (1963) in applying imagination to the practical problems encountered in the business and professional worlds, Parnes (1977, Note 3) attempts to develop the most comprehensive process possible for stimulating the use of imagination in practical situations. He uses his own applied research on the development of creative thinking in the program at SUNY as well as the applied and theoretical research of others to come up with a process that is comprehensive, theoretically sound, and, above all, effective. He is continually involved in modifying this process as new information becomes available. His institutes are attended yearly by many of the most widely known researchers and theorists in creativity development as well as individuals just beginning to be interested in their own or others' progress.

The Parnes *Creative Problem Solving* Model provides a structured method of approaching problems in an imaginative way. It is different from other methods in its emphasis on the generation of a variety of alternatives before selecting or implementing a solution. In each of the five steps of the process—fact finding, problem finding, idea finding, solution finding, acceptance finding—the problem solver defers judgment during ideation or generation of alternatives to avoid inhibiting even the wildest possibilities, which may turn out to be the best ideas. Judgment is exercised at a more appropriate time. The purposes of the model are twofold: (1) to provide a sequential process that will enable an individual to work from a mess to arrive at a creative, innovative, or effective solution, and (2) to enhance the person's overall creative behavior.

Of the many teaching-learning models used in programs for the gifted, the Parnes model provides the most hard data attesting to its effectiveness. It also demonstrates the most versatility based on its successful practical application in business, government, the health care professions, and education. However, as a *total* approach to curriculum development for the gifted, the Parnes *Creative Problem Solving* Model is difficult to justify as qualitatively different and/or comprehensive. It can be combined easily with other, different approaches in a way that can minimize or eliminate the disadvantages of lack of comprehensiveness.

Joseph S. Renzulli: The Enrichment Triad

Several teaching-learning models have been developed for education and used in programs for the gifted, but a popular one designed specifically for teaching gifted children is Renzulli's (1977) *Enrichment Triad*. Educators of the gifted as well as critics of special provisions for such pupils have long been concerned about providing qualitatively different (see Chapter 1) learning experiences for these children. Therefore, Renzulli presents an enrichment model that can be used as a guide in developing defensible programs for the gifted that are qualitatively different. Renzulli's model provides for moving the student through awareness, the learning of process, and the development of a product using three different but interrelated types of learning activities.

The *Enrichment Triad* has three types of enrichment:

Type I: General Exploratory Activities
Type II: Group Training Activities
Type III: Individual and Small Group Investigations of Real Problems

The first two are considered appropriate for all learners; however, they also are very important in the overall enrichment of gifted and talented students for two important reasons. First, they deal with strategies for expanding student interests and developing thinking and feeling processes, necessary elements in any enrichment program. Second, they represent logical input and support systems for Type III enrichment activity, which is the one uniquely appropriate for the gifted.

Type III enrichment is the major focus of this model since it is the element considered the most important for gifted learners. Renzulli recommends that approximately half of the time that gifted students spend in enrichment activities be in these types of experiences. Type III enrichment consists of activities in which the student becomes an actual investigator of a real problem or topic by using the methods of scientists in the field, even if they are not as sophisticated. The students must spend enough time in Types I and II to develop independence skills necessary for conducting a real study before starting Type III activities.

According to Renzulli, students must have three basic clusters of characteristics to benefit from his model: (1) above-average intelligence, (2) above-average creativity, and (3) task commitment (motivation-persistence). There is a definite interaction among these three that results in superior performance.

The *Triad* model does have its drawbacks, mainly because of its newness and the tendency of educators to adopt it blindly without considering its philosophical basis and the requirements for implementation. However, teachers can implement it appropriately, giving careful consideration to its philosophical base, its specific strategies, and how these aspects fit into an individual's unique situation. With the benefit of longitudinal studies of its effectiveness, educators may be able to develop qualitatively different programs for gifted children that are defensible to anyone who would question their existence.

Hilda Taba: Teaching Strategies Program

One of the most promising process models for use with gifted children is the generic teaching strategies program developed by Taba. Her series of four sequential questioning techniques resulted from almost 15 years of research on children's thinking and how it could be developed (Taba, 1964, 1966). Few of the approaches used frequently in this field can provide similar evidence of their effectiveness in producing the growth in abstract reasoning that educators cite as their goal. Yet, only scattered programs for the gifted employ the Taba strategies. Perhaps this spotty use results from the fact that much of the literature is unavailable or difficult to find, or from the lack of an advocate—one who sees its potential and pushes for its acceptance. More importantly, perhaps, Taba's insistence that all children can develop abstract reasoning skills if assimilation and accommodation activities are paced appropriately has led educators of the gifted to dismiss the teaching strategies developed by someone with this attitude as inappropriate for their pupils.

Regardless of the reasons for only scattered inclusion of the Taba strategies in current programs, there is a more than adequate basis in theory and research to justify their use alone or in combination with other approaches in the education of the gifted.

The *Hilda Taba Teaching Strategies* are structured, generic methods in which the teacher leads students through a series of sequential intellectual tasks by asking them open-ended but focused questions. There are four strategies—concept development, interpretation of data, application of generalizations, and resolution of conflict (also called interpretation of feelings, attitudes, and values). The four, although not designed to be hierarchical or serial, can be used sequentially since they build upon each other. Within each strategy, however, there is a definite sequence to the questions, with a theoretical and practical justification for the order.

Learning how to use the *Hilda Taba Teaching Strategies* Program (Institute for Staff Development, 1971a, 1971b, 1971c, 1971d), is not simple. The strategies are complicated. Differences between an inappropriate and an appropriate teacher question or behavior that can throw a whole discussion off track often are subtle. Demonstrations, practice with critiques from experienced leaders, classroom tryouts, and self-analysis are necessary components in the learning process. Many teachers feel that it has taken them years to perfect their use of the Taba strategies. However, they also attest to the effectiveness of the strategies when implemented appropriately.

The Taba model suggests modifications of the regular curriculum that are appropriate for the gifted in all four areas discussed earlier. Although it is primarily a process approach, because of Taba's (1962, 1964) comprehensive approach to curriculum development and implementation, the model provides for many changes that are important in programs for the gifted. Suggested content modifications are in the areas of abstractness, complexity, organization, economy, and methods of inquiry while process changes emphasize higher levels of thinking, open-endedness, use of discovery, requiring students to verbalize their reasoning or evidence, and pacing. One product modification (transformation), and most of the learning environment changes (except complexity and high mobility), are suggested.

Calvin Taylor: Multiple Talent Approach

According to Taylor (1968a) all individuals, especially children of school age, have far more talents than they use. Much of this talent is wasted by allowing it to lie dormant for so many years while children are in school. By recognizing and developing these varied talents, several positive benefits can occur: many more persons will be able to excel in at least one area, thus making more individuals feel good about themselves; people will become more self-directed as they experience and display their unique talent profiles (Taylor, 1968b); schools will not lose so many students through drop-outs (Taylor, 1968b); and conversely, some individuals who are always at the top in academics will experience the feeling of being closer to the bottom in some talent area, thus gaining a more realistic picture of themselves in relation to others (Taylor, 1968b).

Taylor (1968a) suggests that a model such as Guilford's (1967), even though accurate, may be impossible to use for classroom practice since it contains so many separate elements. His suggested alternative is to group together certain of these abilities into six or seven world-of-work areas: academic, communication, creative planning, decision making, and forecasting. Thus, his is a practical model for classroom teachers as well as a way to make education more relevant by concentrating on real-world talents and abilities.

Adaptations of Taylor's *Multiple Talent Approach* can enhance a program even though, in its entirety, it may not be appropriate for use in categorically funded projects for the gifted because of its philosophy that most children are talented in some way. It provides a new way of looking at students and can serve as a model for making education more relevant to the real-life needs of adults. Gifted students, who may be very skilled academically, may need help in developing some of the practical skills addressed by this model. Taylor's approach encourages the development of thinking skills and the acquisition of knowledge as well as the evolution of practical talent areas.

Donald J. Treffinger: Self-Directed Learning

One of the important priorities expressed by educators of the gifted is a need to develop self-directedness or independent learning skills in students so they can continue their progress without constant supervision or assistance from an adult. Often these educators, along with parents, assume that because children are gifted they automatically are—or will become if simply turned loose—self-directed learners. Indeed, one of the characteristics of gifted children is that they are more independent than are others. However, not all of the gifted are independent learners, and even if they are more so than other children, they probably do not possess the skills that will enable them to completely direct their own learning or conduct their own research unless they have had some practice in being self-directed. Children who have been told what to learn, and how and when and where, and who always have had their learning and products evaluated by someone else cannot suddenly be expected to be able to take over these responsibilities and handle them.

Treffinger's (1975) model provides the structure needed to gradually develop in students the skills necessary to become self-directed learners. In fact, it is a model for moving both teacher and student toward a setting in which self-directed learning can occur. Its primary goal is the sequential development of skills in the student for managing the student's own learning, which builds upon the strengths of gifted children, enhances their involvement in their own learning, and increases their motivation by allowing them to study in areas of interest to them.

Within each of four instructional areas (identifying goals and objectives, assessing entering behavior, implementing instruction, evaluating performance), Treffinger identifies four levels. These levels are examples of the movement from teacher direction to self-direction and involve two intermediate steps between teacher direction and self-direction. In the first step toward self-direction, the teacher creates options from which the students choose. In the second, the students are involved in creating the choices. At the last level, self-direction, the student is in complete control of creating and choosing the options, although teacher advice or assistance is available.

Treffinger's model for self-directed learning can provide a valuable complement to other approaches used in programs for the gifted. It is a developmental, practical approach that builds upon some of the more salient (and often troublesome) characteristics of gifted children: their stubbornness when told what to do, their curiosity about a wide range of topics, their constant questions, their nonconforming nature, and their tendency to direct the activities in which they are engaged. It is not difficult to learn or understand but may be difficult for some to implement.

Frank E. Williams: Teaching Strategies for Thinking and Feeling

One of the most commonly used approaches in programs for the gifted is Williams's model for developing thinking and feeling processes. It provides an inexpensive idea book (Williams, 1970) and a total kit (Williams, 1972) that includes books, tapes, inservice training materials, and many practical materials for implementing the approach such as forms for recording student progress and for needs assessment of children. Since the approach is simple and practical, many school districts bought the program and have based their entire gifted program's curriculum on this approach.

The Williams (1972) program was not developed specifically for use with gifted children. In fact, its major purpose is to provide a model for enhancing the cognitive and affective processes involved in creativity or productivity in all children. The thinking processes of fluency, flexibility, originality, and elaboration along with the feeling processes of curiosity, risk taking, complexity, and imagination, are developed through the traditional subject matter content. The teacher uses a series of 18 strategies or modes of teaching.

Williams assumes that for a good education or optimum learning to occur, there must be a proper mix or interaction among three basic elements: what children are or can become (pupil behaviors), the curriculum (subject matter content), and what teachers can do with both the curriculum and the students (teacher behaviors). Because of this interaction, the design of any learning experience for any child should consider pupil behaviors, teacher behaviors, and content areas.

From this basic philosophy, Williams (1970) developed a morphological model with three dimensions: the curriculum, teaching strategies, and student behaviors. As with other morphological frameworks, this model depicts these components as interrelated parts of a whole. There is no hierarchy of strategies or behaviors either implied or intended. The framework can be used as a structure for curriculum planning, instruction, and teacher training. In short, it provides a vehicle for intersecting a given subject area with any teaching strategy to produce student behavior that is creative.

As with the other approaches discussed in this section, Williams's model does not provide a comprehensive program for curriculum development for gifted students. However, it offers certain unique features that highly recommend its use with the gifted: its process modifications, individualization, and concentration on the cognitive and affective behaviors necessary for creativity development.

Readers who decide to implement this approach, however, are urged to develop procedures for assessing the effectiveness of the strategies since such data are not available. Use of the needs assessment instruments for evaluation of progress is strongly advised as is comparison of this method with others to determine the most effective strategies for use with gifted children.

COMBINING THE MODELS

As can be discerned from these descriptions, a number of teaching-learning models are available for use, singly or combined, in programs for the gifted. These vary in their purposes as well as in the content, process, product, and learning environment modifications appropriate for the gifted that they address directly. For example, Bruner modifies content through suggesting that it be organized around basic concepts. He also addresses the process of discovery, although his major modifications are in the area of content. The cognitive and affective taxonomies, on the other hand, provide modifications mainly in the process area—and in especially one aspect of process, the development of higher levels of thinking.

Guilford provides a unifying model for changes in content, process, and product as dimensions of a learning task. However, he does not make all the suggested curricular changes in any of the areas. Thus, even though his theory is somewhat more comprehensive than many others, it alone does not provide a complete curriculum. The same is true of Renzulli's *Triad*. Although it offers a comprehensive framework for an overall approach, the educator must add other process models such as Bloom, Taba, Taylor, Kohlberg, and Krathwohl to provide guidance in the development of Type II activities. Treffinger's developmental approach to self-direction can provide the teacher with methods for moving students toward the development of their Type III investigations.

Some similarities also should be noted. Most of the models modify process but few consider content changes at all. In fact, many of them make very similar process changes because of their emphasis on higher levels of thinking and on development of creative or divergent thought processes. Most also include an emphasis on the thinking skill of evaluation (e.g., Bloom, Krathwohl, Guilford, Parnes) or decision making (Taylor).

Whether these models are combined or used separately, their similarities and differences must be considered. In other words, they must be combined so that the total curriculum is comprehensive; however, the degree of overlap also must be considered. It is not desirable to place undue emphasis on process skills or on one process skill simply because more methods and materials are available for use. The chapters that follow provide a suggested process to follow in the development of a comprehensive curriculum that is qualitatively different and appropriate for gifted children.

NOTE

1. References for information about these models are given in this section and are not repeated in later chapters.

Chapter 5

General Considerations: Their Effect on Adaptation or Selection of Models

When making decisions about the types of teaching-learning experiences to provide for gifted pupils, factors related to the setting, the students, the teacher, and the theoretical models all must be considered. Factors involving the setting include both the school system and the individual school and their philosophies, administrative structure, support services, resources, other students and teachers, the regular classroom program, the community, and the parents. Factors related to the models include their authors' theoretical assumptions about learning, teaching, and giftedness, the curricular modifications they provide that are appropriate for gifted students, the elements of the approaches, and research on their effectiveness.

THE SETTING

School System Structure and Philosophy

One of the first aspects of the setting that provides either facilitation or constraints is the school system's structure and philosophy regarding the gifted program. In some cases, a well-developed philosophy and well-defined curricular emphasis dictate the kind of model each teacher should use. Although these cases are somewhat rare, the district curriculum needs to form the basis for each teacher's curriculum to provide some consistency across the program. Other models then can provide different dimensions based on individual school, teacher, or child factors. For example, if the district philosophy indicates that the emphasis in gifted programs should be on creativity or the development of divergent thinking skills, a teacher could choose *Creative Problem Solving* (Parnes), *Teaching Strategies for Thinking and Feeling* (Williams), *Multiple Talent Approach* (Taylor), or the *Structure of Intellect* (Guilford) with an emphasis on the divergent thinking section. If district policy further dictates the use of the *Structure of*

Intellect (SI), any one of the models having a similar philosophy can provide a complement. Even those focusing on other aspects of a differentiated program can be used with the basic model. *Self-Directed Learning* (Treffinger), for instance, allows children independence in their choice of SI-type activities.

Type of Service

A second aspect of district policy and philosophy to be considered is the type of service gifted students are receiving. Are they being served in the regular classroom by an itinerant teacher whose primary responsibility is as consultant to the classroom teacher? Are they in a resource room—for part of each day, or one day a week for one hour, or for several hours on several days, or for a majority of each week? Is the program one of semiseparation or a full-day class? Are they in a separate school for gifted children?

Each of these situations has different implications for choosing or adapting a model. For example, with a consulting teacher, it is impossible to implement a method such as Bruner's totally unless it or a similar approach already is a part of the regular curriculum. If a Brunerian philosophy is important, it probably will be possible to encourage emphasis on the more abstract and complex concepts through extending activities or possibly to encourage the teacher to allow student inquiry into some area related to the regular curriculum. If an emphasis on basic concepts is the focus, the abstract ideas presented to gifted children need to be those that can be developed from existing content. The consulting teacher looks at the scope and sequence, concepts, and data being taught in the classroom, consults an authoritative source of generalizations, and chooses those that can be developed. Extending activities can be devised to lead students toward discovery of more abstract ideas.

With varying degrees of separation from the regular classroom, fewer constraints are placed on selection or adaptation of a model for the gifted program. In a special school, unless system or school policy dictates a specific curriculum, choice of an approach is almost unlimited. A special class, being more a part of the regular curriculum, still will have a wide range of choices, constrained only by school policy or philosophy. In resource rooms, or semiseparation programs, the percentage of time spent in the gifted program is a factor to consider. When students spend a small amount of time, such as an hour each day or an hour every two or three days, the regular curriculum plays a big part in their education and the gifted program must build more upon it. Of course, the gifted program can be completely separate, as often is the case. However, a separate program, often including only playing games, is impossible to justify as a comprehensive approach to educating gifted children.

In building upon the regular curriculum, a resource room teacher of the gifted can use models such as *The Taxonomies of Cognitive and Affective Behaviors* to extend children's thinking into the higher levels. To do this, the first step is to ascertain what skills and knowledge are being developed and to what extent. In other words, does the teacher handle application, analysis, and higher level activities, or concentrate on the lower levels of knowledge and comprehension? If the regular classroom teacher concentrates on these lower levels, activities that take the children further up the taxonomies then can be devised for the gifted program to extend their thinking. Other models can be used in a similar manner.

Another consideration with resource room programs is frequency of contact. If children come to the resource room or to a districtwide center once a week or two weeks, it is difficult to maintain continuity in the program. Each experience almost needs to be a separate one unless two conditions are met: (1) there is some contact with children between the times they are in the program, and (2) regular classroom teachers are very much a part of the process. When trying to use an approach such as the *Enrichment Triad,* for example, unless children can work on their Type III activities and get assistance on them during the intervening weeks or days, they tend to lose interest in their projects. One of the most frequent criticisms of resource room or center models for delivery of services is the absence of continuity in the program itself as well as the lack of coordination between the regular and special programs. Even when special teachers are allowed planning and consulting time to develop this coordination, it is difficult to achieve.

Individual School Structure and Philosophy

When considering the individual school as an aspect of the setting, two of the above factors also are present—administrative structure and philosophy. The school philosophy may be similar to or in conflict with the district's, or may be concerned with a different dimension of children's learning. A conflict situation may be the most difficult to resolve but if the teacher is creative, problems often can be handled.

Assume, for example, that school district policy is to develop divergent thinking skills in gifted children and that it dictates the use of Williams's model as a basic approach. The individual school, on the other hand, is concerned that the gifted program teach academic content, particularly the abstract concepts not treated in the regular classroom. Since children, or anyone for that matter, must have something to be creative about, the two goals are not really incompatible although they may appear to conflict. Divergent thinking skills can be developed in the context of academic subjects. The teacher chooses the abstract concepts to serve as an extension of the regular curriculum as discussed earlier, and the thinking exercises build upon and extend knowledge gained in the regular classroom. Another way to deal with a similar conflict if district policy does not suggest a specific model is to use the *Hilda Taba Teaching Strategies* since they meet the dual objectives of developing knowledge and abstract ideas while also enhancing flexibility and fluency in ideas.

Service Delivery

The type of service delivery in individual schools influences the program in the ways discussed earlier with regard to the school district. Another aspect of the administrative structure to consider at the school level is the amount of flexibility allowed in both scheduling and providing freedom for children to go beyond the limits of the building. If the restrictions cannot be eliminated, the teacher will not be able to fully implement a model such as the *Enrichment Triad,* which requires that students be able to learn anywhere. They will not always be able to get everything they need at the school or be able to do all their off-campus work after class hours. With little flexibility in scheduling, a model such as the *Enrichment Triad* is difficult to implement. Students will want to work with other teachers or off-campus mentors. If students as a group are interested in working together on a project, their schedules may need to be rearranged to enable them to meet regularly. They should not be expected to do all of their group work after school hours.

Resources

A third school-related factor is the availability of resources. To implement such approaches as Bruner's and Renzulli's, a variety of methodological as well as content resources is needed and must be available when required. Advanced equipment should be provided or the children should be allowed to go off-campus when necessary to use equipment made available through other entities. Additional resources such as other special educational programs, and support services such as counselors, speech therapists, and psychologists will have an effect on the curricular approach.

If, for instance, a learning disabilities resource program is available in the school, it can serve gifted children with learning problems. The learning disabilities teacher is responsible for remedial activities, leaving the teacher of the gifted free to concentrate on talents and strengths. Ready access to the services of a school psychologist allows the teacher of the gifted to plan more carefully for individual needs than if all the testing were the latter's responsibility. Counselors can provide support in affective areas by leading discussions about moral dilemmas using Kohlberg's model, conducting sessions to resolve family or other conflicts using the Taba strategy, and guide children to higher levels of affective behavior through use of the *Affective Taxonomy.* If such support is available, the teacher of the gifted can concentrate on other areas.

Students

Another factor that will influence curriculum development is the other students in the school—their level of ability/intelligence, their achievement, and their reactions to the gifted pupils in the program. Since instruction in a school and/or classroom normally is directed toward the average pupil, the ability and achievement levels of other students have a great deal of influence on instruction in regular classrooms. If the general ability level is high, the curriculum for the special program builds from a higher base and may need fewer modifications of content, process, and products to meet the needs of gifted children. For instance, the subjects taught in regular classrooms may already be complex and abstract and may be paced rather rapidly so that they are appropriate for many gifted students. On the other hand, if the general ability and achievement levels are low, many curricular modifications may be needed to compensate for the lower level of classroom instruction.

A related factor is the percentage of the total school population eligible for special services or being served by the gifted program. In schools where a high percentage of children are identified as gifted and in need of curricular modifications, the educator may consider implementing an approach such as the *Enrichment Triad* with Type I and Type II activities in the regular classroom and Type III available for students who have a well-developed interest area and are ready to carry out an investigation. The teacher also may consider an approach such as Treffinger's, where the regular classroom teachers gradually move students toward more self-direction. When they reach a high level of independence, they begin to work with a special teacher of the gifted. Williams's model also is appropriate for use in all classrooms. The program for the gifted then can focus on areas other than creativity development. If very few students are gifted, a more comprehensive approach such as Bruner's may be needed to form the basis for the curriculum and be implemented with a few children for longer periods during the day.

The reactions of other students to the gifted may influence the type of program. If there is a great deal of hostility toward someone who is taken out of the regular classroom for special instruction, a consulting teacher model may be required. With such a method, the choice of a curricular model for the gifted program is restricted of necessity since its implementation depends largely upon the regular classroom teacher. An individualized approach such as Williams's or Guilford's may be the most appropriate for this kind of setting.

Other Teachers

Perhaps the most important factor in the school setting is the other teachers and their attitudes toward gifted students, special provisions for these pupils, and the curriculum in their classrooms. There seem to be two general continuums of attitudes toward gifted students. At one extreme of the first continuum are those who believe that the gifted will make it on their own and that no special educational provisions are necessary at all; at the other extreme are those who believe that special programs are an absolute necessity and that educators should be doing everything possible to meet these students' needs. Attitudes on the second continuum are related to the type of services gifted students need and range from simply turning them loose to providing a structured program that force-feeds them according to what educators feel is necessary.

These two general continuums, as well as other personality and school-related factors, result in some degree of willingness or reluctance to provide curricular modifications appropriate for the gifted students. If the gifted program consists of self-contained classrooms, attitudes of other teachers will not have a great deal of effect on curriculum development. However, if the program for the gifted uses a resource room or consulting teacher model, the faculty's negative attitudes and reluctance to provide modifications will impose substantial restrictions on the kind of program that can be developed. Any approach that depends on the willingness of the regular classroom teachers to be flexible in allowing students to leave the classroom to conduct investigations or make presentations (as does the *Enrichment Triad* or a comprehensive Brunerian approach) will be limited by the lack of cooperation. If follow-up is needed through SI exercises in the classroom or through independent research, a lack of cooperation again will be a limiting factor.

Regular Classroom Programs

Attitudes of teachers also are reflected in the quality of the regular classroom provisions for gifted students. Other than the general level of instruction based on the ability of the majority of students, two aspects of the regular classroom program are of primary importance. One is the overall degree of individualization for all children, the other is the number and type of curricular modifications made for gifted students. If, for instance, the overall philosophy is that of providing for individual differences in learning rates, interests, and achievement levels, these modifications will not need to be made for the gifted program. The curriculum can concentrate, for example, on abstractness, complexity, and development of higher levels of thinking rather than pacing and variety. Depending on the amount of independent work or self-directed learning in the regular classroom, there may be a need for an emphasis on Type II activities (e.g., simulation games, discussions) that require small-group interaction. If no individualization is occurring, then the gifted program must be comprehensive enough to satisfy many individual needs.

Some regular classroom teachers may be providing curricular modifications already in a few or several areas. One teacher may be a firm believer in a discovery approach, another may be using Bloom's *Taxonomy* as a basis for encouraging higher levels of thinking, still another may be placing a great deal of emphasis on creativity and divergent thinking, while yet another may not be making any appropriate modifications. As the regular classroom program becomes more suitable to the characteristics of gifted children, their teacher gains more flexibility in the choice of a curricular approach.

THE COMMUNITY

A key aspect of the setting is the community, both its general characteristics (i.e., socioeconomic status (SES) level, philosophy regarding the purpose of education, philosophy on special provisions for the gifted) and those of the parents of gifted children in the school. The socioeconomic level may have its greatest impact in the overall feelings of the value of education. Middle-class society and upwardly mobile groups tend to place great emphasis on the value of education, lower and upper classes seem to value it less. In communities where the overall emphasis on education is low, there is less likelihood that a program for the gifted will seem important and be supported. Often, the emphasis on the basics in low SES communities precludes any concern for gifted or talented children. Thus a program for the gifted in such a community would need to be low key, which indicates that a model such as the *Triad* is not acceptable since it is quite likely to become a high visibility program as children go out into the community and do research, then present their results to outside audiences.

In general, the community philosophy regarding the purpose of education influences the focus of the program, whether the emphasis is on talent or creativity development for all children or on accelerated academic achievement for those who are capable. Although the teacher of the gifted should not respond to all the whims of the community, these values must be considered. If the emphasis is on creativity development for all children, for instance, *Creative Problem Solving* or the Williams model are good choices, while the Taylor model can be implemented for an entire school if talent development for all is important. For a combined emphasis on academic learning and creativity, the teacher can select the *Hilda Taba Teaching Strategies* alone or combined with another approach.

Community values and philosophy as well as those of parents perhaps have their greatest impact on a program's emphasis on moral reasoning and affective development. In conservative communities where the belief is that moral reasoning and values are the sole responsibility of the home, it is difficult to implement Kohlberg's *Moral Dilemma* discussions or use Krathwohl's *Affective Taxonomy* on a regular basis. Parents of students in the program, of course, are the most important consideration in this respect.

The Parents

In addition to the more general influences of values, SES level, and perception of the purpose of education just cited, the parents of gifted children have an impact on the curricular model(s) chosen because of (a) their knowledge of the alternatives available for programs, (b) their general familiarity with the effectiveness of different types of programs, (c) the level of involvement they desire, and (d) their perceptions of the needs of their children.

Although these are factors that can be changed through education and through positive interactions between parents and professionals, they certainly are factors to consider when beginning a new program. If parents are not familiar with the full range of options, they may have in mind a certain kind of program and be opposed to other types. They may not be familiar, for example, with the research showing the effectiveness of creativity development programs in enhancing divergent thinking and problem solving and thus be opposed to this sort of approach. A lack of familiarity with research showing the importance of motivation and creativity to later professional productivity can result in the belief that emphasis on these characteristics also is unnecessary.

Parents, of course, may perceive their children differently from educators since they see them in a completely different setting. Students who may appear bored in school and perhaps never show real excitement about any project may have a million projects going on at home. Thus, the teacher may perceive that the student needs to develop new interest areas while the parent may feel that the child needs to narrow those interests and follow through on a few of them. Children who are creative and divergent at home may be so concerned with getting right answers and competing with friends that they are afraid to offer different answers. They also may be more creative in a nonacademic setting than in an academic one. Because of these differing perceptions, parents may seek emphasis on an aspect of the child's development different from what the teacher may deem important. These differing perceptions eventually must be resolved but at first the teacher may need to supplement the chosen approach to satisfy parental wishes.

A final characteristic of parents is the level of involvement they desire in the education of their children. Kroth (1980) has identified four levels of involvement that professionals must respect. The first is informational. At this level, parents want to know why their child is considered gifted, what special programs are being provided, and what the pupil's progress is. They also are willing to share their information about the child. At the second level, participation, parents join in making decisions about special class placement, attend IEP conferences, open house activities, science fairs, and field trips, and assist their child in school-related projects. The third level is interactive. Parents at this level want to become involved in the actual planning of educational experiences for their child. These parents do not want an IEP or a placement decision handed to them but seek to assist in its development. Parents no doubt are interested in educational workshops on topics such as "What the Research Says About Creativity Development," "How to Educate Your Child at Home," or "Alternative Programs for the Gifted—Pros and Cons." Education through workshops may have to precede the parents' involvement in planning. Those at this level certainly need to be involved in some program advisory capacity. The fourth level, deep involvement, is appropriate for only a few parents. They are involved in work with other parents as buddies, workshop leaders, and officers in parent groups. They can be extremely helpful to professionals in their attempts to work effectively with other parents.

As for influence on the adaptation or selection of a model, parents at the informational level do not tend to have a great deal of effect since their main desire is to know what is happening. However, as they become more deeply involved, they will have a greater influence. Those at the interactive level, for example, may assist the teacher in developing an educational plan, including perhaps the selection of teaching-learning models to be used with their children. Parents at the highest level assist not only in the development of their child's plan, but also in the overall program approach. Since the special program will be more effective if parents are involved more than peripherally, a goal should be to move them beyond the informational level, respecting the fact that at first they may not feel comfortable as participants in planning. When implementing a model that requires the participation of parents at home (e.g., working on Type III activities outside the school), the teacher also should consider their willingness to be involved.

THE STUDENTS

The gifted students, of course, are the most powerful influence on curriculum development since the thesis of this book is that a special curriculum should be based on the unique traits of those to be served. Since the general curricular modifications presented in this book are derived from the research on characteristics of the gifted, the needs of such children as a group can be met by making these changes. However, within this general framework, the particular characteristics and needs of the children in a given program should receive further consideration as they may dictate how many of the content, process, product, and learning environment modifications are absolute musts and how many can wait for a while. These student characteristics also may influence the ways in which these modifications are made (i.e., what particular combination of teaching-learning models is used).

Both the common characteristics (average) and the range of characteristics (differences) will influence curriculum development. In general, the more homogeneous the group, the easier it is to choose a curricular approach. One or two models can be combined to form an overall approach, with others as supplements.

The more heterogeneous the group, the more difficult the task of designing a curriculum appropriate for all. It certainly is important with a heterogeneous group to choose a model that lends itself easily to individualization.

To illustrate the possible influence of group and individual characteristics on overall curriculum design, return to Table 1 in the introduction to Section I. In this chart, characteristics often found in gifted children are listed according to the clusters of learning, motivational, creativity, and leadership characteristics as in the *Scales for Rating the Behavioral Characteristics of Superior Students* (SRBCSS) (Renzulli et al., 1976). Across the top of the chart are the recommended curricular modifications in all four areas. An X has been placed in the intersecting columns and rows to indicate that a particular curricular modification is necessary because of a specific child characteristic. This chart actually is a summary of the material in the first section. To use it, first look at the column labeled Abstractness. Moving down this column, the reader can see that the content modification of abstractness builds mainly on the cluster of learning characteristics of the gifted. There is an X in every row in this cluster. In the process area, Higher Level Thought also is indicated by all of the learning characteristics. The process modification of open-endedness is justified by many of the learning, motivational, and creativity characteristics.

Application of the analysis in this chart to the present discussion leads to the conclusion that the common characteristics of the children to be served should indicate which of the curricular modifications are most important to implement. For example, if all the students to be served exhibit a strength in the cluster of learning characteristics, abstractness of content will be a must. Further, if all students exhibit a strength in the motivational characteristic "Prefers to Work Independently; Requires Little Direction from Teachers," the following curricular modifications are indicated: variety, methods, open-endedness, discovery, realistic evaluation, and the learning environment changes of student-centered, encourages independence, openness, and high mobility.

When there are fewer characteristics common to the group, modifications may be needed in all areas for at least one or two of the students, so the range of characteristics or the degrees of difference in its members also are important. Each child's characteristic strengths can be compared to those of the group and then analyzed with respect to the type of curricular modifications needed. Table 1 can be helpful in this process also.

In addition to these general characteristics of gifted students, both the commonalities and ranges of the following traits are influential: achievement, age, general level of intelligence, interests, socioeconomic level, background experiences, other talents, handicaps, self-concept, and learning style preferences. The curricular approach(es) should be adaptable to the ranges of characteristics and appropriate for the common and unique traits. Although most of the teaching-learning models recommended for use in gifted programs seem adaptable to all levels of these characteristics, some are more appropriate for selected groups. For example, Kohlberg's *Moral Dilemma* discussions can be most productive when students in the group are at different stages of moral reasoning. Discussions are much more stimulating and exciting if the students are challenging each other rather than if the teacher is providing the stimulus. Although moral dilemma discussions can be held with pupils of any age, it is much easier to identify content-related moral issues that are appropriate for junior and senior high school students than with younger children. When considering these elements, the teacher also should examine the assumptions of the model to determine how they match the particular characteristics of children in the program.

THE TEACHER

After the students, perhaps the second most powerful element to take into account in the development of a curriculum is the teacher(s) who will be responsible for its implementation. Research on the effectiveness of educational approaches has shown repeatedly that the single most important variable in determining success is the teacher (Callahan & Renzulli, 1977; Dunkin & Biddler, 1974; Gage & Berliner, 1979). If the educator does not have the skills necessary for implementing the methods and does not believe in their value, it is hopeless to expect a program to be effective.

Characteristics of teachers can be separated into three groups: philosophical, personal, and professional. Philosophical characteristics can have a general influence on curriculum development and are most likely to affect decisions regarding a strength vs. deficit approach, a focus on individual vs. group needs, separation vs. integration of children, and stress on social responsibility vs. development of individual needs. These issues are discussed in other sections of this chapter, particularly with reference to community and parental philosophy, so they are not covered again here. However, they should be considered either as a means of selecting teachers or as guides to the selection of teaching approaches. In other words, the philosophies of both the teacher and the curriculum cannot be incompatible if the program is to succeed.

Professional characteristics of teachers include traits related to skills as well as those resulting from their educational and experiential background. Usually these traits (except experiential background) can be changed if the individual is willing to acquire new skills and the opportunities to learn them are both available and affordable. Personal characteristics, on the other hand, are not changed easily—if at all. They include intelligence, motivation, self-confidence, and other personality traits. Again there are two choices, depending on the resources available and the timeline for implementing a program. One is to decide on the curricular approach and then choose teachers who have the skills and personal traits to implement that method. The other is to choose the teacher because of certain personal or professional traits and then have that person develop a curricular approach. Regardless of the choice of strategy, the problem of selecting a teacher will not go away.

Much has been written and a number of studies have been conducted on the subject of teacher selection. Space does not permit a review of the literature here. However, it may be useful to review the recommendations by Maker (1975) as a result of a thorough review of the literature and research. She recommends that the minimum criteria for selection of a teacher be (a) "an ability to relate effectively to the particular group of youngsters one is planning to teach" and (b) "an openness to change" (p. 17).

In addition, the special characteristics of the students to be taught necessitate consideration of other traits. For example, teachers of the intellectually gifted or academically talented must have a high degree of intelligence and self-confidence. Teachers of the creatively gifted should have a "high regard for imaginative ideas, a respect for the potentialities of the individual, a high regard for the teacher's responsibility to the child and the group's responsibility to the child, and a belief in the importance of enhancing pupils' self images" (p. 18).

Training can be expected to accomplish certain changes with regard to specific skills, attitudes, and competencies if teachers with these characteristics are selected initially. Minimum competencies expected of the trained teacher include both skill and willingness in the following areas: identification of children with a variety of talents, being student-directed more than teacher-directed, individualizing instruction, and assuming a variety of roles in teaching. These teachers also need skill and willingness in using questioning techniques or strategies that stimulate higher levels of thinking and familiarity with basic concepts, media, and methods in the academic areas being taught. The ability and willingness to provide a psychologically safe environment for the expression of ideas is especially critical.

These minimum criteria can form the basis for teacher selection. However, the particular curricular approach or theoretical model to be used can provide additional criteria or can suggest that certain of these traits be emphasized. For example, in implementing Treffinger's self-directed learning model, or guiding Type III investigations in Renzulli's, a student-directed attitude and skills in guiding pupils rather than prescribing for them are necessary, not just desirable. The Parnes, Taba, or Kohlberg models require a willingness on the part of the teacher to elicit ideas from students rather than present them.

In implementing most, if not all, of the models, two dimensions of personality are critical: the tendency to be judgmental vs. accepting and to be rigid vs. flexible. An individual who has a tendency to make judgments about the value of each student's answers or even quick decisions about what is generally right or wrong will have difficulty with the general principles of open-endedness, use of a discovery approach, proof/reasoning, freedom of choice, realistic evaluation, and the development of an environment of acceptance. Those with a tendency toward rigidity in their behavior as well as in their thinking no doubt will find many of these same principles difficult to implement. This personality trait also will have a more general impact on the individuals' willingness to acquire new skills as needed or to adapt their own methods to the school situation.[1]

One final characteristic to consider within the school is that of status with other teachers. What often occurs is that a new, inexperienced teacher is hired to begin the special program. If the program is self-contained, there may be no difficulties. However, if the support and cooperation of the well-established, experienced, well-respected teachers are needed, the new one (who may not have any background in the regular classroom and thus no common experiences) may have a myriad of problems. To expect such a person to implement an approach requiring the support and cooperation of most of the regular classroom teachers in a school is foolish indeed.

THE MODEL

The third major consideration (after the students and the teacher) is the model itself—its assumptions, effectiveness, comprehensiveness, purpose, and adaptability. A teaching-learning model is a structural framework that serves as a guide for the development of specific educational activities and environments. A model can be highly theoretical and abstract or it can be a more practical structural framework. Regardless of how theoretical or practical, the distinguishing features common to teaching-learning models are

a. an identified purpose or area of concentration
b. underlying explicit and implicit assumptions about the characteristics of pupils and about the teaching-learning process
c. guidelines for developing specific day-to-day learning experiences
d. definite patterns and requirements for these activities, and
e. a body of research surrounding their development and/or evaluation of their effectiveness.

Each of these common elements is described briefly along with some of the variations to be found in the models presented in the introduction to this section. The reader who may have skipped that introduction (as readers often do) is encouraged to read it before this section since it provides necessary background information.

Each model has an identified purpose, a focus, or an area of concentration. The concentration or focus area can be very broad or quite narrow. Renzulli's *Enrich-*

ment Triad, for example, was developed as a total enrichment program for the gifted, focusing on content knowledge, a wide range of intellectual skills, and the development of an investigative attitude. The Williams model, on the other hand, was developed to enhance creative abilities—a narrower range of intellectual and affective skills. Because it says something about a lot of things, the Renzulli model goes into each practice in less depth than does Williams since the latter is narrower in its scope.

Each model must make some theoretical assumptions regarding both the nature of the learner (e.g., the pupil's learning, motivational, intellectual, and emotional characteristics) and the nature or effectiveness of certain teaching methods. These assumptions can range from highly theoretical and complicated ones such as Kohlberg's assumption that all individuals progress through identifiable, invariant stages in their development of moral reasoning to one of Taylor's simple assumptions that individuals possess a variety of types of talent. The stage of development or proof of these assumptions also varies from model to model. A related aspect of assumptions is how clearly they are stated. Some authors clearly reveal the assumptions they reject and state the ones they accept, while others describe some but leave out other critical ones. Still others say nothing about either their implicit or explicit assumptions, and teachers are left to their own devices in uncovering the underlying ideas.

The third and fourth aspects of models are their guidelines for development of specific learning experiences. Along with these are associated requirements or standards by which their appropriateness is judged. The Bloom and Krathwohl *Taxonomies,* for example, provide definitions of cognitive and affective behaviors to enable the educator to design activities that systematically develop behaviors at each level in the hierarchy. One requirement, or standard, associated with the implementation of the models is that each lower level behavior is necessary before the next higher level behavior can be reached effectively. Associated with the Taba *Strategies* is a broad range of teacher attitudes and competencies that involve much more than simply knowing what sequences of questions to ask the children.

All teaching-learning models have some basis in research, either as a background for their development or as a justification for their use through measures of their effectiveness. There has been extensive research on the elements in the Parnes program, for instance, as well as numerous longitudinal and experimental studies of its effectiveness with various groups. The Taba strategies were developed and evaluated over a period of ten years. On the other hand, there has been little, if any, research on the effectiveness of the Williams strategies. Renzulli's model was developed out of his experience in evaluating programs for the gifted and based on reviews of research on the characteristics of gifted individuals; however, to date, there is very little research showing his model's effectiveness.

To summarize these considerations and to assist in selection, the following checklist is presented as a summary of the criteria educators can use in evaluating the teaching-learning models to decide if and how to incorporate them into the program. The five general criteria of appropriateness to the situation, comprehensiveness as a framework for curriculum development for the gifted, flexibility or adaptability, validity, and practicality are followed by specific questions teachers can ask themselves in making judgments.

Appropriateness to the Situation

1. To what extent do the purposes of the model match the needs of the students, the school philosophy, parental values, and teacher characteristics?
2. To what extent do the model's underlying assumptions fit reality? (e.g., if the model makes assumptions about the characteristics of gifted students in general, are they true of those in the program?)

Comprehensiveness

1. What content modifications are provided by the model?
2. What process modifications are provided by the model?
3. What product modifications are provided by the model?
4. What learning environment modifications are provided by the model?
5. Which of the modifications, not actually provided by the model, could be generated easily by the approach?

Flexibility/Adaptability

1. How easily can the model be adapted to all content areas or subject matter covered in the program?
2. How easily can the model be adapted to the present administrative structure(s) of the school and program?
3. How easily can the model be combined with others to provide a comprehensive program?
4. How easily can the model be used with the age level(s) of children served by the program?
5. How adaptable is the model to individual differences in gifted children?

Practicality

1. What materials or services are available to implement the approach?
2. What is the cost of these materials or services?
3. How much training of the special teacher and/or regular classroom teacher is needed to implement the model effectively?
4. How easily could the approach be implemented in the present situation?

Validity

1. How appropriate were the methods used in developing the model?
2. How much research is available to show its effectiveness as an educational approach?
3. How much research is available to show its effectiveness as an approach to use with gifted children?
4. How much evidence is there to indicate that the model is internally valid (or structurally sound)?
5. How defensible is the approach as a qualitatively different program for gifted students?

SUMMARY

This section has presented factors that can influence the selection or adaptation of teaching-learning models in curriculum development for gifted students. Now perhaps the task seems impossible. It isn't. A great deal of creativity may be necessary, but by adopting a problem-solving attitude, enlisting the support and assistance of key individuals in the school and community, and gradually implementing changes, an appropriate and comprehensive curriculum can be developed for gifted children. The rest of Section II presents a step-by-step problem-solving process that can be used in the development of a curriculum.

NOTE

1. For a further discussion of these personality types and their effect on the teaching of gifted children, see Maker (1975).

Chapter 6

A Step-by-Step Curriculum Development Plan

By adopting a positive attitude as well as enlisting the assistance and support of other individuals, educators can create a curriculum that fits each setting, the teacher, and the students. To develop this individualized curriculum, the educator must follow a step-by-step process in a systematic manner rather than haphazardly collecting a set of activities or games. This chapter describes such a process. It also includes work sheets that can be adapted or reproduced as they are to provide additional help for the curriculum developer. These work sheets were developed using the basic philosophy and methodology of *Creative Problem Solving* taught by Sidney Parnes (Noller, Parnes, & Biondi, 1976) in the annual Creative Problem Solving Institutes sponsored by the State University of New York, Buffalo.

INVOLVEMENT OF KEY INDIVIDUALS

No curriculum can be developed effectively by one person in isolation. There are too many factors to consider, too many people to satisfy, and too many problems to solve. The extent of others' involvement, however, is a variable that depends on the situation and the other individual(s). Some persons who can be helpful are parents, students, other teachers, support personnel in the school, administrators, and influential community members. In selecting people to assist in curriculum development, the educator should choose a majority of (a) influential, well-accepted individuals, (b) persons who are positive toward the program and toward education for the gifted, and (c) knowledgeable individuals. Sometimes involvement in planning can change negative attitudes but most of those selected should be positive already.

These individuals can be involved in a number of ways: they actually can write parts of the curriculum, they can simply react to what has been developed, or they can participate in identifying problems and possible solutions. Generally, the most effective involvement is in an advisory capacity. However, these persons should be involved from the beginning rather than after the curriculum has been developed.

To begin the curriculum development process, then, select an advisory group consisting of a variety of types of people, then plan an initial brainstorming meeting. At this session, provide a brief overview of the task and how the individuals are to be involved. Spend most of the meeting in brainstorming at the fact-finding step in the Parnes process. Use a chart or work sheet similar to Exhibit 6-1 either individually or in a group situation. A group brainstorming session seems to be the most productive but the work sheets can be used on an individual basis. First, list all the situational factors that might be important in the development of a curriculum. Next, choose from the list the ones that seem most important and identify limitations they might impose. Again, choose the most important ones from that list for further work. Using the list of limitations, develop as many ways as possible that these problems can be overcome. This list of solutions will be helpful as the process is continued.

At the same meeting or the next one, continue the fact-finding process by listing the unknown situational factors, their possible effect, and possible sources of answers. A chart or work sheet similar to Exhibit 6-2 can be used. First, list all the information about parents, students, the school, and the community that is unknown but needs to be known before the curriculum is developed. Choose the most important needs. Identify the possible effects this information might have and the sources for it. At this point, depending on the extent to which the advisory group is to be involved, assignments can be made. If the group or some of its members are to be actively involved in the process, this list can be used to assign the task of obtaining the needed information. Without the aid of the group, the teacher will have to obtain all the data.

DEVELOPING A DEFINITION

At this point, it is important to either develop or adopt a definition of the population to be served. If the school district, state, or school already has an accepted definition, the task is merely to modify it to fit the present situation. If there is no existing definition, then a longer process is necessary. There are numerous definitions of giftedness and talent with varying degrees of inclusiveness. Each of these should be examined before decisions are made. Following are some examples of definitions:

United States Office of Education (1972)

Gifted and talented children are those identified by professionally qualified persons who by virtue of outstanding abilities are capable of high performance. These are children who require differentiated educational

Exhibit 6-1 Work Sheet for Overall Curriculum Design

Work Sheet #1: Known Situational Factors

Known	Possible Limitation	Possible Solutions
List all the known factors about the school, community, and parents that may influence the development of a curriculum for the gifted.	List the limitations that might be placed on the development of the curriculum by important situational factors.	List all the ways the limitations might be overcome or avoided.
Now go back and circle the most important ones.	Now go back and circle the most important ones.	

Source: Adapted from *Creative Actionbook: Rev. Ed. of Creative Behavior Workbook* by R.B. Noller, S.J. Parnes, and A.M. Biondi by permission of Charles Scribner's Sons, © 1976.

Exhibit 6-2 Work Sheet for Overall Curriculum Design

Work Sheet #2: Unknown Situation Factors

Need to Know	Possible Effect	Source
List all the information that needs to be known about the school, community, parents, and students before a curriculum can be developed.	List the effects these unknown factors may have.	List all possible sources for the important information needed.
Now go back and circle the most important ones		Now decide who will gather the data from these sources.

programs and services beyond those normally provided by the regular school program in order to realize their contribution to self and society.

Children capable of high performance include those with demonstrated achievement and/or potential ability in any of the following areas, singly or in combination.

1. General intellectual ability
2. Specific academic aptitude
3. Creative or productive thinking
4. Leadership ability
5. Visual and performing arts
6. Psychomotor ability. (p. 2)

New Mexico State Department of Education (1975)

The quality of giftedness is a complex, multi-faceted human dimension which takes many forms. The gifted child is a productive or potentially productive individual who is original, fluent, flexible, or divergent in his behavior and is superior in intelligence and/or creativity. (p. 27)

Armijo, Atrisco, East San Jose, Kit Carson, Longfellow and Old Town Elementary Schools, Albuquerque Public Schools

Gifted and talented students are those children and youth whose abilities, talents, and accomplishments are outstanding in comparison with their peer group and/or the total school population. These are persons of exceptional promise in any of several fields including the following:

General intellectual ability
Specific academic aptitude
Creative thinking
Leadership ability
Visual or performing arts ability
Psychomotor development. (Kerr & O'Dell, Note 5, p. 12)

When examining these definitions, consider their common characteristics (e.g., capable of high performance, outstanding) as well as their differences (demonstrated or potential ability, areas of talent included). Note the elements that are considered important in your situation. The advisory group could be involved in this process by being (a) given copies of several definitions and asked to modify, select, or write one, (b) asked to write down all the elements the members feel are necessary to include in a definition, or (c) asked to react to the definition selected or developed and suggest modifications. The first alternative may be the most effective but it definitely will require that more time be spent on the activity than would the others.

NEEDS ASSESSMENT

Now that the population has been defined and selected, the time has come to identify its needs—both group and individual. In this process, it is helpful to begin with a comprehensive listing of characteristics of the gifted such as the *Scales for Rating the Behavioral Characteristics of Superior Students* (SRBCSS) (Renzulli et al., 1976) or a similar one and making an assessment of individual and group strengths and weaknesses. A work sheet such as Exhibit 6-3 provides a way to review the student characteristics and compile them. When using this work sheet (or a similar one), names of the children are listed in the column on the left, with the clusters of characteristics to be assessed across the top. The numbers correspond to a listing of the description of characteristics in Renzulli et al. (1976). For example, in the grouping of learning characteristics, if the SRBCSS is being used, characteristic 3 is "Has quick mastery and recall of factual information." Other characteristics can be listed on a separate sheet and keyed to a number on the work sheet. To complete the work sheet, consider each child carefully and make a $\sqrt{}$ or X to indicate whether the characteristic is a definite strength or a definite weakness. If unsure, put a ? in the square. If a finer distinction is desired, numbers from 1 to 4 could be assigned on each characteristic to indicate the degree to which the student possesses that trait; however, the numbers make the task more complicated. After completing the chart, it is helpful to eliminate the question marks by obtaining the needed information, if possible, before analyzing it. If not, the question marks are counted separately.

To interpret the chart, several aspects should be analyzed. First, calculate the group totals for each characteristic. Then examine the individual totals by cluster. Are the student's strengths clustered mainly in one area or are they spread evenly throughout the different areas? Where do the weaknesses cluster? The group's common characteristics also should be examined by cluster to see what, if any, patterns exist. After going through this process, using all ten scales of the SRBCSS, two teachers in one of the author's classes were surprised to find that the strengths of their children were clustered in the nonacademic areas, especially those related to creativity and leadership. Their perceptions of the most appropriate curriculum then underwent a radical change.

The common characteristics of the group as well as the amount and kind of individual differences are used in the planning process to decide which curricular approach(es) will form the basis of the program. If the actual population is unknown at the time the curriculum is being planned, it is helpful to review the characteristics of children now in the program, examine the procedures used to

Exhibit 6-3 Work Sheet for Overall Curriculum Design

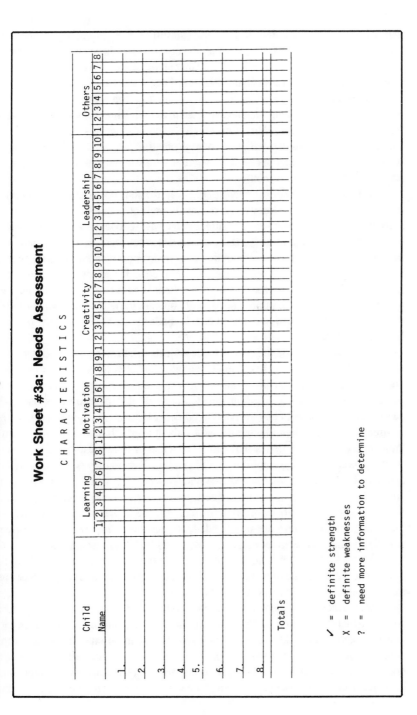

Work Sheet #3a: Needs Assessment

C H A R A C T E R I S T I C S

Child Name	Learning 1 2 3 4 5 6 7 8	Motivation 1 2 3 4 5 6 7 8 9	Creativity 1 2 3 4 5 6 7 8 9 10	Leadership 1 2 3 4 5 6 7 8 9 10	Others 1 2 3 4 5 6 7 8
1.					
2.					
3.					
4.					
5.					
6.					
7.					
8.					
Totals					

✓ = definite strength

X = definite weaknesses

? = need more information to determine

identify those to be included, and/or look carefully at the general population at the school or in the district. If, for example, the criterion for entrance into the program is an IQ score of 130 or above, it is likely that all the students will have strengths in most if not all of the learning characteristics. They may or may not exhibit clusters of strengths in creativity, motivation, and leadership. If a second criterion of high creativity is added, students can be expected to exhibit strengths in both these areas but not necessarily in the others. On the other hand, if identification is based on the students' exhibiting high intelligence or high creativity, there is likely to be a group with clusters of strengths in one area, another with strengths in the other, and still another with strengths in both.

A further assessment of the needs of each child also is necessary for planning to meet individual needs. One way to do this is presented in Chapter 7. However, since the method discussed there assumes that a basic curricular approach has been developed or selected already, the process described here is more general and perhaps more useful in overall planning than in developing an individual plan for one child. After or during the process of completing the needs assessment work sheet for the whole class (Exhibit 6-1), teachers should compile the student and parent perceptions of the pupil's needs and compare these to their own. Based on these perceptions of need, a decision can be made about the focus of the program for each student.

There are several ways these needs assessments can be accomplished. One is to ask the parents and student to complete the relevant SRBCSS scales. After ratings are made according to the directions on the forms, an asterisk or star can be placed beside the characteristic needing development. If this procedure is used, the parents and child should be reminded to consider both strengths and weaknesses, or strengths alone, when making decisions about needs. It also is helpful to limit the number of characteristics that can be checked or to request that the areas be ranked according to their importance. Otherwise, all areas may be checked and no priority of importance established. Another procedure is simply to have parents and student respond to open-ended questions regarding their perceptions of areas of need. A questionnaire developed for this purpose is presented in Exhibit 6-4. Since the questions here are open-ended, the responses may be very different, resulting in difficulties in comparing parent, student, and teacher perceptions of need. However, the task is not impossible since the general areas are at least the same. The same form can be used with both parents and students if the latter are mature enough to understand the instructions.

After all needs assessment information is collected, it can be compiled on a form similar to that in Exhibit 6-5. The first column should list the characteristics in each general area mentioned by at least one individual as important. In the next three columns, note whether the student, parent, or teacher perceives this as an area of need. These notes should indicate both the priority (e.g., most important, least important) and the type of need (strength needing development, weakness needing

Exhibit 6-4 Work Sheet for Overall Curriculum Design

Work Sheet #3b: Needs Assessment Questionnaire

Name _____   Date_____

<u>Instructions</u>: Please list below in order of importance no more than three specific strengths or weaknesses you feel need to be a focus of the gifted program this year.

LEARNING CHARACTERISTICS

Strengths needing development:

1. _____
2. _____
3. _____

Weaknesses needing remediation:

1. _____
2. _____
3. _____

MOTIVATIONAL CHARACTERISTICS

Strengths needing development:

1. _____
2. _____
3. _____

Weaknesses needing remediation:

1. _____
2. _____
3. _____

CREATIVITY CHARACTERISTICS

Strengths needing development:

1. _____
2. _____
3. _____

Weaknesses needing remediation:

1. _____
2. _____
3. _____

LEADERSHIP CHARACTERISTICS

Strengths needing development:

1. _____
2. _____
3. _____

Exhibit 6-5 Work Sheet for Overall Curriculum Design

Work Sheet #3c: Needs Assessment Summary

Child Name _____

Area/Characteristic	Perception of Need			Decision
	Student	Parent	Teacher	
Learning				
Motivation				
Creativity				
Leadership				
Other				

remediation). A useful code is $\checkmark$ = strength, X = weakness, 1 = most important, 2 = medium importance, 3 = least important. When these perceptions are compiled, everyone can discuss the work sheet and decide what the emphasis should be. To continue the process of overall curriculum design, the teacher can develop a second needs assessment (duplicating Exhibit 6-3) that summarizes the cooperative decisions on areas of need.

DEVELOPING A PHILOSOPHY

The next step in the process of curriculum development is to write a statement of philosophy to guide everyone's efforts. If a district and/or school philosophy already exists, it should be examined carefully and modified or expanded if necessary. Philosophy statements that relate to the program need to be considered so that inconsistencies can be resolved if necessary. Both district and school philosophies regarding education for all children and for the gifted should be considered. A philosophy statement also should address two general areas: (1) the purpose of education for the gifted and of this program and (2) the particular educational approaches that should be used in gifted programs.

In the first general area—purpose—the philosophy should address at least two major issues. The more difficult is the question of societal responsibility vs. individual need. Is the major purpose of the program to provide for the development of the potential of gifted students so they can become more effective and/or productive members of society? Or is its major purpose the development of talent for the benefit of the individual? Although some may argue that the two positions are not incompatible, it often is true that most people (if being honest with themselves and others) actually subscribe to one position or the other—not both. A second issue related to purpose is the question of division of responsibilities between the regular curriculum and the special program. In other words, what purposes are the same and what are different?

In relation to the second area, the philosophy statement should address general questions on the type of curriculum to be provided to achieve the purposes listed. It should look at the general relationship between the regular and special programs as well as between those at one school and the districtwide effort. The statement also should answer questions as to the extent of involvement allowed and expected from parents and students in the design of the program, and should address issues related to the assumptions made in teaching-learning models. Other areas to be covered in this general statement include (a) the number and kind of content, process, product, and learning environment modifications believed important; (b) the relative importance of individual and group needs in the planning process; and (c) the strategies to be used for assessing student progress. A final consideration is the relative emphasis on strengths, weaknesses, or a combination of these.

The philosophy statement should make clear the program's major emphasis as well as who is responsible for the decisions—the parent, the teacher, the student, or any combination of these.

An advisory group also can be helpful in the development of a philosophy statement. One way to involve this group is to provide some examples of philosophy statements such as these:

> The philosophy of the elementary school is to create a variety of learning environments which stimulate the interests and facilitate optimum development of each child. Within the framework of the "General Goals of the Albuquerque Public Schools Board of Education" and the *State Department of Education Minimum Standards,* the total EDUCATIONAL PROGRAM WILL DEVELOP AND EXTEND basic skills in communicative arts, quantitative thinking, environmental awareness, science, and social studies and will promote positive attitudes and respect toward self and others. Individual children's programs will be developed through ongoing assessments and diagnosis of strengths and needs. Because of the varied and ever-changing world and society we live in, we must constantly review the relevancy of our educational program. Recognizing the integrated nature of learning, the elementary program will be based on the cognitive, affective and psycho-motor domains of the learning process. (Kerr & O'Dell, Note 5, p. 21)

> Within the framework of the unique quality of giftedness these students will be provided with the skills to:

> 1. Acquire independence
> 2. Demonstrate development of affective skills
>   a. Acceptance of self
>   b. Maturity in accepting responsibility
>   c. Respect for others
>   d. Willingness to participate in groups
> 3. Demonstrate ability to plan
> 4. Implement creative thinking
> 5. Implement critical thinking (Kerr & O'Dell, Note 5, p. 22)

Albuquerque Public Schools (Armijo, Atrisco, East San Jose, [Kit Carson, Longfellow] and Old Town Elementary)

We are committed to an educational program designed to challenge the student through a multidimensional academic teaching approach involving special curricula and enrichment in the content areas of language development, social science and mathematics. We are also committed to the development of skills in creative problem-solving, and in critical, elaborative, and evaluative thinking processes. The ultimate goal of our program is to develop within the student a desire for excellence and a sense of responsibility to self, school, community, and to our changing society. (Kerr & O'Dell, Note 5, p. 23)

The group should, of course, be provided with copies of any local philosophy that pertains to the program. The members can be given the examples before a meeting and asked to think about these philosophies and what elements from each should be included in their own. At the meeting, the group can list ideas using Exhibit 6-6 as a work sheet or a chart.

First, the general philosophical considerations are listed. These include factors related to existing philosophies that can affect the philosophy of this program. The list is then reviewed and the most important factors noted. Next, the group lists elements that relate to the purpose of the program and notes the most important ones. The group then lists elements related to program approaches and again identifies the most important. At this point, it probably will be necessary to return to the list of purposes and the list of approaches and discuss each of the ideas, especially if they appear to conflict.

If the advisory group is expected to actually write the philosophy, the process may need to be extended. However, another way to handle the situation is to write the philosophy based on the group discussion, then send it to each member for individual reactions. One person in the group other than the developer also can assume the responsibility of writing, asking for reactions, and reviewing the philosophy.

DEVELOPING PROGRAM GOALS

Once a statement of philosophy is developed, the overall program goals must be written. These relate to the earlier needs assessment data and can be separated into yearly targets for program development if necessary. Program goals must be distinguished from student objectives. The former are overall statements of what the curriculum should or will accomplish for all pupils; student objectives are more specific statements of the desired behavioral results for each child. Stated program goals can correspond to the general areas of curriculum modification described in Section I.

To facilitate the process of development of goals from student needs, a work sheet similar to Exhibit 6-7 can be used. Major child needs that are to be developed in the program are listed in the left column according to the general areas of learning, motivation, creativity, leadership, other needs, etc. In the next column,

Exhibit 6-6 Work Sheet for Overall Curriculum Design

Work Sheet #4: Developing a Philosophy

General Philosophical Factors to Consider	Suggested Purposes	Suggested Approaches
List the general philosophical constraints or considerations that must be made. They may result from community values, district philosophy, or school policy.	List the elements you feel should be included in a statement of philosophy pertaining to the purpose of the gifted program.	List the elements you feel should be included in a statement of philosophy pertaining to the educational approaches to be taken in the gifted program.
Now go back and circle the most important ones.	Now go back and circle the most important ones.	Now go back and circle the most important ones.

Source: Adapted from *Creative Actionbook: Rev. Ed. of Creative Behavior Workbook* by R.B. Noller, S.J. Parnes, and A.M. Biondi by permission of Charles Scribner's Sons, © 1976.

Exhibit 6-7 Work Sheet for Overall Curriculum Design

Work Sheet #5a: Translating Needs into Program Goals

Child Needs/Area	Content Goals	Process Goals	Product Goals	Environment Goals

write program goals for content modification that will meet the child's needs. The third, fourth, and fifth columns are for listing the process, product, and learning environment goals.

Exhibit 6-8 illustrates how to complete this work sheet. In this example, only four child needs have been selected for the overall program focus; actually, in most instances, several such needs can be involved. To examine this example, refer back to Table 1 in the introduction to Section I. The child need "further development of insight into cause-effect relationship" is developed directly from the learning characteristic and focuses on the development of this strength in the pupils. Program goals are developed from the chart indicating which modifications are implied by each characteristic. For example, in this case, the program goals are to provide content that is abstract, complex, varied, and organized in a way that will facilitate economy, and includes the study of productive people. Process goals pertain to higher levels of thinking, open-endedness, discovery, and pacing. Product goals deal with investigations of real problems and presentations to real audiences. Environment goals are in all areas.

The second child need, "strengthen task commitment," is developed from the motivational characteristic "becomes absorbed and truly involved. . . ." Referring back to Table 1, the educator finds that some of the curricular implications are the same for this characteristic; therefore, some of the program goals are the same. Additional goals are in the process area (e.g., freedom of choice). To meet needs in the other areas (Exhibit 6-8), many of the program goals are the same, so they are not listed again.

This process can be the complete responsibility of the teacher or can be a task of the advisory group. However, unless the advisory panelists are familiar with the principles of curriculum development in education of the gifted, they may need considerable advance education. A more effective way to involve the group may be in decisions about child needs that should be the focus of the program or what goals need to be implemented (or added) each year.

CHOOSING TEACHING-LEARNING MODELS

After general program goals have been established and before the development of specific objectives, the teaching-learning models should be evaluated to determine their appropriateness for the situation. A decision about the model(s) to be used in the program must be made so that objectives can be developed from its framework. To facilitate this process, a work sheet has been developed that lists the criteria and questions described earlier in this chapter (Exhibit 6-9). To use this work sheet, write the criteria to be used in assessing the model in the column on the left and the model name across the top. Using the system of 1 = poor, 2 = average, and 3 = excellent, assign a rating to each model on each criterion. Next, total the

Exhibit 6-8 Work Sheet for Overall Curriculum Design

Work Sheet #5a: Translating Needs into Program Goals

Child Needs/Area	Content Goals	Process Goals	Product Goals	Environment Goals
Learning				
1. Further development of insight into cause-effect relationships	1a. Provide abstract content in all areas	1g. Provide for structured development of higher levels of thinking	1k. Provide situations allowing students to address real problems	1m. Provide an environment that is student-centered
	1b. Provide content with complex ideas in all areas	1h. Provide open-ended activities and ask open-ended questions	1l. Provide situations in which students can direct their products toward real audiences	1n. Provide an environment that encourages independence
	1c. Cover content areas that are different from the regular curriculum	1i. Provide experiences using a discovery approach		1o. Provide a climate that is free from restrictions and encourages divergence
	1d. Organize content around basic concepts and abstract generalizations	1j. Pace the presentation of new material rapidly		1p. Provide an environment that is accepting rather than judging
	1e. Strive for economy in learning experiences			1q. Provide a complex environment
	1f. Provide for the study of creative, productive people			1r. Provide an environment that permits high mobility
Motivation				
2. Strengthen task commitment	2a. Cover content areas that are different from the regular curriculum	2b. Provide open-ended activities and ask open-ended questions	2d. Provide situations allowing students to address real problems	2e. Provide an environment that is student-centered
		2c. Provide opportunities for students to choose topics and methods of studying them		2f. Provide an environment that encourages independence
				2g. Provide a climate that is free from restrictions and encourages divergence
				2h. Provide a complex environment
				2i. Provide an environment that permits high mobility

Exhibit 6-8 continued

Child Needs/Area	Content Goals	Process Goals	Product Goals	Environment Goals
Creativity				
3. Stimulate curiosity	3a. Cover content areas that are different from the regular curriculum	3b. Provide opportunities for students to choose topics and methods of studying them 3c. Pace the presentation of new material rapidly	3d. Provide situations allowing students to address real problems	3e. Provide an environment that is student-centered 3f. Provide an environment that encourages independence 3g. Provide an environment that is free from restrictions and encourages divergence 3h. Provide an environment that is accepting rather than judging 3i. Provide a complex environment 3j. Provide an environment that permits high mobility
Leadership				
4. Strengthen self-confidence		4a. Provide structured group interaction activities	4b. Provide situations in which students can direct their products toward real audiences	4c. Provide an environment that is student-centered 4d. Provide an environment that encourages independence 4e. Provide a complex environment 4f. Provide an environment that permits high mobility

Exhibit 6-9 Work Sheet for Overall Curriculum Design

Work Sheet #6a: Evaluating Models

Assign a rating to each model on each criterion question using the following code: 1 = Poor 2 = Average 3 = Excellent

Criteria and Questions

	Bruner	Bloom	Krathwohl	Parnes	Renzulli	Taba	Kohlberg	Taylor	Williams	Guilford	Treffinger	Totals	Comment
Appropriateness to the Situation													
1. To what extent do the purposes of the model match the school philosophy, parental values, and the teacher?													
2. To what extent do the underlying assumptions made in the model fit reality?													
Flexibility/Adaptability													
1. How easily can the model be adapted to all content areas of subject matter covered in the program?													
2. How easily can the model be adapted to the present administrative structure(s) of the school and program?													
3. How easily can the model be combined with others to provide a comprehensive program?													
4. How easily can the model be used with the age level(s) of children served in the program?													
5. How adaptable is the model to individual differences in gifted children?													
Practicality													
1. To what extent are materials and services available to implement the approach?													
2. To what extent is the cost of these materials and services within the program's budget?													
3. To what extent is the necessary training of regular and/or special teacher(s) available and affordable?													
4. How easily can the approach be implemented in the present situation?													

Exhibit 6-9 continued

Assign a rating to each model on each criterion question using the following code: 1 = Poor 2 = Average 3 = Excellent

Criteria and Questions	Bruner	Bloom	Krathwohl	Parnes	Renzulli	Taba	Kohlberg	Taylor	Williams	Guilford	Treffinger	Totals	Comment
Validity													
1. To what extent are appropriate methods used in the development of the model?													
2. To what extent is there research available showing its effectiveness as an educational approach?													
3. To what extent is there research available showing its effectiveness as an approach for gifted students?													
4. To what extent is there evidence that the model is internally valid?													
5. To what extent is the approach defensible as a qualitatively different program for gifted students?													
Totals													

ratings for each model to give an indication of overall effectiveness. This grid, with its individual ratings on each criterion and its totals for each approach, can be used as a guide in the selection of the particular combination of elements that will fit your situation. Additional criteria can be listed if appropriate to a situation or a completely different set can be developed.

One final assessment of the models needs to be made. As the reader may have noticed, the criterion of comprehensiveness was eliminated from the list provided earlier. To assess this factor, a more effective method is to list the curricular modifications in the column at the left as criteria and the models across the top (Exhibit 6-10). A checkmark is placed in the column and row if the modification is made, and left blank if it is not. The totals for each column indicate the comprehensiveness of the model. A similar method can be used to assess the model's comprehensiveness in providing the modifications serving as program goals. Using the same grid, checkmarks are made only in the rows pertinent to program goals. The column totals indicate the model's effectiveness in meeting those goals. Using the same format, other program goals can serve as the criteria in a similar evaluation process. If the advisory group is familiar with the models, it can assist in this process; if not, the task should be done by the teacher.

DEVELOPING OBJECTIVES AND STRATEGIES

Objectives should be separated into those dealing with content, processes, and products. Content objectives relate to the information and ideas that will be taught; process objectives involve the thinking processes or skills that will be developed; product objectives define the types of products expected of the students. Each of these types of objectives and their development is discussed separately. The following analysis assumes that the reader wishes to develop objectives in each of the areas that will form a comprehensive, appropriate curriculum for the gifted—in other words, one that will implement the modifications presented in Section I of this book. Readers can make their own decisions about what to eliminate if not all changes are to be made in the program.

Content Objectives and Plans

If the curriculum is to satisfy the requirements of abstractness, complexity, organization, and economy, the educator must begin by making decisions about the abstract ideas that will guide in the selection of specific data and will serve as a way to organize the presentation of this material. The first step is to develop or select abstract, complex, different, and methodological generalizations to be developed within each content area (or cutting across each content area) in the program. Several sources of generalizations as well as methods for judging them

Exhibit 6-10 Work Sheet for Overall Curriculum Design

Work Sheet #6b: Evaluation of Models

Rate each model on each criterion by placing a ✓ in the column if the modification is made by the model. If not, leave the space blank.

	Curricular Modifications	Bruner	Bloom	Krathwohl	Barnes	Renzulli	Taba	Kohlberg	Taylor	Williams	Guilford	Treffinger	Totals	Comment
Content Modifications	1. Abstractness													
	2. Complexity													
	3. Variety													
	4. Organization													
	5. Economy													
	6. Study of People													
	7. Methods													
Process Modifications	8. Higher Level Thought													
	9. Open-Endedness													
	10. Discovery													
	11. Proof/Reasoning													
	12. Freedom of Choice													
	13. Group Interaction													
	14. Pacing													
	15. Variety													
Product Modifications	16. Real Problems													
	17. Real Audiences													
	18. Evaluation													
	19. Transformation													
Learning Environment Modifications	20. Student Centered													
	21. Encourages Independence													
	22. Openness													
	23. Accepting													
	24. Complex													
	25. High Mobility													
	Totals													

are presented in Section I. Another source of generalizations is a college text in the specific content area. Such a text can provide ideas that are important to the understanding of the discipline. After choosing these generalizations, consult with content specialists in these areas to determine their validity and importance as basic ideas in that discipline. Rewrite them if necessary. In addition, since the Bruner (and Taba) models suggest that the key concepts be revisited as the children become more mature, these generalizations will have to be restated in differing degrees of complexity and abstractness if the curriculum spans several years.

After an acceptable set of generalizations has been devised, each element should be examined to determine the key concept(s) that must be known or developed for the generalization to be understood. Next, the data (e.g., specific illustrations of the concepts or specific information to be taught) are listed for each concept (Exhibit 6-11). Since this process is for the purpose of planning, the reader must realize that not all these data need to be taught. Plans should be made to assess the students' understanding of each concept before presenting new information. A work sheet for use in this process is illustrated in Exhibit 6-11. At the top of the work sheet, the generalization to be developed is listed and coded with a number or letter for later reference. In the first column, the key concepts necessary for understanding the generalization are listed. In the second column are the specific data or information that can be used to develop the concept. Since this is a brainstorming activity, list several sources or types of data. Later, go back and examine the list to determine the most economical data to use in developing all concepts.

If the program for the gifted uses a resource room, consulting teacher, center approach, or any other pull-out administrative model, the most economical and effective approach is to build the curriculum of the special program upon what is taught in the regular classrooms and extend it to higher, more complex levels. This requires more work in the planning stages but will result in a more efficient, coordinated program for the students.

After the initial development of generalizations, the content of the regular curriculum should be examined to determine to what extent these abstract ideas are being developed already. To facilitate this process, Work Sheet #6d (Exhibit 6-12) can be used. Regular classroom teachers, textbooks, and school curriculum guides all are sources of information for this analysis. Several of these work sheets are needed—at least one for each generalization. To complete this form, first write the generalization to be developed, along with its code number or letter. After examining what is taught in the regular program, list these data (according to each concept) in Column 1. Put an asterisk in the generalization above the concept(s) that need to be developed. In Column 2, list the additional data that need to be taught in the special program in order to develop that concept. As with Work Sheet #6c (Exhibit 6-11) all data are listed at this stage. Later, the list can be evaluated and the most appropriate data chosen.

Exhibit 6-11 Work Sheet for Overall Curriculum Design

Work Sheet #6c: Developing Content Plans

Generalization # _____ :

Concept	Possible Data to Be Used in Developing Concept

Exhibit 6-12 Work Sheet for Overall Curriculum Design

Work Sheet #6d: Building Content Plans upon the Regular Curriculum

Generalization # _____ :
Key Concepts To Be Developed

Data Taught in the Regular Curriculum	Data Needing to Be Taught in the Special Curriculum

* Key concepts to be developed

An example of this process is taken from the development of a science curriculum in a special program (Exhibit 6-13). The generalization is a methodological one, pertaining to the value and use of the scientific approach. It is complex, abstract, methodological, and it is important to the understanding of science. First, the key concepts involved in the generalization are listed or marked. Next, each concept is listed, along with the data taught in the regular classroom program. In this case, the only type of observation taught is how to observe and record changes in temperature. Students also are taught the importance of careful observations. To understand the concept of observation fully, additional data need to be taught in the gifted program, including different types of observations that can be made, different ways to measure them, experimental and control observations, and examples of incorrect inferences that can result from careless ones. The same process is followed with the second concept "organization of data."

This process, which begins with generalizations, selecting concepts, and listing data, can be long. However, the result is that a good deal of information is available for later use in the actual design of learning experiences. All the data and concepts for each content area and generalization need not be developed at this time. It can be a continuing process as the curriculum becomes more fully rounded.

Process Objectives and Plans

Now that the generalizations have been developed and content plans made, process objectives and strategies should be designed. These objectives follow directly from the process model(s) used in the program. The definitions of each step in the process or each level of thinking are used to develop objectives. To plan objectives and strategies, a work sheet such as Exhibit 6-14 is helpful. Several of these work sheets are needed, perhaps one for each concept. However, several concepts actually may be developed with the same activity.

As in the designing of content objectives and plans, if the curriculum for the gifted needs to be built upon the regular classroom program, the latter should be examined to determine what thinking skills or levels are being developed. A work sheet such as Exhibit 6-15 can be used in this process. First note the generalizations, key concepts and the data to which the processes pertain. Next, using the model as a guide, list the processes being used in the regular program that pertain to the concepts being examined. In the second column, list processes that can extend the regular curricular activities to higher levels.

As an illustration of this procedure, the example presented earlier can be extended (Exhibit 6-16). Using Bloom's *Taxonomy of Cognitive Objectives* as a guide, the teaching activities in the regular classroom are analyzed. In this case, the teacher is only developing the concept of observation at the comprehension level. To extend it higher, activities are developed at the application, analysis synthesis, and evaluation levels. In addition, these activities are designed so they

Exhibit 6-13 Work Sheet for Overall Curriculum Design

Work Sheet #6d: Building Content Plans upon the Regular Curriculum

Generalization # ___1___ : The growth of knowledge in science occurs through questioning, observation, experimentation, manipulation of materials, observation of results, and revision of original theories.

Key concepts To Be Developed:

Observation*	Organization of Data*	Control Groups
Prediction	Classification	Hypothesis
Environment	Inferences	Energy
Scientific Method	Contamination	Variable
	Raw Data	Brainstorming

Data Taught in the Regular Curriculum	Data Needing to Be Taught in the Special Curriculum
Observation	*Observation*
Ways to observe and record changes in temperature	Different types of observations that can be made: checklists, coding schemes, timed observation, use of microscope, changes in color from use of chemicals
The importance of careful observation	Types of measurement of observations: weight, length, color, density, temperature
	Experimental and control observations
	Examples of incorrect inferences resulting from careless observations
Organization of Data	*Organization of Data*
Keeping records of observations in notebooks	Types of graphs: bar, line
Grouping like observations together	Choosing units for graphs
	Separating experimental from control observations

* Concept(s) developed in this work sheet

Exhibit 6-14 Work Sheet for Overall Curriculum Design

Work Sheet #7a: Developing Process Plans

Content Generalization # _____

Concept(s) Developed: _____

Process Objectives	Sample Teaching Activities	Materials or Resources Needed	Possible Student Products

Exhibit 6-15 Work Sheet for Overall Curriculum Design

Work Sheet #7b: Building Process Plans upon the Regular Curriculum

Generalization # _____   Key Concept(s) _____

Data_____

Processes Used in the Regular Curriculum	Processes to Be Developed in the Special Curriculum

Exhibit 6-16 Work Sheet for Overall Curriculum Design

Work Sheet #7b: Building Process Plans upon the Regular Curriculum

Generalization # _____   Key Concept(s) __observation_____

Data __importance of careful observation, how to make observations, **examples of incorrect**__

inferences from careless observation _____

Processes Used in the Regular Curriculum	Processes to Be Developed in the Special Curriculum
Knowledge Teacher lecture on importance of careful observation *Comprehension* Teacher questions on why observation is important	*Application* Teacher sets up an experiment with two solar collectors (one tilted, one flat); records temperature systematically with-out knowledge of children; puts one collector where shade will cover for part of day; children are told to observe, record temperature, & make conclusions (they are not told how to make observations) *Analysis* Observations made by children are compared with those made by the teacher—similar-ities and differences in observations and conclusions are noted Discuss which inaccuracies caused incorrect conclusions or inferences *Synthesis* Children develop a plan for making more systematic observations to overcome prob-lems Students implement plan in a problem/exper-iment of their own choice (can be chosen from alternatives offered by teacher or generated by children) *Evaluation* Students judge the effectiveness of the plan and its implementation

satisfy the other general principles important in the processes used with gifted children. A discovery approach is used in that the children are not told why careful observation is needed or how to make observations. They are led to discover important aspects of the process. The activity also is open-ended in that there are several ways of making the observations. Teacher questions when discussing the activity also can be open-ended. A variety of methods is used, freedom of choice is encouraged, and students are asked to give their reasoning in the discussions.

By continuing a process such as this throughout the year as well as in the initial development of a curriculum, the educator will have comprehensive, detailed plans available whenever needed. Each year, new areas can be added, old ones expanded, or ineffective ones discarded. If several teachers work together using a similar process and format, ideas can be exchanged or shared.

Products

Since the actual product to be developed often is the student's option, objectives should pertain to the criteria used to evaluate them. The program goals provide a general framework for these criteria. For example, the first program goal (Exhibit 6-8, supra) states that the teacher will "provide situations allowing students to address real problems." A student objective developed from this goal could be:

"Products address real problems _____ percent of the time," or "_____ percent of products address real problems."

Specific product objectives addressing the evaluation criteria also can be developed for each major content area.

DEVELOPING EVALUATION PROCEDURES

The next step in any curriculum development process, after objectives and methods have been developed, is to devise procedures for evaluation. This evaluation involves two types of assessment: (1) of student progress and (2) of the overall success of the curriculum. Evaluation of the overall effectiveness includes a compilation of the results of the assessments of student progress as well as analyses such as students' perceptions regarding the importance or practicality of various aspects of the curriculum. Each of these types of evaluation is discussed separately. Because of the complexity of the subject, this treatment focuses on a few general issues and methods for selecting evaluation procedures. Since numerous publications are available on the subject, and since several of these contain sample instruments and summaries, actual instruments are not described.[1] Some examples of evaluation procedures can be found in the sample curricula in Section III.

Assessing Student Growth

Student growth in all areas—content, process, and product—should be evaluated. This can be accomplished by using both formal and informal procedures. Formal procedures include mainly pretests and posttests on standardized instruments. Informal procedures include observation, questionnaires, peer evaluation, self-evaluation, and various rating scales. In designing or selecting means of evaluation, it is important to distinguish between criteria for determining success and the methods used to make the judgment. For example, criteria for evaluating the attainment of content objectives can include accuracy/correctness of ideas, comprehensiveness/completeness of expression, or number of specific instances cited to support conclusions. Methods for evaluating content objectives can include standardized achievement tests, teacher-designed tests of content, analysis of taped class discussions (focusing on accuracy, comprehensiveness, and amount of specific data cited in students' answers to teacher questions), or rating scales based on observations.

Criteria for evaluating process objectives can include number of ideas expressed (fluency), number of categories of ideas (flexibility), or level of thinking evidenced by a student's answer. Other criteria are generated from the model being used. For instance, to identify a child's level of self-direction for the purpose of developing this characteristic further, several behavioral indicators are identified (e.g., can determine criteria for evaluation of own products, can accurately use card catalog). These also can be used as criteria for measuring success. The same is true of Taylor's model. Several publications (e.g., Eberle, 1974; Stevenson et al., 1971) provide detailed lists of child characteristics for identification of talent in each area. These can be used for judging progress. In effect, the development of criteria for judging student progress in the process area is a matter of selecting from the existing literature those elements that apply to the particular situation. Methods include many of the same ones used to evaluate progress in the content areas as well as instruments such as the *Ross Test of Higher Cognitive Processes,* tests of creativity, and tests of critical thinking.

Criteria for judging student products can be generated by audiences that assess them as well as by the pupil. General criteria include originality or uniqueness, degree of elaboration or detail, evidence of synthesis (i.e., integration of ideas rather than separateness), quality of organization, degree of transformation (distance of the final product from the original sources used in its development), or appropriateness to the audience for which it is intended. Other methods can include peer evaluation and simulated audience assessment.

To facilitate the process of development of plans for evaluating student progress, the criteria, methods, and grading procedures (Exhibit 6-17) should be developed for the key concepts, process objectives, and product objectives. Work Sheet 8 is applicable for this purpose. First, note the code for the generalization.

Exhibit 6-17 Work Sheet for Overall Curriculum Design

Work Sheet #8: Developing Plans for Evaluating Student Progress

Content Generalization # _____

Key Concepts and Process and Product Objectives	Criteria	Method	Grading Procedure

Next, list the key concepts to be evaluated (Column 1), then for each concept list the criteria for determining mastery (Column 2), the method of evaluation (Column 3), and the grading or reporting procedure (Column 4). If the criteria, methods, and grading procedures are the same for all concepts, they can be grouped together, but if there are differences, each should be listed separately. Next, list the process objectives in Column 1, criteria for determining success in Column 2, evaluation method in Column 3, and the grading procedure in the last column. Product objectives and their evaluation are treated in the same way.

As a group, the procedures for evaluation of student progress should satisfy the same requirements of comprehensiveness, variety, and validity as the instruments used to assess students initially. Each criterion for evaluating instruments is explained in Chapter 8 along with questions that should be asked to determine whether the requirement has been met. These questions are not presented again. However, Work Sheet 9a (Exhibit 6-18) was developed from this list and can be used to analyze the comprehensiveness and variety of evaluation procedures employed to assess student progress.

To use this work sheet, list criteria on the left that are important in the areas of child characteristics and intellectual abilities or talents. Other criteria are listed already. Next, enter all the instruments or procedures proposed for use. (The procedures shown on the work sheet are those used in the examples in Chapter 8 and are not necessarily the ones on your list. Next, place a check (√) in the column if the criterion applies to that instrument or procedure. If it does not, the column is left blank. Now, total the checks for each column and row. The row totals indicate the overall comprehensiveness and variety of the whole battery of procedures while the column totals provide the same ratings for each instrument.

After this analysis is completed, the collection of procedures can be assessed on the remaining criteria (Exhibit 6-19) to determine the appropriateness of the overall methods. To use this work sheet (9b), simply assign a rating of 1, 2, or 3 to each criterion and then obtain a total for the whole group of procedures.

Assessing Program Effectiveness

Evaluation of the effectiveness of the curriculum should be a part of a larger assessment of the entire program, including administrative arrangements, identification procedures, and teacher selection. However, this discussion focuses only on the development of procedures for assessing the curriculum's effect. As with the evaluation of student progress, some data should be collected throughout the year to make immediate changes if necessary. Data collected at the end of a year or period of years can be a summary of the continuing evaluation but also should include perceptions of program effectiveness for the longer period. One aspect of this assessment definitely must be a summary and evaluation of the data on student growth. Other aspects are the teacher's recordkeeping of what actually happens

Exhibit 6-18 Work Sheet for Overall Curriculum Design

Work Sheet #9a: Assessing Evaluation Procedures

Rate each assessment procedure by placing a ✓ in the column if the criterion applies. If not, leave the space blank.

Criteria	Instruments/ Procedures: SOI-LA	DAP	TICT	CTBS	PIAT	PPVT	WRAT	WISC-R	SRBCSS	Totals	Comment
Child Characteristics (Comprehensiveness)											
1.											
2.											
3.											
Intellectual Abilities (Comprehensiveness)											
1.											
2.											
3.											
Settings (Variety)											
1. Home											
2. Special classroom											
3. Regular classroom											
4. Extracurricular activities											
Perceptions (Variety)											
1. Self											
2. Parents											
3. Special Teacher											
4. Regular Classroom Teacher											
5. Psychologist											
Types of Measurement (Variety)											
1. Objective											
2. Subjective											
Totals											

Exhibit 6-19 Work Sheet for Overall Curriculum Design

Work Sheet #9b: Assessing Evaluation Procedures

Assign a rating to each model on each criterion question using the following code: 1 = poor
2 = average
3 = excellent

Criterion	Evaluation Procedures	Comment
Validity		
1. To what extent are the measurements recent?		
2. To what extent are the instruments valid?		
3. To what extent are the instruments reliable?		
4. To what extent are the instruments valid for assessing gifted students?		
5. To what extent are the instruments valid for assessing children from different cultural or racial groups?		
6. To what extent are the instruments valid for assessing children from low-income (disadvantaged) homes?		
7. To what extent are the instruments valid for assessing children who do not speak English or who speak English as a second language?		
8. To what extent are the instruments valid for assessing children with handi-caps?		
Comprehensiveness		
1. To what extent does the information assess intra-individual as well as inter-individual differences?		
2. To what extent are the measurements comprehensive in their assessment of child characteristics?		
3. To what extent are they comprehensive in their measurement of intellectual abilities or talents?		
Variety		
1. To what extent is the measurement made in a variety of settings?		
2. To what extent does it reflect a variety of perceptions?		
3. To what extent do the procedures use different types of measurement?		
Totals		

and people's perceptions of the program's effectiveness. These individuals include students, parents, others at the school (administrators, regular classroom teachers, counselors), and self-evaluation by the teacher(s) who implement the program.

In designing the procedures for evaluation, it is important to make certain that all aspects of the program are analyzed. One way to do this (Renzulli, 1978) is to develop a matrix of key features in which the indicators of success to be evaluated are listed across the top and the individuals supplying the information on the side. In the intersectional squares, list the instrument to be used in evaluation. This procedure has been adapted slightly (Exhibit 6-20) to produce a work sheet that can be used in designing a curriculum evaluation. In this matrix, program goals in the areas of content, process, product, and learning environment are listed on the left v/hile the indicators of success (student growth, meeting of intent, and positive perceptions by those associated with or served by the program) are at the top.

The work sheet can be used in two basic ways. The first is as a means for assuring that all program goals are assessed on all relevant criteria. To do this, the educator simply lists the instruments to be used in the applicable boxes. For example, to assess student growth related to the process goal of "higher levels of thinking," the instrument used could be the *Ross Test of Higher Cognitive Processes*. The instrument to assess parent perceptions can be a scale for rating student growth in thinking skills.

A second use of the work sheet is in designing the actual questions or items to include in the assessment instruments. Used in this way, the matrix still is the same, with each program goal on the side and indicators of success at the top. Each square serves as a guide to the development of questions or items to be included on instruments. For example, to assess regular classroom teachers' perceptions of the content goal of "covering content areas that are different from the regular curriculum," the questionnaire could ask, "What overlap did you notice between the content of the special program and the content taught in your classroom?" To assess the feature of "meeting of intent" on this same goal, an item in the teacher's log of actual activities is, "List the content areas covered in the program." The advisory group can be a great asset in the development of procedures and actual questions for evaluation, especially on the phrasing of items for the questionnaires.

GAINING ACCEPTANCE FOR THE CURRICULUM

The final step in the development of curriculum plans is to devise a method for implementation. Before it can be implemented, however, the plan must be accepted or approved by the school, the parents, and others. The advisory group can be most helpful in this process, especially if it has been involved throughout the development of the curriculum. Usually, those involved have invested so much time and energy that they are willing to work toward its acceptance. The advisory

Exhibit 6-20 Work Sheet for Overall Curriculum Design

Work Sheet #10: Developing Plans for Evaluating Program Effectiveness

PROGRAM GOALS	Student Growth	Meeting of Intent	Positive Perceptions		
			Students	Parents	School	Teacher(s)
Content						
1.						
2.						
3.						
Process						
1.						
2.						
3.						
Product						
1.						
2.						
3.						
Environment						
1.						
2.						
3.						

I N D I C A T O R S   O F   S U C C E S S

group should meet again after the majority of the development has been accomplished. It should review and approve the curriculum, then assist in the development of plans for implementation. To help in such a meeting, Work Sheet 11 (Exhibit 6-21) can be given to each person or used as a chart for a group discussion. Using a brainstorming format, list in Column 1 the steps to be followed in implementing the plan. Initially, they can be put in any order, then examined to decide on the most appropriate sequence. When the steps have been selected and sequenced, use the second column as a guide to making decisions about who will be responsible for each step, when it will be done, and where. Divide the tasks as much as possible among the group members. After these decisions have been made, spend the remainder of the meeting brainstorming ideas for implementation. Everyone should participate and must refrain from evaluating the ideas. Later, each individual responsible for a task can evaluate the idea list and make decisions about which ones to use.

As the implementation plan is followed, new problems and challenges may arise for individuals and for the group. If necessary, the group can meet again to devise creative solutions to these new issues.

SUMMARY

This chapter has described a step-by-step process that can be followed in the development of a curriculum for gifted students. No assumptions are made about what individual(s) will assume the primary responsibility for its development. This can be taken on by a districtwide coordinator of gifted programs (with subgroups for particular schools), a teacher of the gifted, a committee of teachers, a curriculum coordinator, a committee of such coordinators, or a special committee selected to represent a school or a district. Regardless of who assumes the primary responsibility, one goal must be to obtain active participation from a wide representation of the community or school for which the curriculum is being developed. Their active involvement and assistance is invaluable in the development of a viable product as well as in gaining acceptance in the school and community.

The process described here follows the general principles of a creative problem-solving approach. Many of the work sheets have been adapted from the Noller, Parnes, and Biondi (1976) workbook but made specifically applicable to this situation. Readers unfamiliar with *Creative Problem Solving* (CPS) may want to review these materials to familiarize themselves with the ideas and principles behind the approach. In all cases, at the idea production stage, it is essential to defer judgment and encourage participants to offer a quantity of ideas. The lists that evolve during individual or group brainstorming can be reviewed and evaluated (as well as kept for later reference) in the production of the final document or plan.

Exhibit 6-21 Work Sheet for Overall Curriculum Design

Work Sheet #11: Gaining Acceptance

IDEA/PLAN:

Steps to Implement	Who, When, and/ or Where	How and/ or Why?
List the steps to follow in implementing the idea or plan.	List the individual responsible, when and where this will occur, and who must accept the ideas.	List some ideas for implementing each step of the plan listed in Column 1.
Now go back and circle the best ideas.		Now go back and circle the best ideas.

Source: Adapted from *Creative Actionbook: Rev. Ed. of Creative Behavior Workbook* by R.B. Noller, S.J. Parnes, and A.M. Biondi by permission of Charles Scribner's Sons, © 1976.

The process described in this chapter is not rigid but is a logical, sequential one that can be adapted to a variety of situations. Feel free to use the work sheets as they are or modify them to meet your needs. However you do it, the author's hope is that your process will result in a comprehensive, qualitatively different curriculum for your gifted children. Good luck!

NOTE

1. Readers wishing further information should consult the following references: The Association for the Gifted Evaluation Committee, 1979; Renzulli, 1976a; White, 1974.

Chapter 7

Adapting the Curriculum for Special Populations

Chapter 6 described a general process for developing a curriculum for gifted students. Chapter 8 analyzes a process of planning to meet individual needs. This chapter focuses on general adaptations that should be made for certain subgroups or special populations of gifted children: disadvantaged or low income, the culturally different, the handicapped, underachievers, high performance/low verbal, highly creative/low IQ, and highly gifted. If the general processes described in Chapters 6 and 8 are followed, the needs of special populations will be met since a major principle in those chapters is that a curriculum should be built upon the unique characteristics of the children to be served and that within this general framework, the needs of each individual must be addressed. What, then, is the purpose of this chapter? It is to provide specific examples of the special needs of typical subpopulations and show how these needs can be translated into general adaptations of the curriculum. In effect, it provides a further illustration of the basic principles espoused by this author.

The organization of the discussion is

a. a brief review of the generalized characteristics of the particular population
b. sample work sheets showing the translation of characteristics into child needs, goals and objectives, teaching-learning models, and academic areas, and
c. a brief discussion of the ideas in the work sheets.

The review of characteristics must be limited to a few basic references since this book is not intended to resolve any differences of opinion or fact regarding these traits. Space does not permit a thorough review.

A GENERAL PLAN

The general principles of curriculum development for the gifted are applicable to special populations. First, the curriculum must be qualitatively different from that of the regular classroom so that the special program is justifiable. Second, it must be designed to enhance or take into account what is different about the children. The curriculum must be built upon the differences that require a special program for these pupils. Herein lies a clue to the adaptations that must be made. Often, children who are considered special populations or special subgroups are those who demonstrate superior potential in spite of or in addition to certain characteristics that tend to inhibit their performance in school or cause learning difficulties. These traits are not necessarily deficits or weaknesses. In the case of children from different cultural backgrounds, for example, bilingualism is a definite asset. However, if English is a second language, learning to read in English may be a slow process. In the case of children who are highly gifted, their rapid pace of learning, superior conceptual understanding, and broad background of knowledge are strengths that benefit everyone. However, the degree of difference between them and the majority of their peers often causes special problems with student interaction, not to mention the problems with teachers who are threatened by such superior children.

Because of these inhibiting characteristics, the thesis of this chapter is that in planning programs for the special populations of gifted children described here, there must be a realistic balance between the development of strengths and of skills in coping with their differences. This could be considered a "weakness through strength approach," but the basic premise is that learning or interactional difficulties cannot be ignored in the special program.

In planning the curriculum, the approach to needs assessment for the group is the same as that described in Chapter 6 and for individuals can be as that described in either Chapter 6 or Chapter 8. To assess group needs, Work Sheet 3a (see Chapter 6, Exhibit 6-3) is helpful. This provides a format for summarizing the common characteristics of the group to be served. It is used in an adapted form in this chapter to summarize the generalized characteristics of each special population. A second work sheet, 5b, "Meeting Their Needs" (Exhibit 7-1), has been devised to assist in making adaptations for group needs of special populations. It is used in this chapter as a way to summarize the curricular adaptations presented for each group of children.

To use this work sheet, begin with a summary of student characteristics. Translate these into needs in the areas of strength and weakness. Next, write a curricular goal and/or objective for meeting that need. Program goals can be numbered or coded so it is not necessary to write them several times. Based on these factors, choose a teaching/learning model that can be used as is or adapted easily to suggest strategies for meeting the need (Column 3). Next, write sample

Exhibit 7-1 Work Sheet for Overall Curriculum Design

Work Sheet #5b: Meeting Their Needs

Special Group _____

Special Populations

Child Needs	Goals/Objectives	Models	Teaching Activities	Academic Areas/Materials
Strengths				
Weaknesses				

teaching strategies (Column 4) along with academic areas and teaching materials that can be helpful. This work sheet is completed as an example for each group discussed.

DISADVANTAGED OR LOW INCOME

Children from low-income areas or whose parents are very poor lack many of the early experiences, opportunities, or materials at home that can enhance their intellectual development. Regardless of the lack of stimulation, there are many gifted children from disadvantaged homes. Often they are from different cultural or ethnic groups, which may cause additional differences that are reflected in school learning.

The literature tends to be difficult to interpret since many authors group together those from low-income areas and those from different cultural groups, implicitly making the assumption that children from inner city neighborhoods are all black or Mexican-American, or that all black or Mexican-American children live in the inner city area and are from disadvantaged homes. Although it may be true that a greater percentage of disadvantaged children are black, Mexican-American, or Native American, there are many Anglo pupils in low-income areas. There also are many Mexican-American, black, and Native American children from advantaged homes. This chapter attempts to distinguish between the two factors of culture and socioeconomic status. Differences mainly attributable to cultural or ethnic group are discussed in following sections while those attributable mainly to family economic status are described in this next section.

Characteristics

In learning characteristics, the most noticeable traits of children from low-income families usually are their weakness in knowledge and vocabulary—factors that result from their lack of exposure to reading materials and information. They may not be as interested in reading as other gifted children who have been exposed to interesting materials and have been read to all their lives. However, they often show strengths in observational skills and in memory or recall—intellectual abilities that are independent of specific knowledge. With regard to motivational characteristics, few generalizations can be made. Some may be independent learners while others require a great deal of attention from the teacher; some may be motivated easily while others may not. However, it does seem clear that as these children progress in school, their motivation decreases. Perhaps this is because of the low quality of some schools they attend and perhaps their lack of academic success if they receive no recognition or stimulation. Thus, weaknesses in task completion and internal motivation often are found (Baldwin, 1978; Frasier,

1979). Much of the research on achievement motivation (Weiner, 1972, 1974; Weiner, Frieze, Kukla, Reed, Rest, & Rosenbaum, 1972; Weiner & Kukla, 1970; Weiner, Nierenberg, & Goldstein, 1976) shows that low-income/disadvantaged children are dependent on external motivators and that they tend to attribute their success to factors such as luck rather than to ability or effort.

In creativity and leadership, however, the picture is much brighter. Torrance (1968, 1971, 1977), for example, concludes that in many ways the life experiences of children from low-income homes actually may be more supportive of creativity than those of children from advantaged homes. Children in low-income families must improvise with common materials to develop toys and must be creative just to get by. They show creative strengths in curiosity; generating new, unique, and clever ideas or solutions to problems; taking risks; and showing a sense of humor. These strengths usually are concentrated in areas other than verbal, showing up in their drawings and actions. They often are perceived as leaders among their low socioeconomic status (SES) peers. They show responsibility and adaptability and are well-coordinated. However, they may not show this self-confidence with children from more advantaged backgrounds or with adults.

Curricular Modifications

One very important aspect of planning for children from low-income homes is the need to provide enrichment programs as early as possible that can stimulate them intellectually as well as offer some of the experiences they may have missed. Generally, studies show that as these pupils progress through school, the gap between what they need to know and what they do know becomes wider (Renzulli, 1973). Passow, Goldberg, and Tannenbaum (1967) report average drops in intelligence of as much as 20 points as these children move through school. These early experiences, as well as later ones, should develop and enhance their creativity and leadership while providing experiences that can make up for lost time in their learning. Exhibit 7-2 shows the translation of some of these needs into curricular modifications.

The strengths in creativity are combined into one needs statement—developing affective and cognitive aspects of creativity. The program goal (Column 2), chosen for major emphasis is the provision of open-ended activities. Since several models provide this kind of activity, there is wide latitude in the selection of an approach. Teaching activities focus on idea production, divergent thinking, and creative production in language arts, music, the visual arts, and science. To strengthen one of the weaker areas—content knowledge and intellectual skills— one objective calls for the development of these abilities while the second emphasizes doing so through the child's strengths in divergent/creative production. The *Cognitive and Affective Taxonomies* can meet the first goal most appropriately while the Taba strategies are an excellent choice for the second. Leadership

Exhibit 7-2 Work Sheet for Overall Curriculum Design

Work Sheet #5b: Meeting Their Needs

Special Group   Disadvantaged

Special Populations

Child Needs	Goals/Objectives	Models	Teaching Activities	Academic Areas/Materials
Strengths:	Provide open-ended activities in all academic areas		Creative dramatics	Language Arts
1. Continued development of characteristics of creative and affective areas			Mime	Music
	Encourage fluency, flexibility, originality, and elaboration in all content areas	Parnes	Emphasize fact-finding and idea-finding steps with problems in all academic areas	Visual Arts
				Science
		Guilford	Emphasize operation of divergent production; use of figural and symbolic content; development of products of units, transformations, implications	
	Encourage curiosity, complexity, risktaking, and imagination	Williams	Emphasize Strategies	
			2 (attributes), 4 (discrepancies), 5 (provocative questions), 11 (intuitive expression), 16 (creative listening skill), and 18 (visualization skill) in all content areas	
		Taylor	Emphasize creative talent	
Weaknesses:	Provide experiences to develop higher levels of thinking in a variety of areas	Bloom and Krathwohl	Develop all levels of thinking but make certain that knowledge is present before moving up taxonomy (may need to spend more time on knowledge and comprehension than with other gifted students)	All content areas, but especially basics such as reading and math
1. Development of intellectual skills and knowledge in all content areas				
	Provide for development of knowledge and higher levels of thinking in open-ended activities that also encourage creativity	Taba	Emphasize development of long lists of information at data-gathering steps; then move further in strategies	

strengths can be developed through group dynamics and group process activities as well as use of behavioral content in Guilford's *Structure of Intellect* model. It should be emphasized, however, that with children who have low self-confidence and low motivation, an approach that combines the development of strong areas with weaker ones will be much more effective than any emphasis on weaknesses alone. The teacher should begin with strengths and gradually start to work on the weaker areas.

THE CULTURALLY DIFFERENT

Three different cultural/ethnic groups are discussed in this section—black, Mexican-American, and Native American. Other groups certainly could be covered but these seem to be the ones most commonly encountered and researched.

Blacks

Characteristics

The greatest difficulty in separating economic from ethnic characteristics seems to be in relation to blacks. Very little, if any, research exists dealing with the differences between blacks and Anglos of the same SES level. There does seem to be some indication of differences in language or intellectual patterns. In one study, for example, Meeker (1978) reports differences between ethnic groups, all of which are disadvantaged. She found that blacks were lower in cognition, evaluation, and convergent production and higher in memory than the Anglo and Mexican-American children in the study. Blacks were lower in abilities involving figural content than were the other groups, and blacks and Mexican-Americans were significantly lower in abilities involving semantic content than were the Anglos. Viewed in the context of learning characteristics, these differences translate into strengths in mastery and recall and weaknesses in the semantic area of vocabulary development. The children also have weaknesses in the evaluation and convergent production areas of cause-effect relationships and grasping underlying principles when dealing with ideas or semantic content.

However, when considering symbolic areas or logical reasoning independent of semantics, black children seem to show strengths. For example, Halpern (1973) found that the blacks in her study scored best on activities involving symbolic content (in the arithmetic and digit span subtests) and on the abstract reasoning/comprehension tested by the comprehension and similarities subtests of the *Wechsler Intelligence Scale for Children—Revised* (WISC-R). Bruch (1971) also identifies many of the same strengths and weaknesses through her work with the *Stanford-Binet*.

In much of Torrance's work, the disadvantaged groups are blacks but he also has summarized research comparing blacks and Anglos of the same socioeconomic backgrounds (Torrance, 1977). He concludes that in 86 percent of the cross-cultural studies using the *Torrance Tests of Creative Thinking* (TTCT), results indicate either no differences or variances in favor of the culturally different group. Generally, the blacks and disadvantaged groups tend to excel on the figural tests.

With regard to motivation and leadership, few generalizations can be made except that blacks tend to excel in physical activities, are sociable, and often are interested in adult social and racial issues (Renzulli, 1973; Torrance, 1967). Because of the lack of recognition of talent, or the racial biases of teachers and classmates, black children are likely to lose their earlier motivation and show weaknesses in task commitment or persistence and a need for external motivation (Baldwin, 1978; Renzulli, 1973).

Modifications of the Curriculum

To develop the modifications work sheet, two strengths are translated into needs (Exhibit 7-3): memory and creativity. In the development of creativity, many of the activities are the same as those for children in low-income families. However, with the added strengths in symbolic areas, activities should be concentrated there as well as in the figural and spatial areas. The second program goal relates to the combination of strength in memory and in divergent production, and weakness in knowledge in other academic areas. In other words, the children's tendencies toward creativity are emphasized as they learn new academic content.

When dealing with low student motivation, it is suggested that (a) opportunities be provided for the pupils' choice of topic areas (to capitalize on any interests they may have), (b) emphasis be placed on self-evaluation (in an attempt to encourage the development of internal motivation), and (c) attention be given to ensuring success, especially in their first attempts at working independently. When using Treffinger's model, for example, these students may begin at a much lower level and progress much more slowly than would be expected of gifted pupils. The teacher must pay careful attention to the possible frustrations students may face because of their lack of knowledge, lack of familiarity with references, or low self-confidence.

Mexican-Americans

Characteristics

The major characteristics of Mexican-Americans resulting from their cultural background seem to involve learning and leadership. Although they acquire English language skills rapidly once exposed, initially they may be lacking in conceptual development, vocabulary, and other traits related to language de-

Exhibit 7-3 Work Sheet for Overall Curriculum Design

Work Sheet #5b: Meeting Their Needs

Special Group _____ Blacks

Special Populations

Child Needs	Goals/Objectives	Models	Teaching Activities	Academic Areas/Materials
Strengths: Development of creative abilities in both affective and cognitive areas	Provide open-ended experiences in figural and symbolic areas	Guilford	Emphasize divergent thinking using figural and symbolic content	Visual Arts Music Math
		Taylor	Emphasize creative talent	
Further exercise of memory in new areas	Provide open-ended experiences that require recall of information with creative application in academic areas	Parnes	Emphasize fact-finding and idea-finding steps with real problems	Social Studies Language Arts
		Williams	Emphasize discrepancies, provocative questions, creative reading, and creative listening	
Weaknesses: Development of internal motivation	Provide opportunities for free choice of problems	Treffinger	Move student slowly through levels but emphasize participation in decisions; attempt to direct student toward areas where teacher knows pupil can experience success	All Academic Areas
	Provide for structured development of independent learning		Convince student that success results from internal factors	
			Emphasize development of criteria and methods for self-evaluation	
	Introduce student to new topic areas that can be explored	Renzulli	Emphasize Type I and II activities until teacher feels student will be successful with Type III	
			When a Type III activity is begun, place student with a very special mentor who can assist in the follow-through and ensure success	

Exhibit 7-3 continued

Child Needs	Goals/Objectives	Models	Teaching Activities	Academic Areas/Materials
	Provide opportunities for self-evaluation	Parnes	After Type III products have been developed, encourage presentation to as many receptive, kind audiences as possible; practice presentations with peer group as much as possible before sharing with an audience	
			Emphasize problem-finding and solution-finding steps	

velopment (Bernal, 1975, 1978; Bernal & Reyna, 1974; Gerken, 1978; Meeker, 1978). Since much of their early school success is dependent upon these language skills, bilingual children who are Spanish-dominant, or monolingual Spanish children, may fall behind in their beginning years. They may not be recognized as gifted or able children and not challenged in school, which can contribute to problems later. Regardless of the problems that may develop later, educators should concentrate on their initial characteristics.

In looking at the intellectual abilities of Mexican-American students, Meeker (1978) found them to be lower in cognition than Anglos (but higher than blacks), higher than Anglos in memory (but lower than blacks), and approximately equal to Anglos in evaluation and divergent production. With regard to content, they showed strengths in the figural area. Bernal (1978) further identifies the following characteristics of the gifted Spanish-speaking pupil. The child:

1. Rapidly acquires English language skills once exposed to the language and given an opportunity to use it expressively.
2. Exhibits leadership ability, be it open or unobtrusive, with heavy emphasis on interpersonal skills.
3. Has older playmates and easily engages adults in lively conversations.
4. Enjoys intelligent (or effective) risk taking behavior, often accompanied by a sense of drama.
5. Is able to keep busy and entertained, especially by imaginative games and ingenious applications, such as getting the most out of a few simple toys and objects.
6. Accepts responsibilities at home normally reserved for older children, such as the supervision of younger siblings or helping others do their homework.
7. Is "street wise" and is recognized by others as a youngster who has the ability to "make it" in the Anglo dominated society. (p. 15)

When these characteristics are viewed in the context of learning, motivational, creative, and leadership characteristics, both strengths and weaknesses can be seen in the area of learning, with definite strengths in leadership and creativity. No conclusions can be drawn about common motivational characteristics except those related to socioeconomic status or a continued pattern of low achievement because of heavy emphasis on language-related skills.

Curricular Modifications

The major educational approach for children with these characteristics should be development of academic skills through the children's strengths in interpersonal relationships and creativity. Some ideas are provided in the sample work sheet shown in Exhibit 7-4. The goals and objectives also emphasize continued development of intellectual skills through academic areas that are less dependent on language. This is an important point to emphasize. Although desirous of increasing the language skills of these children, educators must not neglect their overall intellectual development. This can be done through a variety of types of activities in such areas as math, science, visual arts, and music. The Bloom, Guilford, and Bruner models all suggest strategies that can be helpful, as can tests and activities developed from Piaget's theories. To develop the children's language skills, there should be an emphasis on their interpersonal relations abilities, their creativity, or a combination of the two (e.g., through creative dramatics, mime). By involving the students in activities such as listing uses of common objects, they exercise their creative ability while practicing their language skills if this is done in a group setting. Listing the ideas verbally or even demonstrating them certainly is more effective than having the children merely write them down. Writing, it seems, means combining so many weak areas that the students cannot exercise their strengths enough to have a successful experience.

Native Americans

Characteristics

Because of the number of different groups of Native Americans, it is difficult to make any generalizations about their common characteristics. The major research in the area of differing characteristics of gifted Native American children has been that by Meeker (1978) in which she examines the *Structure of Intellect* (SI) abilities of Navajo children in New Mexico and Arizona. In this continuing study, she reports high auditory memory and high figural ability with low semantic scores and very low classification abilities. Further investigation shows that the Navajo language is learned aurally and has almost no words for classification. This obviously contributes to these cultural differences.

Patricia Locke (Note 6), herself Native American, has summarized the intellectual, motivational, and leadership characteristics sometimes found in gifted Anglo children that educators would *not* expect to find in gifted Native American children:

- Very rapid answers;

- Tends to dominate peers or situations;

- Individualistic—likes to work by self;

- Body or facial gestures very expressive;

- Impatient—quick to anger or anxious to complete a task;

Exhibit 7-4 Work Sheet for Overall Curriculum Design

Work Sheet #5b: Meeting Their Needs

Special Group   Mexican-American

Child Needs	Goals/Objectives	Models	Teaching Activities	Academic Areas/Materials
Strengths: Continued development of intellectual skills	Provide opportunities for structured development of higher level thinking skills	Bloom	Emphasize higher levels of application, analysis, and synthesis in areas of child's interest and strength	Math Science Visual Arts
	Increase thinking skills through figural or symbolic content as well as semantic content in the dominant language	Guilford	Emphasize figural and symbolic content	Music
			Emphasize classification, systems, relations, transformations, and relations in the product dimension	
	Provide opportunities for development of inductive thinking by use of a discovery approach	Bruner	Have children conduct experiments with heat, light, and other common sources of energy	Science
			Use formal logic exercises with symbols rather than ideas	Math/Science
Weaknesses: Development of language skills	Provide for development of language skills through students' strengths in interpersonal relations		Have child tutor others in academic areas of strength	Areas of interest and strength
		Bruner	Have child teach others Spanish Play simulation games in which group interaction is used to learn and report	"Dig" simulation
		Taba	Discuss results of simulation games	
			Use resolution of conflict strategy to discuss classroom problems	
		Guilford	Emphasize content dimension of behavior; combine it with verbal answers and any operations or products dimensions where child shows a strength	

Exhibit 7-4 continued

Child Needs	Goals/Objectives	Models	Teaching Activities	Academic Areas/Materials
	Provide for development of language skills through strengths in creativity	Parnes	Creative Dramatics Mime Emphasize brainstorming of uses of common objects, listing all the words child can think of to describe color, texture, etc; List the many meanings of a certain word	Language Arts Music Visual Arts Social Studies

- Great desire to excel even to the point of cheating;

- Frequently interrupts others when they are talking;

- Frank in appraisal of adults. (p. 3)

These are not identifying characteristics in Native Americans because most American Indian tribes place a negative value on such traits. Children do not tend to develop in this way because of the expectations of their parents and the influences of their tribe. In a different vein, the characteristics used in identifying gifted students in an experimental project serving Native Americans in North Dakota are the following:

1. Independence of thought
2. Perceptiveness
3. Understanding
4. Trustworthiness
5. Conscientiousness
6. Strength of influence on others
7. Persistence
8. Devotion to distant goals
9. A desire to excel
10. A longer attention span than normal for children his age
11. A persistent curiosity
12. A good memory
13. An awareness and appreciation of people and things
14. A wide range of interests
15. An ability to solve problems
16. A tendency to prefer the companionship of older children
17. Rebelliousness due to frustration and lack of challenge (Grey Bear, Note 7, pp. 1-2)

Although there are differences of opinion in the two lists, there appear to be some commonalities. For example, this list indicates that gifted Native Americans exhibit leadership through an ability to influence others but may accomplish this in a quiet, unobtrusive manner. They may be independent in their thinking but prefer to work together rather than alone. Based on a synthesis of the ideas of Meeker, Locke, and Grey Bear, Native American gifted children might be expected to show weaknesses in vocabulary and information (e.g., low semantic scores) with strengths in memory/recall (e.g., high auditory memory), observation/sensitivity, and problem solving in other than the semantic and classification areas. It also might be found that they are persistent and internally motivated but prefer group work or teacher-directed activities. They may show curiosity and skills in interpersonal relations, but do so without aggressiveness or assertiveness.

Curricular Modifications

If these expectations are accurate, the curriculum should emphasize intellectual strengths in the memory and figural areas while developing semantic abilities and classification skills. This should be done in an atmosphere where cooperation rather than competition is emphasized. Curiosity should be encouraged and interpersonal skills strengthened.

In Exhibit 7-5, some of these general ideas are translated into specific teaching strategies using Work Sheet 5b. As with the work sheet for Mexican-Americans, this one emphasizes the continued development of intellectual skills in the children's areas of strength while at the same time working on their classification weaknesses through other intellectual and interpersonal strengths. Helpful teaching-learning models are Guilford, Taba, Renzulli, and Taylor, with emphasis on their use in cooperative group situations. With the Renzulli approach, it is suggested that students be taught methods of classification in the context of both Type I and II enrichment.

THE HANDICAPPED

Common Characteristics

Although it generally is impossible to make valid statements about the common characteristics of the gifted handicapped because of the differing types and effects of disabilities, some common characteristics should be noted. As a result of the emphasis, by both society and by educators, on deficits rather than on talents, those who are intellectually gifted but have a handicap of any kind are thought of as handicapped—not as gifted. Educators tend to forget that a deficit in one area does not necessarily imply a deficit in others (Maker, 1977; Maker, Redden, Tonelson, & Howell, Note 8). For this reason gifted handicapped individuals often must cope with a major gap between what they perceive themselves as capable of doing (based on what they know about their talents) and what others discern (based on their concepts of the debilitating effect of a handicap). Associated with this problem is the frustration of not being able to achieve the perfection they desire (Maker, 1977; Maker et al., Note 8).

A second area of possible commonality is creativity. Certainly, all gifted handicapped students cannot be assumed to have strengths in creativity but there is some evidence (White, Note 9) that a substantial percentage of them are creative. He speculates that this higher creativity may result from the need for persons with disabilities to practice their divergent thinking skills just to accomplish everyday tasks that nondisabled individuals perform with ease. Certainly it is difficult for a deaf child to exhibit creativity in verbal areas or a blind child to show creativity in the visual arts, but their abilities can be recognized easily through their unimpaired

Exhibit 7-5 Work Sheet for Overall Curriculum Design

Work Sheet #5b: Meeting Their Needs

Special Group ____Native American____

Child Needs	Goals/Objectives	Models	Teaching Activities	Academic Areas/Materials
Strengths: Enhancement of non-verbal intellectual abilities	Provide structured exercises for development of higher levels of thinking in content areas of strength	Bloom	Emphasize higher levels of thinking (analysis, synthesis, evaluation, and feeling)	Math Visual Arts Music
		Guilford	Emphasize memory operation, figural and symbolic content, and units in the product dimension	
		Taylor	Emphasize decision-making talent in nonverbal areas	
Weaknesses: Development of classification skills	Provide opportunities for developing these intellectual skills through strengths in memory and symbolic areas	Guilford	Emphasize product dimension of classes combined with all operations and all types of content except semantic Concentrate on logic exercises presented auditorially	Math Visual Arts Music
	Provide opportunities for development of classification skills through interpersonal cooperation and leadership skills	Taba	Emphasize concept development strategy in small groups; have children classify or categorize in groups rather than individually; begin with concrete objects; move to symbols, next use behavioral information, and, finally, semantic	Visual Arts Math Music
		Renzulli	Concentrate on Type I and II activities related to science investigations (which often are concerned with classification) Teach methods for classification and encourage small groups to work together	Social Studies Language Arts Science <u>Search</u> simulation game

talents. Learning disabled children, in contrast, seem to show creative strengths in areas such as fluency, originality, and elaboration, but have difficulty with flexibility (Torrance, Note 10).

With regard to motivational traits, there is some evidence that the gifted handicapped (with the possible exception of those with learning disabilities) are strong in persistence, internally motivated, and independent (Maker, 1977; Maker et al., Note 8). Negative public perceptions and attitudes often serve as a goad to success, making people with handicaps persist in their efforts and determined to show others they are wrong. It is important to realize, however, that these motivational traits may be precisely what brings gifted handicapped adults and children to educators' attention. Perhaps those who have not been recognized are those who lack persistence. Certainly, it cannot be assumed that, because the successful handicapped adults in this author's research showed extreme persistence, independence, and internal motivation, all able handicapped individuals have these same traits. These characteristics may have resulted from their success rather than contributing to it (Maker et al., Note 8). However, it does seem that the gifted handicapped, like the gifted nonhandicapped, generally show strengths in motivation.

Perhaps as a result of some of the frustrations and difficulties discussed above, gifted handicapped students may not show leadership skills except when dealing with similar children. They may not be well liked by their classmates, who perceive them as having a chip on their shoulder or who are unable to recognize their abilities because of emphasis on the handicap. However, most gifted handicapped individuals who have accepted or adjusted to their disability show the same strengths in leadership as do their nonhandicapped gifted peers. They show these qualities when working with both handicapped and nonhandicapped individuals.

Most of the variances among the handicapped involve learning characteristics because of the different types and effects of the disabilities. The following sections present some of these different learning characteristics for four groups of disabilities.

Unique Characteristics

Sensory Handicapped

Included in this group of handicaps are deafness or hearing impairment and blindness or visual impairment. Obviously, since these very different disabilities are grouped together, it is difficult to make general statements about their common characteristics. However, there are some data to indicate that both blind and deaf children's rate of cognitive development is slower than that of the nonhandicapped but that they do catch up later (Maker, 1976, 1977). If true, this fact indicates that children with sensory handicaps may show weaknesses in many of the learning characteristics, especially those requiring abstract thinking abilities. However, because of the necessity of exercising unimpaired sensory channels, these children may show definite strengths in visual memory (deaf and hearing impaired) or auditory memory (blind and visually impaired).

Learning Disabled

Based on analyses of profiles of performance of gifted children with learning disabilities (Maker, 1976, 1977) a pattern of abilities seems to emerge. These children show intellectual weaknesses in information, memory, and perceptual areas, with strong abilities in fields requiring abstract reasoning but not dependent on memory. Their logic, classification abilities, and grasp of general trends seem to be unimpaired by learning problems. Of course, such impairments might result in IQ scores so low that they would not be considered gifted. This idea, however, presents questions too complicated to treat in this short discussion. Suffice it to say that the children recognized as gifted learning disabled seem to have the characteristic pattern just described.

Other characteristics expected in these pupils include a lack of persistence (perhaps the result of continued failure) on certain types of tasks, low internal motivation, low self-direction, and a highly self-critical attitude. As indicated earlier, these children may show creative strengths in fluency, originality, and elaboration but have low flexibility. They often have difficulty with peer relationships (Bruininks, 1978a, 1978b) and may lack flexibility in adapting to new situations (Torrance, Note 10).

Mobility Impaired

There seem to be no generalizable characteristics for this group in the learning area. These individuals basically have different strengths and weaknesses, as would a group of nonhandicapped gifted children. Two characteristics that seem to be related to the combined effect of their disability and their giftedness are (1) a striving toward perfection and (2) a great concern over interpersonal relationships. This group, more than any of the others, often consists of perfectionists who are very frustrated at their inability to meet their own standards of excellence (Maker et al., Note 8). They often seem very concerned with peer relationships. Perhaps this is because of how their physical appearance can determine others' initial reactions or first impressions. Physical appearances seem to play a big part in forming opinions about competence.

Social/Emotional Disabilities

A discussion of the characteristics of children with behavior disorders or emotional disturbances is difficult since in many cases these conditions seem to be associated with or result from other handicaps. They also seem to be an aspect of the whole syndrome of underachievement (Whitmore, 1980). Rather than attempting to separate the syndrome of underachievement from the syndrome of behavior disorders/emotional disturbance, these difficulties are not discussed as an aspect of underachievement. However, two types of characteristics should be noted. One is the lack of adaptability or flexibility in many disturbed children, both gifted and nongifted. A second type is noted by Meeker (1969) in her analysis of profiles of boys classified as "incorrigible." They seem to have a deficit in the evaluation area. There is some evidence to support the belief that this same deficit is present in gifted children with behavior disorders.[2]

Curricular Modifications

Unlike most of the special populations discussed in this chapter, most gifted handicapped students already are being served in a special educational program and have been identified because of their deficits. The one possible exception is the learning disabled who are coping with academics well enough to avoid being discovered. However, in most cases, the service these children are receiving is deficit oriented. It focuses on their weaknesses without developing, or even recognizing, their superior abilities. For these reasons, the curriculum in a gifted program should focus on the child's strengths or on the development of weaknesses through strengths. That is the basic principle followed in the curricular modifications suggested in Exhibits 7-6 through 7-9. In these work sheets, needs and curricular modifications are based mainly on the characteristics that distinguish them from other gifted handicapped children. However, some of the strengths through which the weaknesses are developed may be common to several or many gifted handicapped groups.

Curricular modifications for the sensory handicapped (Exhibit 7-6) center on the development of abstract thinking capabilities through exercising perceptual abilities using unimpaired senses. The generation of information also can be encouraged through intuition (e.g., using other knowledge to create new perceptions). As Maker (Note 11) suggests, a step can be added to Taba's concept development strategy in which students are encouraged to use all five senses plus their intuition to list attributes of objects before attempting to group them by similarities. Since they are most likely to be participating in a group situation, they also have the benefit of the perceptions of the other members.

For the learning disabled (Exhibit 7-7), suggested curricular modifications use their abstract reasoning capabilities as a way to generate missing information resulting from their weaknesses in memory or as a way to organize information so it can be remembered more easily. Several teaching strategies can be used for these purposes; those especially helpful are Williams's analogies and organized random search on Taba's concept development.

Exhibit 7-6 Work Sheet for Overall Curriculum Design

Work Sheet #5b: Meeting Their Needs

Special Group ___Sensory Handicapped___

Child Needs	Goals/Objectives	Models	Teaching Activities	Academic Areas/Materials
Extension of auditory or visual memory along with development of abstract reasoning skills	Use existing knowledge, unimpaired sensory channels, and intuitive perceptual modes along with memory to develop reasoning capabilities	Taba	Add a second step to concept development strategy (e.g., after listing, have students describe objects, pictures, or other data using sensory or intuitive mode) (Maker, 1981)	All academic areas, but begin with concrete materials and move gradually to more abstract content
		Guilford	Use strengths in memory to develop weaknesses in semantic areas	
		Williams	Use strategy of attribute listing from memory as well as imagination. After this, develop categories integrating all these attributes	
			Use strategy of analogies involving known attributes or those perceived through unimpaired senses or intuitive mode	

Special Populations

Exhibit 7-7 Work Sheet for Overall Curriculum Design

Work Sheet #5b: Meeting Their Needs

Special Group _____ Learning Disabled

Child Needs	Goals/Objectives	Models	Teaching Activities	Academic Areas/Materials
Development of abstract reasoning abilities along with skills in memory and perception	Provide learning experiences that can use abstract reasoning to aid memory and perception	Williams	Use analogies strategy to help remember attributes of objects, numbers, items, or characteristics of things	All areas, but stress those in which student shows unusual strengths or unusual interests
			Make analogies or comparisons between traffic signs and punctuation marks if a child is having difficulty remembering when to use a certain punctuation mark (have the children, not the teacher, generate the relationships)	
		Taba	Use strategy of organized random search by providing children the structure and having them generate applications of that structure	
			Stress concept development strategy and generation of abstract categories; individual items belonging in categories can then be generated	

Special Populations

With children who are mobility impaired or have social/emotional disabilities, their intellectual strengths can be used to help them generate ways of coping with problems they may have in social interaction or emotional disabilities (Exhibits 7-8 and 7-9.) Obviously, this strategy is not enough by itself but if accompanied by simulations or analysis of the student's actual experiences, its effectiveness definitely can be enhanced. Among the strategies suggested are group dynamics activities, videotaping of group interaction, the Taba resolution of conflict strategy, and creative problem solving related to interpersonal problems or coping skills. Taylor's decision-making talent activities can be stressed as can Williams's strategy of evaluation of situations.

In these cases, the reader should be reminded again that the needs addressed are only examples and that each individual child must be assessed before needs are determined. In most instances, many needs will be addressed rather than only one.

UNDERACHIEVERS

Characteristics

Most studies of underachieving children and adults have shown them to be different from achievers mainly in motivation and social/emotional characteristics (Gallagher, 1966; Purkey, 1969; Terman & Oden, 1947; Zilli, 1971). Most authorities also have noted that these characteristics are persistent and can be identified early in the child's academic life. In Terman's and Oden's (1947) follow-up, for example, the same characteristics that differentiated their successful from unsuccessful individuals could have identified the groups when they were 10 years old. Others also have shown that the pattern of underachievement begins early and persists throughout the school career (Gallagher, 1966).

In his review of the research, Gallagher (1966) identifies low self-concept, negative attitudes toward school, choice of less socially acceptable friends, lack of persistence, and poor study habits as consistent characteristics of underachievers. Purkey (1969) concludes that the problems of underachievers can be categorized into five areas: self-confidence, social relationships, perseverance, self-expression, and philosophy of life. Zilli (1971) includes the usual factors of motivation, social pressure, personality, and home environment but adds school factors such as inadequate curriculum content, poor teaching, and lack of challenge.

Based on her case studies of underachieving gifted children and the evaluation of the success of a program for them, Whitmore (1979) separates traits of underachievers into psychological or personality, physical or developmental, and the school environment. She concludes that the etiology of underachievement centers on the interaction "between the child, his personality and behavior, and the social environment of home and school" (p. 47), an idea also posed by Gallagher

Exhibit 7-8 Work Sheet for Overall Curriculum Design

Work Sheet #5b: Meeting Their Needs

Special Populations

Special Group   Mobility Impaired

Child Needs	Goals/Objectives	Models	Teaching Activities	Academic Areas/Materials
Development of more adequate peer relationships and social skills along with enhancement of intellectual strengths	Develop effective ways of (a) accepting limitations and (b) coping with and overcoming negative attitudes of others through use of student's intellectual and creative strengths		Place student with a well-adjusted, successful handicapped adult as a mentor Have handicapped adults speak to class or student Conduct group dynamics activities Hold fishbowl discussions Tape and self-analyze group interaction	Social Studies List of coping strategies used by successful handicapped scientists (Maker et al., Note 8)
		Taba	Emphasize resolution of conflict and interpretation of behavioral data	
		Parnes	CPS on strategies for coping or other personal problems	
		Guilford	Emphasize behavioral content	

Exhibit 7-9 Work Sheet for Overall Curriculum Design

Work Sheet #5b: Meeting Their Needs

Special Group   Social/Emotional Disabilities

Child Needs	Goals/Objectives	Models	Teaching Activities	Academic Areas/Materials
Development of more effective social interaction and ways of coping with emotional problems	Use intellectual and creative strengths to enhance abilities in social/emotional areas	Taylor	Stress use of self-evaluation and self-criticism in all situations rather than outside evaluation. Teach students structured ways to evaluate their own performance.	Social Studies
			Stress development of decision-making talents	
			Stress communication talent and forecasting talent in social situations	
		Williams	Emphasize strategy of examples of habit, especially in social situations	
			Emphasize strategy of evaluation of situations, especially real ones in which student is or has been involved	
		Taba	Stress resolution of conflict strategy at all steps	

Special Populations

(1966). Because of past emphasis on personality and home factors as causes of underachievement, Whitmore reports teachers have tended to believe they can have little or no effect on changing the patterns of achievement and thus have used only out-of-class remedies such as counseling rather than modifications of the school environment or curriculum.

Curricular Modifications

Since the classroom environment does seem to play a part in the continuation or aggravation of underachievement problems, it is imperative that the teacher provide as supportive and challenging a setting as possible. Whitmore (1979) makes the following general recommendations:

1. Gain understanding and empathy for the highly gifted child, striving to see the world as he sees it and to feel what he feels.
2. Reduce external pressures perceived by the child in school.
3. Plan for the child to experience genuine success he values, adjusting unrealistic goals and making short-term objectives to be accomplished through small steps.
4. Evaluate the appropriateness of the curriculum—does it provide opportunities for the child to build upon his strengths and to pursue his interests? Does it allow him to develop a readiness before building skills that are weak? Is it appropriate for his learning style and mental abilities?
5. Teach the child skills for coping—i.e., methods of reducing body tension, relieving frustration and anger, and handling teasing, criticism, compulsive perfectionism, etc. A significant part of those coping skills is having a rational understanding of his difficulties in the classroom, recognizing the consequences of his behavior, and knowing it is possible to develop control over his behavior in order to control the outcomes and gain desired rewards. In the experimental UAG [Underachieving Gifted] program, class meetings and private individual or small group conferences were the most effective vehicles for this learning.
6. Communicate genuine respect and acceptance of the individual, valuing him highly for his unique personhood.
7. Be flexible and involve students in planning and evaluating, allowing them to develop a high degree of self-management skill. Structure the day to allow student choice and pursuit of interests in relatively unstructured time periods. An extended day program can allow daily workshops to provide time for more informal learning and social activity.

8. Work closely with the parents through monthly conferences and frequent parent meetings, as well as with other professional personnel available within the school system and community. (p. 48)

Using the work sheets, four child needs have been translated into educational goals and curricular modifications (Exhibit 7-10). The weaknesses selected for development are knowledge and skills in academic areas and development of the ability to resolve conflicts between personal characteristics and the demands of others. Treffinger's *Self-Directed Learning* model provides a structured way to develop an environment where children can pursue interest areas and learn to manage their own time. The Parnes *Creative Problem Solving* (CPS) model is useful in developing a positive attitude (and skills) related to perceiving these problems as solvable. The method also can be used to develop personal coping skills.

Strengths should be a primary focus of the program since the students need to experience success as a way to break out of a pattern of underachievement and failure. Concentration on thinking abilities that do not depend upon previously learned academic skills are valuable, as is development of any nonacademic talent areas in which the student shows some potential. Taylor, Kohlberg, and Guilford provide helpful suggestions and methods.

HIGH PERFORMANCE/LOW VERBAL

Characteristics

Little has been written about the special traits of children who fit into this group, mainly because in the past only those with high verbal ability have been considered gifted. However, with the current concern over a broadened conception of giftedness along with the increased use of the WISC-R and other intelligence tests that have separate sections or scales evaluating nonverbal or performance abilities, more children are being identified who show strengths in performance and weaknesses in verbal abilities. Performance areas include such abilities as perceptual organization as assessed by mazes, object assembly, and block design on the Wechsler scales and concrete intelligence assessed by the Guilford and Meeker items involving figural or symbolic content.

Other abilities include perception of the gestalt as a whole when only parts are given, as assessed by the picture arrangement subtest of the Wechsler scales or other visual closure tests. A common element in all these tests is that the child must manipulate figural or symbolic content rather than words and meanings. Eye-hand coordination, speed, and perceptual-motor abilities are included along with the intellectual abilities of visualization, memory, and reasoning. The production or

Exhibit 7-10 Work Sheet for Overall Curriculum Design

Work Sheet #5b: Meeting Their Needs

Special Group _____ Underachievers

Special Populations

Child Needs	Goals/Objectives	Models	Teaching Activities	Academic Areas/Materials
Weaknesses: Development of knowledge and skills in academic areas	Use child's interests to plan activities in which success can be experienced	Treffinger	Begin at child's level of self-direction but progress as rapidly as possible, exercise care in selecting projects or activities that can be accomplished	Any area of interest to the child Any area where the child has experienced previous success
	Provide psychologically safe learning environment where students are encouraged to express their ideas freely, defer judgment, and provide and experience constructive criticism	Parnes	Teach children coping skills used by others Adopt list of coping skills of handicapped scientists as a starting point. For examples of those who have succeeded, use idea-finding step of CPS to develop ways of applying these strategies to child's own life Use entire strategy of CPS to identify problems and develop (as well as implement) creative solutions	List of coping strategies of successful handicapped scientists (Maker et. al., 1978)
Development of ability to resolve conflicts involving personal character-istics, home environments, and the expectations of an academic environment		Krathwohl	Emphasize identification of personal values (valuing step) and their organization while resolving the conflict between child's own values and those of parents and the school; stress values related to achievement and social or interpersonal relationships.	
Strengths: Further development of abstract reasoning capabilities	Provide activities stressing higher levels of thinking without building upon areas in which the child's achievement is lacking	Guilford	Identify strong areas of content, process, and product, then work only on strengths or combine one weakness with two strengths until child gains more confidence	All content areas

	Kohlberg	Taylor	
Development of nonacademic talent areas	Provide for development of wide range of talent areas and abilities within classroom	Discuss moral dilemmas in which very little new background knowledge is needed	Social Studies Science
		Use talent areas (except academic) as target areas, depending on child's unique characteristics and talent profile	All content areas, both traditional and nontraditional

output phases, however, involve use of perceptual and motor skills rather than verbal ones.

Thus, the characteristics of high performance/low verbal children include strengths in some or all of these concrete or perceptual areas, with weaknesses in one or all of the verbal areas such as vocabulary, information, rapid insight into cause-effect relationships, and other similar learning characteristics when the content is verbal rather than visual or concrete. Motivational, creative, and leadership characteristics may show either strengths or weaknesses, depending on each individual, so there are no consistent patterns in these areas. The student may show a high degree of creativity but this usually involves figural rather than verbal content.

Modifying the Curriculum

There is some question about the appropriateness of including students with high performance abilities and low verbal skills since verbal ability often is considered the most important component of giftedness. However, if a concept of intelligence such as Guilford's (1967) is the theoretical basis of a program, such children definitely should be included. If high performing, low verbal children are included in a program for the gifted, however, it is essential that they not be treated in the same way as their highly verbal peers. They have been identified because of their strengths and talents in the performance areas, so these are the elements that should be addressed in the program.

Serving these children and developing their talents does not require a separate program, although different methods can be appropriate. High performing students can and should be allowed to express their abilities in nonverbal ways. Their abstract or semantic experiences should always be preceded by a good foundation in concrete experiences related to the verbal ones. For example, when reporting or developing projects, these students should be allowed and encouraged to develop nonverbal products such as slide-tape presentations, dioramas, flow charts, or three-dimensional models rather than written reports. Their thinking skills should be exercised through manipulation of symbolic, figural, and concrete information rather than through concentration on words and ideas.

Using the curriculum development work sheet (Exhibit 7-11), two student needs have been identified and curricular suggestions made. Most, if not all, of the gifted program activities should be concentrated on the development of strengths, so the needs selected are in those areas: development of abstract reasoning or thinking skills involving strong areas and development of self-expression through nonverbal modes. Useful models are Guilford (because of his sections on abilities that are concerned with concrete intelligence), Treffinger and Renzulli (for their emphasis on the development of products and investigations in areas of interest), and Williams and Parnes (because of their stress on creativity using any type of content, including nonverbal).

Exhibit 7-11 Work Sheet for Overall Curriculum Design

Work Sheet #5b: Meeting Their Needs

Special Group High Performance/Low Verbal

Special Populations

Child Needs	Goals/Objectives	Models	Teaching Activities	Academic Areas/Materials
Strengths: Development of higher levels of thinking through areas of strength	Provide learning activities that will exercise children's thinking abilities through concrete, figural, and symbolic content	Guilford	Combine figural and symbolic content with all other operations and products; stress complex products such as transformations and implications	Math Science Logic Sculpture Art and Music
		Treffinger	Encourage development of independent projects in areas of strength	
		Renzulli	Provide Type I and II enrichment in performance and mechanical areas to expand exposure	Cuisenaire Rods Tangrams Puzzles Mazes Blocks
			Have speakers who are involved in the visual arts, mechanics, and other similar areas discuss their work	
		Williams	Use strategies of evaluating situations, tolerance for ambiguity, organized random search, examples of habit, examples of change, analogies, discrepancies, provocative questions, and paradoxes using concrete, figural, and symbolic content.	Perception Stimulators (D.O.K. Publishers) Computers

Exhibit 7-11 continued

Special Populations

Child Needs	Goals/Objectives	Models	Teaching Activities	Academic Areas/Materials
Development of skills in self-expression through nonverbal areas	Provide opportunities for development of products using other than a verbal format; encourage all to use this mode	Renzulli	Encourage development of Type III products using other than verbal mode Assist student in making presentations to audiences using these modes	Math Science Logic Sculpture Art
		Williams	Emphasize strategy of visualization and intuitive expression with nonverbal production	Music and any other areas of interest to the student
		Parnes	Use all steps of CPS with figural problems	

Students also need to be exposed to careers in which their type of intelligence is needed and can flourish. They need exposure to practicing professionals and creative or eminent individuals in these careers so they can learn to value their own abilities as well as develop creative ways of using them.

HIGHLY CREATIVE/LOW IQ

Characteristics

Much has been written about the intellectual, motivational, and personality characteristics of creative adults and of youngsters who perform well on tests of creativity. A series of studies—the most significant being by Getzels and Jackson (1962), Wallach and Kogan (1965), and Torrance (1962)—also has focused on the relationship between intelligence and creativity. The fact that this relationship seems to be moderate rather than high has led to a great deal of interest in the possible differences between individuals who are high in creativity but do not score in the gifted range on IQ tests and those who score in the gifted range on the tests but are low in creativity. It is not possible to review the results of this research thoroughly because of limited space but some of the material is summarized.

The basic design of these studies has been to separate the subjects into four groups based on their scores on IQ and creativity tests: those with (a) high creativity and low IQ, (b) high creativity and high IQ, (c) low creativity and low IQ, and (d) low creativity and high IQ. Getzels and Jackson (1962) and Torrance (1962) studied only groups (a) and (d), while Wallach and Kogan (1965) analyzed all four. The group that is of interest in this review is (a)—high creative, low IQ.

A consistent finding of these studies as well as others (Gallagher, 1966; Dellas & Gaier, 1970) is that even though the low IQ groups have lower measured intelligence than the high IQ groups, there are no differences between their levels of achievement. In other words, creativity may be just as important in predicting achievement as is an IQ score. It should be noted, however, that an IQ score of at least 120 is necessary for high achievement even if a child is highly creative (Gallagher, 1966). Other characteristics of the high creative, low IQ groups are the following (Getzels and Jackson, 1962)

1. show a preference for humor, social stability, and wide range of interests rather than IQ scores, character, and goal-directedness;
2. are more interested in seeking satisfaction for their interests and aspirations than in pursuing success as defined by society; and
3. write stories that are less stimulus-bound and that use more humor, novel situations, and unexpected endings than the high IQ group.

Wallach and Kogan (1965) characterized members of this group as being in angry conflict with themselves and their school environment, possessing feelings of unworthiness and anxiety. In a stress-free environment, they conclude, these children can perform well cognitively.

The major strengths of this group, then, are in the area of creativity characteristics, with weaknesses concentrated in leadership and, somewhat, in learning. These children seem to have more of a sense of personal responsibility than a social responsibility and are more concerned with developing their own interests than responding to the wishes of others.

Curricular Modifications

If only IQ tests or if a combination of such measures as IQ tests, achievement scores, and teacher recommendation are used as identification procedures, many of the high creative, low IQ children will be excluded from a gifted program (if the usual IQ cutoff of 130 is used). However, many of the children whose IQ scores are 130 or slightly above also might fit into this category. They cannot be ignored, and should be treated differently from those who are not so creative so that these positive traits will flourish.

Educational programs for children with these traits should focus on the development of their highly creative strengths and should allow a substantial degree of self-selection or self-directedness in the choice of learning activities. Some time can be spent in development of more effective social relationships and in assisting these students to resolve some of the conflicts they face when their personal values conflict with those of the school. However, the majority of time should be spent on development of their creative strengths.

Using the familiar work sheets, two needs are identified (Exhibit 7-12) and program goals developed. The ideas above are simply extended and shown in the familiar form. Helpful models for development of creative strengths are Parnes, Williams, Taba, Guilford, and Taylor. For developing other cognitive abilities, and for enhancing achievement, the Treffinger and Renzulli models provide a valuable framework for allowing the freedom of choice these students seem to need.

HIGHLY GIFTED

Characteristics

Included in the group considered highly gifted are children described as "first order gifted" (Gallagher & Crowder, 1957) or "one in a million" (Terman & Oden, 1947). They have a measured IQ of above 160 or 180 on a standardized test.

Exhibit 7-12 Work Sheet for Overall Curriculum Design

Work Sheet #5b: Meeting Their Needs

Special Group ____Highly Creative/Low IQ____

Child Needs	Goals/Objectives	Models	Teaching Activities	Academic Areas/Materials
Strengths: Development of cognitive and affective abilities involved in creativity	Provide experiences that develop the full range of creativity characteristics	Williams	Use all strategies to develop all thinking and feeling behaviors	All content areas, but focus on those of special interest to the student
		Parnes	Use all steps	
		Taba	Use all strategies but emphasize a variety of answers at each step, a variety of groupings, and different, original answers rather than "good" ones	
		Guilford	Stress divergent production using all content and all products	
		Taylor	Stress creativity talent, communication talent, and planning, with emphasis on originality and flexibility rather than correctness	
Weaknesses: Development of knowledge and convergent production necessary for school success	Provide for expression and development of convergent pursuit of own interests	Treffinger	Move student as quickly as possible to highest levels of self-direction; begin at a level higher than past experience might indicate, then change if student cannot handle this much freedom	All content areas of interest to student
		Renzulli	Concentrate on Type III activities as quickly as possible	
		Parnes	Allow students to select problems of their own choice	

Special Populations

Most of the research on children of this level of intelligence has used a case study approach since there are so few pupils who fall into the category. Hollingworth (1942) studied 12 children with Binet IQs above 180, Terman and Oden (1947) 25 with the same IQ, and Gallagher and Crowder (1957) compared 15 children with IQs of 165 and above with 15 who had IQs from 150 to 165. Kerstetter (1953) assessed 25 children with IQs over 160 while Anastasiow (1964) evaluated 23 with IQs of 145 and above on the WISC or 155 and above on the Binet.

The somewhat consistent results of these studies indicate that these children have a common problem in social and emotional adjustment. They seem to have a difficult time in finding challenging and interesting work at school, in tolerating those with lesser ability, and in accepting authority. However, the problems in social adjustment seem to be influenced greatly by their social and intellectual environment. Gallagher and Crowder (1957) conclude that if a highly gifted student is a member of a group of average or below-average children, the pupil is more likely to experience adjustment problems than if a member of an above-average group. In other words, it seems important that these children be grouped with their intellectual peers as much as possible. No conclusions about commonalities in creativity and motivational characteristics can be made. These pupils may or may not be creative, may show independence and self-direction, and may be highly motivated. Some will not have these traits. They certainly show definite strengths in learning characteristics.

Curricular Modifications

The educational program for highly gifted children should be designed to enhance their intellectual strengths. It needs to be different from the curriculum for the majority of gifted students in much the same way that the program for the gifted should be different from the regular one for all children. For instance, the pacing of instruction must be quicker, with a greater emphasis on higher levels of thinking, more complex and abstract content, and a more flexible environment with more sophisticated references. In addition, these children should be grouped with their intellectual peers or at least with older gifted students when possible.

These two curricular changes are summarized as before using the work sheet (Exhibit 7-13). The first need, development of intellectual strengths, suggests that the basic curriculum for all gifted students be modified for the highly gifted and that when models using a discussion or sharing format are involved, the pupils should be grouped with either their intellectual peers or older, gifted peers. The second need, independence, may be either a strength or a weakness, depending on the student. Teaching methods for this need involve the instructor's development of the ability to learn what the pupil wants to learn without the help of an adult, an important coping skill needed by highly gifted students.

Exhibit 7-13 Work Sheet for Overall Curriculum Design

Work Sheet #5b: Meeting Their Needs

Special Group   Highly Gifted

Special Populations

Child Needs	Goals/Objectives	Models	Teaching Activities	Academic Areas/Materials
Strengths: Development of intellectual strengths without boredom	Provide intellectual challenges and stimulation beyond that provided for other gifted children	Taba	Group together students with remarkable intelligence for at least a part of their program	All content areas Many new content areas not usually included
			Group students with older gifted children when possible; use all strategies	
		Bloom & Krathwohl	Stress higher levels of thinking more than with other gifted students	
	Provide instruction paced more quickly than with other students	Kohlberg	Discuss moral issues at higher levels and with older students	
	Use a variety of methods, and vary them often	Williams	Emphasize discrepant events, examples of change and habit, tolerating ambiguity, development rather than adjustment, and evaluating situations	
Strengths or Weaknesses: Development of skills in self-direction and independence	Provide for development of inquiry skills so students can direct their own learning when teachers must work with slower children	Treffinger	Move students as quickly as possible to higher levels of self-direction	All content areas
		Renzulli	Stress methods of inquiry in all areas of professional inquiry during Type I exploration and Type II process development	
		Williams	Emphasize organized random search and provocative questions	

SUMMARY

This chapter has presented summaries of the common characteristics of special subgroups of gifted children. A summary of the learning, creativity, motivation, and leadership characteristics of each of these groups is shown in Exhibit 7-14. Renzulli's basic lists of characteristics are used as the groupings. In many cases, no generalizations can be made, and in all cases there are notable exceptions to the generalizations that are presented here. Each child should be considered on an individual basis. However, these modifications provide a sample of the kinds of changes that can and should be made for pupils with the needs identified on the work sheets. It is hoped that this chapter will serve as a stimulus to further creative thought rather than as a cookbook of ideas.

NOTES

1. Those interested in this topic are encouraged to read the research report on successful handicapped scientists (Maker et al., Note 8).
2. The source of this belief is in *Structure of Intellect-Learning Abilities* (SI-LA) testing done with children in the summer enrichment program operated by the University of New Mexico.

Exhibit 7-14 Summary of Characteristics of Special Groups of Gifted Students

	Disadvantaged/ Low SES	Mexican-American	Native American	Black	Sensory Handicapped	Learning Disabled	Mobility Impaired	Social/Emotional Problems	Underachievers	High Performance/ Low Verbal	Highly Creative/ Low IQ	Highly Gifted
		Culturally Different			Handicapped							
Part I: *Learning Characteristics*												
1. Has unusually advanced vocabulary for age or grade level; uses terms in a meaningful way; has verbal behavior characterized by "richness" of expression, elaboration, and fluency.	X	X	X	X		✓		✓		X		✓
2. Possesses a large storehouse of information about a variety of topics (beyond the usual interests of youngsters his age).	X	X	X	X		X				X	X	✓
3. Has quick mastery and recall of factual information.	✓	X	✓		✓	X	X		✓	X	X	✓
4. Has rapid insight into cause-effect relationships; tries to discover the how and why of things; asks many provocative questions (as distinct from informational or factual questions); wants to know what makes things (or people) "tick".					✓	X			✓	✓		✓
5. Has a ready grasp of underlying principles and can quickly make valid generalizations about events, people, or things; looks for similarities and differences in events, people, and things.			✓	X	X	X	X	X	✓			✓
6. Is a keen and alert observer; usually "sees more" or "gets more" out of a story, film, etc., than others	✓	✓	✓	X	✓	X	X				✓	✓
7. Reads a great deal on his own; usually prefers adult level books; does not avoid difficult material; may show a preference for biography, autobiography, encyclopedias, and atlases.	X			X	X	X	X		✓			✓
8. Tries to understand complicated material by separating it into its respective parts; reasons things out for himself; sees logical and common sense answers.		✓	✓	✓	✓	X			✓	✓		✓
Part II: *Motivational Characteristics*												
1. Becomes absorbed and truly involved in certain topics or problems; is persistent in seeking task completion. (It is sometimes difficult to get him to move on to another topic.)	X	X	✓	✓	✓	X			X	✓		✓

NOTE: A ✓ indicates a possible strength, or possession of the characteristic to a high degree. An X denotes a possible weakness, or a trait that may be present to a low degree.

Exhibit 7-14 continued

	Disadvantaged/Low SES	Mexican-American	Native American	Black	Sensory Handicapped	Learning Disabled	Mobility Impaired	Social/Emotional Problems	Underachievers	High Performance/Low Verbal	Highly Creative/Low IQ	Highly Gifted
		Culturally Different			Handicapped							
2. Is easily bored with routine tasks.	X											✓
3. Needs little external motivation to follow through in work that initially excited him.			✓	X		X			X			✓
4. Strives toward perfection; is self-critical; is not easily satisfied with his own speed or products.			X			✓			✓			✓
5. Prefers to work independently; requires little direction from teachers.						X	✓		X			✓
6. Is interested in many "adult" problems such as religion, politics, sex, race— more than usual for age level.			✓									✓
7. Often is self-assertive (sometimes even aggressive); stubborn in his beliefs.			X					✓				✓
8. Likes to organize and bring structure to things, people, and situations.												✓
9. Is quite concerned with right and wrong, good and bad; often evaluates and passes judgment on events, people, and things.								X				✓

Part III: Creativity Characteristics

	Disadvantaged/Low SES	Mexican-American	Native American	Black	Sensory Handicapped	Learning Disabled	Mobility Impaired	Social/Emotional Problems	Underachievers	High Performance/Low Verbal	Highly Creative/Low IQ	Highly Gifted
1. Displays a great deal of curiosity about many things; is constantly asking questions about anything and everything.	✓		✓								✓	
2. Generates a large number of ideas or solutions to problems and questions; often offers unusual ("way out"), unique, clever responses.	✓	✓		✓							✓	
3. Is uninhibited in expressions of opinions; is sometimes radical and spirited in disagreement; is tenacious.		✓									✓	
4. Is a high risk taker; is adventurous and speculative.	✓	✓							X		✓✓	
5. Displays a good deal of intellectual playfulness; fantasizes; imagines ("I wonder what would happen if..."); manipulates ideas (i.e., changes, elaborates upon them); is often concerned with adapting, improving, and modifying institutions, objects, and systems.		✓									✓	
6. Displays a keen sense of humor and sees humor in situations that may not appear to be humorous to others.	✓			✓							✓	

7. Is usually aware of his impulses and more open to the irrational in himself (freer expression of feminine interest forboys, greater than usual amount of independence for girls); shows emotional sensitivity.

8. Is sensitive to beauty; attends to aesthetic characteristics of things.

9. Nonconforming; accepts disorder, is not interested in details; is individualistic; does not fear being different.

10. Criticizes constructively; is unwilling to accept authoritarian pronouncements without critical examination.

Part I: Leadership Characteristics

1. Carries responsibility well; can be counted on to do what he has promised and usually does it well.

2. Is self-confident with children his own age as well as adults; seems comfortable when asked to show his work to the class.

3. Seems to be well liked by his classmates.

4. Is cooperative with teacher and classmates; tends to avoid bickering and is generally easy to get along with.

5. Can express himself well; has good verbal facility and is usually well understood.

6. Adapts readily to new situations; is flexible in thought and action and does not seem disturbed when the normal routine is changed

7. Seems to enjoy being around other people; is sociable and prefers not to be alone.

8. Tends to dominate others when they are around; generally directs the activity in which he is involved.

9. Participates in most social activities connected with the school; can be counted on to be there if anyone is.

10. Excels in athletic activities; is well coordinated and enjoys all sorts of athletic games.

Chapter 8

Developing an Individualized Program for Gifted Students

With the current emphasis on individualized education programs (IEPs) in special education (HEW, 1977), many teachers have become concerned about legal and practical matters resulting from the requirements of Public Law 94-142, the Education for All Handicapped Children Act of 1975. Although the concern for meeting the needs of individual children is appropriate, there seems to be a greater attempt to meet the letter of the law rather than its intent. The purpose of the IEP requirement in P.L. 94-142 is to ensure that each child is treated as an individual with unique characteristics and that the special education program be designed with these characteristics in mind.

Congress included other aspects of the required individual planning process to assure that this program was developed in an appropriate manner (i.e., by including parents, the student, and other teachers in the planning process) and that the program for each child was reviewed periodically to determine its continued relevance. Because the IEP development process has these legal requirements, the concern seems to be more for legal responsibilities than for the philosophical and educational concerns such as how to make a valid assessment of individual characteristics, how to involve parents in more than a cursory manner, and how to design a program directed toward individual as well as group needs.

The purpose of this chapter is not to discuss the legal requirements but to describe how teachers can design individualized programs for each gifted child they serve. Because of this focus, the ideas here are directed to all teachers whether or not they are required by district, state, or federal regulations to develop a formalized educational plan or an IEP. In effect, this chapter is an extension of or a supplement to Chapter 6, which discussed the general process of curriculum development. This focuses on the process of curriculum development for specific children, or how to modify the basic program for all gifted pupils to meet the needs of one of them.

The process described is similar to that of overall curriculum development: (a) involving key individuals, (b) assessing needs, (c) developing a profile,

(d) developing objectives, (e) designing learning experiences, and (f) evaluating progress. The general principles are similar to those in overall curriculum development for the gifted: the program should be built upon the unique present and potential future characteristics of each child.

INVOLVEMENT OF KEY INDIVIDUALS

All too often in the development of IEPs and individual programs in general, parents and other key people, including the child, are involved after the plan has been developed. The extent of their involvement seems to be reaction and approval rather than input into development or assistance in decision making. When parents are called in for a conference only after the fact, they are under considerable pressure to agree with the plan, and the teacher manifests a great deal of defensiveness. Who wouldn't be defensive after spending months working on a plan for a child? What parents wouldn't feel pressured to agree when they know teachers have spent such a long time on their child's program and developed it to the best of their ability and knowledge of the pupil?

To avoid this pressure and defensiveness, and more importantly to develop the best program for each child, key individuals (parents, other teachers, the students) should be involved in every step of the process. They should be consulted about their perceptions of the child's characteristics and needs, in making decisions about areas in which to concentrate, and in choosing objectives and developing means for meeting them. Key individuals also should be a part of the assessment process. They should provide their evaluation of changes that have occurred in the child. The following sections contain suggested ways to involve these key individuals, but first, some general considerations related to parent involvement need to be discussed.

Ideally, parents will want to be involved to a great extent in their child's educational program. This way, educators can be more certain that home and school expectations for the child are consistent. However, the level of involvement the parent desires must be respected. Many factors affect that participation, including job and family commitments, general educational concern, knowledge of opportunities and restrictions affecting the program, and how comfortable the parents feel about making educational recommendations. Educators first must respect the parents' present levels of involvement and allow participation to that extent. They also must encourage greater involvement through educational programs, activities designed to develop interest, and constant attempts to develop a cooperative rapport to make parents feel comfortable about making contributions.

As described more fully in Chapter 6, there are four levels of parent involvement (Kroth, 1980): informational, participation, interactive, and deep involvement. At the informational level, the extent of involvement probably is the sharing of information about the child—characteristics, interests, strengths, and weaknesses. Parents share their knowledge of what the child is like at home, educators share their understanding of the child at school as well as the kind of educational program developed. For parents who are at the next three levels, active participation is necessary and desirable. It is to be hoped that through the educator's respecting parents' present level of involvement and providing positive experiences at that level, they will be encouraged to become a more integral part of the planning process.

DEVELOPING A PLAN

This section presents a step-by-step process for the development of individualized programs. This is followed by a case study to illustrate its application to one particular student.

Assessment

Obviously, the first step in the process of individualization is to assess the child's present characteristics. The first substep is to analyze existing information to determine whether additional assessments are needed and whether the data satisfy the criteria of (a) comprehensiveness, (b) variety, and (c) validity. Following are some of the questions teachers can ask to determine the quality of the data.

Comprehensiveness

To determine, first, its comprehensiveness, ask: Does the existing information cover all the child characteristics important to the overall curricular approach? For example, when the *Enrichment Triad* is used, assessment should cover the three clusters of traits Renzulli (1978) includes in his definition of giftedness (abilities, creativity, task commitment) as well as interests and learning styles since a major assumption he makes is that the curriculum for gifted students should respect their individual interests and learning styles. If Treffinger's (1975) *Self-Directed Learning* model is used, the assessment should include information on the student's degree of self-direction.

A second question is: Do the data include information about intraindividual as well as interindividual differences? In other words, do the data provide a self-comparison of the child's characteristics? To obtain a complete picture of the individual's abilities, the teacher should compare the pupil to other gifted students and other children in general, but often the most important data come from comparisons within the person. It is important to examine strengths and weaknesses at one point and to study developmental changes over time. For example, in examining a child's achievement scores, it is helpful to note that the pupil's achievement in mathematics is at the 80th percentile using national norms and reading scores are at the 98th percentile. Further analysis is necessary to determine whether the achievement in math has dropped recently or whether the pattern is well established. If it has occurred recently, the cause could be poor teaching, a need for different math skills instruction, a drop in interest, or a lack of challenging subject matter. If the pattern is well established, it might be inferred that the child has a general lower level of interest in this area, a possible underlying learning problem, or a general lack of curricular emphasis.

Comparison with other children (nongifted) tends to keep test scores in their proper perspective for parents as well as teachers. A math score in the 80th percentile is really not low—the child still is achieving higher than 80 percent of those who have taken the test. Comparison with other gifted students also is important in the design of individual programs. If others of equal ability in the same program are achieving much higher, then the math curriculum may not be meeting the needs of this particular child, so some changes may be necessary.

A final question to determine comprehensiveness is: Do the data include assessment of a variety of talent areas or intellectual abilities? The principle behind this question is very simple—an IQ score, achievement levels, or overall ratings on behavior rating scales are not enough. Educators now know enough about giftedness to realize its multidimensional nature, so there should be no excuse for the use of single scores in the planning of a program for any gifted child.

Variety

The second criterion, variety, is determined by asking three basic questions:

1. Do the data include assessment in a variety of settings?
2. Do they reflect the perceptions of a variety of individuals, including the student, parents, regular classroom teachers, a psychologist or diagnostic specialist, and the special teacher?
3. Do the data include a variety of types of measurement, including, for example, both objective and subjective assessments?

Actually, the teacher could consider the criterion of variety as an aspect of comprehensiveness. However, it is somewhat different, so it is presented here separately.

The first question, variety in setting, is important in understanding the child's abilities as well as motivations. It also can aid in developing the best educational program. For example, if a child's performance on standardized tests generally is inferior to that in class discussions (based on observational data) or during informal assessments, one reason for the difference could be anxiety in testing situations.

There also could be a lack of motivation to perform well in such settings. In another case, a student may show a great deal of task commitment when working on a special project after school hours but fail to complete any homework assignments. Perceptions of a number of individuals not only contribute to the information about a student's behavior in a variety of settings (since most of the individuals observe the student in different places) but also serve as a check on others' viewpoints. As everyone knows, individuals' particular biases and values often determine what they look for or see in others. Individuals' particular characteristics also have an influence on students and how they behave around teachers. Thus it is important to check these perceptions to form a clearer or more accurate picture of a student.

Obtaining a variety of types of assessment simply provides a check on the validity and reliability of the measurement itself. Perhaps the best example of the value of different types of measurement is a comparison of two ways of assessing achievement—grades and standardized tests. As is well known, grades all too often are influenced by a teacher's subjective perceptions of a student or by factors such as completion of homework, neatness of written work, or attitude toward the instructor and the class. Gifted students who are bored in a class may show lack of interest, stubbornness, or refusing to complete assignments and may receive low grades in a subject they know well. Even students who are not bored but are eager to share their knowledge may be irritating to a teacher through constant questions, calling out instructor errors in pronunciation, and correcting of other students, and cause the educator to assign a lower grade than the pupil deserves. Thus, if grades are the sole indicator of achievement, the picture may indeed be distorted. Similar anomalies can occur in other cases if only one type of measurement is used.

Validity

The third criterion for analysis of existing information is its validity. Four questions can be asked to determine validity:

1. How recently was the measurement taken?
2. What is the established validity and reliability of the instruments or procedures?
3. What is the validity and reliability of the instruments for use with gifted students?
4. What is the validity of the instruments for use with the following children (if applicable): those from different cultural or ethnic groups, from low-income (disadvantaged) homes, who are handicapped, and who do not speak English or use it as a second language?

The first question merely deals with how up to date the information should be. Some characteristics, such as those assessed by an IQ test, are not expected to change as much as interest or even creativity, so such a test that is several years old is not considered out of date while an interest inventory given three or four years ago is seriously dated. Creativity characteristics seem to be more situationally determined as well as more amenable to educational intervention than those assessed in intelligence tests, so it is helpful to give a second creativity examination if the only scores available are those that initially determined entrance into the special program.

With regard to the second question, the established validity and reliability of the instruments, the teacher is well advised to consult with an educational diagnostician, a school psychologist, or a counselor if not familiar with a particular test rather than tracking down all the data on examinations given to each student in a program. Generally, objective measurements are more reliable (i.e., more likely to yield the same results if repeated at a different time) but they are not necessarily more valid. The concept of validity pertains to the ability of the instrument to assess what it purports to measure. An instrument does need to be reliable to be valid but its reliability does not ensure its validity. For a complete reference on tests, teachers can consult the latest issues of the *Mental Measurements Yearbook* (Buros, 1978), and *Tests in Print* (Buros, 1974), or the latest editions of manuals of the tests to be used.

The third question involves the validity of a particular instrument for use with gifted students and may be more difficult to answer. A major concern is test ceilings and the number of items included for evaluating abilities at higher levels. Usually tests are developed to be the most effective at their middle ranges so they include a greater number of items of average difficulty. Since few items are at the upper ranges, a score can be affected greatly by performance on only one question. With achievement tests, for example, a student may get all or almost all items correct and will have a score in the 99th percentile. The following year, on the same test, the pupil may miss one or two more items (which may have been correct through guessing the first year), lowering the score by several percentile points and even several raw score points. Even if the same number of items are correct, the student may have a lower percentile score because of being a year older and a year further along in school. On the surface, in both cases it appears that achievement is not at a rate commensurate with the student's ability; the pupil even may have regressed. In reality, the student probably has achieved at the same high rate but there are not enough items at the appropriate level of difficulty to measure progress accurately.

Although standardized, group-administered achievement tests are most likely to be affected by low ceilings, other examinations may have the same problem. Even IQ tests have a low ceiling at their upper age ranges. For example, the *Stanford-Binet,* considered the most reliable and valid instrument for assessing intelligence at the highest levels, permits much higher scores by preschool and primary aged children because of its greater ceiling at those ages. To overcome these problems, the teacher of course can select additional tests with higher ceilings. The teacher also can administer the next higher level of the test (i.e., if the form designed for ages 4 through 6 does not have a high enough ceiling, the form for ages 7 and 9 is used). However, if the latter is chosen, the percentile or raw scores should be used rather than grade equivalents and caution exercised since the child is being compared with those who are older.

The fourth question relates to the appropriateness of the instruments for use in identifying children who may be penalized in some way by traditional testing procedures. Since volumes have been written on the subject of test bias, there is no attempt here to discuss all the relevant issues.[1] Few tests or testing procedures are acceptable to all individuals concerned about a particular group, nor are any tests or procedures acceptable to a variety of special groups. There are numerous perceptions as to how to eliminate or minimize test bias. For example, one approach with children from different cultural groups is to attempt to develop culture-free instruments based on information equally unfamiliar to all groups. A second approach is to develop culturally loaded or environmentally based instruments derived from information all children from a particular culture or living in a particular environment have a high probability of knowing. These are distinctly different approaches, resulting in completely different procedures, and there is little or no agreement among testing specialists about what constitutes the best method.

One important issue is verbal loadings of tests. Generally, tests based on figural information with little verbal or semantic content show the least bias from cultural, economic, or handicapping factors. Some examples are the figural form of the *Torrance Tests of Creative Thinking* (TTCT), the performance section of the Wechsler Scales (WPPSI, WISC-R, and WAIS), and the *Leiter International Performance Scale*. It must be noted, however, that criticism of these instruments stems from the belief that nonverbal tests do not predict academic success as well as verbal tests since verbal abilities are an integral part of academic performance. A related belief is that nonverbal tests do not predict giftedness as accurately since, according to these critics, verbal ability is the most important component of intelligence. However, even if this point of view is accepted, it seems obvious that it is highly inappropriate to use a verbally loaded test with a child who has been deaf from birth or one who speaks only Spanish. Equally obvious is the fact that a figural or visual task should not be used with a blind child.

A second issue concerns the common practice of translating tests into other languages or administering them in a child's native language. Although this is superior to testing in a child's second language, there are two problems:

1. The validity of the translation of concepts is of concern. Often, a literal or direct translation does not capture the essence of an important concept or

results in confusion between two possible meanings. There also may be no conceptual counterpart for an idea in the second language.

2. The difference in a language's use in different geographical areas also is of concern. For example, the Spanish spoken in Mexico is very different from that used in most small towns in northern New Mexico (where many families still speak no English).

Generally speaking, if a battery of tests is comprehensive and varied, as discussed in this section, it also is more likely as a group to meet the third criterion of validity. In other words, the whole analysis of a child's ability is more likely to present a true (valid) picture of ability if it includes (a) evaluation of a variety of characteristics, (b) intraindividual as well as interindividual differences, (c) observation/assessment in a variety of settings, (d) the perceptions of a number of individuals, and (e) a range of types of assessments (e.g., objective as well as subjective) than if it does not meet these criteria. However, educators who must be concerned about the validity of assessment procedures for any of the special populations of gifted children discussed in Chapter 7 should consult test manuals, testing specialists, and publications reviewing the research on this issue rather than assuming that this chapter provides an adequate basis for answering questions about special groups.

After the test information is analyzed, it is time to decide whether new data should be collected and, if so, what kind is needed, who will administer the tests or make the observations, and how this will be accomplished. For the sake of practicality, the teacher should attempt to identify the smallest number of new assessments that will add the most to the existing information in terms of these criteria. For example, in a program based on Renzulli's *Enrichment Triad,* if the earlier analysis showed there had been no assessment of creativity, no information was available from regular classroom teachers or from parents, and all data were from tests administered by the school psychologist, two types of measurement could add enough comprehensiveness and variety to complete the assessment.

A test of creative thinking administered by the special teacher in a playful setting can provide one measurement of the cluster of characteristics important in Renzulli's model as well as generate an additional type of test setting. A second measurement of creativity as well as the perceptions of other individuals can be obtained if the regular classroom teachers, parents, and the special teacher complete a set of behavior rating scales that include creativity characteristics as well as other learning, intellectual, motivational, and personality characteristics of interest in the development of the child's profile. At this point, the educator also could share the existing data with parents, other teachers, and the student, and ask their perceptions of its comprehensiveness, variety, and validity. They may have suggestions for additional areas to be assessed to resolve discrepancies between the data and their perceptions of the student's characteristics.

Compilation of Information

Data on the student are compiled to form an individual profile. Its usefulness is increased if (a) a table of norms with a corresponding weighting system is developed so that all pupils in the program can be compared with each other and with themselves, using a standard procedure; (b) all assessments of a particular trait or ability are grouped together; (c) characteristics are organized or categorized according to the model(s) being used; (d) the profile includes both the scores and a graphic representation of them; and (e) all information is contained in a one-page form that is standard for all students involved. The suggested procedure for developing a profile with all those characteristics is a modification of the identification matrix developed by Baldwin (Baldwin & Wooster, 1977). If such a matrix, or a modified one as proposed by Maker (Note 11) is used, this step is made easier by the availability of scores, weights, and ranges.

The first step in the process is to develop a table of instruments on which scores are available for students in the program. This table should list the instruments, a system for weighting their scores, and the ranges of scores receiving a certain weight (Table 8-1 infra is an example). A weighting system is developed to compare scores obtained on different instruments and essentially is a primitive way of standardizing results. In most identification matrices, weights range from 1 to 5, but in using one for developing an individual profile, weightings from 1 to 10 are recommended since a greater degree of differentiation is needed.

To assign weights to ranges of scores, the teacher must decide first whether to compare the student to others in the school or program (local norms) or to all who have taken the test (national norms). If comparisons are made on a local basis, average scores and ranges from lowest to highest must be computed for the local group. Weights are assigned, with 1 the lowest and 10 the highest. If comparisons involve national norms, the standard scores, percentile ranks, or stanines can be used. Since most of the children will be above average, it usually is more helpful to assign a weight of 1 to scores in the average range and 10 to the uppermost. In this case, the point spread for each weight is determined by subtracting the median score from the upper limit, then dividing by 10.

For example, if scores are reported in percentiles and the 50th percentile is the average, it is assigned a weight of 1 and the upper percentile is weighted as 10. The average score, 50, is subtracted from the upper limit, 100, which leaves 50. This range of scores then is divided by 10, resulting in a point spread of 5 for each weighted score, as follows:

Weighted Score	1	2	3	4	5	6	7	8	9	10
Score (%)	50-54	55-59	60-64	65-69	70-74	75-79	80-84	85-89	90-94	95-99

For additional examples of weighting systems, see Table 8-1.

The next step in the development of a profile is to decide on the most helpful clustering of characteristics and instruments. If the theoretical model makes certain assumptions about characteristics or if it provides a structure for viewing them, that grouping should be used. For example, when the Renzulli triad is used, it is helpful to group together all measures of ability, of creativity, and of task commitment, and all information about interests and learning styles. If the Guilford model is used (Figure 8-1), the most helpful grouping is by the three dimensions of content, process, and product, with each type of ability as a separate heading. On the profile sheet, each trait is listed, and the instrument or procedure that provides an assessment of it is entered under it. At the top of the form, a column is provided for instruments and traits, scores, and weighted scores. The weighted scores can be arranged to produce a graphic representation. In Figure 8-2 infra, a bar graph is used.

If the process just described is followed, the result is a profile form that satisfies all the criteria of usefulness outlined earlier. All information is organized to facilitate its use in planning individual programs within the existing curriculum. Furthermore, all scores are represented graphically and contained on a single form to avoid the problem of shuffling through hundreds of papers and test protocols to find needed data.

Development of Objectives

Once a profile is developed, it is time to interpret it, conduct additional testing or observation if needed to resolve discrepancies, and make decisions about areas of emphasis for the educational program. It is helpful to share the profile with parents, other teachers, and the student, asking for their perceptions of its accuracy and validity. If there seems to be major discrepancies or ambiguities in the measurement, additional tests or observations may be warranted. If the profile seems satisfactory, these individuals can assist in the decision-making process. Decisions must be made about whether to focus on strengths, weaknesses, or a combination of the two. Unless a student has learning problems, a gifted program should focus on the development of strengths, because talent development is the real purpose of these plans. Exceptions to this general principle are the special populations discussed in Chapter 7.

Decisions about areas of focus actually can become the long-term goals for each child. Within each long-term or annual goal is a series of short-term objectives. Goal areas can be broader statements in terms of overall development while specific objectives pertain to the special program and what will be done there. Both short-term and long-term goals can be developed directly from the profile since it is individualized as well as based on the model that forms the framework for the gifted program. If, for instance, the program is based on a combination of the

Renzulli triad and Williams's (1970, 1972) model, one long-term or annual goal can be developed for each of the types of enrichment activities:

Type I: Student will explore at least five new topics or subjects within each content area.

Type II: Student will develop thinking and feeling behaviors involved in creativity to a greater extent.

Type III: Student will develop at least one area of interest by conducting an in-depth investigation of a real problem and presenting it to a real audience.

In Type I, specific objectives can pertain to either the further exploration of some content area already of interest to the child or to the investigation of completely new areas. A combination also can be helpful—further in-depth exploration of subtopics within an area of interest along with a branching out into new fields. The particular needs and desires of the student, along with the wishes of the parents and the particular restraints of the program, determine both the number of new topics explored and their particular combination.

In Type II activities, specific objectives are based on Williams's model and on decisions made cooperatively by parents, teachers, and the student after reviewing the profile of strengths and weaknesses in the behavior area. For example, a student with strengths in the thinking areas of fluency and originality may have as a specific objective the development of fluency and originality in new content fields. In this way, the student develops risk taking by exploring new areas but the major purpose is to enhance the pupil's strengths. The weaker area also can be combined with the strengths through having the student present original ideas to the class or to a different audience. Specific objectives can pertain to other research skills needed for particular kinds of investigations as determined by the student's interests.

Specific objectives in Type III are developed as the student decides on a particular investigation and pertain directly to that study. These objectives can be detailed on the student's Project Management Plan (proposal for project).

Development of a Program Plan

After both long-term and specific goals have been written, the next task is to cooperatively develop methods and materials for achieving the objectives. In general, the first decision is to determine which ones can best be met, and where—the regular classroom program, the special program, support services, or at home. One way to resolve the problem of weak areas is to meet these needs through the regular classroom program, support services, or exercises at home. In this way, talent development can be the major focus of the special program. Using the earlier example, objectives in Type I can be accomplished in the regular program and at home, Type II through the regular classroom program and the special program with some practice exercises at home, and Type III as the major responsibility of the special program with parental support.

The specific activities, materials, and learning experiences in the special program are selected from or designed around the particular teaching-learning model(s) upon which the curriculum is based. Content, process, product, and learning environment modifications are needed to meet each student's needs. Since much of this volume is devoted to the generation and/or selection of learning experiences for particular purposes, such a discussion does not seem needed here. For an example of the application of this process in an individual case, the reader is referred to the case study later in this chapter.

Evaluation of Progress

Progress toward objectives and goals should be assessed informally as a continuing process and should be evaluated more formally at the end of each year or marking period. Informal assessment can include teacher observation, teacher rating scales, student self-evaluation using rating scales, parent rating scales, or parent observation. It also can involve teacher-designed tests, structured situational tests, interaction analysis of discussions, and peer evaluation. Formal assessment can include many of these same instruments or procedures as well as posttesting on the instruments used initially as diagnostic or identification procedures. Based on the collection of informal assessments throughout the year, immediate changes can be made in the objectives and/or program plans. As a result of the formalized evaluation at the end of the year, major redirections can be made in the program and objectives for the following year if necessary.

CASE STUDY OF AN EXCEPTIONAL CHILD

The following section presents a case study of a highly intelligent, highly creative boy. As an outsider, the author was asked to assist in the development of a profile and an educational program plan for him. This is the process followed.

David M. first came to the attention of his teachers because of his outstanding creative writing and drawing ability. He has always enjoyed creative writing, making up long, elaborate stories and creating imaginary animals or families. These stories always were illustrated with drawings showing an ability far superior to what one would expect from a child his age. He was always an excellent reader, good in science and most subjects, but having trouble in math. His third grade teacher noted that he had particular difficulty with multiplication tables. David is a rather quiet, reserved boy who always seems to be thinking. He can amuse himself all day—writing, drawing, reading, and thinking.

When the public schools began to develop programs for gifted children, David was in the third grade. His teacher referred him for testing but his IQ score was not high enough to qualify him for placement (it was a few points below the 130 criterion). Throughout his school career, however, David continued to show his superior talents in writing, drawing, and thinking. When his aunt was appointed vice principal of a middle school, she asked him (by then in the seventh grade) for suggestions and told him to think about the situation for a while and write them down. His response was so thoughtful it was published in the *Middle School Journal:*

As you may well know, the writer feels that the V.P. must gain the students' respect as well as not becoming a tyrant.

The second objective is to let the students know who you are, to inform them of your status on the faculty, and to let them know exactly what a Vice-Principal does.

The above are the primary objectives. To be efficient, you must do the little things, too:

1. You must be firm and loud, but don't let the students think that the only thing you do in the school is scream at kids in the hall.
2. The writer highly recommends a complaint box be established if none exists. Complaints should be read at least weekly, and doing something about the legitimate complaints (lousy lunchroom food is possible exception) should be considered. Optional: At the end of the year, call a general assembly to read some of the *most* legit complaints and what you've done about them. More practical measure, call anyone who wants to come. Do this at least a week before the 5th of June.

    Also put the complaint box in the main office in the front. Students aren't going to search the grounds and enter a possibly strange building to turn in a complaint.
3. Try to concentrate as much stuff (activity info, etc.) in the front office as possible without overloading. Single class project info and stuff like that ought to be kept in the class in the display case.

In order to fulfill the two primary objectives, you must:

1. Let them (the students) know you're a nice gal.
2. Let them know of your punishments you plan to use on the bad students.

3. Visit as many classrooms as you can. Figure out a schedule of speaking times conforming to the students' schedule.
4. Do not visit classes with the Principal. (This sets up a "big Principal hurt us bad, little Vice-Principal inferior" sort of attitude.)
5. Have a good, well-written speech generally memorized in your head. Talk to the students as equals, except on the discipline part. Power flaunting (limited, of course) is allowed here. Have *short* question/answer period after speech.
6. I am uninformed as to what exactly the V.P. does. This is up to you.

This is all I can think of. Be determined, don't go overboard (kitchen duty for running in the halls for example) on your reprimands. Do not be too soft, either. (Morris, 1979, p. 31)

When David's mother and I began talking about his unique creative talent and his difficulties in math, we decided to give him a complete battery of tests and develop as comprehensive a profile of intellectual strengths and weaknesses as possible. Since the SOI model provides the most comprehensive system for developing such a profile, we used it as a basis for the areas to explore.

A profile was developed using the procedures described earlier in this chapter. Following that procedure, we first analyzed the existing information to determine its comprehensiveness, variety, and validity. Information available on David was rather limited. His folder contained the *Comprehensive Tests of Basic Skills* (CTBS) scores for three years, a WISC-R protocol and write-up from four years ago, and some miscellaneous creative work and anecdotal notes from previous teachers. There were no ratings or measures of divergent thinking, no diagnostic or individualized tests of achievement, and no systematic teacher ratings of ability or motivation.

Thus, the measurement lacked comprehensiveness in that there was no assessment of all the dimensions in the Guilford *Structure of Intellect* model (i.e., not all are assessed by the WISC-R), particularly as to divergent thinking and some of the product areas involved in creativity. The information lacked comprehensiveness in its assessment of David's own pattern of strengths and weaknesses in a variety of intellectual abilities. Also lacking was variety in the perceptions of individuals (there were no rating scales completed by other teachers or by parents), assessment in different settings (only standardized testing situations had been used), and variety in types of evaluations (all were standardized, objective tests that required one right answer). The data lacked validity in that the IQ scores were not recent and the only achievement results were group measures in which he performed at or near the top in almost every area.

On the basis of this analysis, the following tests were given:

a. the *Structure of Intellect-Learning Abilities* (SOI-LA) test to provide a basic assessment of each operation, content, and product, and to give a picture of David's own strengths and weaknesses;
b. the WISC-R to obtain a current evaluation of intelligence;
c. the *Peabody Picture Vocabulary Test* (PPVT), the *Peabody Individual Achievement Test* (PIAT) and the *Wide Range Achievement Test* (WRAT) as additional measures of achievement on an individual basis; and
d. the *Differential Aptitude Tests* (DAT) for a different type of analysis of intelligence.

We also asked that both the parents and the regular classroom teacher complete four subscales of the *Scales for Rating the Behavioral Characteristics of Superior Students* (SRBCSS) to provide subjective perceptions of David's abilities in different settings.

Still following the process, we next developed a table of ranges and weights for the scores on tests and procedures administered (Table 8-1). We were concerned with comparisons of David's performance to other children his age as well as within himself. By developing weightings based on percentile rankings, a set of scores was produced that compared his performance with others his age. Using the percentages of the total possible items, we compared his performance to the "absolute" criterion of the total possible. Since he was near the top of the age scale for the WISC-R, these scores, although based on percentage of total, are interpreted similarly to the percentile rankings. For the behavior rating scales, weightings are based on the total possible points that can be received as 10 and an approximately average score as 1. These weightings also could have been based on the averages and ranges of other students in David's school or class had these been available.

The next step was to group the measurements according to the model being used and to put this information on one form that included a graphic representation. We first developed a rough draft of a chart showing the intellectual abilities categorized according to Guilford's dimensions, along with the tests measuring each of the abilities. To develop a profile of SI abilities from the WISC-R scores, Meeker's (1969) templates were used with the test protocol. A Profile and Tally Sheet (Figure 8-1) was developed from the analysis. The numbers in the blanks in each cell (e.g., MSU, MMU, MMR, etc.) indicate the number of items David answered correctly on a particular ability of the model while the numbers in the boxes in the right corner of each cell indicate the total number correct in that cell over the expected number (based on test norms and Meeker procedure) for a person David's age. For example, in the cell MSS (Memory of Symbolic Systems), he received a

Table 8-1 Ranges and Weights of Scores for SOI Analysis

Instruments	Ranges of Scores with Weights									
	1	2	3	4	5	6	7	8	9	10
SOI-LA Test [1]	50-54%	55-59%	60-64%	65-69%	70-74%	75-79%	80-84%	85-89%	90-94%	95-99%
DAP (Percentile)	50-54%	55-59%	60-64%	65-69%	70-74%	75-79%	80-84%	85-89%	90-94%	95-99%
TTCT (Percentile)	50-54%	55-59%	60-64%	65-69%	70-74%	75-79%	80-84%	85-89%	90-94%	95-99%
CTBS (Percentile)	50-54%	55-59%	60-64%	65-69%	70-74%	75-79%	80-84%	85-89%	90-94%	95-99%
PIAT (Percentile)	50-54%	55-59%	60-64%	65-69%	70-74%	75-79%	80-84%	85-89%	90-94%	95-99%
PPVT (Percentile)	50-54%	55-59%	60-64%	65-69%	70-74%	75-79%	80-84%	85-89%	90-94%	95-99%
WRAT (Percentile)	50-54%	55-59%	60-64%	65-69%	70-74%	75-79%	80-84%	85-89%	90-94%	95-99%
WRAT (Percentile)	50-54%	55-59%	60-64%	65-69%	70-74%	75-79%	80-84%	85-89%	90-94%	95-99%
WISC-R [1]	50-54%	55-59%	60-64%	65-69%	70-74%	75-79%	80-84%	85-89%	90-94%	95-99%
SRBCSS (Raw Score)										
Creativity	20-21	22-23	24-25	26-27	28-29	30-31	32-33	34-35	36-37	38-40
Learning	13-14	15-16	17-18	19-20	21-22	23-24	25-26	27-28	29-30	31-32
Motivation	17-18	19-20	21-22	23-24	25-26	27-28	29-30	31-32	33-34	35-36
Leadership	20-21	22-23	24-25	26-27	28-29	30-31	32-33	34-35	36-37	38-40

1. Weightings for scores on these tests are based on the percentage of the total possible items in all categories of operations, content, and products.

score of 6 on the ability in the Digit Span Subtest, 1 in Picture Completion, and 1 in Information. His total for MSS was 8, and the total expected for someone his age was 5.

To complete the profile and obtain results needed to interpret David's strengths and weaknesses, the total scores obtained, the expected figures for his age, and the totals possible were computed for each operation (e.g., cognition, memory, evaluation, convergent production, divergent production), type of content (figural, symbolic, semantic), and product (units, relations, systems, transformations, implications) tested by the WISC-R (Table 8-2). As the table indicates, his scores were higher than expected for his age on all but one ability—the product area of relations. Convergent production, units, and implications were extremely high. The percent total and all his other scores were transferred to the rough draft of his Talent/Ability Profile.

The next step was to examine the tentative profile and determine whether any additional tests needed to be given to resolve discrepancies or assist in the interpretation. Since all observational data showed him to be high in creativity, the SOI-LA test indicated a deficit in the product areas of transformations and implications, and the WISC-R provided little information on these abilities, it seemed necessary to administer the TTCT Verbal (V) and Figural (F) forms to resolve the discrepancies. The weighted scores for this instrument were developed based on percentiles (see Table 8-1) using national norms.

It was now time to develop a Talent/Ability Profile for use in planning David's educational program (Figure 8-2). As described earlier, a form was designed for listing the clusters of abilities and the exact scores obtained. A graph of the scores based on the weighting system was developed. Average weights were computed for each ability and these averages circled to distinguish them from the other weights. The figures in the "score" column are either percentages, percentiles, or standard scores rather than raw figures.

Before interpreting the scores, one last profile was taken from the computer analysis of the SOI-LA that we received from the SOI Institute (Figure 8-3). This plot of scores provides an analysis of an individual's ability scores based on his own average to provide a graphic way of viewing differences (relative strengths and weaknesses) within each individual.

Armed with the profiles and scores, David, his teacher, his mother, and I then were ready to examine them and develop an educational program for him. His clear areas of strength were in divergent production, figural and semantic content, and the product areas of units and implications. The weaker areas seemed to be in products—classes, relations, systems, and transformations. Cognition, memory, and evaluation also were somewhat lower than his average. When discussing weaknesses, however, it should be noted that none of his scores fell below average or the 50th percentile and that most were in the 70s, 80s, and 90s. The scale and weights were developed as a way to look at children who were likely to be superior

Figure 8-1 Profile and Tally Sheet for SOI Analysis of WISC-R for David M.[2]

Profile and Tally Sheet for S.O.I. Analysis of the WISC-R

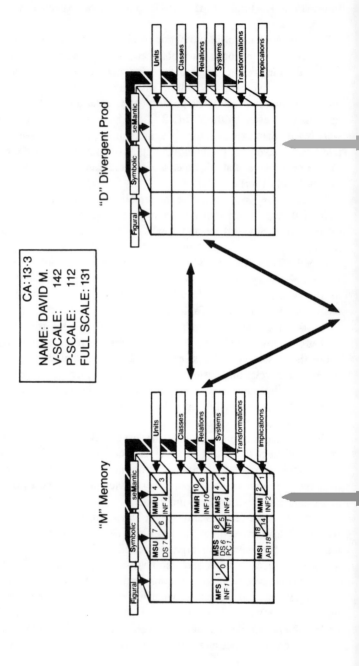

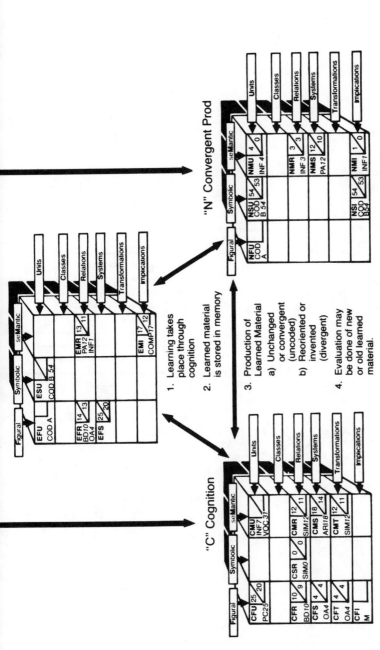

Note: Each large box represents an operation in Guilford's *Structure of Intellect* model, while each small box within these represents one of the separate abilities in the model.

Source: Reprinted from *The Structure of Intellect: Its Interpretation and Uses,* by permission of Charles E. Merrill Publishing Co., © 1969.

Figure 8-2 Talent/Ability Profile Based on SOI Analysis

Name _David M._   Date _July 8, 1979_   Age _13_

Ability/Procedure	Score	1	2	3	4	5	6	7	8	9	10
Intellectual Abilities											
I. Operations											
A. Cognition								⊗			
1. SOI-LA	76%						x				
2. WISC-R (115%)	90%									x	
B. Memory								⊗			
1. SOI-LA	79%						x				
2. WISC-R (131%)	93%									x	
C. Evaluation								⊗			
1. SOI-LA	72%					x					
2. WISC-R (123%)	94%									x	
D. Convergent Production									⊗		
1. SOI-LA	71%					x					
2. WISC-R (153%)	95%										x
3. DAP	142										x
E. Divergent Production											⊗
1. SOI-LA	100%										x
2. TTCT-V&F	99+%										x
II. Contents											
A. Figural									⊗		
1. SOI-LA	77%						x				
2. WISC-R (118%)	95%										x
3. TTCT-F	99.9%										x
4. DAP	142										x
B. Symbolic								⊗			
1. SOI-LA	75%						x				
2. WISC-R (132%)	87%								x		
C. Semantic										⊗	
1. SOI-LA	88%								x		
2. WISC-R (135%)	93%									x	
3. TTCT-V	99.9%										x
III. Products										x	
A. Units										⊗	
1. SOI-LA	90%										x
2. WISC-R (142%)	90%										x
3. TTCT-F	99.9%										x
B. Classes			⊗								
1. SOI-LA	63%			x							

Figure 8-2 continued

Ability/Procedure	Score	1	2	3	4	5	6	7	8	9	10
							Weighted Score				
C. Relations							⊗				
1. SOI-LA	74%					x					
2. WISC-R (91%)	84%						x				
D. Systems							⊗				
1. SOI-LA	75%					x					
2. WISC-R (110%)	82%						x				
E. Transformations						⊗					
1. SOI-LA	74%					x					
2. WISC-R (106%)	80%						x				
3. TTCT-V (Activities 4,8,5)	99.9%										x
F. Implications								⊗			
1. SOI-LA	69%				x						
2. WISC-R (140%)	100%										x
3. TTCT-V (Activities 1-3,7)	99.9%										x
Achievement											
I. Verbal											⊗
A. CTBS	99%										x
B. PIAT	135										x
C. PPVT	163										x
D. WRAT	140										x
II. Numerical									⊗		
A. CTBS	87%							x			
B. PIAT	135										x
C. WRAT	100	x									
Ratings											
I. Creativity	39.5										⊗
A. SRBCSS-Parent	39										x
B. SRBCSS-Teacher	40										x
II. Motivation	33								⊗		
A. SRBCSS-Parent	35										x
B. SRBCSS-Teacher	31							x			
III. Learning	29.5								⊗		
A. SRBCSS-Parent	29								x		
B. SRBCSS-Teacher	28							x			
IV. Leadership	34.5								⊗		
A. SRBCSS-Parent	31						x				
B. SRBCSS-Teacher	38										x

Figure 8-3 SOI Profile for David M.

PLOT OF SUMMARY SCORES

	Weakness	*	Strength
Operations:			
Cognition	 X		
Memory	 X		
Evaluation	 X		
Convergent	 X		
Divergent	 X
Contents:			
Figural	 X		
Symbolic	 X		
Semantic	 X		
Products:			
Units	 X		
Classes	... X		
Relations	 X		
Systems	 X		
Transformations	 X		
Implications	 X		

*Student's own average (.77).

Source: Reprinted from SOI-LA test results by Mary Meeker with permission of the SOI Institute, 343 Richmond Street, El Segundo, California, 90245, © 1980.

Table 8-2 Total Scores for Interpretation of WISC-R Ability Profile Based on SOI Profile Analysis

Ability	Total Possible	Expected for Age	David's Score	% of Total [1]	% of Expected [2]
Operations					
Cognition	123	96	111	90	115
Memory	58	41	54	93	131
Evaluation	73	56	69	94	123
Convergent Production	21	13	20	95	153
Contents					
Figural	87	70	83	95	118
Symbolic	38	25	33	87	132
Semantic	161	111	150	93	135
Products					
Units	82	52	74	90	142
Relations	59	55	50	84	91
Systems	76	57	63	82	110
Transformations	20	15	16	80	106
Implications	38	27	38	100	140

1. These percentages were obtained by dividing David's score by the total possible.

2. These percentages were obtained by dividing David's score by those expected for his age.

in almost everything, so it would not be helpful to analyze a profile made up completely of 9s and 10s.

In further examining the profile, we looked for discrepancies that might need further explanation. One of the most interesting was between WRAT and PIAT scores in math. On the WRAT, his score was in the 50th percentile, on the PIAT in the 99th. On the WRAT, the student actually must make the computations but on the PIAT chooses the correct answers from several possibilities. The CTBS scores and the SOI Analysis of Ability offered a further explanation. His "math application" scores on the CTBS were much lower than "math concepts," and his ability in dealing with symbolic content was much lower than in any other content area. The lower abilities in systems and relations also might contribute to such low scores on the WRAT. With the PIAT, he could be using his strengths in the semantic areas to compensate.

Following Meeker's (1969) recommendations and based on a concern about his math achievement, we chose several specific weaknesses for remediation and several specific strengths for development. We also decided upon some general areas of focus that combined strengths with weaknesses and developed long-term goals and specific objectives for each. The goals, objectives, educational approaches, and means of evaluation were written into an Individualized Education Program (Exhibits 8-1 and 8-2) as required by the public schools. The exhibits show how teaching strategies based on the *Structure of Intellect* approach can be translated into a written plan as required by P.L. 94-142 if such a plan is required.

Although most of David's work in the gifted program was concentrated on the development of strengths, he chose to work on some of his weak areas because of his difficulties in math. The long-term goals correspond to Meeker's two general strategies: (1) focusing on specific abilities by targeting individual cells and (2) focusing on general abilities by combining strengths with weaknesses. Within the specific abilities element, objectives list the areas to be strengthened and those to be remediated. Within the general areas, the objectives target certain combinations of strength and weakness. The general approach was to combine two strengths with one weakness because the major emphasis was on talent development.

Methods and materials to be used involved both individual and group activities. David was to work for an average of 30 minutes per day in the SOI workbooks on activities at his level in each ability area. The plan was to average this much time each day but to allow him to choose when and how much to do each day. The workbook activities also could be accomplished at home. David's regular classroom teacher used the *New Directions in Creativity* program (Renzulli, 1976b) with her whole class, and David participated in this program, emphasizing the listed activities. The teacher of the gifted uses the *Creative Problem Solving* Model and the Taba strategies so these activities occurred in the special program, as did

(Text continues on page 250.)

Exhibit 8-1 Individualized Education Program Implementation Plan

Name ___David M.___   School ___Hoover___   Implementor ___1___

Long Term Goal D. will develop specific areas of intellectual strengths and weaknesses through concentration on specific "cells" in the Structure of Intellect Model of Human Intelligence

Dates Init.	Ach.	Short-Term Objectives	Teaching Methods/Materials	Method of Evaluation	Comments
		1. D. will increase at least two grade levels in the following areas of intellectual strength: a. Cognition of figural units b. Cognition of figural transformations c. Divergent production of figural units d. Divergent production of semantic units e. Divergent production of symbolic relations f. Cognition of semantic relations g. Memory of symbolic units	1. D. will complete exercises in the SOI Workbooks (Advanced Cognition, Advanced Divergent Production, Advanced Memory) chosen, beginning at his present level of functioning and progressing sequentially. He will work in these for an average of 30 minutes per day.	Posttesting on SOI-LA Test Posttesting on TTCT	Regular classroom or home
		2. D. will increase at least two grade levels in the following areas of intellectual weakness: a. Evaluation of figural classes b. Convergent production of figural units c. Memory of symbolic systems d. Cognition of figural systems e. Cognition of symbolic systems f. Evaluation of symbolic systems	2. D. will complete exercises in the SOI Workbooks (Basic Evaluation, Basic Covergent Production, Basic Memory, and Basic Cognition) chosen beginning at his present level of functioning and progressing sequentially. He will work in these for an average of 30 minutes per day	Posttesting on SOI-LA test Posttesting on WRAT and PIAT	Regular classroom or at home

1. In this IEP, responsibility for implementing the plan has been divided among the special program, regular classroom program, and home. Implementors for each method are listed in the "Comments" Column.

Exhibit 8-2 Individualized Education Program Implementation Plan

Name ____ David _____   School ____ Hoover _____   Implementor _____

Long-Term Goal ____ D. will develop general areas of strength and weakness through concentration on combining strengths with weakness using the Structure of Intellect Model of Human Intelligence

Dates		Short-Term Objectives	Teaching Methods/Materials	Method of Evaluation	Comments
Init.	Ach.				
		1. D. will increase at least two grade levels in intellectual areas that combine his strengths in divergent production, semantic content, and figural content with his weaknesses in classes. This leads to the exercise of the abilities DMC and DFC	1a. Complete exercises in Divergent Production Workbook for these specific abilities.	Posttesting on SOI-LA Test Taping with self-evaluation using posttesting on TTCT	1a. Regular classroom or at home
			1b. Participate in class activities using the New Directions in Creativity Program, especially "Words with Feeling" (DMC) and "Figure Families" (DFC).		1b. Regular classroom
			1c. Self-evaluation of ability to produce different categories or classes of items during brainstorming or listing activities.		1c. Special program
			1d. Participate in class activities using Taba's Concept Development Strategy, emphasizing a modification of the grouping task at Steps 3 & 5 in which he concentrates on generating categories not on the list. Emphasize a modification of Step 4 by adding items to the new categories developed.		

Exhibit 8-2 continued

Short-Term Objectives	Teaching Methods/Materials	Method of Evaluation	Comments
2. D. will increase at least two grade levels in intellectual areas that combine his strengths in semantic and figural content, units, transformations, and implications with his weakness in convergent production. This leads to the exercise of the abilities NMU, NMT, NMI, NFU, NFT, & NFI.	2. Complete appropriate exercises in Convergent Production Workbook for these specific abilities.	Posttesting on SOI-LA test Posttesting on WRAT and PIAT	2. Regular classroom or at home
3. D. will increase at least two grade levels in intellectual areas that combine his strengths in semantic and figural content and in units, transformations, and implications with his weakness in evaluation. This leads to the exercise of the abilities EMU, EMT, EMI, EFU, EFT, & EFI.	3a. Complete exercises in Evaluation Workbook for these specific abilities. 3b. Participate in class activities using Creative Problem Solving, emphasizing strategies for problem finding and solution finding. 3c. Participate in class activities to develop critical thinking as described by Ennis (1964) (see Chapter 2). 3d. Self-evaluation of abilities in all areas. Teach new methods for evaluating own performance.	Posttesting on SOI-LA Test Posttesting on Cornell Test of <u>Critical Thinking</u>	3a. Regular classroom or at home 3b. Special Program
4. D. will increase at least two grade levels in intellectual areas that combine his strengths in divergent production, units, transformations, and implications. This leads to the exercise of the abilities DSU, DST, & DSI.	4a. Complete exercises in Divergent Production Workbook for these specific abilities.	Posttesting on SOI-LA Test Taping using self-evaluation with coding system	4a. Regular classroom or at home

5.	D. will increase at least two grade levels in intellectual areas that combine his strengths in divergent production, figural content, and semantic content with his weakness in relations. This exercises DFR and DMR.	4b.	Participate in class activities using New Directions in Creativity Program emphasizing "Fun with Words," "Time to Rhyme," "Making Words with Prefixes and Suffixes," "Building Words" (DSU) & "Wandering Words" (DST).	Observation of products from New Directions work-sheets	4b. Regular classroom
		5a.	Complete exercises in Divergent Production Workbook for these specific abilities	5a. Posttesting on SOI-LA Test Observation of products from New Directions work	5a. Regular classroom or at home
		5b.	Participate in New Directions in Creativity "Say It with Symbols" and "Make a Character" (DFR).		5b. Regular classroom
		5c.	Participate in Creative Problem Solving process emphasizing fact-finding, idea-finding, and acceptance-finding steps.	5c. Posttesting on SOI-LA Test	5c. Special program
6.	D. will increase at least two grade levels in intellectual areas that combine his strengths in figural and semantic content and in units, transformations, and implications with his weakness in memory. This exercises MMU, MMT, MMI, MFU, MFT, & MFI.	6a.	Complete exercises in Memory Workbook.	6a. Posttesting using Group Memory Test	6a. Regular classroom
		6b.	Participate in individualized activities using the SOI Group Memory Test and Training Manual.		6b. Home

the emphasis on self-evaluation. Activities from the *SOI Group Memory Test and Training Model* (Meeker, 1973) were done at home along with his parents and brother since all were interested in improving their abilities in this area.

The basic method of evaluation was posttesting on the SOI-LA test. However, for different abilities, other posttest scores (on the TTCT, Cornell, WRAT, and PIAT) were used to supplement the basic test. Self-evaluation by listening to taped brainstorming or other group activities was continuous, as was teacher observation of his products on work sheets or other written activities.

SUMMARY

This chapter has presented a detailed process for developing individualized programs for gifted students. A major thesis has been emphasis on the development of comprehensive profiles and program plans based on the particular model(s) forming the basis for overall curriculum development. It is not necessary to base these profiles on a particular approach. The teacher could develop an eclectic approach based on the general characteristics of gifted children presented in the introduction to Section I of this book and described in Chapter 6 as a means for general curriculum development for all gifted students or for special populations of gifted students. However, since the teaching/learning models normally provide the basis for developing specific curricular modifications, their use for individual planning seems advantageous.

NOTES

1. For additional references on this topic, the reader is referred to the following publications: Baldwin, Gear & Lucito, 1978; Maker, 1976; Torrance, 1977.

2. For an explanation of Meeker's procedure for analysis of tests according to Guilford's *Structure of Intellect* model, the reader is referred to Meeker, 1969. Space does not permit a thorough explanation of the process here.

3. Each separate ability in Guilford's *Structure of Intellect* model is referred to by a combination of three letters. The first denotes the operation (Cognition, Memory, coNvergent production, Divergent production, Evaluation). The second denotes the content dimension—Figural, Symbolic, seMantic, Behavioral—while the third indicates the type of product (Units, Classes, Relations, Systems, Transformations, Implications). Thus, DMC means Divergent production of seMantic Classes.

Integrated Approaches

Introduction to Section III: The Developmental Nature of Curricula

The most challenging and difficult aspect of providing a qualitatively different curriculum for gifted students is to design a program that incorporates the best elements of theory yet operates within the constraints of a public school structure. Often, compromises must be made and beautiful plans discarded in the face of harsh reality. However, with a creative attitude and a developmental perspective, educators can begin with the best possible plan, try it, evaluate it, then refine it until it represents the best possible program for that situation. Perhaps the process never ends. Students are different, parents are different, the school staff changes, the school changes, and the community changes. If educators do not respond to these changes, the curriculum no longer will be tailored to the situation.

The author was hesitant to publish these examples for just that reason. Someone might perceive the programs in this section as ''models'' and expect to incorporate them immediately into a different situation. Worse than that, someone might visit Albuquerque five years from the date of this writing (or even two), and expect to find the same programs in existence. As this book was being published, several changes were being made in the curricula presented in this section. This is as it should be: the teachers are responding to the differing needs of their students and the situational constraints placed upon their programs.

Curricula in this section have been developed by teachers of the gifted in the Albuquerque Public Schools. All of these teachers are or have been students of the author so their programs reflect some influence of their training. Their programs also reflect their differing personalities, styles of teaching, and philosophies. Many other teachers and students also have developed exemplary curricula that could easily have been included in this book. Four representative programs have been selected that are different in grade levels, school population, overall structure, and philosophy to illustrate how teachers can plan different programs using the same general principles, the same choices of theoretical models, and the same basic developmental process.

The first section in each chapter describes the curriculum, covering such important aspects as a definition of giftedness, philosophy, program goals, student objectives, individualized plans, sample teaching activities, and pupil and program evaluation procedures. Although many of the same program elements are discussed in each chapter, their descriptions do not follow a consistent outline. To do so would have required that each be fitted into a structure that was much too rigid.

The second section of each chapter analyzes the curriculum. Since this analysis is different in each case and focuses on varying aspects of the program, no consistent outline is followed. The purpose of the analysis is to call attention to particular program elements: how the general principles described in Section I are being implemented, how the processes in Section II are followed, and how certain teaching-learning models are combined to form a comprehensive, qualitatively different approach. The analysis directs attention to the curriculum's strengths and presents alternatives that might work in different situations.

The developers, implementers, and evaluators of the curricula presented here are: Patti Williams, Chapter 9; Suzanne Keisel-Stagnone, Chapter 10; Evelyn Morris, Chapter 11; Jan Bodnar, Chapter 12.

World Cultures: A Partially Self-Contained Program in a Middle School

DESCRIPTION OF THE CURRICULUM

Overview

This program serves 21 seventh grade gifted students. They are in the special classroom for three 50-minute periods each day. All are together for the first period, then are in the program for two other consecutive periods during the day. In the large group setting, students report progress on their investigations and projects or play simulation games. Small-group settings are used for discussions, problem-solving activities, individual project work, learning packets, and writing practice. The teacher is responsible for covering English and Social Studies requirements as outlined in the school Curriculum Development Plan. The content of the program is dictated by the prescribed curriculum. Several generalizations stemming from the mandatory coursework become the focus of study during the year. The specific data examined and concepts explored relate to these generalizations.

Renzulli's *Enrichment Triad* model forms the framework for the program. Time for Type III Enrichment is provided daily. Type I activities are available constantly in the classroom. The Type II activities are structured according to *Hilda Taba's Teaching Strategies* or Sidney Parnes's *Creative Problem Solving* techniques. Both models enhance the triad framework at the group training level. There also is much carry-over into Type III investigations. Students are armed with deductive problem-solving tools such as truth tables and the rudiments of formal logic to apply to their chosen problem area

Simulations are a crucial element of the program. They provide an organized means of presenting students with selected aspects of reality. The game format allows them to manipulate specific concepts and to see and experience their interrelationships as the exercise unfolds. Simulations serve to test generalizations and solution-finding techniques, allow exchange and observation of group dynamics, and provide a data base. The students use this data base as a springboard to understanding the more integrated complex situations likely to be encountered in later investigations.

Philosophy

The educational philosophy of the program is stated in its most skeletal form: a list of beliefs, assumptions, and biases, the gestalt of which represents an operational framework for an educator of gifted individuals.

It is believed:

- that educational systems, informal or formal, are based on a vision of the future. Learners are provided with a selected set of concepts, skills, and information that an educator has deemed essential to equip them for things to come.

- that the future facing today's adolescents will be highly technological and rapidly changing, will involve an immense data bank, and, of course, will be pervasive and personal.

- that the youths of today will not be victims of the future but are the helmsmen of its course if they are allowed to assume their responsibilities.

- that highly intelligent individuals are indeed gifted and have the potential to affect the future in a profound and special way.

- that education is the interplay between an individual and the changing world, not wholly an internal or external process.

- that learning experiences that contribute significantly to individuals' understanding of themselves and their world are self-initiated and evaluated, involve cognitive and affective aspects, and are actively sought after by the students.

- that gifted youths are more readily able to engage higher levels of thinking in solution-finding situations.

- that change is constant.

It is believed that an educator's job is to:

- encourage the development of generalizations and concepts that serve as an organizing framework for the new perceptions and information discovered by the learner.

- develop the students' abilities to exploit those generalizations to accommodate a vast array of new and diverse knowledge and materials.

- provide the pupils with tools to formulate, test, and modify concepts and generalizations. These tools may be cognitive, such as specific inductive and deductive problem-solving techniques, or affective, such as awareness and new perceptions of their evolving value systems.

- create situations in which the participants are provoked, and their own sense of curiosity excites them, into further inquiry.

- assist children in permeating the relationship between the schoolroom and the outside community—first under contrived, protected circumstances such as a simulation game and then in authentic situations involving real problems, professional means of inquiry, and dissemination, with the possibility of failure.

- respect the individuals' right to use their critical facilities to evaluate and possibly reject learning experiences encountered in an educational system.

- help the students to find alternate meaningful constructs to order and validate their own experiences and images of the future.

- challenge the individuals at the highest levels—cognitive, affective, social, creative—that they are capable of stretching toward.

- ensure interactions—solitary, dyads, small groups, and herds—that will develop understanding of group dynamics, personal preferences, and different learning styles.

Content Objectives

A public school system regulates to some extent what is taught within its confines. Regulations are found in the guise of curriculum guides and development plans. The purpose of these documents is to lend a degree of universality to the education the students receive in the system. Therefore, seventh grade students in classes for the gifted must be exposed to the same content as those in developmental classes. The content objectives around which that program was developed originate in the school district's curriculum guide.

After assuring administrators and parents that the children would leave class with the requisite skills and knowledge held by all seventh graders, the teacher transforms those basic skills and that data base into a qualitatively and quantitatively different program of studies. Using the principles of Jerome Bruner and the criteria of Hilda Taba, the teacher distills a number of generalizations and subsequent concepts that seem important, to offer opportunities for discussion, manipulation, expansion, and modification and, bluntly, are interesting to the educator and within that person's field of expertise.

It is essential that the generalizations stimulate the teacher, for that serves to titillate the students and gives the material an immeasurable edge fostered by real inquisitiveness. Teachers can save time by admitting a biased point of view and pinpointing the facets and anomalies of the information that attract and puzzle them personally. But with that investment of interest in a topic, teachers must realize and explain that generalizations are not truisms and may be found to be too abstract, irrelevant, or lacking upon examination of contingent material. In other words, teachers must use their experience and education to choose valuable information but must not value it more than they value the children/people.

Generalizations

- One must speak in descriptive rather than evaluative terms when discussing other individuals or groups.

- By observing the proxemics and nonverbal components of a culture, one can begin to discern certain values, characteristics, and patterns important to that culture.

- People encounter many difficulties and problems when interacting with those who are different from themselves.

- All people, past and present, have shaped their beliefs and behavior in the face of universal human needs and problems.

- Concrete remnants of a culture do not reflect its abstract beliefs accurately.

Concepts

cultural universals
artifacts
cultural evolution
change
values
proxemics
concepts
patterns
human needs
culture
archaeology
ethnology
problem solving

Process Objectives

Process objectives are dictated by the models chosen. They often are the reason for adopting a particular model since they are the promises that the program's implementation will fulfill. The objectives described next are paraphrases or quotes from the model's originator about what the students are meant to accomplish after a learning experience structured in terms of the established framework and criteria.

Type I Enrichment (Renzulli)

The student will (a) be exposed to a wide variety of topics, concepts, and issues not ordinarily covered in the regular curriculum, and (b) be granted some insights into areas of study that may serve as the foundation for a Type III activity.

Type II Enrichment (Renzulli)

The student will (a) master skills and techniques necessary to solve problems in a variety of areas, (b) develop a sensitivity to and awareness of self and others, (c) experience open-ended problems, and (d) be exposed to processes of study they might find useful in pursuing during advanced studies.

Type III Enrichment (Renzulli)

The student will (a) become an actual investigator of a real problem using the appropriate means of inquiry, (b) take part in the formulation of a problem to be investigated and the suitable methods of resolution to be used, (c) use information as raw data, (d) direct inquiry actively toward the production of a tangible result, and (e) apply thinking and feeling processes to real situations.

Application of Generalizations (Taba)

The student will (a) predict consequences of a given set of circumstances, (b) support predictions with evidence and reasoning, (c) limit predictions by stating and supporting necessary prior or attendant conditions, and (d) draw warranted conclusions and suggest modifications or extensions of previously made generalizations on the basis of verified predictions.

Resolution of Conflict (Taba)

The student will (a) draw inferences about the feelings of persons involved in a conflict situation, (b) identify possible solutions and consequences in dealing with such a situation, and (c) form generalizations about the ways individuals handle such problems.

Interpretation of Data (Taba)

The student will (a) make and support inferences, (b) draw conclusions based on well-supported inferences, and (c) generalize from a specific instance to other similar instances.

Concept Development (Taba)

The student will (a) list items, (b) organize lists by grouping and labeling, (c) refine groups by subsuming items under labels, and labels under labels, and (d) regroup, label, and subsume in a different way.

Creative Problem Solving (Parnes)

The student will (a) identify a problem, (b) generate possible solutions to it, (c) select the most feasible, (d) have the solution accepted, and (e) implement it.

Activities

Each unit and activity relates to the concepts around which the class is based.[1] Some units emphasize a particular concept, others are designed to involve all the closely linked concepts. Thus, in dissecting the units presented during the year into separate components related to specific concepts, the elements appear to be more discrete than they actually were. To avoid redundancy, the units are listed once and are not repeated through every concept to which they may pertain. It is particularly difficult to categorize the simulation games because they are so multifaceted.

Cultural Universals

"Dig" is a simulation game in which the class invents, constructs, and reconstructs cultures. This simulation relates to every concept listed. "Time Capsule" is an interaction unit in which the class examines contemporary culture and chooses artifacts that best represent their culture for a future generation. It also involves the concept of artifacts.

Artifacts

The class took a field trip to La Cienega, a colonial Spanish outdoor museum where persons in costume simulate the life style of that time using the tools and methods available then. Using state-of-the-art videocassette equipment, a visual record of the class experiences and products was taped. The class members viewed this material as artifacts on two levels, first as a representation of a time period, then as concrete examples of the technology and machinery of 1980.

Cultural Evolution

"Connections" is a ten-part television series that traces the evolution of some inventions. Technological development and humankind's relationships with technology, as master and as dependent, are examined. *Future Shock* is a book that focuses on the tremendous cultural changes caused by the rapidly expanding and immense amount of information society has generated.

Change

In the Super Dictionary Unit, a set of Ditto masters teaches efficient use of the resource with etymology as content. Through discussion and reading, the class identified a huge group of words that defined meanings in a jaded manner. The use of fresh expressions rather than tiresome cliches was emphasized. During poetry reading, the class recorded the recitations; the linguistic changes from Shakespeare to Silverstein became more evident when heard from the tapes.

Values

Junior Great Books, a collection of short stories that express different values, were examined and discussed in relation to authors, characters, and readers. Mock trials were used as the vehicle for discussion of the issues of right and wrong, good and evil, fair and unfair. The traditional values embodied in working at home were reflected and reinforced by that great American institution—homework.

Proxemics

After opening a school-wide Christmas Shop, in addition to stocking, inventorying, and accounting, the class members were exposed to the science of the use of space. They had to decide how to arrange the displays, floor plan, and cash box for maximum sales. On an informal outing to Skate Ranch, the students noted the use of space in public places. The class sponsored a St. Patrick's Day dance, the Shamrock Shuffle, and pondered the problem of converting the gymnasium into an intimate, exciting ballroom. Sometimes, when students arranged themselves on an $8' \times 15'$ rug for a discussion, they discussed the fact that Americans were a noncontact nationality with certain space requirements.

Concepts

The study of law as a conceptual framework and the Bill of Rights as a catalog of abstract ideals was investigated. "Cope," a simulation game that forces participants to develop a coping mechanism to deal with rapid change, provided the topic of how concepts were formed and how they were changed. The unit "Drawing on the Right Side of the Brain" used drawing as a visual representation of how the right and left hemispheres of the brain form and relay concepts.

Patterns

Deductive thinking was presented by using *Mind Benders,* the rudiments of formal logic, and syllogisms; students became aware of the patterns of processing information by elimination and stricture. Through traditional texts and unorthodox means, such as student-generated *Mad Libs,* class members focused on the grammar patterns of the English language. The spelling unit was a continuing element. When students misspelled words in writing assignments, they made out spelling cards. These cards were the basis for weekly individual tests. Each student kept the spelling cards and examined them for patterns of errors.

Culture

Each student chose a New Mexican culture group, past or present, and created materials that presented a realistic insight into that culture to the other pupils.

Human Needs

Project C.A.I.R. is a kit designed to analyze a sample of American culture and to see how basic human needs are met within a family, a subculture, and a culture. "If you don't know where you are going you will probably end up somewhere else" is a set of Ditto masters that explain how personal needs and interests can be identified and how these needs must be integrated into realistic career choices.

Archaeology

A Journey through New Mexico History is a textbook that presents archaeological information chronologically and on a knowledge level.

Ethnology

"U.S.S.R." is a teacher-made simulation that incorporates the ethnic variations among the Soviet people with the history, geography, and political ideology of that country. *People of the Deer* is a nonfiction account of Canadian Eskimos and their relationships with industrialized culture.

Problem Solving

"Shipwreck" is a journal-writing activity. Students had to resolve such problems as leadership, division of labor, ownership, and stress, that occurred in an island microcosm. "Flight" is a simulation using geographical information. Students learned physical geography while practicing decision-making skills in a team. Type III activities were individual or small-group problem-solving endeavors, each unique, so methods of attack varied widely. "Search" is an interaction unit whose purpose is to get the most information from the library with the least amount of extraneous work.

All Concepts

Some activities and skills, pervasive throughout the year, defy categorization. Type I activities are so dependent upon an individual's prior experience that they could go under all, or none, of the concepts with which the teacher is concerned. Sustained Silent Reading and companion Sustained Silent Writing are not presented as a whole in a single concept. In addition to discussions, the class used writing skills from paragraphs to monographs to discover, supplement, develop, dispute, expand, and explore every single concept.

Sample Lesson Plans

The *Hilda Taba Teaching Strategies* (Institute for Staff Development, 1971a, 1971b, 1971c, 1971d) form the basis for most class discussions. To provide examples of how these discussions integrated the process and content objectives of the curriculum, four sample discussion plans are presented next. In these plans, focusing questions asked at each step in the discussion are listed sequentially. Supporting questions are asked as needed but are not included since they depend upon student responses to initial focusing questions.

Concept Development—Artifacts

1. What kinds of things will be left of our civilization for others to find 6,000 years hence?
2. Which of these artifacts go together because they are alike? For what reasons?
3. What are some labels that could be used to name these groups?
4. Which artifacts or groups of artifacts fit under other labels? Which labels fit under other labels?
5. What, in looking at the original list of artifacts, are some other ways of grouping the artifacts?

Interpretation of Data[2]

1.   What did you see in this show?
2. a. What are some causes for (the decline of the longbow)?
   b. Why do you think (the invention of the moldboard plow) is a cause (for the decline of longbow use in warfare)?
3. a. What are some causes of (the invention of the moldboard plow)?
   b. Why do you think (the invention of the horse collar) led (to the invention of the moldboard plow)?

4. a. What could you conclude about the causes for technological change?
   b. What would lead you to conclude that, based on what we have discussed?
5. a. What can you say generally about the effect of one invention on the development of other inventions?
   b. What in this discussion would lead you to make that statement?

Application of Generalizations

1. a. What if archaeologists far in the future excavate the American Southwest and find these (aluminum poptops) scattered across the terrain? What do you think they will conclude about the use of this artifact?
   b. Why?
2. a. What else would have to be true for (the archaeologists to conclude that these were jewelry rings)?
   b. Why do you think (that the future archaeologists would have to have a humanoid form) for them to make that conclusion?
3. a. What do you think will happen as a result of (their considering this artifact as a ring)?
   b. Why do you think they will (stop looking for other uses for this artifact)?
4. a. What would you conclude is likely to happen if future archaeologists find these and interpret them in the ways we have discussed?
   b. What, from our discussion, would lead you to that conclusion?
5. a. What would you say now about this generalization in light of our discussion: The concrete remnants of a culture may not accurately reflect some aspects of that culture?
   b. What in our discussion leads you to say that?

Resolution of Conflict[3]

1.   What have you read so far in *The Overcoat* by Nikolai Gogol?
2. a. Why do you think Akaky Akakevich acted the way he did?
   b. How do you think he was feeling in this situation?
   c. What are some of the reasons you think Akaky was feeling that way?
3. a. What are some things that Akaky Akakevich *could* do?
   b. How do you think (the police, his boss) would react if Akaky did that?
   c. Why do you think (the police, his boss) would react that way?
4. a. What do you think Akaky Akakevich *should* do?
   b. Why do you think (trying to recover the coat) is the best solution?
   c. What do you think would be the consequences of (trying to recover the coat)?
   d. What reasons do you have for predicting that (he would get the coat back)?

5. a. Have you or has anyone you know ever been involved in a situation in which something valuable and very important has been stolen?
   b. What did you do about it?
6. a. How did you feel? How do you think (your mother) felt?
   b. Why do you think (she) felt that way?
7. a. What are your reasons for (confronting the major suspect)?
   b. How effective do you think the confrontation was? Why?
8. a. How could you have handled the situation differently?
   b. What do you think would have been the consequences if you had done that?
   c. Why do you think that would have happened?
9. a. Thinking back over the whole discussion and the different situations we've explored, what could you say generally about the way people deal with situations in which something valuable and very important has been stolen?
   b. What leads you to say that this is generally true of people?

Evaluation of Student Progress

An IEP is provided (Exhibit 9-1 and continued on 9-2) as an example. The   management plan and progress report are shown in exhibits 9-4 and 9-5. An IEP is provided (Exhibit 9-1) as an example. The same student's management plan and progress report also are included (Exhibit 9-2).

The student catalogs Type I activities on 3″ × 5″ index cards, and is solely responsible for recognizing, experiencing, and documenting these elements (Exhibit 9-3). Only the student can recognize a general exploratory activity that is new to that individual since each one comes to the class with different experiences. Besides this primary reason, an ancillary to student recording of these experiences is that, to earn more credits, they constantly ask themselves, ''Is this a Type I?,'' which coerces them into looking at everything they do as a learning experience. The only restriction on Type I activities is that no more than 20 percent can be of the same material. This prevents excessive television viewing and last-minute *National Geographic* reading.

Type II activities are the responsibility of the teacher to document. They are recorded in the grade book and include marks for in-class assignments, homework, tests, and projects. Since these activities closely resemble conventional classroom experiences, the methods of evaluating them are conventional. The criteria may be more exacting, the number missed fewer, and a required degree of mastery higher, but the evaluation techniques are similar to those used in many classes.

Type III activities are the responsibility of the teacher and student jointly. Conferences and written communications are frequent and are used to evaluate student progress toward product completion. Each student develops a management

Exhibit 9-1 Individualized Education Program Implementation Plan

Name _____   School __Cleveland__   Implementer __Wms.__

Long-Term Goal   Student will execute activities, according to own abilities, within the bounds of the Renzulli Enrichment Triad Model

Dates		Short-Term Objectives	Teaching Methods/Materials	Method of Evaluation	Comments
Init.	Ach.				
		Student will have at least 100 Type I experiences.	interest centers field trips T.V. programs task cards brainstorming filmstrips av materials books periodicals speakers	checklists charts observation anecdotal records conferences self-evaluation commercial mater- ials teacher-made mater- ials fulfillment of management plan	
		Student will participate in at least eight Type II activities a week	interviews discussions simulations mock trial teacher-made material		

		Student will attempt at least one Type III activity in the course of the school year.
		
		  area of research: (write in
		    individual areas)
		  method of inquiry: (write in
		    individual's method)
		  final product: (write in
		    proposed product)
		  intended audience: (write in
		    student's intended audience)			

Exhibit 9-2 Individualized Education Program Implementation Plan Continued

Name _____   School ___Cleveland___   Implementer ___Wms.___

Long-Term Goal ___To master the prescribed curriculum for seventh grade, as outlined in the school's Curriculum Development Plan for Language Arts and Social Studies.___

| Dates | | Short-Term Objectives | Teaching Methods/Materials | Method of Evaluation | Comments |
Init.	Ach.				
		See Curriculum Development Plan for short-term objectives. (Plan is attached in actual student IEPs.)	commercial materials textbooks teacher-made materials	teacher-made tests commercial tests peer grading observation standardized instruments student self-evaluation	

Exhibit 9-3 Sample Student Record of Type I Activities

Date Achieved	Description	Materials
1979		
10-29-30	"Freedom Road"	Movie
11-4	"Connections"	TV show
9-20	State fair	Fair
9-20	Indian Village	Fair
9-20	Spanish Village	Fair
11-6	"HEADLINES"	Game
11-7	*A Chocolate Moose for Dinner*	Book
11-8	*Adventures of Tom Sawyer*	Book
11-9	"Fiddler on the Roof"	Movie
11-10	"60 Minutes" (Vietnam war, old card)	TV show
11-10	Sylvia Plath poems	Book section
9-28	Inventory	Work
10-2	Learned salary system	Check/Dad
11-30	Read *By Balloon to S.*	Book
12-3	"Norm Ellenberger"	TV show
12-5	Lobo basketball	Game
12-5	Read Chris's *Book of Idioms*	Book
12-2	Learned to play Menin	(Comp. game)
11-28	Read Kenneth Rexroth's	Poem book section
12-6	Listened to Arthur Fiedeler's Encore	Music
12-6	*Break A Leg Betsy Mayle*	Book
10-11	*The Magician's Nephew* (Nernia)	Book
10-14	"The Miracle Worker" (Helen Keller)	Movie
10-15	*The Hot Header*	Newspaper
10-19	"The Scarlet Letter"	TV show
10-21	"Connections"	TV show
10-21	Article on psychosurgery	Newspaper
10-23	Task card (Mass media 16)	"Tee" world
10-28	"60 Minutes" (depression, marijuana)	TV program
10-28	"Connections"	TV program
10-26	Book on witches, demons, etc.	Story collection
11-10	Sylvia Plath poems	Book section
11-14	Taught Lorna chess	Game
11-15	"2 attorneys _____?_____" (etc.)	Newspaper article
11-15	Learned different chess approaches	Game
11-16	*Newsweek* article on Iran	Magazine
11-16	*Newsweek* article on 1970s	Magazine
11-18	"Prime Time" section on Iran	TV show
11-19	"Life Story of the Quintuplets"	Movie
11-25	"60 Minutes"	TV show
11-29	*Escape from Warsaw, Silver Sword*	Books

Exhibit 9-3 continued

Date Achieved	Description	Materials
12-25	Learned to play "Othello"	Game
12-25	Read Osmuraid penguide	Writing (calligraphy)
12-26	Watched "A Shining Season"	Movie (TV)
12-27	Watched "Star Trek"	Movie (theater)
12-27	"20/20"	TV show
12-27	"The Last Battle"	7th chron of Narnia
12-24	"Iran Report"	TV special news
12-22	*Guideposts* magazine	Magazine
9-7	Learned about typewriter	Mom, typewriter
12-31	Went to Pelican–ate crab	Crab, Mom
1980		
1-10	Learned "Automatic Detective"	Game
1-9	Read about "Snit's Revenge"	Game
1-8	"Juke Box Awards"	TV show
1-12	Journal Gymnastics	Exhibit
1-13	"Nazi War Criminals in U.S."	TV show
1-13	"Guinness Book of World Records"	TV show
1-24	"People's Choice Awards"	TV show
1-24	Read about publishing book	Pamphlet
1-18	*Born Free*	Book
1-28	Read *Bananas*	Magazine
1-30	Learned about model rockets	David, model supplier
2-3	Watched "World Chmpshp Arm Wrestling"	TV
2-3	"60 Minutes"	TV
1-28	*What's in A Name*	Name origin book
2-1	*The Girl Who Had No Name*	Book
2-1	*Freaky Friday*	Book
2-14	"Olympics"	TV
2-16	Saw newspaper office	*Tribune*
2-16	Read *National Geographic*	Magazine
2-9	"Prime Time"	TV show
3-2	*The Russian Book*	Book
3-15	Whitehouse Replica	Exhibit
3-16	"The Coal Miner's Daughter"	Movie
3-15	Lemon cups	Recipe (cook)
3-20	Play "The Magic Touch"	Play
3-24	Learned about Acapulco	Mom, Dad
4-8	Saw Acapulco pics	Pictures
4-6	"When Time Ran Out"	Movie
4-8	Article–sea creatures	*National Geographic*

Exhibit 9-3 continued

Date Achieved	Description	Materials
4-26	Spelling Bee	*
4-23	*Other Side of the Mtn. Pt. II*	*Book*
4-25	*Snowbound!*	Book
4-27	"Lady Sings the Blues"	Movie
4-28	Spelling article	Newspaper
4-27	"Save the Burros"	Article
4-27	"Artichokes"	Article
4-26	Encyclopedia Brittanica	Lookover
4-30	Botan rice candy	Japanese food
4-25	Honor Society	Meeting
5-18	Party (13)	
5-17	*Calico Captive*	Book
5-26	*Karen*	Book
5-23	"Muhammad Ali" (life story)	Movie
5-24	Jumping spiders	Experience
5-14	Learned to use typewriter	Skill
5-22	Ate fried zucchini	Food
5-21	Learned about print reader for blind	
5-18	*6,000 Words*	Book

plan (Exhibit 9-4) before embarking on an investigation. This plan defines the problem, methods, and product for both teacher and investigator. After teacher and student discuss the master plan and determine the scope and depth of the Type III, the parents are called in for a conference and the specifics of the investigation are entered in the IEP. The students are aware of the legal ramifications of this procedure and the commitment to which their signature obligates them. For some students, this conference occurs during the second week of school, but for others much more time is needed to devise an acceptable motivating Type III activity. All Type IIIs are finalized by the end of the first nine-week grading period.

Each nine weeks, three different modes of evaluation are used. First, a progress report (Exhibit 9-5), in a symposium setting, is presented to classmates. This format helps maintain interest in the investigation, causes a certain amount of progress because of peer pressure, and provides a forum for much constructive criticism and suggestions. All students also evaluate themselves, using an open but standardized simple system. Then, using the management plan, the student and teacher, in a conference, candidly discuss the investigation, evaluate it, and determine the direction the study is taking. In this conference the investigator self-assigns a quarter grade and, unless it obviously is askew with the supporting

Exhibit 9-4 Student Management Plan

NAME ___Mary M._____   TEACHER ___Williams_____   GRADE __7__

MANAGEMENT PLAN FOR INDIVIDUAL OR SMALL GROUP INVESTIGATION

GENERAL AREA OF STUDY ___publishing_____

SPECIFIC AREA OF STUDY ___Braille and poetry_____

BRIEF DESCRIPTION OF THE PROBLEM TO BE STUDIED. WHAT DO I HOPE TO FIND OUT?

   how books for visually handicapped people are published

INTENDED AUDIENCES: WHICH INDIVIDUALS OR GROUPS WOULD BE INTERESTED IN THE FINDINGS? LIST THE ORGANIZED GROUPS, CLUBS, SOCIETIES AT LOCAL AND NATIONAL LEVELS. LIST NAMES AND ADDRESSES OF CONTACT PEOPLE IN THESE GROUPS.

   audience-visually handicapped people

   contact librarian - public library for names and addresses of organizations

   Library for the Visually Handicapped

INTENDED PRODUCTS: WHAT FORM WILL THE FINAL PRODUCT TAKE? HOW, WHEN, AND WHERE WILL I COMMUNICATE THE RESULTS OF MY INVESTIGATION TO AN APPROPRIATE AUDIENCE? WHAT OUTLET VEHICLES (JOURNALS, CONFERENCES, ART SHOWS, ETC.) ARE TYPICALLY USED BY PROFESSIONALS IN THIS FIELD?

   an illustrated book of poems written in Braille but enjoyable for seeing people also. This book may be published on a wide scale or may be only a single copy. Regardless of the size of the edition, it will be donated to the library for the visually handicapped.

METHODOLOGICAL RESOURCES: LIST THE NAMES AND ADDRESSES OF PERSONS WHO MIGHT PROVIDE ASSISTANCE IN ATTACKING THIS PROBLEM. LIST THE HOW-TO-DO-IT BOOKS THAT ARE AVAILABLE IN THIS AREA OF STUDY. LIST OTHER RESOURCES (FILMS, COLLECTIONS, EXHIBITS, ETC.), SPECIAL EQUIPMENT (e.g., CAMERA, TRANSIT, TAPE RECORDER, QUESTIONNAIRE, ETC.)

   1. itinerant teacher of the visually handicapped— Ms. Bloom for: Information, stylus, Braille typewriter, training with Braille

   2. encyclopedia for Braille

   3. publishing and writer's manual for information

   4. fiction for inspiration - Light a Single Candle—Butler

NECESSARY INFORMATION: WHAT TYPES OF DATA WILL BE NEEDED TO SOLVE THE PROBLEM? IF RAW DATA, HOW CAN IT BE GATHERED AND CLASSIFIED? IF ALREADY CATEGORIZED DATE, WHERE IS IT STORED?

   publishing techniques— library
   patenting laws— U.S. government
   Brailling techniques —various places

Source: Adapted from *The Enrichment Triad Model: A Guide for Developing Defensible Programs for the Gifted and Talented* by J.S. Renzulli by permission of the author, 1977.

Exhibit 9-5 Type III Project Progress Report

NAME: Mary M.

September, 80
DATE

CATALOG WHAT YOU HAVE DONE SO FAR.   INCLUDE THE FOLLOWING:

INTERVIEWS: (PEOPLE TALKED TO)

PHONE CALLS MADE: (INDIVIDUALS & ORGANIZATIONS)

Need to call Elizabeth Paak, John Baker School, ask for other phone numbers and also if pencil has been invented yet, ask if she thinks it has a chance of being patented.

BOOKS READ: (TITLES, AUTHORS)

Light a Single Candle by Beverly Butler

Certain encyclopedia articles

MATERIALS PRINTED: (FLYERS, BROCHURES, ATTACH COPIES)

Page explaining Braille alphabet for class—30 copies

RESEARCH DONE: (HYPOTHESES & RESULTS)

Learned Braille: 6-point alphabet, 5 symbols, capital and numeral signs

Need to study patenting laws.

SUCCESSES TO DATE:

Perfection of Braille pen and learning of Braille

Prospect Park librarian said no pencil like this has been invented/patented yet (she thinks)

FAILURES TO DATE:

EXPECTATIONS:

I expect, of course, to patent my Braille pencil, but not to manufacture it, because of the costs.

IF POSSIBLE, DEMONSTRATE YOUR PROGRESS (SHOW & TELL). PLAN A 5-MINUTE PRESENTATION WITH PROPS (SPIDERS, DOGS, PICTURES, POEMS, ELEPHANTS, AARDVARKS, ETC.)

evidence, it is entered on the report card with no changes. If the evidence does not match the student's assessment, the individual is asked to provide documentation that corresponds with the grade assigned. When new evidence of the investigation comes to light, the grade is reassessed in conferences until it is acceptable to both parties. Only once was a grade viewed as too high by the teacher, and the students sometimes underestimated their progress; usually they were fair and realistic in their assessments.

Using very different means of evaluation and evaluators, the goals and objectives of the IEP were met and accomplished in full by all the students participating in the program.

Evaluation of Program Success

After a year of study, growth, and interaction, only a few tangible items remain as artifacts indicating progress and achievement.

By using a product-oriented model such as the Renzulli *Triad,* a quantifiable measure is a built-in component. Of 21 participants, 80 percent completed their individual or small-group investigations into real-life problems. Each investigation was a bona fide Type III, meeting all the criteria (Exhibit 9-6). Completion of the projects was determined by the presentation of the product to the real audience for which it was intended. Audiences were as diverse as gallery goers and entomologists, geologists and neighborhood residents, commuters and blind people.

Products were presented in various ways, all professionally acceptable: videotapes, manuscripts, recipe cards, Braille, exhibits, television and radio announcements, and newspaper advertisements.

Investigative methods included research, using existing publications, surveys, experiments, polls, and correspondence, to mention a few. Eighty percent of the students had the motivation and were equipped with the skills to accomplish a self-selected, independent research project within the given and rather arbitrary time frame of a school year. This percentage is quite high and indicates some degree of program success.

Another available quantifiable measure is standardized achievement test scores. The *California Test of Basic Skills* (CTBS), High School Form, was given as a pretest and posttest (see Tables 9-1, 9-2, and 9-3). Only 17 students' pretest and posttest scores were available because four students entered the program after the first nine weeks and so were not pretested using this instrument. The first table (9-1) indicates pretest scores in reading, language, reference skills, and social studies in the form of grade level equivalents. Posttest gains also are indicated. The key explanations are important since many of the students were achieving as high as possible (13.6) on the pretests. The second table (9-2) provides class averages in all areas. As can be seen, because of the extremely high scores of students and the

Exhibit 9-6 Progress Report

Name ____Mary M.____

Date ____April 13____

PROPOSED TYPE 3

My proposed Type III was to write and publish a poetry book, <u>The Token of Images</u>, and to Braille it and donate it to the Library for the Visually Handicapped. When I began my project, I didn't know how to type, and I didn't know a single bit of Braille.

EXPERIENCES ENCOUNTERED

My experiences (of the learning kind) were writing the book, typing the manuscript up (I now know how to work a typewriter, although I'm not exactly speedy), researching the publishing process, in which I had to do a little calling, check out a book and read the two million rules, and select a prospective sounding publisher. After I learned the publishing process for both books and magazines, I began the Braille part, which proved to be the most trying. I had been practicing Braille all this time, but all I had was the basic Braille alphabet, not the contractions and punctuation which I needed to learn. I contacted a teacher at my school who taught blind children and she helped me in getting all the Braille I needed in a booklet and a stylus and slate, along with a Brailler (a Braille typewriter) to use to Braille my book, which I plan to do this summer.

PROGRESSION SO FAR

As a summary, I've written a poetry book, learned Braille, gotten a Brailler (equipment) and learned the publishing processes and rules for typing a manuscript. This summer I plan on completing my half typed-up manuscript and sending it in to a publishing company. If at first I fail, I'll try again; after all this hard work I see no point in stopping. I'll Braille my book this summer too and I'll donate it to the Library for the Visually Handicapped whether it gets published or not.

FAILURES

At the beginning of the year, my proposed Type III was to invent a <u>Braille Pencil</u> and patent it, but things never seem to work out, and I soon discovered that "Braille pencils" had already been invented. This totally shattered my project, so I . . . started over! This was my only REAL failure; although I encountered many difficulties (such as typing, being able to contact people, and having to totally learn Braille), I never actually ran into a barrier which stopped me cold in my tracks.

Table 9-1 Individual Student Records

Pretest Reading Total	Posttest Gains	Pretest Language Total	Posttest Gains	Pretest Reference	Posttest Gains	Pretest Social Studies	Posttest Gains
11.0	1.0	11.5	2.1*	11.5	2.1*	13.0	.6*
13.6	T	13.6	T	13.6	T	10.8	2.8*
12.6	1.0*	11.0	.7	13.6	T	13.0	.6*
9.1	1.8	7.7	.8	8.6	1.1	11.4	1.1
13.6	T	13.6	T	13.6	T	13.6	T
11.7	.6	12.5	1.1*	12.4	1.2*	13.6	T
13.6	T	13.6	T	13.6	T	13.6	T
13.6	T	13.6	T	13.6	T	13.6	T
11.2	1.0	11.8	1.2	11.5	2.1*	13.5	.1*
11.6	2.1*	13.6	T	12.4	1.2*	13.6	T
11.4	1.1	10.6	3.0*	12.4	1.2*	13.6	T
11.4	2.2*	11.0	2.6*	12.4	-.9	13.6	T
12.8	.8*	13.6	T	13.6	T	13.5	.1*
12.4	1.2*	11.8	1.2	13.6	T	13.0	.6*
11.0	-1.6	10.7	1.0	13.6	T	11.4	2.8*
13.6	T	12.1	1.5*	12.4		13.6	T
10.7	.5	10.4	2.6	10.8		11.7	1.9*

Key: T - Ceiling of test reached in pretest. No gains measurable using this instrument.

* - Test ceiling reached with this gain. Gain probably is depressed.

---

low test ceilings, few gains were recorded. Even when raw scores were used, gains were not evident since many students achieved perfect raw scores on the pretests. In an attempt to identify changes that would reflect gains accurately, each student's lowest subtest score was identified in pretesting. The posttest score (Table 9-3) for that subtest was noted and the gains computed. At the time of pretesting, the students' actual grade placement was 7.0 and at posttesting was 7.9. The picture still is unclear since many students reached the ceiling at posttesting.

Another measure of program success was how well the concepts and generalizations that formed the basis for the course were assimilated. These factors were implicit in classroom activities throughout the year of study. Sometimes they were

Table 9-2 Class Averages

Subtest	Pretest	Posttest	Gain
Reading	11.0	13.6*	2.6
Comprehension	10.8	13.6*	2.8
Spelling	10.3	13.6*	3.3
	3.8	7.5	3.7
	11.2	13.6*	2.4
	10.7	10.9	.2
	8.9	10.9	2.0
	8.4	12.5	4.1
Language	5.7	6.4	.7
Mechanics	9.7	13.6*	3.9
	11.8	10.9	-.9
	9.7	12.0	2.3
	8.4	13.6*	5.2
Language Expression	11.7	13.6*	1.9
Social Studies	10.8	13.6*	2.8

*Test ceiling reached with this gain. Gain probably is depressed.

Table 9-3 Gains Made on Lowest Subtests

	Reading Total	Language Total	Reference	Social Studies
Mean Pretest Grade Equivalent	12.0	11.9	12.5	12.9
Mean Gain Using Only Measurable Gains[a]	1.2	1.6	1.4	1.2
Mean Posttest Grade Equivalent	12.72	12.9	13.2	13.5
Class Gain, All Scores Incorporated	.72	1.0	.7	.6

[a]These averages only include those student scores in which, the test ceiling was not reached on either the pretest or posttest.

present in only an oblique form of awareness; sometimes they were generated in an alternate form by students in discussions and simulations; rarely did they enter the classroom uncloaked as the topic of a discussion to be manipulated by the students.

In a final exam setting, students were asked to define ten of the concepts. The degree of mastery was amazing. A grasp of the complexity, surrounding issues, and key words involved in the concept definitions was outstanding. In another session students were asked to write statements containing a selected group of the concepts, which applied not only to specific classroom situations but also to humankind in general (Exhibit 9-7). Each generalization was restated adequately by at least one individual. The student's lexicon was not always exact but the general underlying grasp displayed did reflect the intrinsic meaning of the predetermined generalizations.

A final evaluation technique was to ask for the students' perceptions of the program. They were asked to list ten things they liked and ten they disliked about the year. Table 9-4 lists classroom activities and the number of students indicating that this activity was among the best or least liked experiences. It seems clear that, although on many activities they were divided, students enjoyed the "Dig" simulation, the Skate Ranch trip, the play, and their Type III activities.

ANALYSIS OF THE CURRICULUM

Curricular Modifications

The World Cultures program incorporates modifications of the basic curriculum in the areas of content, process, product, and learning environment. Since the students spend a majority of their day in the special program, the teacher must make certain that they have acquired the basic knowledge and skills from the regular curriculum. This is done by incorporating the prescribed curriculum into the program as data to be used in developing abstract concepts and generalizations. These concepts and generalizations then become the content focus of the special curriculum, with the facts and skills to be taught organized around these basic ideas. The concept of variety is included since the focus is on ideas above and beyond the regular program. The integration of Type I experiences also assures that students will be exposed to new and different subject matter. Methods of inquiry are included in several of the units but are particularly emphasized in the "Dig" simulation, the mock trials, and the "Search" simulation.

Process changes incorporated into the curriculum are the following: development of higher levels of thinking, open-endedness, discovery, explanation of reasoning, freedom of choice, group interaction, pacing, and variety. Higher levels of thinking are emphasized through discussions using the Taba strategies and Parnes's *Creative Problem Solving* process, as well as through the *Junior Great*

Exhibit 9-7 Students' Approximations of Generalizations

At the end of the year, the words that represented the concepts the class experimented with were written on the board. The students were asked to make statements they believed were true about those concepts, based on what they had learned. The statements below were selected randomly to represent the class's grasp of the generalizations used to organize the curriculum content.

Original:	Many difficulties and problems are encountered when interacting with people who are different from you.
Student-generated:	Humans have strange customs and superstitions that an onlooker might find confusing. Humans react differently at different times. All humans don't act well when they are under stress.
Original:	Concrete remnants of a culture do not accurately reflect the abstract beliefs of a culture.
Student-generated:	Artifacts tell about cultures of the past and can often be misinterpreted. All artifacts may be interpreted incorrectly.
Original:	All people, past and present, have shaped their behavior and beliefs in the face of universal human problems and needs.
Student-generated:	All artifacts represent something from the universals of culture. Universal human needs show how even the most different people have things in common.

Books program, mock trials, deductive thinking exercises, *Project C.A.I.R.*, and the "Shipwreck" simulation. Open-endedness is apparent in all the questions in discussion plans. The principles of discovery and group interaction were incorporated through the use of the Taba strategies which emphasize guided discovery and interaction as well as through the simulation games. Students could choose areas of study, methods, audiences, and means of evaluation through their designing of Type III activities as well as through their choice of Type I exploratory activities. Any environment, media, or type of activity was acceptable as long as it was new to the student.

Because of the teacher's use of the Taba strategies which require that students provide evidence of reasoning or support for ideas, this principle was incorporated. Variety was present in the methods used; these included discussions, simulations, lectures, work sheets, projects, field trips, guest lectures, solo research, and

Table 9-4 Favorite and Least-Liked Activities as Perceived by Students

	Liked	Disliked
"Dig"	11	0
Dictionary Notebooks	0	4
Cultural Universals	0	0
Deductive Thinking	1	0
How to Use Those Little Gray Cells	0	5
"Shipwreck"	0	1
"Connections"	0	0
Contextual Spelling	0	0
"Search"	0	5
Grammar (commas, phrases, clauses, letters, paragraphs)	0	7
"Junior Great Books"	2	1
Cliches	0	4
New Mexico Learning Packets	2	5
N.M. Textbook	0	4
La Cienega Trip	5	0
Type Is	3	2
Type IIIs	7	1
Courthouse/Law	7	0
Mock Trials-Moot	8	0
"Flight"	4	5
Soviet Union	3	4
Career Education	0	0
Christmas Shop	3	1
"Time Capsule"	6	1
Project C.A.I.R.	2	11
"Cope"	1	12
Skate Ranch Trip	10	0
Play	9	0
Sustained Silent Reading	2	0
VTR Training (videotaping)	9	0
Dance Sponsorship	5	0
Writing Mad Libs	3	1
Discussions	0	1
"Drawing on the Right Side of the Brain"	3	1
Homework	0	2
Poem Reading	0	2
Sustained Silent Writing	0	4
Research Methods—Hypothesis Testing	0	0
Future Shock	0	0
Eskimos, *People of the Deer*	0	0
Writing:		
instructions	0	0
book reviews	0	0
essays	0	0
outlines	0	0
thesis statements	0	0

team research. Although the pace of instruction is not completely apparent from the description of the curriculum, since the content included the regular courses in two subjects as well as full development of abstract concepts and generalizations along with individual research, it is clear that the speed was rapid.

Students' development of Type III investigations and presentation to real audiences form the basis of product changes recommended for gifted pupils. Many of the Renzulli (1977) methods were incorporated into the development and implementation of these investigations, including design of a management plan, presentation to real audiences, and collection of raw data. In addition, a group forum was developed for progress reports and the Type III activities were formalized to the extent that they were included in a student's IEP and thus agreed upon by the parents, teacher, and pupil. Self-assessment and an evaluative conference with the teacher were integral parts of the process.

It is difficult to determine elements of the learning environment from a description of the program. However, with the amount of emphasis on student research, simulation games, and discussions, the environment definitely is student centered, encouraging of independence, and open. From observation of the teacher, the author also can attest to the fact that that individual is a very accepting person who permits a high degree of movement in and out of the room and who has developed a complex physical and psychological environment.

Combination of Models

The overall framework of this program is the Renzulli *Enrichment Triad*. General exploratory activities are interpreted somewhat differently from what the model may have intended in that the responsibility for seeking out and recording Type I activities is the student's rather than the teacher's. Some guidelines are provided for these activities, but students generally make their own choices. In this way, they truly are exploring their own areas of interest. Type II activities include discussions based on the Taba and Parnes models as well as simulation games in which students learn research and decision-making skills and methods specific to different scholarly fields.

No other formal teaching-learning models are involved in the program although many other materials and strategies actually were used. Some of these include the *Great Books* discussions and logic games. Skills development in several areas was incorporated into the general framework rather than separated from it.

Comparison to Other Curricula

Of the four programs presented in this section, the World Cultures curriculum shows the greatest emphasis on Renzulli's approach. This is appropriate because of the age and experience of the children as well as the overall structure of the program. Because students are in the special class for at least four periods out of a seven-period day, time there can be spent in group process activities as well as on work toward the full development of individual and small-group investigations. In the high school seminar program, work with the teacher on individual research projects is difficult, if not impossible, since the students meet with the special instructor for such a short time.

Other programs described in this section are designed for younger children as well as being in a different setting. With the early childhood program, for example, students lack many of the basic language and academic skills that will enable them to be successful in school. Thus, the program must provide accelerated development of these skills while enhancing the creative strengths of the children.

Some of the strengths of the curriculum include (1) its emphasis on abstract generalizations and basic concepts, (2) its organization of content around these concepts, (3) the variety and interest of methods used, and (4) the creative development of a program at the middle school level that must cover the basic curriculum as well as provide enrichment. The program is comprehensive in that it incorporates content, process, product, and learning environment modifications appropriate for the education of gifted students.

RESOURCES

British Broadcasting Co. — T.V. *Connections* (A videotape series). New York: Author, 1979.

Campbell, D. *If you don't know where you are going you will probably end up somewhere else*. Niles, Il.: Argus Communications, undated.

Edwards, B. *Drawing on the right side of the brain*. Los Angeles, Ca.: J.P. Tarcher, 1979.

Farley, M. *People of the deer*. New York: Pyramid Books, 1976.

Ford, J., & Ferguson, J. *Project C.A.I.R.: Cultural awareness through inquiry and research*. Intercultural Awareness, undated.

Interact. *Dig, Search, Moot, Flight, Time Capsule, Cope* (Simulation games). Lakeside, Ca.: Author, undated.

Lavash, D.R. *A journey through New Mexico history*. Portales, N.M.: Bishop Publishing, 1971.

Moldof, E.P., & Dennis, R.P. (Eds.). *Junior great books, series seven*. Chicago: The Great Books Foundation, 1975.

Montgomery, R.A. *Journey under the sea* (Choose Your Own Adventure Series). New York: Bantam Books, 1979. (a)

Montgomery, R.A. *Space and beyond*. (Choose Your Own Adventure Series). New York: Bantam Books, 1979. (b)

Packard, E. *The cave of time* (Choose Your Own Adventure Series). New York: Bantam Books, 1979. (a)

Packard, E. *Your code name is Jonah* (Choose Your Own Adventure Series). New York: Bantam Books, 1979. (b)

Packard, E. *The witch's curse* (Choose Your Own Adventure Series). New York: Bantam Books, 1979. (c)

Perfection Form Co. *How to use the little gray cells: The practical logician info lab.* Logan, Ia.: Author, 1976.

Price, R. & Stern, L. *Mad libs.* Los Angeles: Price/Stern/Sloan Publishers, Inc., 1980.

Terman, D. *By balloon to the Sahara* (Choose Your Own Adventure Series). New York: Bantam Books, 1979.

Warriner, J.E., Griffith, F., Graham, S.L., Mersand, J., & Whitten, M. *English grammar and composition: Third course.* New York: Harcourt Brace Jovanovich, 1977.

Writing Improvement Project Staff. *Building english skills.* Evanston, Ill.: McDougal, Littell, & Co., 1977.

NOTES

1. Sources for the materials listed in each of the units can be found in the Resources section.

2. This discussion is based on *Connections: Technology and Change* by Burke, a television series.

3. Prior to this discussion, students read the first portion of *The Overcoat* (Gogol, 1956). Reading stopped at the point where Akaky loses the coat.

Chapter 10

An Elementary Resource Room Program

DESCRIPTION OF THE CURRICULUM

Definition

The gifted child is one whose high potential and psychological differences result in the need for a range and type of study different from what most pupils require. These are not the elite students of the school but a unique group whose needs are not entirely met by the regular classroom program. Differences often exhibited by gifted children include these factors:[1]

1. Extreme Curiosity: These children have the need to know about a lot of things.
2. Outstanding Creative/Cognitive Ability: Gifted children often are able to think of things in ways that are quite different from most children.
3. Leadership Ability: Many gifted children are able to organize groups and work with them efficiently while causing little or no friction.
4. Independent: Gifted children may have the ability to direct their own investigations into areas of interest and be able to work without adult supervision.
5. Perceptive/Sensitive: Gifted children often are very much in tune with the feelings of other persons in their environment and can identify others' needs or wants. Their own personal feelings may be deep and they may exhibit greater extremes of emotion.
6. Self-Expressive: Gifted children tend to express themselves well from very early ages. However, with all their interests and abilities, they need many different ways to present their thoughts, feelings, and inspirations. They need many avenues to the outside world.
7. Rapid Learning Pace: Some gifted children can move through various school subjects or interest areas at a very rapid pace.

Not every gifted child exhibits all of these characteristics at any one time but all may benefit from exposure to a program designed to cultivate and expand the skills associated with these seven identifying characteristics.

Philosophy

The reason for the existence of a gifted program is to serve the needs of children who have potential far beyond that of others. It is important that all children be given the opportunity to develop to their greatest potential, and the gifted need help beyond the regular class program to reach this goal.

The characteristics just listed are exhibited by the gifted population as a whole rather than by any one individual. However, they are considered important in the development of a gifted child's full potential. These seven areas are the focus of this school's gifted program. Within the context of developing and using these characteristics, individual attention is given to the specific needs and strengths of each student.

Overview of Curriculum Emphasis

The curriculum focuses on development of abilities in each of the listed areas. As can be seen, the program goals, or overall program emphasis, is on the development or strengthening of the characteristics considered attributes of giftedness. The program for each area is described briefly.

Stimulation of Curiosity and Interest

The encouragement and cultivation of a gifted child's natural curiosity form an important component of the pupil's program. It includes exposure to a wide variety of topics not covered in the regular curriculum. The topics are chosen to stimulate further investigation as well as to provide exposure to new areas of possible interest. Examples of topics that may be covered are the human body, archaeology, and appreciation of the fine arts.

Development of Creative Cognitive Ability

A child having outstanding creative ability often is unable or unwilling to use it in a school setting. Many activities in the program allow the pupil to use materials, ideas, and words in ways that are unusual and original. The use of higher level thinking skills is emphasized in activities throughout the program to promote an increase in the child's ability to think at these levels. Methods that may be included are Parnes's *Creative Problem Solving,* brainstorming, and brainstretching; the *Hilda Taba Teaching Strategies;* and various activities based on Bloom's *Taxonomy.*

Development of Leadership Skills

The need to develop appropriate leadership skills is addressed by allowing children to be leaders of small groups at various times. Emphasis is placed on concepts and skills such as group organization, fair play, using talents of each group member, planning and evaluation of activities, and taking several perspectives on a problem. The role of the teacher is that of an observer and facilitator, with major responsibilities resting on the group leader.

Development of Independence

Development of self-management skills in learning involves acquiring skills in organization of information and conducting actual research in and out of the classroom. Additional work on learning and processing information should result in an increased ability to locate, gather, and utilize information independently. Areas that may be included are goal-setting techniques, flow charts, library skills, using community resources, and exploration through empirical scientific methods.

Development of Perception and Sensitivity

The program deals with the emotional sensitivity of the child through acquisition of effective techniques to deal with personal and social problems, issues, and situations. Evaluative and reflective thinking skills are used in analyzing and reacting to problem situations. Methods such as Kohlberg's *Moral Dilemma* discussions, transactional analysis, and Simon's *Values Clarification* activities are used, as are sessions with the school counselor.

Development of Self-Expression

The child's course of study requires the use of various methods of self-expression, with activities focusing upon the development of new means of communication such as drama, photography, poetry, art, and advanced use of language.

Provisions for a Rapid Pace of Learning

The program deals with these children's rapid pace of learning through acceleration of learning in areas of special interest or skill. Children may learn more about a subject on their own level or may move on to a more advanced set of skills than they normally would encounter in the regular classroom. An example of this is a child with an intense interest in geometric shapes. This pupil can be exposed to the uses of and problems involving these forms, or can go on to learn techniques in trigonometry or analytic geometry through a mentor or an independent study program.

Needs Assessment

Each child's abilities are evaluated using a variety of procedures. Each of the assessments is keyed to one or more of the seven identifying characteristics stated in the definition (Exhibit 10-1). The purpose is to pinpoint each child's strengths and weaknesses within each broad area.

Exhibit 10-1 Characteristics and Measures Used in Needs Assessment

CHARACTERISTIC	MEASURE
Curiosity	Interest-A-Lyzer (Renzulli, 1977)
	Teacher-Made Interest Survey[2]
Creativity/	
Self-Expression	The Torrance Tests of Creative Thinking (Figural Form B)
	Teacher-Made Creative Dial-a-Story (written)[2]
	Taba Discussion with Tape Analysis (verbal)[2]
Critical Thinking	Taba Discussion with Tape Analysis[2]
	The Ross Test of Higher Cognitive Processes
Leadership	SRBCSS (Renzulli et al., 1976)
	How I See Myself Survey
Independence in	
Learning	Teacher-Made Research Skills Test[2]
	Teacher-Made Goal-Setting Inventory[2]
	Teacher-Made Resource Use Inventory[2]
Perceptiveness/	
Sensitivity	Observation/coding of Kohlberg Moral Dilemma Discussion implementing Taba Strategies[2]
	Observation of participation in values clarification activity[2] (Simon et al., 1976)
	What Kind of Person Are You? (WKOPAY?)
Rapid Pace of	
Learning	The Wide Range Achievement Test (WRAT)
	CTBS/Stanford Standardized Measures
	Observation of regular class performance

Each test or survey is selected on the basis of how much information it provides about the particular characteristic(s) concerned. When the data are compiled on each student, basic prototypes emerge. Children then are grouped on the basis of ability (strengths), personality, and maturity level. Program goals are established based on each group's needs, and a curriculum is developed for the group prototype.

Content Objectives

Each student will

1. Acquire extended knowledge and insight into the content covered by the regular curriculum through different though related subject areas.
2. Explore a wide variety of topics not covered in the regular curriculum. Although new and highly differentiated materials may be introduced, skills taught in the regular class are required as well as extended.
3. Cultivate new opportunities to extend interest areas through exploration of specific topics within each unit. Exploration of existing personal interests is encouraged.

In each of these areas, the content is different from the regular classroom curriculum because of its depth and breadth.

Process Objectives

Throughout the entire program the following five process objectives are integrated:

1. independent discovery and formulation of problems
2. independent organization and use of information
3. generation of ideas
4. evaluation and improvement of ideas
5. creation of new perspectives

These processes are incorporated primarily through (a) using the teaching-learning models in a flexible and accepting manner, (b) allowing for and cultivating opportunities within the units and activities, and (c) developing a physical and psychological environment that is flexible, accepting, and encouraging of individuality.

One process goal is established specifically for the creation of products. Each child must follow this process when developing a product in a unit, activity, or interest area. The following sequence states these objectives:

Step 1: Generation of many different ideas using brainstorming or problem-solving techniques in the proposed area

Step 2: Analysis of the ideas in a systematic, organized manner until a final choice is selected

Step 3: Establishment of a goal that relates to the choice and to the product to be developed

Step 4: Setting of goals, using a flow chart that outlines time, materials, expertise, and specific steps

Step 5: Research and production

Step 6: Evaluation by student and teacher

The product must be completed in a form agreed upon by both student and teacher.

Product Objectives

Products are extensions of a person's thoughts related to a particular subject or idea. They are statements—commentaries directed by the individual's feelings, creativity, and thinking abilities. This definition reflects the product objective. Thus, the following criteria are established to aid children in cultivating self-discipline and quality in their own products:

1. Reflection of Synthesis: The product must show a different combination of thought that results from the child's forming a new idea or "whole." This synthesis is formed from the pieces of information the child has been exposed to or has gathered.
2. Reflection of Original Thought: The product must reflect a "freshness" in some aspect of its design. It must demonstrate a newness in style or character, and constructive imagination.
3. Reflection of Detail: The child must expand the detail in the product beyond that of only a simple or immature expression.
4. Self-Evaluation: The child must establish criteria for evaluation of performance and of the end product before completion of the project. Criteria must include each of the above factors as well as any other the child may wish to add. The actual evaluation process must take place within one week of the completion of the product.

Involvement of Key Individuals

After the needs assessment is reviewed and objectives established, the overall goals of the program become clear. Activities, units, and content areas can be developed within the established framework. Various individuals contribute time and ideas. Following is a brief description of those consulted and the type of information provided. All ideas then are compiled to form the general plan.

Children in the Program

Each group of children is consulted on content and skills (processes). They provide much information, including specific interest areas not recorded in the initial interest surveys. As a result, the majority of the units developed is based upon the children's interests.

School Staff

Various members of the staff contribute suggestions for skills and content areas that relate to or extend the regular curriculum each year. At least one teacher from each grade level is consulted. Most provide excellent ideas that are incorporated into the program in conjunction with the children's interests.

Parents

Each parent is invited to an individual conference at the beginning of the school year. At that time the basic ideas and emphasis of the program are explained. The parents then are consulted about their perceptions of the program. Most contribute information about their own child's needs rather than about the overall program. These suggestions are noted and incorporated on an individual basis.

School Principal

The school principal contributes ideas for the overall program emphasis. This person's highest priority is a curriculum that places a heavier accent on science and math, so units that coincide with students' interests are developed in both of these areas.

Implementation

Students are placed in groups according to the criteria in the needs assessment. Each group meets four days a week for nine months. Each session lasts an hour and 15 minutes. No more than six children are placed in one group.

On Mondays, Tuesdays, and Thursdays, the first activity involves thinking warm-ups (30 minutes) followed by units and discussions (45 minutes). On Fridays, the schedule includes thinking warm-ups (25 minutes), discussions with the counselor (30 minutes), and sharing time/free selection (20 minutes).

Thinking warm-ups consist of various brainstretching activities involving both creative and critical thinking. Taba discussions, *Thinklab* problems, timed mystery puzzles, analogy, and deductive thinking problems as well as imagination and guided fantasy are some of the elements. Counseling is provided by the school counselor for each group half an hour each week. Activities involve self-image, social interaction, and various levels of reflective and evaluative thinking. These then are reinforced throughout the week by the teacher. Sharing time consists of a small segment of the week when, if the children are so inclined, they can bring anything they wish to share. This activity is extended beyond traditional "show and tell" in that the children also bring opinions, world concerns, or comments for group discussion. Free selection provides a needed break from the regular schedule. Games such as chess, "Evolution," and "Circulation" are available as well as various manipulative centers such as tangrams, geoboards, and metric measuring. Other choices also are available.

Units and discussions[3] are the mainstay of the program. Investigations into new and exciting subjects using varied approaches fill the major portion of the week. Since units are the most important aspect of the program, each one is described next in more depth in chronological order.

Goal-Setting Skills

Children learn through discovery how to set goals, plan steps, implement steps, and evaluate a goal. They determine the differences between the goals' success and their own success as the implementer. The rationale for this unit, as well as for the two others that follow, is the need for acquisition of specific skills based on the needs assessment. Subsequent units requiring independent investigation and production also require this knowledge.

Community Resource Skills

This unit is implemented with the help of the book *A Children's Guide to Albuquerque*. The main goal is to teach children that people and places in their own community are an important and viable research source. Students are required to set a goal in an interest area that involves the community in some way. Interviews and visitations are recorded in each child's logbook. Each student then reports these findings to the group.

Library Skills

This unit is taught through modifying the simulation game "Search" (for specific skills taught, see sample IEP (Exhibit 10-3)). Children are divided into teams by classes. After learning library and research skills, each team develops a unique problem using the proper goal-setting procedures. Problems are traded, research is conducted, and products from the investigations are presented.

World Cultures

This unit is predominantly an exposure and discussion section. The children are introduced to cultures such as the African Pygmies, the Southwest Anasazi, the Amish of Pennsylvania, and contemporary America. Vehicles such as life style simulation, food preparation, movies, and role playing are used. Taba discussions follow each segment. Comparisons with previous cultures, and an analysis of each, are explored. This unit is designed as a preparation for the development of their own cultures.

Anthropology—"The Dig"

This unit is adapted from the simulation game "Dig." Two teams of children develop imaginary cultures containing the same elements that all cultures possess universally. After using appropriate research and goal-setting techniques, each team decides upon its own original culture. Artifacts representing cultural universals such as technology, monetary system, division of labor, and food production are created. Upon completion, the artifacts are carefully broken and buried in a systematic manner. These "remains" then are excavated, using professional archaeological techniques, by the opposite team. As soon as analysis of the artifacts is completed, the two teams meet to discuss the results and compare records. Visits to museum displays, speakers from the local university anthropology department, and films are excellent aids in the enrichment process.

Self-Expression Methods

Again the children are involved in an exposure/discussion format. This section is designed to provide a hands-on learning experience for each child. The goal is to present an environment and activities conducive to self-expression in various forms. Sign language, acrylics, water colors, clay, pantomime, drama, photography, dance, and music are explored with the help of professionals. A specialist in each field presents a lecture and experience session in each medium. The children are given time to explore the new method with the lecturer and/or alone.

Individual Interest

At this point, classroom norms and standards of work have been established. Children now are expected to assume responsibility for their own investigations into an area of special personal interest. Proper goal setting, research, and product objectives are to be accomplished. The only stipulation placed on the product is that it must involve a method of expression that the child has not used previously.

Human Body Systems

Working closely with university medical students, in tours, and in-class exploration, children learn aspects of the human body. Each student is paired with a medical student for a day and, through this activity, learns more about medical care of the body. Before this field investigation, however, skeletal and body functions are learned. This knowledge makes the out-of-class experiences more interesting and meaningful. After compiling all data collected, the class as a whole brainstorms, sets goals, researches, designs, and creates a product.

Leadership Techniques: Teach a Lesson

Each unit in the program requires leadership within the group. In the beginning, the teacher is leader and mediator. However, as units progress through the year, the teacher assumes the role of facilitator and the children become the leaders. At that point, a specific unit is designed for more intense study and mastery of leadership techniques. Children list the qualities of leaders and discuss specific characteristics that appear to make them successful in their roles. Discussion skills, group dynamics, public speaking, and group control techniques are analyzed and practiced through role playing and simulated teaching sessions. Once the children feel comfortable with the techniques, each designs a unit in an interest area. Each student then teaches a group of six children in a regular class setting for three consecutive days. Evaluation procedures follow. Each pupil evaluates the "teacher" and the unit's effectiveness. "Teachers" also are required to evaluate their own performance.

Scientific Method

This unit emphasizes learning and implementing the scientific method through experimentation. Chemistry, electricity, and energy as well as other scientific areas are offered for exploration. After mastering the method and safety precautions, children proceed with investigations into areas of specific interest.

Career/Work-a-Day Program

After brainstorming fields of career interest the children arrange for speakers in each area. They then set goals and research a chosen career, using both library and community resources. Important factors such as job availability, salary, and required education are important facets of the research. Aptitude tests and interest/job surveys help the students become involved in the process. After the research is completed, each pupil is paired with a professional in the chosen field. Students work with community members who indicate desire and motivation, and are allowed to be participants rather than just observers during their career day. Discussion, analysis, and evaluation follow the work-a-day experience.

Sample Lesson Plans

The following are sample lesson plans from a small portion of the *Culture Unit:*

MONDAY

1. *Thinklab Cards*—77, 78, 79, orally in group—15 minutes.
2. *Two-Minute Mysteries*—"The Case of the Candlelight Thief," orally in group—15 minutes.
3. Exposure to the concept of "culture." Taba concept development discussion with the focusing question "What Is Culture?"—20 minutes.
4. Purse activity related to contemporary American culture—20 minutes. A purse is filled with objects that the children silently analyze, then try to answer:
   a. Who and what type person is this?
   b. To what type of culture does this person belong?
   c. What things does this person value?

TUESDAY

1. *Experiences in Visual Thinking*—Imaginary and sensation—25 minutes.
2. Finish purse exercise: Discuss questions using Taba techniques—30 minutes.
3. Film on the Amish of Pennsylvania—15 minutes.

THURSDAY

1. Work on deductive logic thinking skills—pose both written and oral problems, including mindbenders—25 minutes.
2. Speaker on "The American Way of Life" (its differences in cultures); discussion and questions follow—50 minutes.

FRIDAY

1. Continued deductive logic problem—15 minutes.
2. Guided fantasy, using imagination and senses—15 minutes.
3. Sharing Time—15+ minutes.
4. Counselor Discussion: Begin working on sex-stereotyping
   a. Make lists of what "women do" and of what "men do"
   b. Discuss whether these "jobs" have cultural or physical reasons for their existence—30 minutes.

In summary, this curriculum builds upon the strengths and talents of gifted students. These characteristics are grouped in areas of curiosity, critical thinking, leadership, independence, perception and sensitivity, self-expression, and creative thinking. Exhibit 10-2 summarizes the units and activities, teaching-learning models, and academic areas designed to meet student needs in each talent area.

Sample Individualized Plan[4]

An Individualized Education Program is developed for the students. Long-term goals are designed for four areas of emphasis: creative and higher level thinking skills, leadership, independence, and affective skills. Only Goal 1, creative/critical thinking, and Goal 2, leadership, are included in this example (Exhibit 10-3). Short-term objectives correspond to specific skills within the goal areas. Methods and materials, as well as evaluation systems, are included for each objective. In the comments section for Goal 1, each skill is keyed to the level of thinking according to Bloom's *Taxonomy*. When the thinking skill is at the synthesis level, the area of creativity (e.g., fluency, flexibility, originality) also is noted.

Parent Program

During the preschool conferences, many parents express a desire to become involved in a formal parent program. Questionnaires[2] are sent home to verify interest, as well as to gather concerns and ideas for program topics. In this case, 12 parents responded with definite interest in participation; they then were asked to list the topics they wished to cover. Two basic areas of concern emerged from their responses: a need to become educated about the gifted and a desire to learn about activities and techniques that could be used at home to enhance the children's abilities. In this program, individual conferences are held at the beginning, midpoint, and end of the year. Five group sessions on the topics of interest are held throughout the year. Following is a brief description of each of these sessions.

Session I

- Presentation and discussion of definitions of giftedness

- A look at the characteristics of gifted children

- Parents' pinpointing of their own child's characteristics and type(s) of giftedness through a "forced choice" Q-sort technique

- All pupils' conducting of the Q-sorts on themselves before the session, with parents then comparing their perceptions of their child with the student's own view

Exhibit 10-2 Summary of Child Characteristics, Activities, Models, and Content Areas

Child Needs	Learning Activities	Models	Academic Areas
Cultivation of Natural Curiosity	*Units:* Introduction to the following topics: Culture, Archaeology, Anthropology, Drama, Photography, Architecture, Painting, the Human Body, Chemistry, Electricity, Energy Forms, Astronomy, Career Opportunities	Renzulli Taba Bruner	Social Studies Science Art Math Reading
Development of Critical Thinking Skills	*Units:* Each unit requires higher levels of thinking *Activities:* Deductive Thinking Skills Series (Mindbenders), Inductive Thinking Skills Series: "Aha!" Thinklab, Two-minute Mysteries, Conceptual Blockbusting Discussions	Taba Bloom Parnes Ennis	Math Reading Language Development
Development of Leadership Skills	*Unit:* Leadership Skill Techniques *Activities:* Role Playing, Body Language, Creative Problem Solving, Brainstorming, Assuming Leadership Roles in Each Unit, Teach a Lesson	Parnes Kohlberg Taba Simon	Language Development
Development of Independence Skills	*Units:* Goal-Setting Research Skills, Library Skills—"Search" Community Resource Investigation Skills (children then are required to use these skills in all subsequent units), Scientific Method of Research Experimentation *Activities:* Setting Goals, Flow Charting, Evaluation of Own Products Using Reader's Guide, Individual Interest Research, Research Projects, Brainstorming, Learning Proper Letter Formats	Renzulli Parnes Taba	Library Skills Research Skills Writing Language Development
Development of Affective Skills	*Activities:* Transactional Analysis, Values Clarification, Discussion of Moral Dilemmas, Sharing Time, Counselor-Led Activities	Taba Simon	Language Development

Exhibit 10-2 continued

Child Needs	Learning Activities	Models	Academic Areas
Development of Self-Expression	*Units:* Self-Expression Methods, Careers *Activities:* Drama, Mime, Creative Writing, Poetry, Photography, Art, Sign Language, Body Language	Taba Renzulli	Art Writing
Development of Creative Thinking	*Units:* Each unit requires creative thinking *Activities:* "Aha!" "Making It Strange," Brainstorming, Creative Problem Solving, "Scamper," "Imagination Express", Guided Fantasy, Experiences in Visual Thinking, 52/62 Ways to Have Fun with Your Mind	Taba Bloom Parnes Ennis	Math Art Language Development

Exhibit 10-3 Individualized Education Program Implementation Plan

Goal 1 Area of Emphasis:: Creative and Higher Level Thinking Skills

Name __I. J.__   School __Kirtland__   Implementer __S.K.S.__

Long-Term Goal __Student will use critical and creative (fluent, flexible, and original) thinking skills, displaying "Higher Level Thinking" (Bloom: analysis, synthesis, evaluation)__

Dates Init.	Ach.	Short-Term Objectives	Teaching Methods/Materials	Method of Evaluation	Comments
		1. S. will determine whether a statement follows from a set of clearly stated premises.	Practice, Tallahassee project materials, Taba Discussion Strategies	Teacher observation, pretest, posttest based on Ross and Cornell tests	Bloom: Analysis
		2. S. will find missing premise or assumptions, given a conclusion statement and incomplete premises.	Great Books, Tallahassee project materials, Taba application of generalization.	Tape analysis & observation	Bloom: Analysis
		3. S. will evaluate whether a simple generalization is warranted and suggest improvements based on knowledge about proper generalizing.	Taba (application of generalizations and interpretation of data) practice in evaluation, generalizations, Parnes-based evaluation criteria decisions	Tape analysis, inspection of student work	Bloom: Synthesis, Evaluation
		4. S. will decide whether a given reason supports an argument, and will support all predictions and arguments with relative statements.	Taba (all strategies) practice in evaluating arguments, debate practice, report criteria	Tape analysis, inspection of student work	Bloom: Analysis, Synthesis, Evaluation
		5. S. will generate a wide variety of possible solutions to a given problem and will decide on the best one using student-generated and/or given criteria.	Parnes CPS, Taba resolution of conflict research problems posed by teacher or student.	Tape analysis, observation, inspection of product	Bloom: Synthesis (fluency), Evaluation
		6. S. will use materials, words, and ideas in appropriate ways that individual has not used before, without being told or shown how to use them.	Project presentations, art lessons, creative time	Teacher observation	Bloom: Synthesis (flexibility & originality)

Exhibit 10-3 continued

Dates Init	Dates Ach.	Short-Term Objectives	Teaching Methods/Materials	Method of Evaluation	Comments
		7. S. will use words or ideas in ways that are unusual, nontraditional, or structured differently from standard use.	Guided fantasy, creative time, story & poetry writing, experiments in "Visual Thinking," "Making it Strange"	Teacher observation	Bloom: Synthesis (flexibility)

Goal 2 Area of Emphasis: Leadership

Long-Term Goal Student will demonstrate effective and appropriate group leadership skills.

Dates Init	Dates Ach.	Short-Term Objectives	Teaching Methods/Materials	Method of Evaluation	Comments
		1. S. will use at least twice as many positive as negative statements in interactions with group members.	Discussions, analysis of group interactions by students, graphing positive/negative statements made by other students and/or teachers.	Observation	
		2. S. will identify feelings conveyed by body posture and facial expressions and use predominately positive body language in group interactions.	"Body Language" game, books on body language, role playing, mime instruction.	Observation, test based on game cards	
		3. S. will teach a minilesson to a small group of peers.	Student research into an area of interest, followed by student teaching	Observation	
		4. S. will lead a small group in project and/or as part of a unit.	S. leads a group: all units have a leadership component	Observation	

Session II

- Presentation and discussion on levels of thinking using Bloom's *Taxonomy*
- Exploration of how Taba questioning technique can help cultivate the higher levels
- Discussion and practice of questioning methods
- Homework assignment to parents to practice techniques and bring back perceptions of the effects on their own child

Session III

- Review of Taba and homework reporting
- Discussion of concomitant problems that relate to a gifted child's characteristics
- Parents' pinpointing of these problems in their own child
- Presentation of two methods for dealing with problems that can arise
- Description of natural and logical consequences
- Introduction of creative problem solving
- Homework assignment to try the methods and to practice Taba questioning

Session IV

- Review and practice of Taba questioning
- Further discussion of concomitant problems and of methods used to deal with them

Session V

- Presentation on the Summer Enrichment Programs available for gifted children
- Overview of program plan for the next year and feedback on this year's program
- General questions
- Evaluation of parent program

The overall results of the parent program were somewhat disappointing. Many of the parents were more interested in discussing only their own child's specific or immediate needs rather than learning the techniques or concepts presented. However, some parents did seem to enjoy and learn from the few sessions held.

Student Evaluation

Four basic methods are used to assess student progress in the program. The first, and perhaps most accountable, is pretesting and posttesting using the same measures—*Torrance Tests of Creative Thinking* (TTCT); the *Ross Test of Higher Cognitive Processes*; the *Wide Range Achievement Test* (WRAT); the teacher-made tests of skills in research, goal setting, and community resources; and tape analysis of Taba discussions focusing on number and quality of responses.

The second method of evaluation is an informal evaluation of products throughout the year. If the child appears to be making steady progress according to the product objectives, the evaluation is positive.

The third method is a continuing report card.[2] This evaluation occurs at the end of each nine-week grading period. A form listing all activities, discussions, and units in which the child participated is sent to both the parents and the regular class teacher. Before the report is sent, however, teacher and student discuss each section and the pupil has an opportunity to make comments and review the program. The following factors are assessed for each activity, unit, or discussion: participation, follow-through, attitude, and quality of work.

The fourth and final measure is a review of the Individualized Education Program. After the initial formulation, the plan is reviewed twice. By then, both the parents and the pupil can see what has and has not been accomplished. Comments about the quality of performance are noted beside completed objectives. Children also have the opportunity to review and check off completed objectives on their own.

Program Evaluation

The overall program evaluation, in addition to the analysis of student progress, includes classroom interaction analysis and evaluation surveys. The focus of analysis is on the pattern of interaction between teacher and pupil and among students (Figure 10-1). This figure is a sample form used in this process. On the form, the observer or listener marks A (asks) or T (tells) for both students and the teacher. Ratios of teacher talk to student talk and teacher asks to teacher talk are computed as are totals for each category. The most effective pattern includes a low percentage of teacher intervention along with a high percentage of student participation.

Figure 10-1 Interaction Analysis

OBSERVATION DATA FORM
FOR
CLASSROOM
APPLICATION OF GENERALIZATIONS DISCUSSIONS

Any or all of these observation data forms can be used to record teacher acts during a classroom discussion. They provide different data than that which is provided on the Discussion Leader Profile or Discussion Analysis Form.

INTERACTION

As the teacher proceeds, mark in the following squares each time the teacher asks (A) or tells (T) and each time the students ask (A) or tell (T). Record in the order that each occurs. Count tallies at the end for ratios and totals.

Teacher															
Student															

Teacher															
Student															

Teacher															
Student															

Teacher															
Student															

Teacher															
Student															

Teacher															
Student															

Totals:
TT ____
TA ____
ST ____
SA ____

Ratios:
TA ____
T Talk ____

TT ____
S Talk ____

Source: Institute for Staff Development, Hilda Taba Teaching Strategies Program, © 1971. Reprinted with permission.

Students, parents, and regular classroom teachers participate in program evaluation through responses to open-ended questions. Students reply in writing and parents and teachers orally in the final parent-teacher conference, which includes the student, parents, and regular classroom teacher.

Results

All evaluation results showed that the program was highly successful. Analysis of pretesting and posttesting produced gains significant at the .05 level or above on all but four subtests of some of the measures. Students' written evaluations showed they were pleased with the program, as were their parents and regular classroom teachers. As to the test results, gains for individual subtests of each measure were analyzed using a t-test for correlated samples. Table 10-1 provides a summary of the pretest scores, posttest scores, average gain, standard deviation, t, and significance level for each subtest of each measure. Even though student scores were high on most measures at the beginning of the program, posttest results showed significant gains in all areas, especially deductive thinking on the *Ross*, WRAT spelling, the goal-setting/research test, and tape analysis of both number and quality of responses.

To summarize student comments about the program, a content analysis was made of all answers. Eleven children responded to the survey. Following is a listing of the questions, the categories of responses, and the number of students responding in each category:

Question One
What things do you like about this class?
Responses

- the people
- units and activities (9)
- the teacher (3)
- everything (1)
- testing (1)

Question Two
What things do you *not* like about this class?
Responses

- nothing (4)
- add some new things (2)

Table 10-1 Summary of Testing Results

Measure/Subtest	Average Pre-test Scores	Average Post-test Scores	Average Gain	Standard Deviation	t	Level of Significance
TTCT	122.6	139.2	+16.6	17.10	2.767	.039*
Ross Test						
Deductive Thinking	59.7%	85.0%	+25.3%	2.61	3.187	.018*
Missing Premises	38.8%	66.0%	+27.2%	2.43	1.40	.211
Questioning Strategies	50.0%	82.0%	+32.0%	2.33	1.42	.197
Analysis of Relevant Information	48.2%	64.0%	+15.8%	2.00	1.41	.200
WRAT						
Reading	8.1	9.8	+1.7	0.93	2.77	.027*
Spelling	6.0	7.3	+1.3	0.95	4.35	.033**
Arithmetic	4.8	6.0	+1.2	2.75	0.46	.657
Goal-Setting/Research Test						
Teacher Made	57.9%	97.2%	+39.3%	3.00	5.54	.000**
Taba Tape Analysis						
Number of Responses	5.0	11.3	+6.3	4.34	4.15	.004*
Quality of Responses	2.12	3.40	+1.28	0.79	4.65	.000**

*p .05
**p .01

- research lab (2)
- testing (2)
- "Dig" (1)

Question Three

If you were the teacher of the special program, what would you do differently? the same?

Responses

- do the same (5)
- more units (1)
- more brainteasers (2)
- more stuff like self-expression and the "Dig" (2)
- take out the "Dig" (1)

Question Four

What kinds of things would you like to do in the program next year?
Responses

- science (1)
- gardening (1)
- culture (1)
- oceanography (2)
- lots of field trips (2)
- crafts (1)
- more experiments (1)
- space (2)
- horses (1)
- art (2)
- chemicals (1)
- biology (1)
- mythology (1)
- the "Dig" again (1)
- medicine (1)
- astrology (1)
- more of sign language (1)

Question Five

What units did you like that we did this year?
Responses

- all of them (11)

Question Six
What activities did you enjoy this year?
Responses

- all of them (11)

Question Seven
What things would you change about our room?
Responses

- put everything against the wall (1)
- change some centers around (1)
- bigger (2)
- get a window (3)
- nothing (2)
- paint it (4)
- fix cabinet (2)
- more supplies (1)

Question Eight
What have you learned in the program this year?
Responses

- 999-1,000 new expressions (1)
- self-expression (1)
- sign language (2)
- how to set a goal (4)
- how to teach (1)
- Dewey decimal system (2)
- card catalog (1)
- how to think better (4)
- how to give a test (1)

- lots of stuff (1)
- how to be more patient with other children (1)
- how not to be so shy (1)
- how to imagine (1)
- what I Am Lovable and Capable (IALAC) means (1)
- archaeology (1)

ANALYSIS OF THE CURRICULUM

Strengths

One of the unique aspects of this program is the thread of consistency running throughout the entire curriculum. This thread begins with the definition of gifted that includes a particular grouping of observable student characteristics. After these are grouped in clusters, the needs assessment instruments are selected because of their potential to assess the traits in each cluster. Instruments are included or developed to measure each cluster. Emphasis in the curriculum then is placed on the development of student strengths/characteristics in each area through units and activities designed around the clusters of traits. The Individualized Education Program also is keyed to the child need areas, and each trait is evaluated by posttesting at the end of the year. The curriculum thus is well organized and consistent across its various components. Exhibit 10-2 (supra) provides a summary that indicates part of this organization.

Another area of strength is the development process. Several key individuals are involved, including the children, regular school staff, parents, and the principal. Because of their involvement, the curriculum truly reflects the emphasis desired by individuals affected by the program. Since there is an extensive diagnosis (needs assessment) of the students, the curriculum can be individualized to meet their needs.

Another innovative and valid aspect is the grouping of students according to their needs rather than by grade levels. This practice facilitates further development of individualization. Still another innovative practice is the involvement of the school counselor. A strong parent education/involvement program is a definite asset even though in this case the teacher was disappointed that the parents were reluctant to discuss anything besides their own children. Evaluation of the program also is extensive and includes objective measures as well as the subjective perceptions of those concerned.

Curricular Modifications

This program also is comprehensive in that it incorporates most of the content, process, product, and learning environment modifications appropriate for the gifted. With regard to content, the unit organization pertains mainly to the child characteristics being developed. Within each unit, however, the content is arranged around the abstract concepts and generalizations to be developed in that entity. The characteristics of the gifted, rather than the generalizations, provide the overriding structure. Other content modifications involve the study of people through the leadership unit and of methods of inquiry through several units: goal-setting skills, community resource skills, world cultures, anthropology, career/work-a-day program, and the scientific method. Variety of content is achieved through various units since none of this material is taught in regular classrooms.

Process modifications form the basis of the program. All process changes are incorporated, along with emphasis on varied content and key concepts. The emphasis definitely is on use rather than acquisition of information, as can be seen in the sample schedule as well as in the unit descriptions. The major vehicles for this process modification are the teaching-learning models used for planning daily lessons. Discussions are based on Bloom, Taba, Parnes, Kohlberg, and Simon's *Values Clarification* techniques. Work sheets and exercises are based on Ennis's conception of critical thinking.

Open-endedness is provided in all discussions through the use of Taba strategies and the teacher's attitude of encouraging diversity of answers. The Taba strategies also assure an emphasis on student reasoning in reaching conclusions and on discovery learning. In addition, many of Bruner's ideas are included in the curriculum to develop discovery processes. Students are encouraged to pursue their own interests through several units: goal setting, self-expression methods, individual interest, and the career/work-a-day program. Group interaction activities are made part of the leadership skill unit, goal-setting research skills, and all elements listed as "affective development." The pacing seems to be rapid and a variety of methods is used.

Product modifications in the curriculum are reflected by product objectives. All products developed by the children must reflect synthesis, original thought, and detail. Pupils are to establish criteria for evaluation and apply them to their own products. The self-expression unit also provides exposure to new and different methods of expression that can be incorporated into the students' products.

Although not completely apparent from descriptive information, the learning environment facilitates success in all areas. This highly student-centered classroom focuses on pupils' ideas and interests, with the entire curriculum being built around their needs and interests as perceived by themselves, their parents, and other teachers. Independence is fostered in a climate where the emphasis is on development of self-directedness in academic areas as well as self-management in personal, nonacademic areas. Other environment dimensions, including physical and psychological complexity and high mobility, are apparent.

Combination of Models

A wide variety of teaching/learning models is combined to form the curriculum. As with the organization of content, these models are combined according to the child characteristics they are designed to extend or enhance. For example, Bruner's ideas are most influential in the cultivation of curiosity through the content-based units, while Kohlberg's are used more in the development of leadership skills. Renzulli's approaches are apparent in the content exploration units designed to stimulate curiosity and in the development of independent research skills. Although Renzulli's ideas are most noticeable in the areas just cited, a philosophy similar to his is pervasive in the framework of the curriculum.

Perhaps the greatest emphasis is on Taba's methods and ideas. These strategies are used throughout the program and in developing all listed child needs. Although many individuals perceive the Taba strategies as entirely process oriented, the teacher in this resource program has recognized their comprehensiveness in providing specific techniques for implementing most of the content, process, and learning environment modifications appropriate for gifted students.

Two approaches not included in the other curricula in this section are a part of the resource room curriculum: Ennis's (1964) critical thinking skills and Simon's (Simon, Leland & Kirschenbaum, 1972) *Values Clarification* techniques. Ennis's approach is used as a guide to the development of both critical and creative thinking skills. It also provides objectives listed on the individualized plan. *Values Clarification* is very much a part of the development of leadership and affective skills.

In summary, the Elementary Resource Room Program's curriculum provides a comprehensive plan for the development of the strengths of gifted children. It is truly a qualitatively different curriculum shown to be successful in the growth of creative and critical thinking, self-management skills, and levels of knowledge and skill in reading and spelling.

RESOURCES

A variety of materials contributed to the success of the program. Following is a list of some of those resources, categorized according to the unit or area of emphasis.

Critical/Creative Thinking

Christie, C.W., & Maraviglia, C.W. *C. P. S. think book*. Buffalo, N.Y.: D.O.K. Publishers, undated.

Davis, G.A. *Imagination express*. Buffalo, N.Y.: D.O.K. Publishers, 1973.

Gardner, M. *AHA! Insight*. San Francisco: W.H. Freeman, 1978.

Greene, C. *Successful problem solving techniques*. Mountain View, CA.: Creative Publications, 1977.

Harnadek, A. *Deductive thinking skills*. Troy, Michigan: Midwest Publications, 1979.

Harnadek, A. *Inductive thinking skills*. Troy, Michigan: Midwest Publications, 1979.

McKim, R.M. *Experiences in visual thinking*. Monterey, Ca.: Brooks/Cole Publishing Co., 1980.

Myers, R.E., & Torrance, E.P. *Can you imagine: Invitations to thinking and doing*. Lexington, Ma.: Ginn & Co., 1965.

Noller, R.B., & Mauthe, E. *Scratching the surface of c. p. s.* Buffalo, N.Y.: D.O.K. Publishers, 1977.

Sobil, D.J. *Two minute mysteries*. New York: Scholastic Book Services, 1969.

Affective/Counseling

Freed, A.M. *T. A. for tots*. Sacramento, Ca.: Jalmar Publishers, undated.

Freed, A.M. *T. A. for teens*. Sacramento, Ca.: Jalmar Publishers, undated.

Simon, S.B. *"Vulture."* Niles, Il.: Argus Communications, 1977.

Simon, S.B. *I am loveable and capable*. Niles, Il.: Argus Communications, 1977.

Thomas, M. *Free to be you and me*. New York: McGraw-Hill, 1974.

Watson, J.W. *Sometimes i get angry*. New York: Western Publishing Co., 1971.

Watson, J.W. *Sometimes i get afraid*. New York: Western Publishing Co., 1971.

Research and Resources

Hill, H.D., Jr., & McKenna, J.M. *Outline building*. North Billerica, Ma.: *Curriculum Associates, undated*.

Interact. *Search* (A Simulation Game). Lakeside, Ca.: Author, undated.

Peterson, L., & Turner, R., (Eds.). *A child's guide to Albuquerque*. Albuquerque, N.M.: Modern Press, 1978.

S.R.A. *Research lab* (Kit). Chicago: Author, undated.

S.R.A. *Newslab* (Kit). Chicago: Author, undated.

Culture and Anthropology

Aranda, C. *N.M. folklore from the Spanish*. Albuquerque, N.M.: Author, 1977.

Education Development Center. *Man: A course of study* (MACOS). Washington, D.C.: Curriculum Development Associates, 1970.

Howell, C. *Early man* (Rev. ed.). Morristown, N.J.: Silver Burdett Co., 1973.

Interact. *DIG* (A Simulation Game). Lakeside, Ca.: Author, undated.

Jackson, A. *People of the world*. New York: Henry X. Walck, 1959.

Nansen, F. *Eskimo life*. New York: AMS Press, 1975. (Originally published, 1893).

National Geographic Society. *Alaska*. Washington, D.C.: Author, 1976.

Reader's Digest Press. *The world's last mysteries*. New York: Author, 1978.

Vivian, R.G. *The three-c site: An early pueblo II ruin in chaco canyon, New Mexico*. Albuquerque, N.M.: University of New Mexico Press, 1965.

Self-Expression

Gay, K. *Body talk*. New York: Charles Scribner's & Sons, 1974.

O'Rourke, T.J. *A basic course in manual communication*. New York: National Association for the Deaf, 1973.

Science Areas

Adams, A., & Coble, C. *Mainstreaming science and mathematics*. Santa Monica, Ca.: Goodyear, 1977.

Brandwein, P.F., & Ruchlins, H. *Invitations to investigate*. New York: Harcourt Brace Jovanovich, 1970.

Freeman, I.M. *Physics made simple*. Garden City, N.J.: Doubleday & Co., 1965.

Hach Chemical Company. *Water test kit*. Available from Hach Chemical Company, P.O. Box 389, Loveland, Colorado 80537.

Kapit, W., & Elson, L.M. (Eds.). *An anatomy coloring book*. New York: Harper & Row, 1977.

Moorman, T. *How to make your project scientific*. New York: Atheneum, 1974.

Youngpeter, J.M. *PROBE: Suggested activities to motivate the teaching of primary science*. Stevensville, Mi.: Educational Service Inc., 1976.

Zim, H.S. *Rocks and minerals*. New York: Golden Press, 1957.

Leadership

Bushman, J.H., & Jones, S.K. *Effective communication—A handbook of discussion skills*. Buffalo, N.Y.: D. O. K. Publishers, undated.

Careers

Goldreich, G., & Goldreich, E. *What can she be* (A Series). New York: Lothrop, Lee & Shepard, 1976.

Free Selection

A number of games and activities were used, including: Geoboards and cards, Tangram pieces and books, Chess, Circulation and Mancala.

All are available from Creative Publications, 1101 San Antonio Rd., Mountain View, California.

NOTES

1. This particular grouping of traits or characteristics of gifted children was developed by Karen Allen, teacher of the gifted for the Albuquerque, N.M., Public Schools.
2. The teacher-made material in this text is available from Suzanne Keisel-Stagnone, Albuquerque Public Schools North Area Office, 120 Woodlands, N.W., Albuquerque, N.M.
3. Sources for the materials listed in each of the units can be found in the Resources section.
4. This IEP was developed cooperatively by Suzanne and James Keisel-Stagnone.

Chapter 11

An Early Childhood Program for Culturally Different, Potentially Gifted Children

The school for which this curriculum was written is typical of those in the inner city. Once surrounded by small, individually owned homes, it now is in a deteriorating neighborhood of mixed ethnicity in houses shared by many "families." The main street of the city is three blocks away. The inner business core with offices and high-rise buildings is nearby.

The school has 350 students with an ethnic breakdown of Anglo 9 percent, black 26 percent, Hispanic 62 percent, Native American 3 percent. Support services consider only low achievement scores and are directed at providing materials and instruction for the nonachieving student. The full-time principal and 11 regular class teachers are augmented by a support team of three remedial reading teachers; one Oral Language, Speech, and Hearing teacher, a half-time Title I social worker, a half-time counselor, a special education resource room teacher, and several educational aides.

Since no high potential students were identified using normal screening and identification procedures, more comprehensive methods coupled with an intensive program of enrichment were needed. It was believed that with special teaching techniques, programs, methods, and Individualized Education Programs, these children could be taught to test and perform as gifted students. Many of them did, but some did not.

Because of the belief that many children from different cultural backgrounds or from low-income homes with high potential were not being served by a gifted program because of their poor scores on traditional tests, an experimental program was designed. The program was to serve for pilot-testing new selection procedures, standardized instruments, and a curriculum that seemed potentially useful with this population.

Certain aspects of this program have been described more fully elsewhere (Maker, Morris, & James, 1981) so they are not explained here. The purpose of this chapter is to present in detail the curriculum and how it was implemented as well as the results in terms of child growth.

DESCRIPTION OF THE CURRICULUM

Philosophy

A project designed specifically to meet the needs of potentially gifted minority students in an inner city area has its base in the fact that all children have the right to be given the opportunity to reach their full potential in learning. For this to happen, these children need a program of enrichment outside the regular classroom.

It is important to note that the norm of achievement for the inner city population is much below that of the national average—or of the city, for that matter. As a result, the teaching in the regular classroom necessarily must fit the needs of an average much below that of a gifted or potentially gifted student. To best serve students, it thus is necessary to devise an enriched program based on individual characteristics as well as group needs, and especially emphasizing language development.

Developing realistic self-concepts is another goal, since one of the reasons for poor performance in testing situations is the students' lack of a positive self-concept. With the cooperation of parents and regular classroom teachers, children can be guided to develop positive attitudes toward themselves and toward learning.

Another important area of emphasis is creativity. Developing the flexibility and original thinking inherent in creative thinking will help these children cope with everyday problems and view them in various ways. Another consideration is that studies indicate that high performance in school often is as much a result of high levels of creativity as it is of high intellectual ability (Getzels & Jackson, 1962).

In such a program, it is important to emphasize developing the children's strengths and capitalizing upon their unique cultural traits. By emphasizing the positive, educators can improve on some of the weaknesses but, perhaps more importantly, can lead the children to an appreciation for their own unique talents and abilities.

Definition

Project staff began with the definition of giftedness developed by the U.S. Office of Education (1972), which includes six areas of talent—general intellectual ability, creativity/divergent thinking, specific academic aptitude, visual and performing arts, leadership, and psychomotor ability. The State of New Mexico recognizes only the first three of these categories in its definition. However, because of the low level of achievement in the school, the staff believed there would be very few children who showed talents in specific academic areas. Thus, the talent area of leadership was substituted for academic aptitude in the definition because it was clear that many of these children did show evidence of ability in this area.

Potential giftedness in this population was defined as performance significantly above the norm for the school in any one or more of the three talent areas selected for emphasis: general intellectual ability, creativity, and leadership. During the selection process, there was an attempt to choose children with high potential in all three areas; however, many also were chosen because of their promise in only one.

Screening, Identification, and Needs Assessment

Because of the experimental nature of the program and the unusual procedures used to select children, the process and results are described briefly to help the reader gain an overall perception of the program. Since the usual screening procedures had not produced any children eligible for referral for testing (an IQ of 115 was the usual referral cutoff and the highest IQ in the school was 112), a comprehensive process in which pupils were compared with their own peers was instituted.

The first step was to select instruments designed to measure each of the three talent areas that realistically could be administered to the whole enrollment to establish school norms. Since the project was planned for kindergarten and first grade, the screening process was limited to those levels. Exhibit 11-1 lists the instruments administered to all children at the school. Two of the measures, vision and hearing screening and the home bilingual usage estimate, produced background information that could be used to provide supporting evidence or to suggest a further look at children whose total screening scores were not high enough for referral. Vision and hearing screening also elicited information about scores that might be depressed because of a handicap.

Parents of all kindergartners were interviewed in their homes by the special class teacher. For the first graders, parent interview information was obtained only for those who were referred for further testing. Since OLSH Screening and the Boehm already were available on all children, those scores were used as a part of the process.

After information was collected from all these sources, frequency distributions and means were computed for kindergarten and first grade separately. A weighting system such as that described in Chapter 8 (Baldwin & Wooster, 1977) was developed. All scores for all children were recorded on a matrix that was used to determine referral for further testing. On this matrix (Maker, Morris & James, 1981), weighted scores were totaled for each of the three talent areas and for all three together. Children with the highest total scores as well as those who had high results in only one or two areas were referred for further testing.

The 40 children referred were given intelligence and language tests. Since the screening process had been so extensive, only a few more instruments were used. This assessment included the *Leiter International Performance Scales,* a nonverbal test of intelligence, that was administered to children from homes where the

Exhibit 11-1 Instruments Used to Screen a School Population for
Potentially Gifted Young Children

Instrument	Area of Talent Assessed	Grade Level
Parent Interview	All	K
Vision and Hearing Screening	Background Information	K
Home Bilingual Usage Estimate	Background Information	K
Peer Referral Interview	All	K & 1
TTCT— Figural Item	Creativity	1
Diagnostic Teaching with Observation Checklist	Creativity	K & 1
Teacher Referral Checklist	Leadership	K & 1
Observation	Leadership	K
Bernal Checklist with Parents	Intelligence	K
Bernal Checklist with Teachers	Intelligence	1
Draw-A-Person	Intelligence	K & 1
Otis-Lennon	Intelligence	K & 1
Boehm Test of Basic Concepts	Achievement	1
Oral Language, Speech, and Hearing (OLSH) Screening	Language Development	K

dominant language was other than English. Children without a language difference were administered the *Wechsler Preschool and Primary Scale of Intelligence* (WPPSI) or the *Wechsler Intelligence Scale for Children-Revised* (WISC-R), depending on their age. A second measure, the *Peabody Picture Vocabulary Test* (PPVT), given in either English or Spanish, assessed receptive language.

The information from these two assessments was combined with some of the screening data (e.g., the *Torrance Tests of Creative Thinking*–TTCT, diagnostic teaching, and peer referral) and placed on a second matrix. This form was used in the same way as the screening matrix. Eighteen children were selected for the program.

After selection, each child was administered an individual *Wide Range Achievement Test* (WRAT) as well as numerous informal tests of achievement, language, and level of cognitive development. All this information, when compiled, provided a profile of each pupil's strengths and weaknesses. This profile was used to develop individual programs as well as the plan for the group.

The Instructional Program

Although the program's major focus was on the development of strengths and talents, it also emphasized language development and basic skills in reading and math. This latter emphasis on the children's weak areas is necessary to enable them to function well in the regular curriculum and to allow them to develop fully in all areas.

Because of the need to provide as much enrichment as possible and avoid overlap between programs, the special classroom teacher worked as closely as possible with the regular teachers. Since the nine kindergartners attended only this program, the task was not difficult; however, since the first graders were in regular classrooms during the morning and the special program in the afternoon, constant communication was necessary. With the kindergarten program, the teacher simply covered all the usual curriculum more rapidly while providing enrichment experiences in language arts, social studies, and math/science. The regular curriculum in first grade emphasized the development of basic skills in reading and math, using the Open Court series (Carus, 1979) in reading and Macmillan (Thoburn et al., 1976) in math. The special teacher provided some enrichment of basic concepts in reading but did not accelerate the children because of the nature of the series. In math, some acceleration was possible but there was more concentration on developing a concrete basis for the abstract concepts being learned and extending them further, using the concrete experiences as a beginning point.

The *Hilda Taba Strategies* were used as the instructional basis of the program, and Bloom's *Taxonomy* as a means of classifying the objectives and focusing on the development of higher levels of thinking. To provide a strong theoretical framework, the content and teaching strategies were planned with Piagetian research as their base.

Content Objectives

Using the regular curriculum as a starting point and following the suggestions of Bruner (1960), the curriculum was organized around a series of basic concepts and generalizations that could be derived from the information. Following are the generalizations in each content area:

Language Arts

- Language is a tool.
- Language can be a better tool for us to use if we can speak, read, and write better.
- Events follow particular sequences.

Social Studies

- Rules are made for the good of all.
- How we treat other people affects how they treat us.
- People of the world make their living from different kinds of work.
- How we value others affects how we treat them.
- People of the world all have the same basic needs.
- All people depend on others in important ways.
- Maps are pictures that represent specific places.
- Knowing directions (N, S, E, W) helps us to find our way.

Science/Math

- Living things depend on each other and on nonliving things.
- Seasons of the year follow a set pattern.
- Natural forces change the earth.
- Numbers follow patterns.
- Objects can be classified according to various criteria.

- Calendars represent days, weeks, months, years.

- Clocks represent the passage of seconds, minutes, hours.

All data used to teach each of the generalizations cannot be presented here. However, to provide examples of the specific facts and skills that were taught, the following key concepts to be used by the teacher were selected. Below each concept is a list of content and skills designed to develop these concepts.

Rules

- Make rules for behavior in the classroom.

- Make rules for playground behavior.

- Make a book of rules with people following and not following them.

- Self-evaluate a day's behavior to determine whether rules were followed.

Different Kinds of Work

- List different things people do, then group them according to their similarities.

- Cut out pictures of people doing different jobs and make them into a bulletin board display.

- Interview parents about their work and report the results of this interview to the class.

- List all the kinds of work *you* would like to do.

Natural Forces

- Read about causes of erosion.

- Watch films of wind and water at work changing the earth.

- Watch film about volcanoes.

- Take field trips to volcanoes.

- Take field trips to mountains.

Language Is a Tool

- Develop puppet plays, including a script as well as costumes, stage, and plot.

- Develop a silent language.

- Take a field trip to the zoo, noticing how animals communicate.

- List all the ways the people in a set of pictures are communicating with each other.

These concepts and generalizations were developed as a program basis. As the year progresses and individual needs are recognized, these objectives are modified to fit the particular needs of the pupils. As student interests are realized, content also is modified to include those special interests.

Process Objectives

Process objectives encompass all content areas. They can be categorized into the following general areas:

1. Students' responses to teacher questions and activities that are open-ended will (a) be on focus 75 percent of the time, (b) show divergent thinking 80 percent of the time, (c) be reactions to other student ideas 50 percent of the time, and (d) be complete thoughts 90 percent of the time.
2. Students given particular subject matter will recall specific data with 80 percent accuracy.
3. Students, after making a conclusion, inference, or statement arrived at through a thinking process at a higher level than recall, will explain or cite evidence to support their answers 90 percent of the time.
4. Students given specific data will state inferences about causes and/or effects of particular events or patterns appropriate to the data 50 percent of the time.
5. Students will make appropriate selections 90 percent of the time without teacher direction when given the opportunity to choose activities.
6. Students will utilize inductive thinking skills to form appropriate conclusions according to particular criterion 80 percent of the time when given specific data.
7. Students will use deductive reasoning to make appropriate predictions about patterns or events with 80 percent accuracy when provided with specific data.
8. Students will employ cognitive thinking skills at or above the application level in 50 percent of the learning activities in which they participate.

Product Objectives

Product objectives emphasize the need for children to be creative and original. These objectives are categorized as follows:

1. Students will develop criteria for evaluating their own products 50 percent of the time. These will approximate the criteria used by a real audience 25 percent of the time.
2. Students will develop products that address real problems 10 percent of the time.
3. Students will develop products that transform rather than summarize information 10 percent of the time.
4. Students will develop products that are directed toward audiences approximating real ones 5 percent of the time.

Teaching Activities

Teaching activities are based on a combination of Piagetian techniques and aspects of the *Hilda Taba Teaching Strategies*. Although the curriculum contains a heavy content emphasis along with the teaching of basic skills, the activities require creative and divergent thinking. Often, the Taba *Strategies* need modification or to be broken into smaller units because of the children's short attention span. Taba's first strategy, concept development, is used more frequently than the others since it is the easiest to use with this age group and develops the most basic intellectual skill.

Since not all teaching activities can be described adequately, to provide as many concrete examples as possible, the following section contains descriptions of different aspects of several sample lessons: (a) the content purpose, (b) the process purpose, (c) the focusing questions at each step, and (d) any supporting activities or materials used.

Lesson 1

Content Purpose: To clarify and extend the concept of transportation.
Process Purpose: To identify and name a variety of relationships among data.
Supporting Activities: Have children observe the ways people travel to and from the places they go. Keep a list of these ways on a piece of butcher paper in the classroom. While on field trips, have children watch for new means of transportation that they may not already have on the list. For each transportation method listed, make up a card with either a picture or drawing of that mode. Use these cards as stimuli for the discussion.

Focusing Questions:
1. What are some of the ways people move from place to place? (Children talk briefly about the pictures.)
2. Which of these ways people go from place to place would you put together because they are alike? (One child at a time makes a group of pictures.) Why do you think _____, _____, and _____ go together? (Child gives reasons why items are alike.)

3. What would be a good name for this group, based on the reasons why you grouped these together? (Get at least three names for each group made at Step 2.) Why is that a good name? (Ask for a reason for each name.)
4. (a) Which pictures that are now under one name could also go under another name? (b) Why would that picture also belong there? (c) What other ways of moving from place to place could go under this name (besides those we have)?
5. What completely new ways could you find to group these pictures because they are alike? (Steps 2, 3, and 4 are recycled.)

Lesson 2

Content Purpose: To clarify and extend the concept of basic human needs, both physical and social/emotional.
Process Purpose: To identify and name a variety of relationships among data.
Supporting Activities: Talk about what the different people studied throughout the social studies units need to survive. Keep a list of these basic needs with pictures or illustrations that can be used later.

Focusing Questions:
1. What are some of the things people need to survive?
2. Which of these things people need would you put together because they are alike? In what ways are these alike?
3. What would be a good name for this group, based on how these things are alike? Why is that a good name?
4. Which pictures that are now under one name could also go under another name? Why could that picture also go there? What other needs do people have that we have not listed that could also go in this group? Why would they go in this group?
5. What completely different ways could be used to group these pictures? (Recycle steps 2, 3, and 4.)

Lesson 3

Content Purpose: To draw warranted conclusions concerning the following relationships:

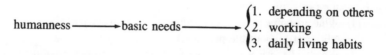

Process Purpose: To make and support inferences, draw conclusions from well-supported inferences, and generalize from a specific instance to other similar ones.

Supporting Activities: Discuss either a representative picture from each group of pictures from among those depicting human need from Lesson 2 (based on that lesson) or a variety of pictures chosen from the list without reference to earlier groups.

Focusing Questions (using the following sequence, discuss each picture separately):
1. (a) Why do you think you need _____? (b) Why do you think (answers to a) causes you to need _____? (Elicit a variety of causes and support for each inference before going to the next step.)
2. (a) What do you think is the most important reason why you need _____? (b) Why do you think that is the most important reason?
3. (a) What would you say, based on what you know about yourself and other people, about why others need _____? (b) Why do you think all people need _____ because of (answer to 3a)?
4. (a) What are some of the things you do because you need _____? (b) Why do you think you (answer to 4a) because you need _____? (Obtain a variety of answers to this question along with support for each answer before going on to the next step.)
5. (a) What do you think are the most important things you do because you need _____? (b) Why do you think those are the most important things you do because you need _____?
6. (a) What, based on what you know about yourself and others, would you say about what others do because they need _____? (b) Why do you think that is true of all people?

After each picture has been discussed separately, review some of the causes given for these needs (answers to questions 1, 2, and 3), then ask the following questions:

1. What could you say generally about what causes all people to need _____, _____, _____, etc., based on what you have said about why you have certain wants? (List all needs discussed.) (Give children time to write a sentence or think about their answer.)
2. What are your reasons for deciding all people have these needs because of (answer to question 1)?

Next, review their answers to your questions about effects of needs (questions 4, 5, 6) and ask the following questions:

1. What would you say generally, based on what you have noted as to what you and others do because you have certain needs, about what happens because people need _____, _____, _____, etc.? (List all needs

discussed.) (Give the children time to think and/or write a complete sentence about what they think.)
2. Why do you think all people (answer to question 1) because of these needs?

Lesson 4

Content Purpose: To modify or extend the following generalization: Living things depend on each other and on nonliving things.

Process Purpose: To predict consequences of a given set of circumstances, to support predictions with evidence or reasoning, to limit predictions by stating and supporting necessary prior or attendant conditions, to draw warranted conclusions, and to suggest modification or extension of the above generalization.

Supporting Activities: Using the previous theme of human needs, draw upon pupils' thinking by having the following discussion.

Focusing Questions:
1. (a) What do you think would happen if suddenly there were no more (human need)_____ ? (Children list their predictions while the teacher listens and records them. Ask this question about a few critical human needs.) (b) Why would you predict that _____ would happen? (Go back to each prediction given and ask why.)
2. (a) What else do you think would have to happen or be true for (prediction) to come true? (b) Why do you think (answer to 2a) would be necessary? (After children have given several necessary conditions for one prediction, select another prediction and ask the same question; continue until a variety of predictions have been explored.)
3. (a) What do you think would be most likely to happen, based on what we have said, if some of the things humans need no longer were here? (b) Why do you think that would be most likely to happen?
4. What, if any, changes would you make in this statement, based on what we have discussed and what you know: Living things depend on each other and on nonliving things. Why would you say _____?

In addition to these kinds of discussions, much time is spent on language development and creative expression. The children tell stories, write and illustrate stories about their field trips, dramatize fairy tales and other stories, and develop puppet shows. During quiet time every day, the teacher reads to them and they often talk about the story. In so doing, the focus can be on summarizing the sequence of events, predicting what might happen next, telling a story about something similar that has occurred, or discussing the feelings of the character in the tale.

Evaluation of Student Progress

To assess the progress of the students, certain of the instruments included in screening, identification, and needs assessment are readministered. These instruments include a TTCT item, diagnostic teaching with observation, Draw-a-Person (DAP) test, the WRAT, and the PPVT. The *Peabody Individual Achievement Test* also is administered to provide additional assessment.

Even though the results of the testing reflect only a six-month span because of the length of the screening and identification process, many of the children made remarkable gains. A few progressed normally as would be expected in this length of time. Table 11-1 summarizes the pretest and posttest scores as well as gains

Table 11-1 Creativity Scores for Early Childhood Program

Child/Class	Instrument/Procedure					
	Diagnostic Teaching			Torrance Test Item		
Kindergarten	Pre	Post[1]	Change	Pre[2]	Post	Change
1	9	—	—	N S	27	+27
2	9	—	—	N S	24	+24
3	3	8	+5	N S	19	+19
4	10	12	+2	N S	55	+55
5	7	16	+9	N S	31	+31
6	11	5	−6	N S	28	+28
7	8	12	+4	N S	29	+29
8	4	14	+10	N S	44	+44
Average	7.1	11	+2.3	N S	32.1	+32.1
First Grade	Pre	Post[1]	Change	Pre[2]	Post	Change
1	10	0	−10	29	37	+8
2	5	13	+8	35	—	—
3	11	11	0	25	38	+13
4	13	—	—	22	—	—
5	10	16	+6	36	40	+4
6	11	12	+1	30	—	—
7	12	10	−2	44	34	−10
8	1	7	+6	31	42	+11
9	4	8	+4	25	—	—
10	5	5	0	38	—	—
11	3	5	+2	N S	30	+30
Average	7.7	8.6	+1.5	28.6	36.8	+9.3

1. Several children were absent at the end of school because of a highly contagious disease. No posttest scores were obtained for them.

2. NS = not scored. The pretests for kindergartners consisted only of scribbles, which are unscorable. One first grade child's test also was unscorable.

made on the creativity measures. Scores on the diagnostic teaching activity are a combination of items measuring such characteristics as quickness of warm-up, problem solving, verbal and nonverbal expressiveness, and ability to improvise with commonplace materials. On the Torrance test item, scores reflect the combination of originality, elaboration, and fluency. Since the raw scores are used, it is difficult to make comparisons except among individual children. Most did make considerable gains, however.

On the measures of intelligence (Table 11-2), positive change also is apparent. Although not a great deal of change would normally be expected in such measures, these children, in a six-month period, showed remarkable gains. For example, one kindergartner (child #4) scored 26 points higher on the PPVT while another (child #7) advanced 12 points. Two first graders advanced 13 and 10 points, respectively, while another's score dropped 10 points. The Draw-A-Person, which is less sensitive to change, reflected smaller gains.

Table 11-2 Intelligence Test Scores for Early Childhood Program

Child/Class	Instrument/Procedure					
	Diagnostic Teaching			Torrance Test Item		
Kindergarten	Pre	Post	Change	Pre	Post	Change
1	6	5	−1	106	106	0
2	7	5	−2	118	—	—
3	4	5	+1	109	117	+8
4	6	6	0	63	89	+26
5	6	5	−1	121	121	0
6	5	7	+2	109	117	+8
7	5	6	+1	103	115	+12
8	7	6	−1	99	108	+9
Average	5.9	5.6	+.3	103.5	110.4	+6.9
First Grade	Pre	Post	Change	Pre	Post	Change
1	5	5	0	101	100	−1
2	5	5	0	143	133	−10
3	4	6	+2	107	112	+5
4	4	6	+2	106	106	0
5	5	7	+2	93	102	+9
6	5	6	+1	101	102	+1
7	4	4	0	127	118	−9
8	5	6	+1	104	106	+2
9	5	5	0	115	120	+5
10	5	5	0	89	102	+13
11	5	5	0	85	95	+10
Average	4.7	5.5	+.8	106.5	108.7	+2.3

Achievement scores also show considerable gain (Table 11-3). In the six-month period, most children gained at least a year; in some cases, the average was more than a year. Kindergarten children's average gain in arithmetic was almost two years. Although the PIAT also was administered, it had not been included as a pretest instrument, so the gain scores were not available. However, the PIAT results provided a second measure of the children's level of achievement that supported their WRAT scores. The average grade level of achievement of the kindergartners was 2.3 in math, 1.5 in reading recognition, 1.4 in spelling, and 2.4 in information. First graders scored an average of 3.2 in math, 2.9 in reading recognition, 2.6 in reading comprehension, 2.6 in spelling, and 3.0 in information. As can be seen, these children were beginning to perform at the level expected of the gifted.

It is interesting to note that the children who made the greatest gains were those who spoke limited or no English at the beginning of the year or who were from the

Table 11-3 WRAT Achievement Scores for Early Childhood Program

Child/Class	Reading			Spelling			Arithmetic		
Kindergarten	Pre	Post	Change	Pre	Post	Change	Pre	Post	Change
1	K.1	1.7	+1.6	1.3	1.4	+.1	P.8	1.7	+1.9
2	K.5	1.5	+1.0	P.8	1.7	+1.9	P.6	1.7	+2.1
3	1.4	1.8	+.4	1.3	1.5	+.2	1.4	2.3	+.9
4	*	1.7	+1.7	*	1.9	+1.9	*	2.6	+2.6
5	K.1	1.0	+.9	P.7	1.4	+1.7	P.4	1.1	+1.7
6	K.5	1.6	+1.1	1.4	1.5	+.1	1.1	1.9	+.8
7	1.3	1.7	+.4	1.4	1.7	+.3	1.4	2.7	+1.3
8	1.3	1.9	+.6	1.4	2.1	+.7	1.1	2.6	+1.5
Average	K.6	1.8	+1.2	K.4	1.9	+1.5	K.2	2.1	+1.9
First Grade	Pre	Post	Change	Pre	Post	Change	Pre	Post	Change
1	—	3.4	—	—	2.8	—	—	3.1	—
2	2.5	3.3	+.8	2.4	3.9	+1.5	2.7	3.3	+.6
3	2.2	2.8	+.6	2.2	2.5	+.3	2.7	3.7	+1.0
4	1.4	3.0	+1.6	1.7	2.8	+1.1	2.3	3.7	+1.4
5	—	4.0	—	—	3.3	—	—	3.1	—
6	1.7	2.8	+1.1	1.7	3.1	+1.4	2.1	3.1	+1.0
7	K.9	3.1	+2.2	K.8	2.6	+1.8	K.9	2.9	+2.0
8	3.8	4.1	+.3	2.2	3.7	+1.5	2.7	3.7	+1.0
9	2.6	4.0	+1.4	2.1	2.6	+.5	2.6	3.3	+.7
10	1.6	2.5	+.9	1.7	2.5	+.8	1.7	2.9	+1.2
11	—	3.1	—	—	2.8	—	—	3.9	—
Average	2.1	3.3	+1.2	1.9	3.0	+1.1	2.2	3.3	+1.1

*This child could not speak enough English to be tested on any of these measures.

poorest families. Child #4 in the kindergarten class, for example, made remarkable gains in all areas. The same was true of child #11 in first grade. These seem to be very bright children who, if given an enriched program, can make outstanding contributions. Even if the program were of benefit to only these children, it would be considered a success.

ANALYSIS OF THE CURRICULUM

Unique Aspects

The curriculum for this program is designed for a unique population—children who show the potential to develop superior abilities but who do not yet perform at an elevated level. Because of these characteristics, the curriculum includes an emphasis on basic skill development while simultaneously enhancing the pupils' creative and leadership capabilities. Thus, the content includes acceleration of basic skill development and self-expression along with exploration of some topics not included in the regular curriculum. Since most of the pupils had never been beyond the confines of their low-income neighborhood, many of these experiences included field trips to places already familiar to most other children: the zoo, local museums, the volcanoes and mountains outside town, the university, the police station, city hall, a courtroom.

Because of the children's basic lack of information, much time is spent on the development of a concrete basis for abstract concepts, particularly in math. This lack of information, coupled with the somewhat slower rate of cognitive development, also influences the rate of development of higher levels of thinking. Many of these children are "preoperational" in Piaget's term (Piaget & Inhelder, 1969) so they have not yet developed the ability to represent objects by words and symbols. As indicated in responses on the figural TTCT of the kindergartners as well as some of the first graders at the beginning of the program (Maker, Morris & James, 1981), they have not yet begun to represent things through their drawings. Most gifted children of this age already have made the transition from preoperational to the concrete operations stage. With this transition comes the ability to make inferences that are far removed from the actual data as well as to make predictions at higher levels than those tied directly to physical reality.

In the teacher's use of the Taba strategies, these developmental aspects are most observable. Except for the first strategy (concept development) the strategies must be simplified because the children cannot understand or perform some of the intellectual tasks. For example, in the second strategy—interpretation of data—the third step requires students to draw inferences based on earlier ones (e.g., prior causes, subsequent effects). Until very late in the year, most of the children could not accomplish this task. In the third strategy, application of generalizations, children have difficulty predicting the consequences of earlier predictions. To keep the discussions based on concrete information as much as possible, all the data that the children are asked to manipulate (i.e., at step one of each discussion) involve either concrete objects or pictures of familiar information.

Combination of Models

In yet a different program, the familiar teaching-learning models are combined. Rather than having one of the models usually used in programs for the gifted as its overall structure, however, Piagetian theory forms the basis of the curriculum. Children's stage of cognitive development is a limiting factor not incorporated into many of the familiar models. Perhaps this is because most programs for the gifted focus on older children. It also is true, however, that children from higher socioeconomic (SES) families are at a higher developmental level before entering kindergarten and first grade. For example, this author has demonstrated that the Taba strategies can be used successfully with little or no modifications in an experimental early childhood program for this same age group from average and high-income families (Maker, in press).

Bruner's ideas form the basis for organization of content around generalizations and basic concepts while Bloom's *Taxonomy* is used as the means for classifying objectives. The *Taxonomy* provides a structure for reviewing all classroom activities and assuring that as many as possible are included at the higher levels.

Curricular Modifications

Although the impoverished background of the children limited the number of curricular modifications necessary or even possible, a surprising number of content, process, and environment modifications were made. Product changes are more difficult because of the pupils' lack of sophistication. As can be seen from the product objectives, the emphasis is on creativity and originality but not on sophistication or potential for presentation to real audiences. The children, their parents, and other interested teachers were the audiences for the art fair and open house.

With regard to the content, modifications were in the areas of variety and organization for economy. Although it could be argued that some of the generalizations and concepts developed were at a higher level of abstraction than those usually taught in kindergarten and first grade, much of the emphasis was on development of concrete referents for these abstract concepts. As noted earlier, this concrete information was lacking because of the children's limited backgrounds. Variety was included through science and social studies material not usually taught at this level.

Many process modifications were made. There was great emphasis on discovery learning, open-endedness, group process and interaction, pacing, and variety. Higher levels of thinking were stressed to the extent possible given the intellectual development of the children. The important point in this regard, however, is that in no instance did the teacher assume that a pupil could not perform an intellectual task. Using concrete information as a reference point, the teacher always asked questions at as high a level as possible, and encouraged the children to try. Within this general structure, too, a pupil's inability to go beyond the concrete was acceptable and the teacher was supportive of all efforts regardless of their success.

Questions and creative activities were open-ended. Children were encouraged to plan and present their own puppet shows and to assist in making decisions about field trips. Much emphasis was placed on self-expression through writing, drawing, and storytelling. A variety of methods was included, such as learning centers, group instruction, tutoring, field trips, workbooks, individual listening to talking books and records, individual and group reading, games, and puppet shows.

The learning environment was a stimulating one that emphasized student interests and ideas. The teacher (and class) responded to the needs of each child individually and planned instruction around group needs and interests. Since the pupils needed practice in expressing themselves, much emphasis was placed on having them talk. Although it was difficult to develop a high degree of independence and self-direction in some of the children, many others already were self-directed because of the necessity of fending for themselves in homes where both mother and father were away most of the day. The teacher emphasized development of independence while attempting to foster a feeling of group responsibility in class management.

The teacher and many of the children had basic value differences, so at times it was difficult to avoid being surprised at the pupils' responses. A teacher can find it difficult to be truly accepting when a bright boy states that he wants only "to work at Taco Bell" when he grows up. The focus, however, should be on assuring that these children know about their alternative career choices and consequences rather than on directing them toward any particular occupation. This is only one example of the many differing values the teacher must accept to develop a truly nonjudgmental attitude.

SUMMARY

Not all components of this experimental program are included in this description. Many are reported elsewhere, including the extensive screening, identification, and assessment process, and the necessary parent involvement program (Maker, Morris & James, 1981). These components all contribute to the overall success of the program. The parent program, for instance, provides an excellent example of how the mirror model (explained in Chapter 6) can serve as a basis for assessing parents' present level of involvement and moving them to higher levels with greater interest and involvement in their children's learning.

The curriculum presented here also is comprehensive in its design as a qualitatively different program. It is built upon the unique characteristics of the children and designed to capitalize upon their strengths as an avenue for remediating their weaknesses in knowledge, language development, and development of abstract thought. The results indicate a high degree of success for most of the children.

Chapter 12

A High School Seminar Program

Rarely do professional staffs at high schools perceive a need for special programs for their gifted and talented students. Many feel that because of the comprehensive nature of most schools, the range of subject offerings along with other opportunities such as advanced placement, clubs, and extracurricular activities, there is no need for additional provisions for such children. Eldorado High School in Albuquerque, N.M., however, is an exception. During the 1977-78 school year, a special task force recommended, as a result of an evaluation and needs assessment, that a special teacher be hired to work with gifted students who were underachieving and/or experiencing emotional or behavioral problems that were interfering with their ability to benefit from the regular educational program. A majority of the staff had expressed a need for such a program.

At first, implementation of the new gifted program was met by resistance and hostility from many staff members. To a large extent this resulted from the fact that the program was not defined clearly and a specific job description for the teacher of the gifted was lacking. This situation was countered by supportive administration and by several teachers who felt strongly about the need for a special program.

DESCRIPTION OF THE CURRICULUM

Philosophy and Goals

The gifted program that provides for direct involvement of and services to students, parents, and staff, is an integral part of the total school program. At Eldorado High School, it is felt that the teacher of the gifted should serve to a large extent as a counselor and advocate for gifted students. The main goals of the program are:

1. To improve the learning environment through curriculum and the implementation of specialized approaches

331

2. To work with students, staff, parents, and others who influence the educational process to develop programs that challenge and motivate gifted students
3. To help students acquire adequate and realistic self-concepts and to become aware of educational and occupational opportunities available to them
4. To facilitate students in problem solving, decision making and communication that will allow them to accept the responsibility for their own actions and choices

The counselor/teacher can provide services for gifted students by suggesting and modeling effective ways to communicate with teachers, peers, and others; by helping them accept the challenge and responsibility for their own learning; by suggesting alternatives in curriculum and problem-solving techniques; and by allowing them the opportunity to express themselves in a supportive atmosphere.

Program Development

The screening began with referrals from administrators, counselors, and teachers of students who seemed bright and who had academic records that indicated high ability but who were underachieving and/or experiencing behavioral or emotional problems that seemed to be interfering with their learning or that of others. Once the staff members had more information about the program and contact with the special teacher, they were more willing to refer students and less resistant to having this instructor work with both achieving and underachieving bright students. As a result of the referral and screening procedures, 29 students were referred for diagnostic testing. Twenty were identified as gifted on the basis of their scores on either the *Stanford-Binet* or a Wechsler individual intelligence test. This reflects an efficiency rate of almost 70 percent. However, because of a shortage of diagnostic personnel, this process was ineffective in identifying all or even a majority of the gifted students at the school.

Assessment of the screening and identification procedures revealed several significant limitations in the instruments used. For instance, the *Peabody Individual Achievement Test* (PIAT) appears to be inappropriate for distinguishing between high achievers and gifted high school students because most of those who are academically high achievers receive scores above the ceiling level on the test. The limitations of the *Stanford-Binet* and Wechsler intelligence tests are numerous. For example, high school freshmen and sophomores fall at the upper age limits on the *Wechsler Intelligence Scale for Children-Revised* (WISC-R), which means that they must make an almost perfect score in order to rank at two standard deviations above the mean, the IQ score usually considered an indication of giftedness. It appears that at the high school level both the *Stanford-Binet* and Wechsler become achievement tests, making the identification of gifted underachievers extremely difficult if only one instrument is relied on heavily for identification. In addition, a sound argument could be made that at two standard deviations above or below the mean, the validity of any test is highly questionable. It seems evident that if emphasis is to be placed on intelligence tests scores, then educators need an instrument that is devised for and standardized on a gifted population. At this point it seems that an emphasis on a score two standard deviations above the mean on a Wechsler or *Stanford-Binet* is an inappropriate measure of giftedness for students of high school age. Based on this assessment of the first year's screening and identification procedures, more appropriate assessment plans were developed and incorporated into the program. These are described in the following section.

The first year of the program also involved the establishment of working relationships with the administration and faculty as well as developing a job description for the teacher and a structure for the program.

Identification and Screening

Most of the students now entering the program have been identified at the elementary and middle school levels since the public schools have a program at every such institution in the system. If eligible for service at these levels, students also may participate in the optional programs offered at the high school. In addition, since the program at this level is designed for both high achievers and underachievers, students who may not have been eligible for other services because of their low achievement may participate.

Criteria for placement and services may vary somewhat from school to school because of the differing achievement levels at each one as a whole and because of the specific services available for gifted students at each. However, as a general rule, the criteria include (a) an IQ score that is at least two standard deviations above the mean for that test, (b) achievement that is above average to superior, and (c) creativity as documented by teacher perception. If a student does not meet the IQ criterion but shows a high degree of intelligence and has other evidence to support the belief that a special program is needed, the individual can be served. Many whose language or cultural backgrounds seem to be limiting factors in the testing process are accepted into a program.

If a student has not been identified previously, but has come to the attention of a teacher or counselor at the high school, the pupil is referred for further testing. In such cases, the *Stanford-Binet* is administered as the measure of intelligence, achievement scores and records are collected, teacher referrals are obtained, and a decision is made about placement based on this combined information. Decisions are made by an Educational Appraisal and Review (EAR) committee consisting of the teacher of the gifted, a regular classroom teacher and/or the person who referred the student, the diagnostician, the parents, and an administrator. Others may be invited if necessary.

The Teacher's Role

Perhaps one of the reasons for so few programs for the gifted at the high school level is the difficulty in defining or establishing a role for the teacher and program. Few precedents exist and, more importantly, each school is different. The teacher of the gifted in this particular school developed a three-part role—advocate, counselor, and facilitator, with specific responsibilities in each.

Advocacy

As an advocate, the special teacher works with all individuals who are concerned about a gifted student, assisting them in understanding and appreciating the uniqueness of the individual. Concerned individuals include regular classroom teachers, parents, counselors, and administrators. The first priority for the teacher is to be available to students, parents, and staff as a consultant should educational or personal problems arise that seem to be interfering with the student's education. Other examples of teacher activities include the following:

- assisting the regular classroom teacher in developing a challenging, individualized program

- assisting the regular classroom teacher in understanding the emotional, social, physical, and psychological needs of each gifted student

- facilitating articulation/communication between the university and the high school through development of college courses on the high school campus

- providing support (e.g., supplying materials, suggesting resources, developing behavior management techniques) for teachers who are attempting to provide individualized programs

- developing parents' understanding of their child's capabilities and/or problems

- assisting parents in identifying ways to enhance their child's abilities through out-of-school activities and to solve social/emotional problems that may be associated with the student's giftedness

As a result of the advocacy of the special teacher in the first year of the program, three bright students who previously had been enrolled in classes for behavior disordered students were entered in the regular program. Mainstreaming these students required frequent conferences regarding instructional problems and behavior management techniques. In addition, the students and their parents needed extra support and counseling from the special teacher.

Counselor

In the role of counselor, the teacher of the gifted assists students in making wise choices in personal, educational, and career areas with the objective of continued growth toward self-actualization and development of potential. Counseling occurs both in small groups and on an individual basis. For example, the teacher conducts sessions regarding curriculum choices, challenging programs or classes available in the school district as well as at the high school, the honors program, College Level Examination Program (CLEP) and Advanced Placement Exams, concurrent enrollment at the university, and other community resources. Students also are instructed in the Guidance Information Service at the Career Enrichment Center, which provides extensive up-to-date information on colleges, universities, and careers.

A somewhat different aspect of the program is a daily teaching/counseling group that involves value clarification, problem-solving techniques, and discussions. Since the group includes both achieving and underachieving students, interaction with other group members is a significant part of the daily sessions. Goals of these and other counseling functions include the following:

- to help the students achieve a better understanding and acceptance of themselves (e.g., their strengths, limitations, aptitudes, needs, values, interests, worth as unique individuals)

- to assist the students in developing problem-solving and decision-making skills

- to help the students in developing successful interpersonal relationships on the basis of mutual respect

- to help students accept increased responsibility for their educational, occupational, and avocational development

Facilitator

As a facilitator, the high school teacher of the gifted uses all available resources to provide for the cognitive and affective needs of students through both in-school and out-of-school activities. The teacher must be knowledgeable about community resources that can be used to help individual students and must arrange for them to take advantage of what is available. Several organized options exist from which a student may choose as many or as few as desired, including:

- an individualized study project with a faculty member in the school or a mentor from the community

- a cross-discipline discussion group that meets two days each week

- career exploration through shadowing (working with a professional for a day), mentorships, and work-study

Program Goals

The goals of the total program can be separated into those pertaining to content, process, and learning environment. Most, however, involve the development of process skills and the provision of a variety of options from which students may choose. The goals, by program area, are:

Content

1. to identify programs or classes in which the content emphasis is on abstract, complex ideas
2. to identify programs or classes in which the content is different from that usually covered in the regular curriculum
3. to identify programs or classes in which the content is organized around basic concepts and generalizations in which the teacher strives for economy in learning experiences
4. to identify programs or classes in which students can study methods of inquiry as well as the characteristics of individuals who are recognized as being successful and/or are creative and productive in their careers

Process

1. to provide for structured development of higher levels of thinking and problem-solving skills
2. to provide open-ended activities and ask open-ended questions
3. to provide assistance in selecting content and process options based on interests and needs
4. to use a variety of methods and provide a variety of program options
5. to use methods that encourage students to interact with each other on both a social and an intellectual basis
6. to provide structured experiences for career exploration and selection

Environment

1. to provide a physical environment that is flexible enough to allow easy access to (a) a variety of learning environments, both inside and outside the school, (b) a variety of references, and (c) sophisticated equipment or facilities
2. to provide physical and psychological environments in which maximum student-to-student interaction can occur

3. to provide a psychological environment that allows and encourages free expression of ideas, constructive criticism, and deferred judgment during idea production

Student Objectives

To accomplish the established program goals, several structured and unstructured program components exist. As described earlier, the teacher serves in the role of advocate, counselor, and facilitator. Many of the activities in the role of advocate and counselor are unstructured and occur on an informal, individual basis. Since these have been presented already, the following description focuses on the structured program components: the cross-discipline seminar, the counseling group, and the career exploration element.

Cross-Discipline Seminar

The seminar is held each semester for any student in grades 9-12 eligible to be served by the school district's gifted program. Participation is optional and students receive one-half elective credit for attendance. Following is the course outline (Bodnar, Note 12).

Course Description

The seminar is designed to provide gifted students with opportunities to express their ideas, reasoning and values, participate in small group discussions, identify cause and effect relationships, make and support inferences, develop substantive generalizations, and modify and extend generalizations to interpret new situations. The seminar is structured to teach students techniques for organizing and processing information rather than concentrating on teaching specific content. The emphasis is on teaching students efficient reasoning strategies, problem solving techniques and critical thinking skills. To a large extent, the content will be drawn from the social sciences with importance placed on having students develop basic generalizations which will enable them to organize, retain and deal more effectively with information.

Method of Instruction

The teaching strategies to be used to conduct the seminar are based on the work of Hilda Taba. The Taba method is a highly structured teaching approach in which the teacher, through the use of open-ended and sequentially ordered questions, requires the students to process information, develop concepts, and formulate generalizations for themselves.

The main objective of the program is to help students acquire cognitive skills that are necessary for productive and autonomous thinking.

1. The Taba method requires that the questions be structured and sequenced to elicit certain cognitive behaviors from the students in accordance with certain assumptions about the developmental nature of both reasoning and valuing skills.
2. The questions are open-ended in that they cannot be answered with one specific correct answer or a yes or no response. The open-ended questions allow for a variety of responses on different levels of abstraction, sophistication and depth. The questions are structured to set the focus of the discussion, maintain direction, and to elicit certain types of cognitive and affective skills from the students.
3. The Taba strategies are successful when the teacher maintains the role of questioner, as opposed to lecturer, evaluator, and censor.
4. The pacing of the questions is geared to insure a variety of responses at each step, to allow students time to think, and to insure that the students are familiar with the skills required at each step.

Objectives of the Four Basic Taba Strategies

Concept Development

Concepts are formed, clarified and extended as students respond to open-ended questions that require them to enumerate items related to an idea from data and/or experience, to identify and name a variety of relationships among the data and to practice organizing and reorganizing the data.

Interpretation of Data

Students respond to questions that require them to make and support inferences about cause-effect relationships, to draw warranted conclusions, and to evolve generalizations from one instance to other such instances.

Application of Generalizations

The essence of this strategy involves having the students make predictions about the future development of a situation based on their own knowledge of similar situations, and limit their predictions by specifying necessary prior or attendant conditions. Students must support all predictions and inferences made.

Resolution of Conflict

The emphasis in this strategy is on having students see the complexity of various conflict situations, to interpret attitudes, values and feelings of individuals involved in the conflict, to generate a variety of solutions, and to analyze these alternatives in relation to their consequences and effects on the people involved.

Specific Objectives for the Seminars

1. Students will show an increase in their ability to express ideas, participate in discussions, listen, react to one another's ideas, identify relationships among data, make supportable inferences, work in small groups, organize information and ideas, and apply what they have learned to new situations.
2. Students will complete readings, assignments and research which will provide them with the information necessary for participation in the discussions.
3. Students will make and support inferences, conclusions and generalizations based on information from readings, research and discussions.
4. Students will recognize the tentativeness and probabilistic nature of conclusions and generalizations.
5. Students will acquire skills in developing, supporting and applying substantive generalizations.
6. Students will combine information, concepts, and generalizations from the various social science fields in order to interpret, analyze, synthesize, and evaluate new information, ideas, issues and values.

Student Evaluation

Assessment of student progress is based on two criteria: their discussion skills and their ability to generalize. Grades reflect an approximately equal combination of self-evaluation and teacher evaluation. In evaluating their progress, students listen to an audio tape of at least one discussion per week, analyzing their discussion skills and ability to generalize as they listen. A different form (Exhibits 12-1 and 12-2) is used for each of the four types of discussions. After completing this self-analysis form, the student completes a rating sheet (Exhibit 12-3). This same rating sheet is also completed by the teacher.

Exhibit 12-1 Seminar Student Self-Evaluation

Key ✓ - when you did
    X - when you should
        have but did not

Interpretation of Data

Name: _____
Date
Topic

Student Behavior	Enumerating	Causes and/or Effects	Conclusion	Generalization
1. Gives appropriate response to question				
2. Provides support for statements				
3. Provides concise extension and clarification				
4. Views situations from a different perspective				
5. Suggests limitations of statements and avoids overgeneralizations				
6. Builds on the ideas of other students				
7. Questions other students by asking them to support, clarify or extend their ideas				
8. Gives inappropriate response				
9. Interrupts another student				
10. Critical of the ideas, values or opinions of others				
11. Makes overgeneralization				

Source: Student Self Evaluation by Jan Bodnar, © 1981. Reprinted by permission of the author.

Exhibit 12-2 Seminar Student Self-Evaluation

Key ✓ -when you did
X -when you should have
but did not

Application of Generalizations

Name _____
Date _____
Topic _____

Student Behavior	Predictions	Reasons for Predictions	Necessary Conditions	Consequences	Conclusion/Generalization
1. Gives appropriate response to question					
2. Provides support for statements					
3. Provides concise extension and clarification					
4. Views situation from a different perspective					
5. Suggests limitations of statements and avoids overgeneralizations					
6. Builds on the ideas of other students					
7. Questions other students by asking them to support, clarify or extend their ideas					
8. Gives inappropriate response					
9. Interrupts another student					
10. Critical of the ideas, values or opinions of other students					

Source: Student Self Evaluation by Jan Bodnar, © 1981. Reprinted by permission of the author.

Exhibit 12-3 Evaluation of Discussion Skills

Evaluation of Discussion Skills

Name _____

Seminar-Gifted
Program, Eldorado H.S.

Discussion _____

CRITERIA/COMMENT   RATING

1. Gives appropriate responses (follows focus   1 2 3 4 5
   of the discussion)

2. Provides support for statements   1 2 3 4 5

3. Provides concise clarification and extension   1 2 3 4 5

4. Demonstrates the ability to view situations from   1 2 3 4 5
   different perspectives

5. Suggests possible limitations of statements and   1 2 3 4 5
   avoids overgeneralizations

6. Builds on the ideas of other students   1 2 3 4 5

7. Questions other students by asking them to support,   1 2 3 4 5
   clarify or extend their ideas

8. Avoids interrupting others   1 2 3 4 5

9. Demonstrates respect for the opinions, ideas and/or   1 2 3 4 5
   values of others

10. Submits an accurate self-evaluation   1 2 3 4 5

General Comments :

Source: Student Self Evaluation by Jan Bodnar, © 1981. Reprinted by permission of the author.

To evaluate the student's progress in developing the ability to generalize, a form listing behaviors categorized according to the steps in a discussion is filled out by the student and later by the teacher while listening to the taped discussion (Exhibit 12-4). In developing this form, attention was given to the identification of specific, observable behaviors that are included in "ability to generalize." Each type of discussion needs a different form. Exhibit 12-4 is the form used with one of the Taba discussions, interpretation of data.

Although the seminar meets every day, students are required to attend only three times each week but may be present every day if they wish. The students choose the broad topic areas. Approximately every two weeks, the teacher asks what they would like to study. Within the broad topic areas they identify, the teacher selects the specific focus of each discussion. Most topics are in the social science areas, particularly current events.

Following the Taba model, each discussion has both a content and a process purpose. The teacher develops these purposes, as well as the discussion plan, to meet the students' needs for content that is abstract, complex, varied, and organized to facilitate economy in an interdisciplinary perspective. Following are the initial focusing questions for some of these discussions during the past few years.

Strategy: Interpretation of Data

Topic: Assimilation

Focusing Questions:

Step 1. What information do you have on the quality of life of the American Indian? What are some of the things you have noticed about the standard of living of New Mexico Indians?

Step 2. (a) What are some reasons for a *high suicide rate* among Indians? (b) Why do you feel that is so?

Step 3. (a) Why would *poverty* lead an individual to consider suicide? (b) Why does poverty lead to a high incidence of suicide?

Step 4. (a) Thinking back on our discussion, what would you conclude is the major factor contributing to a poor quality of life for the American Indians? (b) Why do you think so?

Step 5. (a) What would you say generally determines whether a subculture will be assimilated into the dominant culture? (b) What makes you believe this is generally true?

Strategy: Interpretation of Data

Topic: Soviet Education

Exhibit 12-4 Student Self-Evaluation

Key ✓ - when you did   Interpretation of Data   Date:
Topic: Critical Thinking   Name:

Student Behavior	Enumerating	Causes and/or Effects	Conclusion	Generalization
1. Provides Data				
2. Infers Causes/Effects	a. Similar			
	b. Different			
3. Supports Inferences	a. No support			
	b. Opinion			
	c. Authority			
	d. Examples			
	e. Evidence			
	f. Logic			
4. States Conclusion		a. Gives Summary		
		b. Identifies Key Ideas		
		c. Gives Abstract Overview		
5. Formulates Generalization			a. Inclusive	
			b. Tentative	
			c. Abstract	
			d. Accurate	
			e. Applicable	
			f. Supported	

Source: Student Self Evaluation by Jan Bodnar, © 1981. Reprinted by permission of the author.

Focusing Questions:

Step 1. What are some of the similarities and differences you noted after reading the article about Soviet and American education? How does Soviet education compare with American?

Step 2. (a) What seem to be the reasons why the Soviets place more emphasis on _____ as opposed to _____? (b) What makes that so?

Step 3. (a) What do you think causes (answer to 2a)? (b) Why is that so?

Step 4. (a) What would you conclude are the major factors accounting for the differences between Soviet and American educational systems? (b) What led you to that conclusion?

Step 5. (a) What in general might you say about making comparisons between institutions found in different countries? (b) Why do you think that is true?

Strategy: Application of Generalizations

Topic: Reinstatement of the Draft

Focusing Questions:

Step 1. (a) What do you predict will be the consequences if President Carter reinstates the draft? (b) What are your reasons for assuming that _____?

Step 2. (a) What other things will have to be true in order for that prediction to occur? Before *women are included in the draft* what other things will have to be considered? (b) Why do you feel that (answer to 2a) is a necessary condition?

Step 3. (a) Assuming that all the conditions you listed are met and there is a *violent protest by students*, what might be the effects of that protest? (b) What leads you to predict that?

Step 4. (a) What would you conclude would be the major effect of the reinstatement of the draft in the U.S.? (b) How did you arrive at that conclusion?

Strategy: Application of Generalizations

Topic: International Politics

Focusing Questions:

Step 1. (a) What do you predict will happen as a result of the discovery of vast oil reserves in China? (b) What led to that prediction? What historical events support that idea?

Step 2. (a) What conditions must be met in order for China to _____?
What will need to occur in order for _____?
(b) Why do you feel that must occur? What makes you think ____?
Why does that depend on _____?

Step 3. (a) Assuming all the conditions that you have listed exist, what do you think will result from *China's significant increase in oil production?* (b) Why do you feel that will be a result? (c) What other conditions would need to be present for _____? What other things would need to be available for there to be _____? (d) What made you assume that? Why do you feel that must be present for _____?

Step 4. (a) What effects on China's development and international status will the vast oil reserves have? (b) Why have you decided that?

Step 5. (a) Considering our discussion, what changes if any would you make in the following statement? (State planning generalization.) (b) Why would you make that change? (Ask after each change is given.)

Although the Taba *Strategies* are the major processes involved, whenever the subject lends itself to the discussion of conflicting moral issues, a modification of Kohlberg's Discussions of *Moral Dilemmas* is used. Students then evaluate their levels of moral reasoning based on Kohlberg's developmental stages. A third model, the Parnes *Creative Problem Solving* (CPS) process, also is used when considering certain types of problems.

Career Exploration Program (SPACE)

This program component has a four-year developmental sequence leading from identification of the student's own competencies and interests through shadowing, mentorship, and work-study. Participation is optional but students can remain with the program for all four years. In order to be eligible for the later phases, however, they must participate in the first phases. The following presents the objectives of the program and describes activities in each phase.

OVERVIEW OF THE SPACE PROGRAM

The Special Program for Advanced Career Exploration (SPACE) is an integrated part of Eldorado High School's Special Education Program for gifted and talented students. The SPACE project is optional and is designed to increase the articulation between the school and the community. With its versatile design, the SPACE project responds to the educational needs and career interests of a broad spectrum of gifted and talented students—individuals with high measured intelligence and strong academic records as well as those with intellectual potential, talent, or leadership that has not been developed adequately through the existing school program.

SPACE introduces students to the world of work through shadow, mentorship, and work practicum situations that provide on-the-job experiences. Students use these experiences to develop a more realistic career outlook by either validating existing career goals or developing new directions for their job explorations.

Rationale

The SPACE program broadens the range of educational options available to gifted secondary school students. "Gifted and talented students, because of the personal significance they attach to careers, need to discover qualities which can be best obtained by direct contact with the career and direct association with people in the career" (Hoyt & Hebler, 1974, p. 54).

It should be noted that SPACE is a new project and is subject to clarification, modification, and—it is hoped—extension as a result of the findings of continuous evaluation procedures.

Performance Objectives

As a special education program, SPACE recognizes the wide range of interests, abilities, motivations, and ambitions of gifted and talented students and seeks to provide each with the career exploration program that best fits that individual's needs. The program has considerable flexibility with regard to both degree of student involvement and type of experience. In each individual case, the student has the opportunity to identify special abilities and strengths and to expand the level of career awareness upon completion of testing and conferences. The students are better able to identify specific career fields that seem compatible with their interests, abilities, and needs. They may choose to examine a variety of different careers with the program coordinator or to concentrate on a specific choice.

Through their placement, it is expected that students will become sufficiently familiar with their career choice(s) to answer such basic questions as the following:

1. What are the entry requirements for the career (education, skills, aptitudes, and specific training)?
2. Which schools, companies, or agencies provide students with the entry requirements?
3. What are the financial expenditures necessary in preparation?

4. What is the occupational outlook as evidenced by salaries, potential for promotion, opportunities for innovation, provisions for health and safety, and the overall working environment?
5. What seem to be the main features of the life style associated with the career, disposition, and personal characteristics necessary for success, and the range of responsibilities that accompany the work?

Besides the objective analysis of a particular career or profession, the program emphasizes the development and/or refinement of personal skills and sensitivities necessary to function effectively in both college and the world of work. The students are expected to demonstrate the following:

1. Self-knowledge: evaluation of their abilities, interests, and aptitudes that will enable them to consider the compatibility of their strengths and interests in relation to the requirements of their career goal.
2. Interpersonal skills: interviewing techniques, responsible assertive behavior, self-confidence, adequate assessment of skills and abilities, and ability to establish a one-to-one working relationship with a professional.
3. Work competencies: seriousness of purpose, willingness to undertake assignments, dependability in meeting commitments, discretion in handling confidential situations, sensitivity in interpersonal relations, independence, accuracy, creative problem solving, promptness, appropriate dress and appearance, and a generally responsive and positive attitude.

Student Application Procedures

The SPACE project is limited to students eligible to be served by Albuquerque Public Schools (APS) gifted programs. Students apply to participate in this program much as they would if they were applying for a job. They receive program information and applications, which they are asked to complete and turn in. At that time, an appointment for an interview is made with the SPACE coordinator. During the interview, an effort is made to learn more about the student's background and interests. Each applicant is requested to take the *Strong-Campbell Interest Inventory,* John Hollan's *Self-Directed Search,* and the *Work Values Inventory.* These instruments help them discover more about themselves. The application process, interview, and testing establish the framework for developing an individualized career exploration program for the student.

Before actual scheduling, students are required to do background reading and research in the career areas they have requested to explore. A resource list of materials is provided.

Program Description

SPACE has a flexible design that accommodates a wide spectrum of career exploration activities. The basic design includes three prototypes:

1. a *shadow* experience—limited to one day of on-the-job experience; no credit because of short duration
2. a *mentorship* (four to ten hours per week) for one semester; variable credit (*maximum one credit per semester*)
3. a *work practicum or internship* (20 hours per week) for one semester; variable credit

As noted earlier, the application procedures are the same for each prototype. In most cases, it is recommended that students follow their career explorations through the sequence of programs just described. For instance, as a freshman or sophomore, the student participates in at least two shadow experiences; as a junior, the individual selects a career in which to pursue a mentorship; as a senior, the person participates in a work practicum experience.

Both the shadow experience and mentorship are possible without interfering with the student's regular academic schedule. The work practicum experience requires substituting job experience for academic credit. The APS now participates in the Executive High School Internship Program in order to provide a structure and comprehensive career exploration program to gifted seniors. A complete description of the work practicum experiences based on the internship program is beyond the scope of this chapter.

Prototypes

The main distinction in the three experiences is their duration and the resulting complexity of the assignments required in each phase. Additional flexibility within each prototype results from the variability of high school credit allowed. In many cases, mentorships result in the establishment of long-standing relationships between the mentor and student that extend beyond the program and/or employment and are independent of it.

Shadow Experience

It is recommended that the student shadow a career choice before making a commitment to a mentorship. The shadow experience is scheduled for a single eight-hour work day. Before this session, the student meets twice with the program coordinator on either an individual or small-group basis to discuss appropriate behavior, specific requirements, current knowledge of the career, questions, and interviewing skills. Upon completion of the shadow experience, the student is required to submit a written report describing observations, perceptions, activities, and personal reactions.

The student, cooperating mentor, and the parents are asked to complete questionnaires regarding the experience. This information is used to evaluate both student performance and program effectiveness. Each student is required to prepare and submit a letter of appreciation to the cooperating mentor or firm. No high school credit is allowed for the shadow experience because of its short duration.

By requiring most students to participate in a shadow experience, the coordinator is better able to identify those who lack the commitment and motivation necessary for successful involvement in a mentorship or work practicum.

Mentorship

The mentorship model is more appropriate for juniors and seniors because it requires more involvement in time and assignments. The hours required vary according to the student's schedule and the amount of high school credit the person wishes to receive. The maximum credit allowable is one per semester. The application process, interview, and testing are the same as for a shadow experience. Students seeking credit must attend a weekly seminar structured to ensure that they are dealing effectively with their placements and are comfortable about the experience. The seminar provides students with an opportunity to share experiences, insights, and problems. Where dissatisfaction or disenchantment with a career field is apparent, participants are placed in an alternate career field of their choosing.

Students also are required to maintain a daily written record of the learning that takes place. The log should reflect their feelings, thoughts, and reactions as participants. One of the initial seminars is devoted to describing the process, purpose, and content of the daily log. Since the student receives high school credit for the experience, the log must be well written. The log is submitted before each seminar for review and comment by the coordinator. It provides a basis for evaluation of the appropriateness of the placement and for identification of areas in which the student may need assistance, suggestions, and/or support. Such data help the coordinator evaluate whether students are being exposed to the appropriate experiences by their mentors. It should be noted that this is not the only criterion by which the coordinator evaluates the placement.

The seminars are designed to ensure that the student is having a successful experience. Some focal questions to the students include:

- Are you a calculated risk taker? What are some specific situations in which you tried something without full assurance of success?

- What are the different ways you have used to get information and insight from your career exploration experiences?

- What is your role as a mentee? How do you feel about that role? How well do you play that role?

- What experiences have you had as a mentee that require you to be flexible? How do you feel about those experiences?

- What would you say are your skills in communicating with professionals, such as your mentor? What things do you have difficulty communicating to your mentor? Why do you think so?

- What is self-direction? What have you done that you consider demonstrates initiative? Why?

- How would you describe your attitude toward this experience? How do you think that attitude developed?

- What motivated you to participate in this program? What motivates you now?

- What are the different ways you can show someone what you have learned?

In addition, the coordinator makes periodic visits to job sites during the semester to monitor the quality of each experience and to assess the students' performance.

One of the short-term experiences provided for a group of students interested in the same career was designed by the Albuquerque Air Routing and Traffic Control Center (ARTCC) in cooperation with the teacher of the gifted. Following is the description developed by the ARTCC coordinator and distributed to his staff (the work schedule is shown in Exhibit 12-5).

The program, as coordinated through Jan Bodnar, will enable the participating students to observe the working of an industry in which they have expressed a career interest.

The students, who are being assigned to Albuquerque ARTC Center, have expressed an interest in the broad field of aviation without any specific mention of air traffic control. Obviously, if we are to fill the need of the student, it would not do to restrict the curriculum to air traffic control, or, for that matter, to attempt indepth instruction in that field.

The Albuquerque ARTC Center program is designed to introduce the student to Government employment in the aviation field. This includes not just air traffic control but the entire FAA, its divisions and functions, and how one relates to the other and to the air traveling public.

Exhibit 12-5 Air Traffic Control Work Practicum Schedule

ELDORADO HIGH SCHOOL SCHEDULE
REPORTING TIMES: Tuesday   - 3:30-4:30 p.m.
                  Thursday - 3:30-4:30 p.m.

Date	Location	Duty	Instructor
February 5, Tuesday	MLSO		L. Greiner
February 7, Thursday	Control Room	Desk AC	Assistant Chief
February 12, Tuesday	Control Room	MLSS	MLSS
February 14, Thursday	Control Room	Area Row	Team Supervisor
February 19, Tuesday	PHX Area Office		J. Lee
February 21, Thursday	Control Room	Sector	Controller
February 26, Tuesday	PHX Area Office		J. Lee
February 28, Thursday	Control Room	Sector	Controller
March 4, Tuesday	ELP Area Office		L. Mitchener
March 6, Thursday	Control Room	Sector	Controller
March 11, Tuesday	ELP Area Office		L. Mitchener
March 13, Thursday	Control Room	Sector	Controller
March 18, Tuesday	ABQ Area Office		C. Tuberville
March 20, Thursday	Control Room	Sector	Controller
March 25, Tuesday	ABQ Area Office		C. Tuberville
March 27, Thursday	Control Room	Sector	Controller
April 1, Tuesday	DSO		DSS
April 3, Thursday	Control Room	Sector	Controller
April 8, Tuesday	DSO	Control Room	DSS
April 10, Thursday	Control Room	Sector	Controller

Exhibit 12-5 continued

April 15, Tuesday	AFS		J. Salinas
April 17, Thursday	Control Room	Sector	Controller
April 22, Tuesday	AFS		J. Salinas
April 24 Thursday	Control Room	Sector	Controller
April 29, Tuesday	Training		G. Reynolds
May 1, Thursday	Training		G. Reynolds

The students will be working in the facility for a period of approximately 14 weeks.

Careful selection of all mentors is an important aspect of the program. When initially contacting possible mentors, for instance, the teacher asks for specific examples of the kind of experiences the person can provide, explains the purpose of the program, and states that students should be involved in all aspects of the expert's job. After these initial contacts, a personal interview is held and the teacher views the site. Only after considering the results of these contacts and the degree of match between student and mentorship placement does the teacher decide to assign a pupil to that setting. This match includes a consideration of such elements as the personalities of both individuals, the interests and abilities of the student, the interests and time commitment of the mentor, and the type of work experiences available at the site.

Counseling Discussion Group

The focus of this group is on the development of problem-solving skills on an individual basis. It is designed to enhance the SPACE career exploration program by assisting in meeting the personal skills and sensitivity objectives of that program component. In addition, this discussion group is a structured method for achieving the counseling objectives of the program:

1. Students will achieve a better understanding and acceptance of themselves (their strengths, limitations, aptitudes, needs, values, interests, worth as individuals).

2. Students will increase their problem-solving and decision-making skills.
3. Students will increase their ability to develop successful interpersonal relationships on the basis of mutual trust.
4. Students will accept increased responsibility for their educational, occupational, and avocational development.

The major vehicles for achieving these objectives are discussions and simulation games in a small-group situation. For these groups to be effective, the students must be able to trust each other and the teacher, there must be open lines of communication, and the discussion topic must reflect the pupils' needs. The teacher may choose some topics and simulation games based on knowledge of the group; others are selected based on areas of interest identified by the students. Some of the games are described briefly in the resource list at the end of this chapter.

Individualization

Much of the program is based on the needs and characteristics of individual students. These needs may change each year or they may remain consistent over the four-year period. An annual plan is developed identifying the activities in which the student will participate. Some students may have no formal contact with the teacher of the gifted while others may be involved in all aspects of the program as well as have daily conferences.

Program Evaluation

Evaluation of the program includes methods for assessing progress as well as its overall success. Assessment of students includes standardized testing using the *Wide Range Achievement Test* (WRAT), the *Woodcock-Johnson Psychoeducational Battery*, and the *Watson-Glaser Test of Critical Thinking*. Student self-evaluation and teacher appraisal of growth through the program's experiences are compiled to assess the overall effectiveness of the seminar component.

Overall program evaluation is accomplished by administering the *Class Activities Questionnaire* (CAQ) (Steele, 1969) and through forms completed by students, parents, and mentors. The CAQ is designed to assess classroom climate in programs for the gifted. It includes five dimensions: lower thought processes, higher thought processes, classroom focus, classroom climate, and student opinions.

Questionnaires are designed to determine participants' perceptions of the effectiveness and quality of the mentorship and work-study experiences. One of them (Exhibit 12-6) is completed by the mentor/supervisor. It assesses student entry and

Exhibit 12-6 Questionnaire on Program Participants' Perceptions

SPECIAL PROGRAM FOR ADVANCED CAREER EXPLORATION
Eldorado High School
Mentor/Supervisor Questionnaire

1. Mentor/Supervisor _____Date _____

2. Profession or Business _____Type of Experience

3. Student Name _____   Shadow
                                                               Mentorship
                                                               Internship

Directions: The purpose of this questionnaire is to gather data which will assist us in
             assessing the strengths and weaknesses of the career exploration program.
             Please indicate the degree to which you agree or disagree with the follow-
             ing statements by circling the letters which most closely reflect your
             opinion.

Key: SA = Strongly Agree

         A = Agree

         U = Undecided

         D = Disagree

         SD = Strongly Disagree

1. The procedures used for placement coordination and follow-up

    (a) were adequate   SA A U D SD

    (b) gave me an accurate perception of my role as a mentor/   SA A U D SD
         supervisor

    (c) were handled in a professional manner by high school   SA A U D SD
         coordinator

    (d) facilitated and encouraged communication between   SA A U D SD
         myself and the student

    (e) included adequate on-site visitation   SA A U D SD

    (f) included appropriate evaluation methods   SA A U D SD

2. At the beginning of the experience, the student displayed

    (a) adequate knowledge of the career upon entrance into   SA A U D SD
         the experience

    (b) a positive outlook on the experience   SA A U D SD

    (c) a willingness to undertake tasks   SA A U D SD

    (d) sound work habits   SA A U D SD

    (e) appropriate appearance   SA A U D SD

    (f) promptness   SA A U D SD

    (g) dependability   SA A U D SD

    (h) maturity   SA A U D SD

    (i) an ability to relate well to a variety of people   SA A U D SD

    (j) willingness to respect the confidentiality of   SA A U D SD
         certain situations

Exhibit 12-6 continued

3. As a result of the experience, the student demonstrates

   (a) more confidence in communicating with professionals   SA   A   U   D   SD

   (b) an ability to ask meaningful questions   SA   A   U   D   SD

   (c) an increased knowledge of the lifestyle required by career characteristics   SA   A   U   D   SD

   (d) an increased knowledge of the necessary personal characteristics   SA   A   U   D   SD

   (e) an increased knowledge of the responsibilities that accompany work in this particular field   SA   A   U   D   SD

   (f) initiative and independence in performing assigned tasks   SA   A   U   D   SD

4. From the experience, as a professional, I

   (a) benefited from my interactions with the student   SA   A   U   D   SD

   (b) experienced no significant inconvenience in the performance of my job   SA   A   U   D   SD

   (c) would be willing to participate as a mentor for another student from the program   SA   A   U   D   SD

5. What suggestions or changes would you offer for improving the overall administration and operation of the program?

6. Please comment on any aspect of the program that draws your immediate attention, either positive or negative.

exiting characteristics, the overall operation of the program, and the value of the experience for the mentor/supervisor. A similar questionnaire asks parents and students to assess each of these same components.

Evaluation Results

Most of the program components had been in full operation so short a time that evaluation results were incomplete as of this writing. Compilation of self- and teacher-evaluations of group participation does show an increase in desirable discussion behaviors as well as in the ability to generalize. Discussion skills showing the most change are numbers of ideas offered (fluency), variety of ideas expressed (flexibility), ability to question each other, willingness to listen to each other rather than just to the teacher, and avoidance of interruptions of others (both students and teacher).

The CAQ was administered in the seminars. Since this was given as only a preliminary assessment of one aspect of the program, the cross-discipline seminar, the results were not computer scored. Exhibit 12-7 presents the factors, the items measuring each, and the mean student response to each item. A low number (e.g., 1 or 2) indicates strong agreement with the item, a high number (3 or 4) strong

Exhibit 12-7 CAQ Results for Cross-Discipline Seminar

Factor/Item	Mean Response

Cognitive Factors[1]

Factor I: Memory

1. Remembering or recognizing information is the students main job. — 2.37

10. Great emphasis is placed on memorizing. — 1.81

Factor II: Translation

9. Restating ideas in your own words is a central concern. — 3.38

21. Great importance is placed on explaining and summarizing what is presented — 2.00

Factor III: Interpretation

6. Students are expected to go beyond the information given to see what is implied. — 1.44

16. Students are expected to read between the lines to find trends and consequences in what is presented. — 1.50

Factor IV: Application

3. Students actively put methods and ideas to use in new situations — 1.94

13. A central concern is practicing methods in lifelike situations to develop skill in solving problems. — 2.44

Factor V: Analysis

7. Great importance is placed on logical reasoning and analysis — 1.69

12. Using logic and reasoning processes to think through complicated problems (and prove the answer) is a major activity. — 1.94

Factor VI: Synthesis

11. Students are urged to build onto what they have learned to produce something brand-new. — 1.81

23. Inventing, designing, composing, and creating are major activities. — 2.81

Factor VII: Evaluation

2. A central activity is to make judgments of good/bad, right/wrong, and explain why. — 2.56

20. The student's major job is to make judgments about the values of issues and ideas. — 2.44

Classroom Conditions Factors

Factor 8: Divergence

17. Students are encouraged to discover as many solutions to problems as possible. — 1.06

Factor 9: Discussion Opportunity/Involvement

5. The class actively participates in discussion. — 1.38

*15. There is little opportunity for student participation in discussions. — *3.81

Factor 10: Enthusiasm

19. Students are excited and involved with class activities. — 2.25

Factor 11: Independence

14. Students are encouraged to independently explore and begin new activities. — 1.88

Exhibit 12-7 continued

Factor/Item	Mean Response
Factor 12: Test/Grade Stress	
8. The student's job is to know the one best answer to each problem.	3.44
22. There is a great concern for grades in this class.	3.00
Factor 13: Lecture	
*4. Most class time is spent doing other things than listening.	*2.56
26. (An estimate of the percentage of teacher talk is 60% or above.)	4.00
Factor 14: Humor	
25. There is very little joking or laughing in this class	*3.69
Factor 15: Teacher Talk	
26. On the average the teacher talks how much of the time: 90% 75% 60% 40% 25% 10%	10%

> * Item is reversed for scoring, so a high score indicates agreement with the factor (but not with the item).

disagreement. It should be noted that results of such an assessment will be much more comprehensive (as well as valid) if appropriate scoring procedures are used. If this is done, the teacher's ideal and real perceived emphasis can be compared easily with the student perceptions. In addition, the consistency of responses, an integral part of the scoring process, is included in the results. However, the instrument did provide an indication that the teacher's objectives were being met in this classroom.

The CAQ results indicate that the teacher is emphasizing all levels of thinking but is stressing analysis and synthesis more than other areas. Translation and memory, the two lowest processes, receive the least emphasis. Divergence, independence, and discussion/involvement are very strong characteristics of the classroom climate. There is little test/grade stress, much humor, and very little teacher talk (69 percent of the students estimated that the teacher talks less than 10 percent of the time and 31 percent estimated less than 25 percent).

To summarize the students' perceptions of the values of the mentorship and work-study experiences, a letter (Bodnar, Note 12, p. 18) written by one of them is most revealing:

To Whom it may concern,

I am a high school student who has reaped many benefits from a work-study program in chemistry. Being fascinated by this field, I desired to learn the political and ethical ramifications of a chemical occupation before I committed myself to a college major in chemistry.

Searching for a job in a lab doing anything, even cleaning test tubes, would make professional chemists available to me and allow me to learn about the field.

After calling many long-established institutions, the Gifted Department of Eldorado High School found a job for me at an analytical chemistry firm in Albuquerque. I have worked there for four months now as a viable part of the lab where I was given responsibility and many challenges. From my experiences at the firm, I now realize the many advantages of a work-study program.

Most importantly, the student learns about working in his field of interest and gets a realistic exposure to the business world. Furthermore, the gifted student finds direct application for the skills he's learned in high school. Not to mention my lab experience, I have found that my background in Calculus has been important not only to my understanding but my operation of various instruments within the lab. Consequently, the hiring institution benefits also. Screening to find a responsible young adult to perform routine laboratory operations is not without its advantages to the firm. For example, a young adult hired for minimum wage frees the lab's analytical chemists from doing simple operations which waste their abilities and creates unnecessary overhead. In the long run, the lab also acquires an employee with a bright future who, after he receives his education, could become an integral part of the company.

Work-study programs for gifted students recognize the valuable resource of these young people and allow them to develop while benefiting a company. Obviously, this is an ideal situation for all parties involved and one which would undoubtedly benefit your institution also.

Thank you for reviewing these thoughts. I hope that you will consider the merits of a work-study program for gifted students.

Sincerely,

Anna Marie Pyle

Based on these preliminary results, it appears that the program is highly successful. Further evaluations should provide specific recommendations for what to continue and what to change.

ANALYSIS OF THE CURRICULUM

At the high school level, a special program for the gifted must be much different from those at other levels unless a large number of teachers or a special school is available. Given only one teacher and a variety of subject interests, academic and nonacademic needs, and differing schedules, the most appropriate approach is to identify and provide as many options as possible. The teacher then becomes a counselor, advocate, and facilitator as in this program, rather than a teacher in the traditional sense. By the time gifted students reach high school (and even while in middle school), they need experts in many content areas. One teacher cannot provide the expertise needed by all students so the best approach is to identify those individuals, both within and outside the school, who can.

Another reason for the teacher of the gifted to assume a different role is the availability of more options for placement of students at this level. Honors classes, advanced placement, university courses (both at the high school and on the college campus), and content outside the usual curriculum are available at most schools. These provide students opportunities to study with experts as well as to interact with their intellectual peers in an academic setting.

Other unique aspects of the program, in addition to the teacher's role, are (1) the emphasis on self-evaluation and (2) the career development component. In this curriculum, students are expected to assess their own class participation. This evaluation focuses not only on discussion skills but also on the development of abstract concepts and higher levels of thinking. Because the students must listen to themselves on tape, they are forced to be realistic in their assessments as they record specific behaviors. This process develops both the habits and the skills needed for realistic and continuing self-evaluation. Career development is connected to self-evaluation in that it contains components emphasizing self-analysis of skills and interests relating to each career. It also includes a developmental sequence leading from the match of career goals and interests through shadowing, mentorship, and work-study experiences.

Curricular Modifications

Curricular changes appropriate for gifted students include those in all areas—either directly through the program or indirectly through the teacher's identification of options and placement of pupils in situations where the learning environment is appropriate. The program goals reflect the curriculum's emphasis and identify whether provision of each modification is direct or indirect. For instance, most of the content modifications are accomplished indirectly while the process changes are an integral part of the seminars. The product modification pertaining to self-evaluation is a direct, strong emphasis in all aspects of the program.

Process modifications addressed directly in the curriculum are higher levels of thinking, discovery, open-endedness, proof/reasoning, freedom of choice, and group interaction. A focus on thinking skill development rather than acquisition of information is very much a part of the seminars and discussions. Use of the Taba strategies, Parnes's CPS process, and Kohlberg's discussions of moral dilemmas assures an emphasis on high-level thinking skills. Self-evaluation by students and assessment by the teacher are consistent with this emphasis. The Taba strategies also indicate open-endedness, guided discovery of abstract generalizations, and emphasis on student justification of inferences, predictions, conclusions, and generalizations. Group interaction is very much a part of both seminars. Students choose general topics to study in the seminars and make a whole range of other choices (with assistance) about classes, career experiences, and other program options. The teacher's emphasis is on assisting in making choices based on students' interests and explaining the later consequences of these selections.

Learning environment modifications also are designed to foster greater flexibility, more interaction among students, and more independence. Students have available a variety of environments for learning through the career exploration program as well as university classes. Freedom of expression, acceptance rather than judgment, and openness are important elements of the program.

SUMMARY

No particular teaching/learning model forms the overall framework of this program, although the Taba strategies may approach this as a basis for the cross-discipline seminars. The curriculum is designed to fit the situation and to provide the best possible program with available resources. Many aspects of the program are unique, including the career exploration component, methods of student evaluation, and the cross-discipline seminar for which students receive credit. Based on a compilation of results of student assessment data and the CAQ outcomes, it seems safe to say that the program is accomplishing its purposes.

RESOURCES

Teacher References

Clark, B. *Growing up gifted*. Columbus, Ohio: The Charles E. Merrill Publishing Co., Inc., 1979, 318-323.

Colson, S., Borman, C. & Nash, W. *Keeping a sense of direction in a snowstorm*. College Station, Texas: Center for Career Development and Occupational Development, 1978.

Gowan, J., Khatena, J., & Torrance, P. *Educating the ablest*. New York: Peacock, 1979, 166-179.

Hoyt, K., & Hebeler, J. *Career education for gifted and talented students*. Salt Lake City: Olympus Publishing Company, 1974.

Perrone, P., & Pulvino, C. New directions in the guidance of the gifted and talented. *The Gifted Child Quarterly*, 1977, *21*, 326-335.

Rodenstein, J., Pfleger, L., & Colangelo, N. Career development of gifted women. *The Gifted Child Quarterly*, 1977, *21*, 340-347.

Zaffrann, R., & Colangelo, N. Counseling with gifted and talented students. *The Gifted Child Quarterly*, 1977, *21*, 305-318.

Student Career Information Materials

American Dietetic Association. *Your future as a dietician* (Rev. ed.). New York: Richards Rosen Press, 1980.

Baggett, H.W. *Exploring data processing careers* (Career Information Series Y. 23). Ormond Beach, Fl.: Camelot Publishing Co., 1975.

Barnewell, G.G. *Succeed as a job applicant.* New York: Arco Publishing Co., 1976.

Booth, A.L. *Careers in politics for the new woman.* New York: Franklin Watts, Inc., 1978.

Cavallaro, A. *The physician's associate—A new career in health care.* New York: Thomas Nelson, Inc., undated.

Criner, B., & Criner, C. *Jobs in personal services.* New York: Lothrop, Lee & Shepard Co., 1974. (a)

Criner, B., & Criner, C. *Jobs in public service.* New York: Lothrop, Lee & Shepard Co., 1974. (b)

Davis, S. *Your future in computer programming.* New York: Richards Rosen Press, 1969.

Dowdell, D., & Dowdell, J. *Careers in horticultural sciences* (Rev. ed.). New York: Julian Messner Press, 1975.

Doyle, R.V. *Careers in elective government* (Rev. ed.). New York: Julian Messner Press, 1975.

Eggland, S.A. *Exploring wholesaling and retailing careers.* Cincinnati: South-Western Publishing Co., undated.

Evers, D.R., & Feingold, S.N. *Your future in exotic careers* (Rev. ed.). New York: Richards Rosen Press, 1980.

Horton, L. *Art careers.* New York: Franklin Watts, 1975.

Kay, E. *Health care careers.* New York: Franklin Watts, 1973.

Karlin, M.S. *Solving your career mystery.* New York: Richards Rosen Press, 1975.

Keyes, F. *Your future in social work* (Rev. ed.). New York: Richards Rosen Press, 1978.

Keyes, F. *Aim for a job in the allied health field* (Rev. ed.). New York: Richards Rosen Press, 1979.

Kirk, W.R. *Your future in hospital and health services administration.* New York: Richards Rosen Press, 1976.

Lee, M.P. *Ms. veterinarian.* Philadelphia: Westminster Press, 1976.

McCall, V., & McCall, J.R. *Your career in parks and recreation* (Rev. ed.). New York: Julian Messner Press, 1974.

McLeod, S. *Challenging careers in urban affairs.* New York: Julian Messner Press, 1976.

Mead, M. *Anthropologists and what they do.* New York: Franklin Watts, 1965.

Millard, R. *Careers in the earth sciences.* New York: Julian Messner Press, 1975.

Peterson, O. *Your future in engineering careers.* New York: Richards Rosen Press, 1975.

Reel, R.M. *Exploring secretarial careers.* Cincinnati: South-Western Publishing Co., undated.

Rettig, J.L. *Careers: Exploration and decision.* Englewood Cliffs, N.J.: Prentice-Hall, 1974.

Ristau, R.A. *Exploring clerical careers.* Cincinnati: South-Western Publishing Co., undated.

Shuff, F.L. *Your future in an occupational therapy career.* New York: Richards Rosen Press, 1978.

Sonnabend, R. *Your future in hotel management.* New York: Richards Rosen Press, 1975.

Splaver, S. *Paraprofessions: Careers of the future and the present.* New York: Julian Messner Press, 1972.

Splaver, S. *Non-traditional careers for women.* New York: Julian Messner Press, 1973.

Splaver, S. *Career choices in psychology.* New York: Julian Messner Press, 1976.

Todd, R.D., & Todd, K.R. *Aim for a job, working with your hands.* New York: Richards Rosen Press, 1975.

Appendix A

Tests

Bennett, G.K., Seashore, H.G., & Wesman, A.G. *Differential aptitude tests.* (DAT) New York: Psychological Corporation, 1973.

Bernal, E.M. *Bernal checklist.* Available from Dr. E. Bernal, 5203 Hedgewood, Austin, Texas 78745.

Boehm, A.E. *Boehm test of basic concepts.* New York: Psychological Corporation, 1971.

Dunn, L. *Peabody picture vocabulary test* (Rev. ed.). Circle Pines, Minn.: American Guidance Service, 1981.

Dunn, L.M., & Markwardt, F.C., Jr. *Peabody individual achievement test* (PIAT). Circle Pines, Minn.: American Guidance Service, 1970.

Ennis, R.H., & Millman, J. *Cornell critical thinking tests, level x and level y.* Urbana, Ill.: Critical Thinking Project, University of Illinois, 1971.

Gonzales, E.G. *Draw-a-person, Koppitz scoring, southwest norms.* Albuquerque, N.M.: University of New Mexico, 1978.

Gordon, I.J. *How I see myself survey.* Gainesville, Fl.: Florida Educational Research and Development C ouncil, 1969.

Gough, H.G. *California psychological inventory* (CPI). Palo Alto, Ca.: Consulting Psychologists Press, Inc., 1969.

Hollan, J. *Self-directed search.* Palo Alto, Ca.: Consulting Psychologists Press, 1977.

Jastak, J.F., & Jastak, S.R. *WRAT: The wide range achievement test* (Rev. ed.). Los Angeles: Western Psychological Services, 1978.

Khatena, J., and Torrance, E.P. *Something about myself* (SAM). Chicago: Stoetling Co., 1976.

Koppitz, E.M. *Psychological evaluation of children's human figure drawings.* New York: Grune & Stratton, 1968.

363

Leiter, R.G., and Arthur, G. *Leiter international performance scale*. Chicago: Stoetling Co., 1955.

McGraw-Hill. *Comprehensive tests of basic skills*. New York: Author, 1973.

Meeker, M. *SOI group memory test and training model*. El Segundo, Ca.: SOI Institute, 1973.

Meeker, M., and Meeker, R. *SOI learning abilities test*. El Segundo, Ca.: SOI Institute, 1975.

Otis, A.S., & Lennon, R.T. *Otis-Lennon mental ability test*. New York: Harcourt Brace Jovanovich, 1970.

Ross, J.D., & Ross, C.M. *The Ross test of higher cognitive processes*. Novato, Ca.: Academic Therapy Publications, 1976.

Strong, E.K., Jr., & Campbell, D.P. *Strong-Campbell interest inventory*. Palo Alto, Ca.: Stanford University Press, 1974.

Super, D.E. *Work values inventory*. Boston: Houghton Mifflin Co., 1970.

Terman, L.M., & Merrill, M. *Stanford-Binet intelligence scale* (revised IQ tables by S.R. Pinneau). New York: Houghton Mifflin Co., 1960.

Torrance, E.P. *The Torrance tests of creative thinking* (TTCT). Lexington, Mass.: Ginn & Co., 1972.

Torrance, E.P. *What kind of person are you* (WKOPAY). Chicago, Ill.: Stoelting Co., 1976.

Wechsler, D. *Wechsler preschool and primary scale of intelligence* (WPPSI). New York: Psychological Corporation, 1967.

Wechsler, D. *Wechsler intelligence scale for children–Revised* (WISC-R). New York: Psychological Corporation, 1974.

Woodcock, R.W., & Johnson, M.B. *The Woodcock-Johnson psychoeducational battery. Part I: Test of cognitive ability*. Boston: Teaching Resources, 1977.

References

Addison, L. Simulation gaming and leadership training for gifted girls. *The Gifted Child Quarterly,* 1979, *23,* 288-296.

Adler, M.J. (Ed.). *The great ideas: A syntopicon of great books of the western world* (2 vols.). Chicago: Encyclopedia Britannica, 1952.

Anastasiow, N.J. A report of self-concept of the very gifted. *The Gifted Child Quarterly,* 1964, *8,* 177-178.

The Association for the Gifted Evaluation Committee (Eds.). *Sample instruments for the evaluation of programs for the gifted and talented.* Storrs, Conn.: University of Connecticut, 1979.

Atwood, B.S. *Building independent learning skills.* Palo Alto, Calif.: Education Today Co., 1974.

Baldwin, A. Curriculum and methods—What is the difference? In A.Y. Baldwin, G.H. Gear, & L.J. Lucito (Eds.), *Educational planning for the gifted: Overcoming cultural, geographical, and socioeconomic barriers.* Reston, Va.: The Council for Exceptional Children, 1978.

Baldwin, A., & Wooster, J. *Baldwin identification matrix inservice kit for the identification of gifted and talented students.* Buffalo, N.Y.: D.O.K. Publishers, 1977.

Baldwin, A.Y., Gear, G.H., & Lucito, L.J. (Eds.). *Educational planning for the gifted: Overcoming cultural, geographical, and socioeconomic barriers.* Reston, Va.: The Council for Exceptional Children, 1978.

Baldwin, L.E. *A study of factors usually associated with high school male leadership.* Unpublished master's thesis, Ohio State University, 1932.

Barron, F., & Welsh, G.S. Artistic perception as a possible factor in personality style: Its measurement by a figure preference test. *Journal of Psychology,* 1952, *33,* 199-203.

Bellingrath, G.C. Qualities associated with leadership in extracurricular activities of the high school. *Teachers College Contributions to Education,* 1930, No. 399.

Bernal, E.M., Jr. Gifted Mexican American children: An ethno-scientific perspective. *California Journal of Educational Research,* 1975, *25,* 261-273.

Bernal, E.M., Jr. The identification of gifted Chicano children. In A.Y. Baldwin, G.H. Gear, & L.J. Lucito (Eds.), *Educational planning for the gifted: Overcoming cultural, geographical, and socioeconomic barriers.* Reston, Va.: The Council for Exceptional Children, 1978.

Bernal, E.M., Jr., & Reyna, J. *Analysis of giftedness in Mexican American children and design of a prototype identification instrument* (Final Research Report). Austin, Texas: Southwest Educational Development Laboratory, 1974.

Bloom, B.S. (Ed.) *Taxonomy of educational objectives: The classification of educational goals. Handbook I: Cognitive domain.* New York: Longmans, Green & Co., 1956.

Bonney, M.E. The constancy of sociometric scores and their relationship to teacher judgments of social success and to personality self-ratings. *Sociometry,* 1943, *6,* 409-424.

Borg, W. *An evaluation of ability grouping* (U.S. Office of Education Cooperative Research Project No. 577). Logan, Utah: Utah State University, 1964.

Bowden, A.W. A study of the personality of student leaders in colleges in the United States. *Journal of Abnormal and Social Psychology,* 1926, *21,* 149-160.

Brandwein, P. *The gifted student as future scientist: The high school student and his commitment to science.* New York: Harcourt Brace & Co., 1955.

Briggs, K.C., & Myers, I.B. *The Myers-Briggs type indicator.* Palo Alto, Ca.: Consulting Psychologists Press, 1962.

Bristow, W. Identifying gifted children. In P.A. Witty (Ed.), *The gifted child.* Boston: D.C. Heath and Company, 1951.

Bruch, C.B. Modification of procedures for identification of the disadvantaged gifted. *The Gifted Child Quarterly,* 1971, *15,* 267-272.

Bruininks, V.L. Actual and perceived peer status of learning-disabled students in mainstreamed programs. *The Journal of Special Education,* 1978, *12,* 51-58. (a)

Bruininks, V.L. Peer status and personality characteristics of learning disabled and nondisabled students. *Journal of Learning Disabilities,* 1978, *12,* 484-489. (b)

Bruner, J.S. *The process of education.* Cambridge, Mass.: Harvard University Press, 1960.

Bruner, J.S. *Beyond the information given.* New York: W.W. Norton & Co., Inc., 1973.

Buhler, E.O., & Guirl, E.N. The more able student: Described and rated. In L.D. Crow & A. Crow (Eds.), *Educating the academically able.* New York: David McKay Company, Inc., 1963.

Burks, F.W. Some factors related to social success in college. *Journal of Social Psychology,* 1938, *9,* 125-140.

Buros, O.K. (Ed.) *Tests in print II: An index to tests, test reviews, and the literature on specific tests.* Highland Park, N.J.: The Gryphon Press, 1974.

Buros, O.K., (Ed.) *The eighth mental measurements yearbook.* Highland Park, N.J.: The Gryphon Press, 1978.

Bushman, J.H., & Jones, S.K. *Effective communication: A handbook of discussion skills.* Buffalo, N.Y.: D.O.K. Publishers, 1977.

Caldwell, O.W., & Wellman, B. Characteristics of school leaders. *The Journal of Educational Research,* 1926, *14,* 1-15.

Callahan, C.M., & Renzulli, J.S. The effectiveness of a creativity training program in the language arts. *Gifted Child Quarterly,* 1977, *4,* 538-545.

Carlson, J.G.H., & Misshauk, M.J. *Introduction to gaming: Management decision simulations.* New York: John Wiley & Sons, Inc., 1972.

Carroll, H. *Genius in the making.* New York: McGraw-Hill Book Company, 1940.

Chaffee, E. General policies concerning education of intellectually gifted pupils in Los Angeles. In L.D. Crow & A. Crow (Eds.), *Educating the academically able.* New York: David McKay Company, Inc., 1963.

Chickering, A.W. *Education and identity.* San Francisco: Jossey-Bass, Inc., 1969.

Cline, S. Simulation: A teaching strategy for the gifted and talented. *The Gifted Child Quarterly,* 1979, *23,* 269-283.

Connolly, M.A. *An assessment by gifted students of teachers' instructional styles*. (Unpublished paper). Available from School of Education, San Diego State University, 1976.

Courtenay, M.E. Persistence of leadership. *The School Review*, 1938, *46*, 97-107.

Cowley, W.H. Traits of face-to-face leaders. *Journal of Abnormal and Social Psychology*, 1931, *26*, 304-313.

de Bono, E. *Lateral thinking*. New York: Harper & Row Publishers, Inc. 1970.

de Bono, E. *Thinking action*. Dorset, England: Direct Education Services, 1976.

Della-Dora, D., & Blanchard, L.J. (Eds.). *Moving toward self-directed learning: Highlights of relevant research and of promising practice*. Alexandria, Va.: Association for Supervision and Curriculum Development, 1979. (ERIC Document Reproduction Service No. ED 171-619)

Dellas, M., & Gaier, E.L. Identification of creativity: The individual. *Psychological Bulletin*, 1970, *73*, 55-73.

Drake, R.M. A study of leadership. *Character and Personality*, 1944, *12*, 285-289.

Dunkerly, M.D. A statistical study of leadership among college women. *Studies in Psychology and Psychiatry*, 1940, *4*, 1-65.

Dunkin, M.J., & Biddler, B.J. *The study of teaching*. New York: Holt, Rinehart and Winston, Inc., 1974.

Dunn, R.S., & Price, G.E. The learning style characteristics of gifted students. *The Gifted Child Quarterly*, 1980, *24*, 33-36.

Durkin, M. Reviewing the concept development task. In Institute for Staff Development (Eds.), *Hilda Taba teaching strategies program: Unit 1*. Miami, Fla.: Institute for Staff Development, 1971.

Eichler, G.A. Studies in student leadership. *Penn State College Studies in Education*, 1934, No. 10.

Ennis, R.H. A definition of critical thinking. *The Reading Teacher*, 1964, *18*, 599-612.

Ennis, R.H., & Millman, J. *The Cornell critical thinking test: Manual for level x and level z*. Urbana, Ill.: University of Illinois, 1971.

Fauquier, W., & Gilchrist, T. Some aspects of leadership in an institution. *Child Development*, 1942, *13*, 55-64.

Flemming, E.G. A factor analysis of the personality of high school leaders. *Journal of Applied Psychology*, 1935, *19*, 596-605.

Frasier, M.M. Rethinking the issues regarding the culturally disadvantaged gifted. *Exceptional Children*, 1979, *45*, 538-542.

Freehill, M.F. *Gifted children: Their psychology and education*. New York: The Macmillan Company, 1961.

Gage, N.L., & Berliner, D.C. *Educational psychology*. Chicago: Rand McNally Co., 1979.

Gallagher, J.J. *Research summary on gifted child education*. Springfield, Ill.: Office of the Illinois Superintendent of Public Instruction, 1966.

Gallagher, J.J. *Teaching the gifted child* (2nd ed.). Boston: Allyn & Bacon, Inc., 1975.

Gallagher, J.J., Aschner, M.J., & Jenné, W. *Productive thinking in classroom interaction*. Reston, Va.: The Council for Exceptional Children, 1967.

Gallagher, J.J., & Crowder, T. The adjustment of gifted children in the regular classroom. *Exceptional Children*, 1957, *23*, 306-312; 317-319.

Gallagher, J.J., Shaffer, F., Phillips, S., Addy, S., Rainer, M., & Nelson, T. *A system of topic classification*. Urbana, Ill.: University of Illinois, Institute for Research on Exceptional Children, 1966.

Garrison, K.C. A study of some factors related to leadership in high school. *Peabody Journal of Education*, 1935, *11*, 11-17.

George, W.C. Accelerating mathematics instruction. *The Gifted Child Quarterly*, 1976, *20*, 246-261.

Gerken, K.C. Performance of Mexican American children in intelligence tests. *Exceptional Children*, 1978, *44*, 438-443.

Getzels, J.W., & Jackson, P.W. *Creativity and intelligence: Exploration with gifted students*. New York: John Wiley & Sons, Inc., 1962.

Gibran, K. *The prophet*. New York: Alfred A. Knopf, Inc., 1972.

Gogol, N.V. *The overcoat*. London: Merlin Press, 1956.

Goldberg, M., Passow, A., Justman, J., & Hage, G. *The effects of ability grouping*. New York: Columbia University, Teachers College, Bureau of Publications, 1965.

Goodenough, F.L. Inter-relationships in the behavior of young children. *Child Development*, 1930, *1*, 29-48.

Goodhart, B.F., & Schmidt, S.D. Educational characteristics of superior children. *Baltimore Bulletin of Education*, 1940, *18*, 14-17.

Gordon, W.J. *Synectics*. New York: Harper & Row Publishers, Inc., 1961.

Gough, H.G. *California psychological inventory manual*. Palo Alto, Calif.: Consulting Psychologists Press, 1957.

Gowan, J.C., & Demos, G.D. *The education and guidance of the ablest*. Springfield, Ill.: Charles C. Thomas, Publisher, 1964.

Guilford, J.P. Three faces of intellect. *American Psychologist*, 1959, *14*, 469-479.

Guilford, J.P. *The nature of human intelligence*. New York: McGraw-Hill Book Company, 1967.

Guilford, J.P. Intellect and the gifted. *The Gifted Child Quarterly*, 1972, *16*, 175-243.

Guilford, J.P. Varieties of creative giftedness, their measurement and development. *The Gifted Child Quarterly*, 1975, *19*, 107-121.

Guilford, J.P. *Way beyond the IQ*. Buffalo, N.Y.: Creative Education Foundation, Inc., 1977.

Halpern, F. *Survival: Black/white*. Elmsford, N.Y.: Pergamon Press, 1973.

Hartshorne, J., & May, M. A summary of the work of the character inquiry. *Religious Education*, 1930, *25*, 607-619.

Heitzman, W.R. *Educational games and simulations*. Washington, D.C.: National Education Association, 1974.

Henry, N.B. (Ed.). *Education for the gifted: The fifty-seventh yearbook of the National Society for the Study of Education* (Part II). Chicago: National Society for the Study of Education, 1958.

Hollingworth, L.S. *Children above 180 IQ*. Yonkers, N.Y.: World Book, 1942.

Hunter, E.C., & Jordan, A.M. An analysis of qualities associated with leadership among college students. *Journal of Educational Psychology*, 1939, *30*, 497-509.

Institute for Staff Development (Eds.). *Hilda Taba teaching strategies program: Unit 1*. Miami, Fla.: Author, 1971. (a)

Institute for Staff Development (Eds.). *Hilda Taba teaching strategies program: Unit 2*. Miami, Fla.: Author, 1971. (b)

Jones, E. *Dimensions of teaching-learning environments: A handbook for teachers*. Pasadena, Calif.: Pacific Oaks, 1977.

Jung, C.G. *Psychological types*. London: Rutledge & Kegan Paul, 1923.

Kagan, J. Impulsive and reflective children: The significance of conceptual tempo. In J. Krumboltz (Ed.), *Learning and the educational process*. Chicago: Rand McNally Co., 1965.

Kaplan, S.N. *Providing programs for the gifted and talented: A handbook*. Ventura, Calif.: Office of the Ventura County Superintendent of Schools, 1974.

Keating, D.P. *Intellectual talent: Research and development*. Baltimore: The Johns Hopkins University Press, 1976.

Keirsey, D., & Bates, M. *Please understand me: An essay on temperament styles*. Del Mar, Calif.: Prometheus Nemesis Books, 1978.

Kerstetter, L. A sociometric study of the classroom roles of a group of highly gifted children (Unpublished doctoral dissertation, New York University, 1952). *Dissertation Abstracts*, 1953, *13*, 606-607. (University Microfilms No. 5405)

Khatena, J. *The creatively gifted child: Suggestions for parents and teachers*. New York: Vantage Press, 1978.

Khatena, J., & Fisher, S. A four year study of children's responses to onomatopoeic stimuli. *Perceptual and Motor Skills*, 1974, *39*, 1062.

Koberg, D., & Bagnall, J. *The universal traveler. A soft-systems guide to: Creativity, problem-solving, and the process of reaching goals*. Los Altos, Calif.: William Kaufman, 1976.

Kohlberg, L. Moral education in the schools: A developmental view. *The School Review*, 1966, *74*, 1-29.

Kohlberg, L. Moral development and the education of adolescents. In R.F. Purnell (Ed.), *Adolescents and the American high school*. New York: Holt, Rinehart and Winston, Inc., 1970.

Kohlberg, L. Stages of moral development as the basis for moral education. In C.M. Beck, B.S. Crittendon, & E.V. Sullivan (Eds.), *Moral education: Interdisciplinary approaches*. New York: Newman Press, 1971.

Krathwohl, D.R., Bloom, B.S., & Masia, B.B. *Taxonomy of educational objectives: The classification of educational goals. Handbook II: Affective domain*. New York: David McKay Company, Inc., 1964.

Kroth, R. The mirror model of parental involvement. *The Pointer*, 1980, *25*, 18-22.

Lawrence, G. *People types and tiger stripes: A practical guide to learning styles*. Gainesville, Fla.: Center for Applications of Psychological Type, Inc., 1979.

Link, H.C. The definition of social effectiveness and leadership through measurement. *Educational and Psychological Measurement*, 1944, *4*, 57-67.

MacKinnon, D.W. The nature and nurture of creative talent. *American Psychologist*, 1962, *17*, 484-495.

Maker, C.J. *Training teachers for the gifted and talented: A comparison of models*. Reston, Va.: The Council for Exceptional Children, 1975.

Maker, C.J. Searching for giftedness and talent in children with handicaps. *The School Psychology Digest*, 1976, *5*, 24-36.

Maker, C.J. *Providing programs for the gifted handicapped*. Reston, Va.: The Council for Exceptional Children, 1977.

Maker, C.J. An experimental program for young gifted children. *New Horizons*, in press.

Maker, C.J., Morris, E., & James, J. The Eugene Field project: A program for potentially gifted young children. In *Balancing the scale for the disadvantaged gifted*. Los Angeles: National/State Leadership Training Institute on the Gifted and Talented, 1981.

Makovic, M.V. The gifted child. In W.F. Jenks (Ed.), *Special education of the exceptional child*. Washington, D.C.: Catholic University Press, 1953.

Martinson, R.A. Guidance of the gifted. In L.D. Crow & A. Crow (Eds.), *Educating the academically able*. New York: David McKay Company, Inc., 1963.

McNaughton, A.H. A generalization is a generalization. In Institute for Staff Development (Eds.), *Hilda Taba teaching strategies program: Unit 2.* Miami, Fla.: Institute for Staff Development, 1971.

Meeker, M.N. *The structure of intellect: Its interpretation and uses.* Columbus, Ohio: The Charles E. Merrill Publishing Co., 1969.

Meeker, M.N. *SOI group memory test and training model.* El Segundo, Calif.: SOI Institute, 1973.

Meeker, M. Nondiscriminatory testing procedures to assess giftedness in Black, Chicano, Navajo, and Anglo children. In A.Y. Baldwin, G.H. Gear, and L.J. Lucito (Eds.) *Educational planning for the gifted: Overcoming cultural, geographical, and socioeconomic barriers.* Reston, Va.: The Council for Exceptional Children, 1978.

Morris, D. How to vice-principal a middle school from a seventh grade student who knows what he wants. *Middle School Journal,* 1979, *10,* 31.

National Education Association. *NEA administration: Procedures and school practices for the academically talented student in the secondary school.* Washington, D.C.: National Education Association, 1960.

Newcomb, T.M. *Personality and social change.* New York: Dryden Press, 1943.

New Mexico State Department of Education. *A plan for the delivery of special education services in New Mexico.* Santa Fe, N.M.: State Department of Education, 1975.

Noller, R.B., Parnes, S.J., & Biondi, A.M. *Creative actionbook: Revised edition of creative behavior workbook.* New York: Charles Scribner's Sons, 1976.

Osborn, A. *Applied imagination.* New York: Charles Scribner's Sons, 1963.

Parnes, S.J. *Programming creative behavior.* Buffalo: State University of New York at Buffalo, 1966.

Parnes, S.J. *Aha! Insights into creative behavior.* Buffalo: D.O.K. Publishers, 1975.

Parnes, S.J. Guiding creative action. *The Gifted Child Quarterly,* 1977, *21,* 460-476.

Partridge, E.D. Leadership among adolescent boys. *Teachers College Record,* 1935, *36,* 320-322.

Passow, A.H., Goldberg, M., & Tannenbaum, A.J. *Education of the disadvantaged.* New York: Holt, Rinehart and Winston, Inc., 1967.

Phenix, P.H. *Realms of meaning.* New York: McGraw-Hill Book Company, 1964.

Piaget, J., & Inhelder, B. *The psychology of the child.* New York: Basic Books, 1969.

Plowman, P., & Rice, J. *California project talent.* Sacramento, Calif.: California State Department of Education, 1967.

Purkey, W.W. Project self-discovery. Its effects on bright but underachieving high school students. *The Gifted Child Quarterly,* 1969, *13,* 242-246.

Renzulli, J.S. Talent potential in minority group students. *Exceptional Children,* 1973, *39,* 437-444.

Renzulli, J.S. *A guidebook for evaluating programs for the gifted and talented.* Ventura, Calif.: Office of the County Superintendent of Schools, 1976. (a)

Renzulli, J.S. *New directions in creativity.* New York: Harper & Row Publishers, Inc., 1976. (b)

Renzulli, J.S. *The enrichment triad model: A guide for developing defensible programs for the gifted and talented.* Wethersfield, Conn.: Creative Learning Press, 1977.

Renzulli, J.S. What makes giftedness? *Phi Delta Kappan,* 1978, *60,* 180-184; 261.

Renzulli, J.S., Smith, F.H., White, A.J., Callahan, C.M., & Hartman, R.K. *Scales for rating the behavioral characteristics of superior students* (SRBCSS). Wethersfield, Conn.: Creative Learning Press, 1976.

Richardson, H.M., & Hanawalt, N.G. Leadership as related to Bernreuter: I. College leadership in extracurricular activities. *Journal of Social Psychology,* 1943, *17,* 237-249.

Rogers, C.R. Toward a theory of creativity. In H.H. Anderson (Ed.), *Creativity and its cultivation*. New York: Harper & Bros., 1959.

Ross, J.D., & Ross, C.M. *The Ross test of higher cognitive processes*. Novato, Calif.: Academic Therapy Publications, 1976.

Rothney, J.W., & Koopman, N.E. Guidance of the gifted. In N.B. Henry (Ed.), *Education for the gifted: The fifty-seventh yearbook of the National Society for the Study of Education* (Part II). Chicago: The National Society for the Study of Education, 1958.

Sigel, I.E. Cognitive development: Classification behavior. In Institute for Staff Development (Eds.), *Hilda Taba teaching strategies program: Unit 1*. Miami, Fla.: Institute for Staff Development, 1971.

Simon, S.B., Leland, W.H., & Kirschenbaum, H. *Values clarification: A handbook of practical strategies for teachers and students*. New York: Hart Publishing, 1972.

Simpson, R.H. A study of those who influence and of those who are influenced in discussion. *Teachers College Record*, 1938, *40*, 247-248.

Spaulding, C.B. Types of junior college leaders. *Sociology and Social Research*, 1934, *18*, 164-168.

Stanford, G., & Stanford, B.D. *Learning discussion skills through games*. New York: Citation Press, 1969.

Stanley, J.C., George, W.C., & Solano, C.H. (Eds.). *The gifted and the creative: A fifty-year perspective*. Baltimore: The Johns Hopkins University Press, 1977.

Stanley, J.C., Keating, D.P. & Fox, L.H. (Eds.). *Mathematical talent: Discovery, description, and development*. Baltimore: The John Hopkins University Press, 1974.

Steele, J.M. *Dimensions of the class activities questionnaire*. Urbana, Ill.: Center for Instructional Research and Curriculum Evaluation, University of Illinois, 1969.

Steele, J.M., House, E.R., Lapan, S., & Kerins, T. *Instructional climate in Illinois gifted classes*. Urbana, Ill.: Center for Instructional Research and Curriculum Evaluation, University of Illinois, 1970.

Stevenson, G., Seghini, J.B., Timothy, K., Brown, K., Lloyd, B.C., Zimmerman, M.A., Maxfield, S., & Buchanan, J. *Project implode: Igniting creative potential*. Salt Lake City: Bella Vista-Institute for Behavioral Research in Creativity, 1971.

Stewart, E.D. Learning styles among gifted/talented students: Preferences for instructional techniques. (Doctoral dissertation, University of Connecticut, 1979). *Dissertation Abstracts International*, 1980, *40*, 4503A-4504A. (University Microfilms No. 8003762)

Strang, R. The nature of giftedness. In N.B. Henry (Ed.), *Education for the gifted: The fifty-seventh yearbook of the National Society for the Study of Education* (Part II). Chicago: The National Society for the Study of Education, 1958.

Suchman, R. Inquiry and education. In J. Gallagher (Ed.), *Teaching gifted students: A book of readings*. Boston: Allyn & Bacon, Inc., 1965.

Taba, H. *Curriculum development: Theory and practice*. New York: Harcourt, Brace & World, Inc., 1962.

Taba, H. *Thinking in elementary school children* (USOE Cooperative Research Project No. 1574). San Francisco: San Francisco State College, 1964. (ERIC Document Reproduction Service No. ED 003 285)

Taba, H. *Teaching strategies and cognitive functioning in elementary school children* (USOE Cooperative Research Project No. 2404). San Francisco: San Francisco State College, 1966.

Taylor, C.W. The multiple talent approach. *The Instructor*, April 1968. (a)

Taylor, C.W. Be talent developers as well as knowledge dispensers. *Today's Education,* December 1968. (b)

Terman, L.M. A preliminary study in the psychology and pedagogy of leadership. *Pedagogical Seminary,* 1904, *11,* 413-451.

Terman, L.M. (Ed.). *Genetic studies of genius (Vol. 1): Mental and physical traits of a thousand gifted children.* Palo Alto, Calif.: Stanford University Press, 1925.

Terman, L.M., & Oden, M. *Genetic studies of genius (Vol. 4): The gifted child grows up.* Palo Alto, Ca.: Stanford University Press, 1947.

Terman, L.M., & Oden, M. *Genetic studies of genius (Vol. 5): The gifted group at mid-life.* Palo Alto, Ca.: Stanford University Press, 1959.

Torrance, E.P. *Guiding creative talent.* Englewood Cliffs, N.J.: Prentice-Hall, Inc., 1962.

Torrance, E.P. *Rewarding creative behavior.* Englewood Cliffs, N.J.: Prentice-Hall, Inc., 1965.

Torrance, E.P. *Understanding the fourth grade stump in creativity.* Athens, Ga.: Georgia Studies of Creative Behavior, 1967.

Torrance, E.P. Finding hidden talents among disadvantaged children. *The Gifted Child Quarterly,* 1968, *12,* 131-137.

Torrance, E.P. Are the Torrance Tests of Creative Thinking biased against or in favor of 'disadvantaged' groups? *The Gifted Child Quarterly,* 1971, *15,* 75-80.

Torrance, E.P. Career patterns and peak creative achievements of creative high school students twelve years later. *The Gifted Child Quarterly,* 1972, *16,* 75-88.

Torrance, E.P. *Discovery and nurturance of giftedness in the culturally different.* Reston, Va.: The Council for Exceptional Children, 1977.

Torrance, E.P. *The search for satori and creativity.* Buffalo, N.Y.: Creative Education Foundation, 1979.

Treffinger, D.J. Teaching for self-directed learning: A priority for the gifted and talented. *The Gifted Child Quarterly,* 1975, *19,* 46-59.

U.S. Department of Health, Education and Welfare, Office of Education. *Education of handicapped children: Implementation of Part B, Education of handicapped act.* Washington, D.C.: Author, 1977.

U.S. Office of Education. *Education of the gifted and talented* (Report to the Congress). Washington, D.C.: U.S. Government Printing Office, 1972.

U.S. Office of Education. Program for the gifted and talented. *The Federal Register,* 1976, *41,* 18665-18666.

Villars, G. (Ed.). *Educating the gifted in Minnesota schools.* St. Paul: State Department of Education, 1957.

Wallach, M.A., & Kogan, N. *Modes of thinking in young children.* New York: Holt, Rinehart and Winston, Inc., 1965.

Ward, V.S. *Educating the gifted: An axiomatic approach.* Columbus, Ohio: The Charles E. Merrill Publishing Co., 1961.

Ward, V.S. *The gifted student: A manual for regional improvement.* Atlanta: Southern Regional Education Board, 1962.

Watson, G., & Glaser, E.M. *Watson-Glaser critical thinking appraisal: Manual for forms ym and zm.* New York: Harcourt Brace Jovanovich, Inc., 1964.

Weiner, B. *Theories of motivation: From mechanism to cognition.* Chicago: Rand McNally, 1972.

Weiner, B. *Cognitive views of human motivation.* New York: Academic Press, Inc., 1974.

Weiner, B., Frieze, I., Kukla, A., Reed, L., Rest, S., & Rosenbaum, R.M. Perceiving the causes of success and failure. In E. Jones, D. Kanouse, H. Kelley, R. Nisbett, S. Valins, & B. Weiner (Eds.), *Attribution: Perceiving the causes of behavior.* Morristown, N.J.: General Learning Press, 1972.

Weiner, B., & Kukla, A. An attributional analysis of achievement motivation. *Journal of Personality and Social Psychology,* 1970, *15,* 1-20.

Weiner, B., Nierenberg, R., & Goldstein, N. Social learning (locus of control) versus attributional (causal stability) interpretations of expectancy of success. *Journal of Personality,* 1976, *44,* 52-68.

White, A.J. (Ed.). *Evaluation of programs for the gifted and talented* (Report of the Connecticut task force on evaluation). Hartford: Connecticut State Department of Education, 1974.

Whitlock, B.W. *Don't hold them back: A critique and guide to new high school-college articulation models.* New York: College Entrance Examination Board, 1978.

Whitmore, J.R. The etiology of underachievement in highly gifted young children. *Journal for the Education of the Gifted,* 1979, *3,* 38-51.

Whitmore, J.R. *Giftedness, conflict, and underachievement.* Boston: Allyn & Bacon, Inc., 1980.

Williams, F.E. *Classroom ideas for encouraging thinking and feeling* (2nd ed.). Buffalo: D.O.K. Publishers, 1970.

Williams, F.E. *A total creativity program for individualizing and humanizing the learning process* (Instructional Materials). Englewood Cliffs, N.J.: Educational Technology Publications, 1972.

Wilson, F.T. Some special ability test scores of gifted children. In W.B. Barbe (Ed.), *Psychology and education of gifted.* New York: Appleton-Century-Crofts, Inc., 1965.

Witty, P. Gifted children—Our greatest resource. *Nursing Education,* 1955, *47,* 498-500.

Witty, P. Who are the gifted? In N.B. Henry (Ed.), *Education for the gifted: The fifty-seventh yearbook of the National Society for the Study of Education* (Part II). Chicago: National Society for the Study of Education, 1958.

Womack, J.G. *Discovering the structure of social studies.* New York: Benziger Bros., 1966.

Youngers, J.C., & Aceti, J.F. *Simulation games and activities for social studies.* New York: The Instructor Publications, 1969.

Zeleny, C. Characteristics of group leaders. *Sociology and Social Research,* 1939, *24,* 140-149.

Zilli, M.J. Reasons why the gifted adolescent underachieves and some of the implications of guidance and counseling to this problem. *The Gifted Child Quarterly,* 1971, *15,* 279-292.

Zuckerman, D.W., & Horn, R.E. *The guide to simulations: Games for education and training.* New York: Research Media, 1973.

REFERENCE NOTES

1. Renzulli, J.S. *Inservice training worksheets for the enrichment triad model: Summary sheets 1, 2, and 3* (Teacher Training Materials). Storrs, Conn.: University of Connecticut, 1979.

2. Lethem, S., & Osborn, M. *Seminar topics and questions for 1980-1981, Jefferson Middle School.* Unpublished paper, 1980. (Available from Dr. C.J. Maker, Department of Special Education, University of Arizona, Tucson, Az.)

3. Parnes, S.J. *Creative potential and the educational experience* (Occasional Paper No. 2). Buffalo, N.Y.: Creative Education Foundation, 1967.

4. Lethem, S., & Osborn, M. *A learning environment for middle school gifted students resource-seminar program, Jefferson Middle School.* Unpublished paper, 1980. (Available from Dr. C.J. Maker, Department of Special Education, University of Arizona, Tucson, Az.)

5. Kerr, P., & O'Dell, D. *Curriculum for culturally different and/or low socio-economic gifted students–Elementary level.* Unpublished paper, 1980. (Available from the authors, Gifted Program, Albuquerque Public Schools, Albuquerque, N.M.)

6. Locke, P. *The gifted and talented American Indian child: A first step.* Paper presented at the Gifted and Talented American Indian Consortium, Bemidji State University/Red Lake Reservation, Bemidji, Minn., November 15-16, 1978.

7. Grey Bear, S. *Teacher's manual: Mathematics for gifted children.* Paper presented at the Gifted and Talented American Indian Consortium, Bemidji State University/Red Lake Reservation, Bemidji, Minn.: November 15-16, 1978.

8. Maker, C.J., Redden, M.R., Tonelson, S., & Howell, R.M. *The self-perceptions of successful handicapped scientists* (BEH Grant No. G00-7701-905). Albuquerque, N.M.: Department of Special Education, University of New Mexico, 1978.

9. White, A. Personal communication, November 1978.

10. Torrance, E.P. Personal communication, April 13, 1979.

11. Maker, C.J. *A model for curriculum development for the gifted handicapped.* Unpublished manuscript, 1979. (Available from Dr. C.J. Maker, Department of Special Education, University of Arizona, Tucson, Az.).

12. Bodnar, J. *Summary of special education gifted program, Eldorado High School.* Unpublished paper, 1979. (Available from Dr. C.J. Maker, Department of Special Education, University of Arizona, Tucson, Az.).

Index

C

About the Author

C. JUNE MAKER is Assistant Professor of Special Education at the University of Arizona, Tucson. In this capacity, she is responsible for the development and coordination of graduate degree concentrations in education of the gifted at both the master's and doctoral levels. She holds national offices in several organizations for the gifted. Her publications are related to the gifted handicapped, teacher training, the development of talents in exceptional children, and teaching learning disabled students.

She has been a coordinator of a graduate degree program at the University of New Mexico, a teacher, a regional supervisor for a state department of education, an administrative intern in the federal office for the gifted, and has consulted with numerous local school districts, state departments of education, and other public and private agencies. Her educational background consists of degrees from the University of Virginia (Ph.D.), Southern Illinois University (M.S.), and Western Kentucky University (B.S.).